Understanding Interpersonal Communication

Fifth Edition

Richard L. Weaver II
Bowling Green State University

▦ HarperCollins*Publishers*

To Robert G. Gunderson and Edgar E. Willis—teachers who have contributed to my growth and development

Picture Credits

Unless otherwise acknowledged, all photos are the property of HarperCollins*Publishers* Page positions are as follows: (t) top, (b) bottom, (r) right, (l) left.

Front Cover: (l) Lawrence Migdale, (tr) Joel Gordon Photography, (br) Jim Whitmer
Back Cover: Jim Whitmer

XVI, Spencer Grant/Monkmeyer Press Photo Service; **3,** Susan Lapides/Design Conceptions; **5,** Elizabeth Crews/Stock Boston; **7,** Rhoda Sidney/Monkmeyer Press Photo Service; **12,** Jean-Claude LeJeune; **21,** Jean-Claude LeJeune/Stock Boston; **36,** Ed Kashi; **43,** Ken Karp/Omni-Photo Communications; **54,** Dean Abramson/Stock Boston; **66,** Joel Gordon Photography; **70,** Kagan/Monkmeyer Press Photo Service; **72,** HI AND LOIS © 1984 Distributed by King Features Syndicate, Inc.; **73,** Lawrence Migdale; **79,** Ellis Herwig/Stock Boston; **84,** Joel Gordon Photography; **87,** George Malave/Stock Boston; **89,** George Bellerose/Stock Boston; **92, 102,** Jean-Claude LeJeune; **107,** PEANUTS © 1970 Reprinted by permission of United Feature Syndicate, Inc.; **111,** Joseph A. DiChello; **116,** Ann McQueen/Stock Boston; **121,** Joel Gordon Photography; **128,** Dean Abramson/Stock Boston; **132,** PEANUTS © 1980 Reprinted by permission of United Feature Syndicate, Inc.; **137, 141, 144,** Joel Gordon Photography; **153,** Peter Vandermark/Stock Boston; **160,** Jean-Claude LeJeune; **164,** Drawing by Frascino © 1985 *The New Yorker Magazine*, Inc.; **173,** Joel Gordon Photography; **178,** Elizabeth Crews/Stock Boston; **182,** Mike Mazzaschi/Stock Boston; **190,** Elizabeth Crews; **195,** Arthur Grace/Stock Boston; **198,** Laimute E. Druskis/Stock Boston; **205,** Peter Southwick/Stock Boston; **213,** Goodwin/Monkmeyer Press Photo Service; **214,** MISS PEACH © 1990 Mell Lazarus; **218,** CATHY Copyright 1979/Universal Press Syndicate, Reprinted with permission; All Rights Reserved; **228,** Jean-Claude LeJeune; **239,** Joel Gordon Photography; **248,** Paul Fortin/Stock Boston; **255,** David M. Phillips; **264,** Elizabeth Crews; **267,** Joel Gordon Photography; **271,** Michael Gregg/Stock Boston; **275,** Michael Kagan/Monkmeyer Press Photo Service; **281,** *THE KEY*, Bowling Green State University; **286,** Harriet Gans/The Image Works; **294,** Frank Siteman/The Picture Cube; **298,** CATHY © 1979 Universal Press Syndicate. Reprinted with permission. All Rights Reserved; **302,** Jean-Claude LeJeune; **306,** *THE KEY*, Bowling Green State University; **314,** Joel Gordon Photography; **316,** Brady/Monkmeyer Press Photo Service; **322,** Camerique/H. Armstrong Roberts; **326,** Sheila Sheridan/Monkmeyer Press Photo Service; **332,** *THE KEY*, Bowling Green State University; **337,** Owen Franken/Stock Boston; **342,** *THE KEY*, Bowling Green State University; **348,** Jean-Claude LeJeune; **350,** Joel Gordon Photography; **353,** MISS PEACH © 1990 Mell Lazarus; **359,** Joel Gordon Photography; **365,** Richard Hutchings; **376,** © 1989 David B. Jenkins; **379,** Susan Lapides/Design Conceptions; **388,** Arlene Collins/Monkmeyer Press Photo Service; **390,** Jim Bradshaw; **394,** Ed Kashi; **408,** Drawing by Koren © 1988 *The New Yorker Magazine*, Inc.; **A–7,** Susan Lapides/Design Conceptions; **A–15,** *THE KEY*, Bowling Green State University.

An Instructor's Manual to accompany *Understanding Interpersonal Communication* is available. It may be obtained through a Scott, Foresman representative or by writing the Speech Communication Editor, College Division, Scott, Foresman and Company, 1900 East Lake Avenue, Glenview, Illinois 60025.

Library of Congress Cataloging-in-Publication Data

Weaver, Richard L.,
    Understanding interpersonal communication / Richard L. Weaver II.—5th ed.
      p. cm.
    Includes bibliographical references.
    ISBN 0-673-38905-7
    1. Interpersonal communication.   I. Title.
BF637.C45W35   1990
158'.2—dc20
                                      89-39228
                                      CIP

Preface

The Fifth Edition of *Understanding Interpersonal Communication*, like the previous editions, is intended to help students understand interpersonal communication and improve their skills in this area. The concepts, principles, and theories of human interaction not only must be learned but also must be made relevant to one's life. Thus, throughout, this book emphasizes the practical skills needed to improve communication with others—indeed, the practical skills that evolve naturally from the concepts, principles, and theories discussed.

Approach and Focus

The dual emphasis on concepts and skills underlies both the overall approach of the book and the organization within chapters. Chapters begin with an explanation of concepts and conclude with a discussion of skills.

My goal has been to write a teachable book that covers essential content, and a readable book that interests students. To these ends, the chapters are organized in a consistent manner that follows the way the course is often taught; however, each chapter is self-contained to permit maximum flexibility. I have tried for prose that is jargon-free and buttressed with numerous, relevant examples.

Key Features

In addition to the dual emphasis on concepts and skills, this text has numerous pedagogical features:

- *Learning objectives* are listed at the beginning of each chapter. There are always ten, representing the most significant concepts in each chapter.
- *Key terms* are printed in boldface in the text.
- *"Consider This"* readings, many new to this edition, appear throughout the text to stimulate thinking and discussion.
- *"Try This"* materials appear throughout the text to encourage students to try new behaviors and practice new skills.
- *Further Reading* suggestions at the end of each chapter are annotated and include both popular and scholarly sources. These have been substantially updated and represent the ten best sources for extending the material of each chapter.

- *Diagrams and models* illustrate the textual material and make the concepts, principles, and theories easier to grasp.
- *Photographs*—several taken by students—add interest and visual reinforcement to the text.

The Fifth Edition

This edition features a greater emphasis on the contexts of communication. A new Appendix on "Interpersonal Communication in the Workplace" has been added. This is a skills-oriented section. The essential communication skills found to promote success on the job are listed. The traits and skills that make up an ideal management profile are offered, as are the communication skills necessary for reflecting on-the-job competence, for influencing others in the workplace, and for getting a job. How one prepares for the job search, constructs a résumé, and engages in the interview are outlined.

There are other changes in this edition as well. The Prologue has been expanded to include a section on ethics. Chapter 1, "Speaking Interpersonally," has been expanded to include a section on the importance of interpersonal communication in personal success, a section that explains how communication relationships develop over time—the developmental perspective—and a section on communication competence.

The chapter on "Perception," formerly Chapter 3, has become Chapter 2 in this edition to facilitate the flow of the material. This chapter is divided into sections on reception, construction, and skills. The chapter on "The Self and Self-Disclosure," formerly Chapter 2, is now Chapter 3. This chapter contains new material on the mediated self, on ways we have for getting in touch with the self, and an expanded section on self-disclosure.

In Chapter 5, "Verbal Communication," much of the material on language has been updated and a new section on "Giving Power to Your Words" has been added. An extensive section on gender differences in language use has also been added, as has one on fine tuning our language behavior.

Chapter 7 on "Interpersonal Persuasion" has been restructured and rewritten. The material on attitudes and values and their relationship to interpersonal communication has been clarified. There is additional material on the process of selecting persuasive strategies, the ethics of interpersonal influence, compliance gaining, and compliance resistance.

Chapter 9 on "Assertiveness" now precedes the chapter on conflict. A new conflict-management model has been added to Chapter 10. The final chapter, "The Course of Intimate Relationships," has been substantially strengthened. I discuss relationship development, relational maintenance, and the promotion of relational growth. After examining relational change and the causes of disintegration, I conclude with a discussion of what happens when relationships are terminated.

Available with the Fifth Edition are an expanded Instructor's Manual, test items (in the Instructor's Manual and on computer diskette), and *Communication: 1940–1989*, a special edition of *TIME* Magazine that offers a historical look at *TIME*'s coverage of major events illustrating the power of communication in 20th-century society.

Acknowledgments

This edition, like those before it, reflects the contributions of many people. I am especially grateful for the suggestions provided by the manuscript reviewers for each edition. For their reviews of the Fourth Edition, thanks go to Joseph Martinez, of El Paso Community College, and Michael Schliessmann, of South Dakota State University. Michael is also a member of the Midwest Basic Course Director's Conference and has provided numerous suggestions and ideas on an informal basis. Thanks, Mike.

For responding to the questionnaires on the Fourth Edition, I would like to thank Roy Beck, Western Michigan University; John Countryman, University of Richmond; Arni Dunathan, Bay de Noc Community College; Ray Ewing, Southeast Missouri State University; Patricia Fox-Callan, Bucks County Community College; Carol Norheim, Pasadena City College; Evelyn Shields, Delta College; Tony Strawn, Henderson Community College; and Jon Williams, Niagara County Community College.

For their reviews of the Fifth Edition manuscript, thanks to Judith Barnes, San Francisco State University; John Countryman, University of Richmond; Denos Marvin, Foothill Community College; William Rawlins, Purdue University; and Jon Williams, Niagara County Community College. You have become close friends and associates as I have worked with your comments and suggestions.

Also, for reviewing portions of the Fifth Edition manuscript, I would like to thank Tom Laga, Adjunct Faculty in Communication, Tunxis Community College, Farmington, Connecticut and Central Connecticut State University in New Britain. The telephone conversations were most encouraging, and the tapes you sent were priceless. I hope the *Instructor's Manual* for the Fifth Edition reflects the many helpful suggestions you made.

At Scott, Foresman and Company, I have worked with Barbara Muller, the former Acquisitions Editor, Vikki J. Barrett, Acquisitions Editor, and Louise Howe, Developmental Editor. Special thanks to Louise for her summary of reviews, suggestions for reorganization, and continuing encouragement. I also worked with Laurie Prossnitz, Project Editor. Laurie is skillful in making certain ideas are couched precisely and that they flow smoothly. Thanks for her skill and precision. The Scott, Foresman team continues to be delightful and cooperative, and their efforts are greatly appreciated. All writing benefits from knowledgeable, experienced, well-intentioned input.

Others who have contributed to the development of the manuscript are Gloria Gregor and Mary Lou Willmarth, whose continuing assistance, interest, and support have contributed to an atmosphere of ease and encouragement in the development of all editions of the book. I am grateful, too, to my friends. Although their names have been changed in the text, many of the examples in the book come from my experiences with them. Thank you, Ken and Sharon Knitt, Jim and Pat Angel, Alan and Connie Swisher, Jim and Shirley Hollars, Hal and Barb McLean, Wayne and Carol Canary, Jim and Amy Strausser, Stan and Sue Seevers, Tom and Mina Briggs, Dave and Chris Hamilton, Edgar and Zella Willis, Steve and Sherrell Earle, Darrel and Brenda Gabbard, Florence B. Weaver, Marilyn Hulett, Paull and Margery Walker, Donald Klopf, and Ronald Cambra. To the assistant directors and teaching assistants connected with the basic speech-communication course at Bowling Green State University, an additional note of appreciation must be added. Thank you, too, to Sue Wenzlaff, Edith Churchman, and Pat Olsen for your suggestions, comments, and unbridled enthusiasm.

My thanks go also to the faculty of the Department of Interpersonal and Public Communication (IPCO) at Bowling Green: Raymond K. Tucker, James R. Wilcox, Donald K. Enholm, and Patricia Arneson. It is a pleasure to work with such a cooperative, supportive, and outstanding group of people.

Several of the photographs used in this edition are from the files of *The Key*, the yearbook of Bowling Green State University. For permission to use these photographs, special thanks to the following staff members: Robert W. Bortel, Director of Student Publications; Brad Phalin, Mark Thalman, Dave Kielmeyer, Jim Youll, Michelle Thornwell, Pat Mingarelli, and Vince Walter, photographers; and Judith K. Miller, Secretary.

I also want to thank my children—Scott, Jacquelynn, Anthony, and Joanna. With each edition, their input has become more relevant and significant. In one way or another, their input and influence appear throughout the book.

Finally, and most importantly, thanks to my wife, Andrea. She read and typed the first edition manuscript. For the second, third, fourth, and fifth editions, she offered thoughtful, critical comments. Throughout all editions, too, she has provided support and love. These editions have emanated from a positive and productive interpersonal family climate that continues to offer rich material from which to draw and rich rewards for participation.

DICK WEAVER

Communication: 1940–1989

Edited by:
James Gaudino, Executive Director of the Speech Communication Association
Gustav Friedrich, University of Oklahoma-Norman
J. Jeffery Auer, Indiana University-Bloomington
Carolyn Calloway-Thomas, Indiana University-Bloomington
Patti Gillespie, University of Maryland
Robert C. Jeffrey, University of Texas at Austin
Mark Knapp, University of Texas at Austin
Jerry Miller, Michigan State University

This exciting new magazine piece, shrinkwrapped into each purchased copy of *Understanding Interpersonal Communication*, is a joint production of *TIME* and Scott, Foresman/Little, Brown. Compiled and edited by members of the Speech Communication Association, *Communication: 1940–1989* contains articles and excerpts relating to communication topics from past issues of *TIME*. It also includes a "You Are There" feature that illustrates the power of the spoken word. Spanning almost fifty years, *Communication: 1940–1989* offers students a unique glimpse of communication in the 20th century.

Contents

Feel free to say "I don't know" ▪ Don't be overly dependent on the goodwill of others ▪ Feel free to be illogical ▪ Feel free to say "I don't understand" ▪ Feel free to say "I don't care" ▪ Learn to make "I messages" ▪ Learn to repeat assertions ▪ Feel free to make requests ▪ Feel free to say "no"

Understanding Interpersonal Communication

Fifth Edition

Prologue
Finding Your Way: Values and Goals

You are beginning a book about interpersonal communication. This book and the course you are taking work toward two goals: (1) increasing your knowledge about interpersonal communication and (2) improving your skills in interpersonal communication.

I am writing this book out of the belief that clear and open communication between people is valuable. Clear and open communication helps me build richer, closer, more effective relationships with people. In my relationships with others I learn more about myself, and growth generally takes place. Self-knowledge, growth, and change are values that are important to me.

I hope that this book and this course will encourage you to think about the values that shape and control your life, how you can gain confidence in the values you hold, how you express these values when you communicate with others, and how these values change as a result of communicating with others. Just as our values affect our interpersonal communication, so our communication skills affect how close we come to fully realizing our values; and certainly weak communication skills can interfere with the fulfillment of some of our values.

Although this book is about interpersonal communication, it is also about values—valuing yourself, your relationships with others, empathic listening skills, effective nonverbal communication, and many others. Some values are implied, others are very explicit. Improving interpersonal communication may mean changing some values, adopting some new ones, even dropping others that are not useful. Values are personal, but so is interpersonal communication.

In the course of the book I will make some assumptions about your desire to grow. I value growth, and I hope it is important to you as well. Growth rarely occurs in total isolation. It requires interacting and communicating with people—understanding them and being understood by them. What motivates a desire for growth? James Jarrett characterizes people who want to grow as having a cluster of needs: to learn, to broaden their range of experience, to repeat pleasant experiences, to internalize insights, to savor feelings, to intensify sensations, to become discriminating, to recognize relevance, to increase human potential, and to create.[1] Let us examine each of these types of motivation in detail.

To learn. The desire to learn cannot be instilled in us from the outside. It must come from within. As children we had a natural desire to explore, to find out about things. To the very young child, learning and playing are the same thing—any new discovery is exciting. As growing adults, we need to recapture that excitement of discovery.

To broaden one's range of experience. Our routine—how we think and behave—becomes a kind of security blanket. Few people are eager to leave their security blankets behind for something they do not completely understand. But it is only by breaking out that we will meet new people, confront new ideas, and discover new frontiers. The more experience we have, the more options we have open to us and the more flexible we become.

To repeat pleasant experiences. We all know what it is to do something for no other reason than that it was enjoyable the last time. We'll

Consider This

At the same time that we are feeling a strong need to be separate we also sense that somehow relationships are very important to our happiness, and so we are presently trying to have both, to be different but have no differences, to be special but one. All anyone has to do is look around to see how complete a failure this approach is.

The answer lies not in avoiding the usual forms that specialness takes but in gently questioning the *need* to stand apart. This never includes formulating rules of conduct such as not buying clothes of good quality, damping down one's humor, or not seeking advancement in one's occupation. Specialness is the wish to be distinguishable in the eyes of other egos, and although this exhibits itself in behavior, there is no catalogue of actions one must avoid. What must be avoided is thinking of oneself as alone and out of context.

—Hugh and Gayle Prather, *A Book for Couples* (New York: Doubleday, 1988), p. 15.

talk to Pam because last time we talked to her she was friendly. We'll talk about our trip to Montana because last time we brought up the subject we got a good reaction. The better we understand interpersonal communication, the better we'll be able to control the variables in a communication situation and re-create pleasant experiences.

To internalize insights.　It is one thing to be able to comprehend an idea; it is quite another to be able to internalize it, to know what it means to us. We need to make insights personal if we're going to grow through them. These insights determine how we look at things, feel about them, and respond to them. Learning empathic interpersonal skills will help us with the internalizing.

To savor feelings.　When we have a good feeling, we want to hold on to it. To know what our reactions are made of and what stimulates them will help us savor such feelings. It can help us make the most of an otherwise unmemorable experience. Do you know what you like? Knowing what we like is the first step toward recognizing pleasure when we experience it. Though of course we never seek them out, even painful feelings can be savored, in a way. That is, we can explore the pain, try to understand what brought it on, and at least appreciate the fact that we are not numb to sensation. That is what savoring means—experiencing a feeling to the utmost.

Consider This

In *The Possessed*, one of Dostoyevsky's most enigmatic (perplexing or obscure) characters has this to say:

> *Everything's good .... Everything. Man is unhappy because he doesn't know he is happy. It's only that. That's all, that's all! If one finds out, one will become happy at once, that minute.*

The situation is hopeless and the solution is hopelessly simple.

—Paul Watzlawick, *The Situation Is Hopeless, But Not Serious: The Pursuit of Unhappiness* (New York: W. W. Norton & Company, 1983), p. 121.

To intensify sensations.   Whenever we can, we are likely to try to control communication situations in order to intensify whatever sensation that situation produces in us. It is like a ride in an amusement park that lets us control the speed or spin of our own car. We can go faster when we want to, slower when we want to. Having communication skills is like having our own controls; we can get the most of what we want out of interpersonal communication situations.

To become discriminating.   We learn in early childhood how to sort color and shape, and to assign meaning—how to be discriminating. This does not mean assigning value, saying one thing is better or worse than another. Discriminating simply means recognizing sameness and differences. A good communicator will be discriminating in this way—not judging "up" as better than "down," but always being able to tell them apart.

To recognize relevance.   In order to deal with the millions of stimuli we encounter every day, we must be selective. We usually base our selection on relevance, not asking "What difference does it make?" but "What difference does it make *to me?*" This is how we begin to make sense out of our environment and our communications. An effective communicator learns to choose and cope with only the most relevant of the many available stimuli.

To increase human potential.   It is not uncommon to hear someone describing his or her philosophy of life as "to be everything I *can* be" or "to do everything I am capable of." There is a strong motivation on the part of many of us to live life to the fullest. The effective communicator wants to explore all known possibilities and, when they are exhausted, to discover even more. This is really what growth is all about: reaching out, discovering how far we can go in any given direction.

To create.   There is a real excitement in the creative impulse, the irresistible desire to invent and to put things together in a new way. We don't have to be artists in the traditional sense of musicians and sculptors to want and be able to create. We have more opportunities to exercise our creativity in communication than in any other area simply because we communicate more than we do just about anything else. As we engage in interpersonal communication we need to find our own personally effective ways of getting along. And this takes real, creative imagination.

Consider This

The link between social well-being and physical health is not bunk, reports S. Leonard Syme of Berkeley. "Part of the human condition is that we are social beings; we need other people," he said at an American Heart Association symposium.

   Syme cited a 10-year study of 2,754 adults conducted at the University of Michigan in Tecumseh. The subjects' health was evaluated along with their marital status, close personal relationships, memberships in organizations outside work, and leisure-time activities. The study showed that those with the lower levels of social contacts had two to four times the risk of dying from serious illnesses than those who had close ties with others.

—Barbara Varro, "That Overwhelmingly Warm, Want-to-Share Feeling," *Chicago Sun-Times*, as cited in *The Sunday Star-Bulletin & Advertiser:* Honolulu, Hawaii, February 14, 1982, p. C-2. Reprinted with permission of Chicago Sun-Times, Inc., 1986.

To be ethical.   If I were to add one item to Jarrett's cluster of needs, based on my teaching and writing about interpersonal communication over the years, it would be the need to be ethical. Because our interpersonal communication may have an impact on others, because it involves choices about communicative means and specific ends (things we want or desire from others), and because it can be judged by standards of right and wrong, it involves ethical issues.[2] My intent in including this section is to try to promote the healthiest communication possible. Whether we are users or receivers, we need to be concerned about ethics.

The problem with ethics is that there are a number of approaches to it, numerous values and perspectives involved in it, and many potential exceptions to ethical standards. But this should *not* deter us from striving to be ethical. Let me list just ten guidelines that need to be considered when communicating with others.[3] We should:

1. Strive to create and maintain and atmosphere of openness, freedom, and responsibility.
2. Reveal an appreciation for individual differences and uniqueness.
3. Seek both sincerity and honesty in our attitudes toward communication.
4. Treat others as human beings who are unique, have feelings, and have inherent worth (as opposed to treating others as objects).
5. Strive for accuracy in our communication with others.
6. Eliminate intentional deception, ambiguity, and obscurity from our communication.
7. Reveal candidness and frankness as we share our personal beliefs and feelings with others.
8. Make every possible attempt to understand the perceptual world of others.
9. Help others make free choices based on accurate bases for those choices.
10. Strive to communicate with others as we would want others to communicate with us.

There is a great deal of complexity involved in judging the ethics of human communication. It is my hope that you will seriously consider these guidelines. In the end, the decision will be yours as you bring your principles, perspectives, and insights to bear on the communication situations you find yourself in.

As you begin to read about interpersonal communication, think about which of these goals and motivations are important in your life. You undoubtedly have others not listed here and you might want to argue about some of the ones I listed. That's fine. The idea is for you to think about the interpersonal communication process in general and to see how it applies to you as a communicator.

Each chapter of this book begins with a discussion of general concepts, then presents skills for implementing these concepts. But you can read and read and not understand unless you not only apply the ideas to your own life but also try them out. The skills section in each chapter suggests how to put concepts into practice. These sections should help you realize some of your values and goals.

Although values and goals are not identical, they are related. The goals we set are often determined by our values. Satisfying a particular value can become a goal. We may value cooperation, for example, and have a goal of becoming more cooperative. We may value knowledge for its own sake and have a personal goal of becoming more knowledgeable. The goal is the ideal end. It is the reality—the product or result—of what we value. It is where we would like to be as a result of valuing certain things above others. (Values and goals are also related to beliefs and attitudes, a topic we will address in Chapter 7.)

Only you know what your own goals are. The goal of this book is to provide the means for understanding interpersonal communication, but throughout the book this ultimate goal is broken down into numerous, achievable subgoals. To make some of these subgoals more recognizable, each chapter begins with a list of learning objectives. Effectiveness in interpersonal communication depends on understanding and practicing a wide variety of concepts and skills.

What makes the study of interpersonal communication so enjoyable and rewarding is that it can be practiced during almost every waking moment, and the rewards can be realized almost immediately. We seem to be involved in communication constantly, even if it is just with ourselves. And the results of our communication are often immediately perceivable. Thus, our lives

Consider This

I have chosen to define communicative competence in terms of the process by which the individual satisfies his or her goals. The literature on learned helplessness and its conceptual relatives helps justify this perspective by pointing to the negative consequences of an inability to satisfy personal goals. Helpless people tend to experience difficulties with tasks, develop negative self-images, and are more likely to develop mental and physical illnesses.

—From "Interpersonal Communication and the Quest for Personal Competence," by Malcolm R. Parks in *Handbook of Interpersonal Communication,* edited by Mark L. Knapp and Gerald R. Miller, p. 175. Copyright © 1985 by Sage Publications, Inc. Reprinted by permission of Sage Publications, Inc.

give us the opportunity to test the ideas we learn in a practical, real, ongoing arena—the arena of life. Interpersonal communication touches us directly, personally, and immediately.

Because interpersonal communication is a people process, I offer throughout the book a viewpoint that is people-oriented. Later, I label the viewpoint "transactional,"[4] but here I simply want to introduce it because it is a central theme and perspective which, if understood, will give you the context into which all the other elements in this book will fit.

To understand this viewpoint, we must first recognize that to get a total picture of any interpersonal communication situation would require getting into the heads of the individuals who are involved. That would be the only way we could identify all the values, goals, and motivations that affect the behavior that takes place. We can never get such a total picture, but we can get an adequate partial picture. Recognizing that the picture is partial adds the personal dimension that is the essence of this people-oriented viewpoint. This awareness or recognition has several benefits. It reminds us, first, that if we truly want to communicate effectively we must *try* to see the world as the other person does. In a sense, we try to enter the other person's reality. This emphasizes cooperation and sharing.

Second, an awareness that the picture is partial also reminds us that the message or words being communicated are not as important as the meanings those words have for those involved in the communication. Communication is a meaning-centered, not a message-centered, process, and meanings reside in people's minds and hearts. Words are simply the vehicles we use to try to accurately communicate our meanings to others.

Thus, interpersonal communication becomes a unique coming together of individuals who are involved in meaning-making and meaning-sharing.

To gain a full understanding of the process we must look inside ourselves and look inside others as well. It is that rich internal experience of two people individually and as they come together that makes interpersonal communication what it is.[5]

Now that you have a better idea about where I am coming from—a values-growth-transactional approach to clear and open communication—we need to find out more about the communication process itself. Chapter 1 provides a perspective on interpersonal communication. It gives an overview so that as I discuss specific concepts within the interpersonal communication process, you will have a better idea of how the parts relate to each other and to the whole.

Notes

[1] James L. Jarrett, *The Humanities and Humanistic Education* (Reading, Mass.: Addison-Wesley Publishing Co., 1973), p. 147. Used by permission.

[2] Richard L. Johannesen, *Ethics in Human Communication*, 2d ed. (Prospect Heights, Ill.: Waveland Press, Inc., 1983).

[3] I have selected these guidelines from Johannesen's book. See especially Chapter 7, "Interpersonal Communication and Small Group Discussion," pp. 91–98.

[4] This view of communication as transactional grew from the work of Dean C. Barnlund. See Dean C. Barnlund, "Toward a Meaning-Centered Philosophy of Communication," *Journal of Communication* 11 (December 1962): 197–211, and "Communication: The Context of Change," in *Perspectives on Communication*, ed. Carl E. Larson and Frank E. X. Dance (Milwaukee: The Speech Communication Center of the University of Wisconsin, 1968), pp. 24–40. The view has been popularized in the work of John Stewart. See John Stewart, "Interpersonal Communication: Contact Between Persons," in *Bridges Not Walls: A Book About Interpersonal Communication*, 4th ed., ed. John Stewart (New York: Random House, 1986), pp. 15–31.

[5] I have taken the position that interpersonal communication is dyadic in nature, based on the work of William W. Wilmot, *Dyadic Communication*, 2d ed. (Reading, Mass.: Addison-Wesley Publishing Co., 1979), pp. 20–30. Wilmot supports the contention that "when a group of three comes together, the communication relationships evolve so that it is normal for one member to be isolated, suppressed, or excluded from complete participation. A primary dyad plus a third party usually evolves" (p. 21).

Further Reading

The suggested readings following each chapter are intended as a starting point. That is, those students who want a wide range of books dealing with interpersonal communication have a place to begin. Some of these books are popular, from the trade market, and some are academic. I have tried to clarify both the level of the book and its relevance to communication in the annotation.

Helen L. Bee and Sandra K. Mitchell, *The Developing Person: A Life-Span Approach*, 2d ed. (New York: Harper & Row, 1984). In this personal and informal textbook on developmental psychology, the authors discuss physical growth, cognition, and social development in each of the major age categories (childhood, adolescence, youth, and adulthood). Interaction, perception, the self, social relationships, intimacy, and personality are all topics considered. This book provides a useful backdrop for the examination of communication.

Andrew J. DuBrin, *Human Relations: A Job Oriented Approach*, 3rd ed. (Reston, Va: Reston Publishing Co., Inc., 1984). Interpersonal communication is one facet of a larger context: human relations. This book examines the larger context in an organizational framework. The author looks at working with others, with small groups, and with the organization. In addition, he discusses managing yourself and provides an overview of human relations. A thorough, well-organized textbook.

Andrew J. DuBrin, *Human Relations for Career and Personal Success* (Reston, Va: Reston Publishing Co., Inc., 1983). DuBrin offers a basic, skills-oriented textbook. Personal topics include setting goals, solving problems, dealing with stress and tension, communication, assertiveness, conflict management, and getting along with the boss and co-workers. Career topics include choosing a career, finding a job, developing work habits, getting ahead, developing self-confidence, and becoming a leader. Offers practical information with little theory or research.

Steve Duck, *Human Relationships: An Introduction to Social Psychology* (Beverly Hills, Calif.: Sage Publications, 1986). In this 271-page paperback, Duck interweaves current research on interpersonal emotions with traditional social psychology topics thus demonstrating that relationships form the basis of our mental and physical well-being. Besides chapters on loneliness, jealousy, and love, Duck includes chapters on sociolinguistics, nonverbal communication, social skills, social anxiety, and the repair of relationships. He provides an excellent examination of the personal experiences and daily lives within which communication flourishes.

Albert Ellis and Robert A. Harper, *A New Guide to Rational Living* (North Hollywood, Calif.: Wilshire Book Co., 1975). Although dated, this book has become a classic. The authors describe RET (rational-emotive therapy), which is a humanistic, educative model that places the reader in the position of choice maker. The authors claim that it is *we* who must choose to reeducate and retrain ourselves. With communication as *the* tool, this book provides the basic structure for self-created, self-directed growth and development.

Richard L. Johannesen, *Ethics in Human Communication*, 2d ed. (Prospect Heights, Ill.: Waveland Press, Inc., 1983). Johannesen offers a readable, comprehensive, and interesting 10-chapter, 244-page textbook on ethics. Because of the author's information and insights, readers will be sensitized to the relationship of ethics to human communication, the complexities and difficulties involved, and the need to become discerning evaluators of communication. A rich, valuable resource.

Mark L. Knapp and Gerald R. Miller, eds., *Handbook of Interpersonal Communication* (Beverly Hills, Calif.: Sage Publications, 1985). This is a 768-page, authoritative assessment of the state-of-the-art in interpersonal communication. It is a comprehensive collection of original reviews that focus on the field's progress since the 1960s. Each chapter offers an extensive review of literature, a comprehensive bibliography, and recommendations for future research. For those interested in the background of and current trends in the field, the authors' "Introduction" (pages 7–24) is outstanding.

Stephen W. Littlejohn, *Theories of Human Communication*, 3rd ed. (Belmont, Calif.: Wadsworth Publishing Co., 1989). Littlejohn presents the best available textbook for examining the present state-of-the-art in communication theory. He discusses the nature of theory and inquiry in communication and includes a summary of general and contextual theories of communication. This book is valuable not only for its chapters on interpersonal communication (Chapter 9, p. 152–173 and Chapter 10, p. 174–201), but because it offers students a look at the whole range of theory and inquiry, of which interpersonal communication is just one part. Readable, thorough, and well-researched, this book is designed for the serious student of speech communication.

Hugh Prather and Gayle Prather, *A Book for Couples* (New York: Doubleday, 1988). Based in part on their own marriage and on the nationwide workshops for couples they conduct, the Prathers take a definite transactional and humanistic approach to relationships. This approach is based on an individual's willingness to communicate with the other member of a relationship. They offer specific suggestions for communication, conflict management, and intimacy. This is a challenging book with innovative ideas designed for the inquisitive student.

J. Melvin Witmer, *Pathways to Personal Growth: Developing a Sense of Worth and Competence—A Holistic Education Approach* (Muncie, Ind.: Accelerated Development Inc., 1985). Witmer provides historical, philosophical, and psychological foundations for the practices needed for achieving personal growth. Witmer discusses the fully functioning person, wellness as a lifestyle, feelings as vital signs, encouragement, problem-solving, creativity, imagery, values, stress, relaxation, and becoming through believing. A practical, 468-page paperback that is comprehensive without being excessively deep. This book provides a valuable additional look at activities that operate alongside effective communication. A useful book in examining values and goals.

1

Speaking Interpersonally: A Perspective

Learning Objectives

When you have finished this chapter you should be able to:

- Describe each of the elements of the interpersonal communication situation.
- Know the three kinds of effects that can occur as responses to messages.
- List and explain the characteristics of interpersonal communication.
- Understand the ten principles of communication that affect what takes place in every interpersonal communication situation.
- Differentiate between the content and the relationship dimension of communication.
- Define and provide one example each of cultural, sociological, relational, and psychological rules.
- Explain what is meant by "communication is transactional" and how this viewpoint affects your way of looking at interpersonal communication.
- Identify the contexts in which interpersonal communication occurs.
- List and briefly explain those characteristics that comprise communication competence.
- Describe the general skills that relate to interpersonal communication as a whole.

We are all interpersonal communicators—that is, we all communicate with other people. We have been communicating since we were born. And most of us are fairly good at it. At least we are usually able to share ideas when we need to and get information that is important to us. Then why read a textbook or take a class in interpersonal communication? The answer is: Just because we communicate a lot does not necessarily mean that we do it as well as we can. We can all improve.

We engage in interpersonal communication innumerable times every day. Whether we are conversing with our family, talking with teammates, discussing a problem with a teacher, or chatting with friends over a cup of coffee, we are sending and receiving messages, and those messages are having some effect. Even when we only wave at someone we know or tap a person on the shoulder in passing, an interpersonal transaction occurs. All these transactions have certain elements in common. The better we understand these elements, the more likely we are to change our communication behavior for the better.

If this is not motivation enough to improve your interpersonal communication, Beverly Sypher and Theodore Zorn, researchers who investigated upward mobility in business organizations, provide more. They discovered that "communication abilities are strong predictors of individual success in organizations."[1] They found that those people who had more developed social skills—that is, greater ability to get along and communicate effectively with others—"were promoted more often than persons with less-developed abilities."[2] It should be clear that the higher people are promoted within organizations, the more involved they are in both written and spoken communication.

Look at this class you are about to embark on as a new opportunity to grow, develop, and change. One purpose of this class will be to label and organize behavior. Another will be raise your awareness of the behaviors that surround you everyday. Yes, some of the material may already be familiar to you. But if you assume that *because* something is familiar there is nothing more to learn, you will be creating an artificial barrier to your growth, development, and change.

In this chapter I will present an overview of the whole interpersonal communication process. I'll discuss what interpersonal communication is and what it isn't. I'll look at ten communication principles that affect every interpersonal situation we are involved in. And I'll examine the human and environmental contexts in which communication occurs. Finally, I will offer some general suggestions on how we can all improve our interpersonal communication skills.

Before beginning our discussion of interpersonal communication, however, it might be useful to see where it fits in with respect to other communication types. Table 1.1 shows one way of categorizing interpersonal communication.

One type is not necessarily better than another, nor does one type necessarily supplant another. It is possible for several to occur simultaneously. Interpersonal communication is likely to be the most familiar type since, normally, we engage in it most often.

Type	Participants	Process
Intrapersonal	One person	Communication that occurs within us.
Interpersonal	Two people	Communication that occurs on a one-to-one basis.
Small-Group	Three or more people (five is ideal)	Communication that occurs when a small number of people meet for a common purpose.
Public	One person and an audience	A person sending a message to an audience for a specified reason.
Mass	Many people	Messages are transmitted to a mass audience through television, film, or some other medium.

Table 1.1
Types of communication.

It should be clear in this table that all categories are *not* necessarily mutually exclusive. They can interpenetrate—that is, interpersonal communication can occur in (penetrate) a small-group or a mass situation just as a small group or a public speaker may occur in (penetrate) a mass situation.

Elements of an Interpersonal Communication Situation

Figure 1.1 on the following page shows the skeleton of the communication process. It depicts in the most basic form the three elements necessarily involved in any communication situation. These elements are **people, messages,** and **effects.**

People

At any point in an interpersonal communication situation we may be a sender of a message, a receiver of a message, or a sender and a receiver simultaneously. Although Figure 1.1 suggests that messages begin with one person and are received by another, the process can be reversed at any time. We send and receive messages simultaneously when the person we're talking to says or does something that influences what we say next. Even as we speak, we are receiving the verbal and nonverbal messages our listener sends us.

Messages

Messages may be **verbal** and/or **nonverbal.** Both kinds of messages are equally valid as communications. Feedback—cues that tell us how our message is being received—may be verbal (e.g., "I don't understand"), but

Figure 1.1
The skeleton of the communication process.

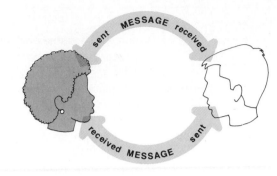

a lot of the feedback we get is nonverbal. We get it in the form of head nodding, eye squinting, large and small gestures, shifts in posture, and in many other ways.

When we think of messages, however, the thing we usually think of first is words, or verbal communication. An important thing to remember is that words mean different things to different people. Words are personal. Words depend for their meaning on the experiences, reactions, feelings, contexts, and ideas of the people using them. All words have these kinds of associations. It is vital to be aware always of the reactions other people have to the words we use.

Effects

Notice that in Figure 1.1 the "message" arrow penetrates the heads: this is to show that the message is having an effect. An effect may be a mental, physical, or emotional response to a message. We may say something that causes another person to reconsider his or her position on a subject: a **mental effect.** We may say something that causes someone to break out in a sweat, run away, or fight: a **physical effect.** Closely tied to physical effects are emotional ones. Our message may cause the other person to feel angry, affectionate, or joyous: an **emotional effect.** The "Try This" on page 18 asks you to categorize comments based on the effect they have on you.

A message that has no effect serves no useful purpose in interpersonal communication. However, we must remember that all effects may not be readily observable. A person might respond to a message with silence. Silence is an effect. It could be based on a mental, physical, or emotional response, and it could have any one of a number of meanings. Also, the communication process may be completed even though the sender is unaware that the message has had an effect. For example, what about advice we give in passing to someone we may never see again? We shout from our car window after a close call, "Next time, watch where you're going!"—and the other driver, unknown to us, begins driving more cautiously and responsibly as a result of our utterance. We may not be aware that the message has had an effect, and yet, clearly, interpersonal communication *has* taken place. This situation admittedly is a bit unusual, as interpersonal communication usually involves *direct* feedback.

Another response that may appear to show no effect is that of boredom or apathy. But just because people do not care about what we are saying does not mean that our message has had no effect. They have chosen not to care, or they have perceived selectively. Just the same, we have produced an effect. No response is a response. Sometimes, too, an effect occurs only after some time has elapsed—a delayed effect. Some effects that take a long time to appear are more significant because they have been thought out more completely. The point is, for communication to take place every message must produce some effect, even if that effect is not immediately apparent.

Characteristics of Interpersonal Communication

Having briefly examined the basic elements of interpersonal communication, let us look at some of the unique features of the interpersonal process that define it and distinguish it from other forms of communication. Interpersonal communication:

1. Involves at least two people,
2. Involves feedback,
3. Need not be face-to-face,
4. Need not be intentional,
5. Produces some effect,
6. Need not involve words,
7. Is affected by context, and
8. Is affected by noise.

Interpersonal Communication Involves at Least Two People

The fact that interpersonal communication involves people may seem too obvious to mention, but by saying it involves people we rule out the communication we have with our pets, with our car (especially when it is running poorly), with our plants, or with any other objects of affection. Such communication may be important and healthy, but it is not "interpersonal" as the term will be used in this book.

To say that interpersonal communication involves at least two people rules out the kind of communication we have within ourselves. *Intrapersonal communication* is the name usually given to these kinds of internal messages. In Chapter 3 we'll look more carefully at intrapersonal communication—

Try This

Pretend that someone made each of the following comments to you. This person is someone you know but do not consider a close friend. Categorize the comments according to the effect they might have on you. Is the effect mental, physical, or emotional?

1. "Have you ever considered changing your major?"
2. "Why don't you grow up?"
3. "You know, you really have a lot of friends."
4. "You're always complaining."
5. "What do you like best about this class?"
6. "For somebody taking interpersonal communication you sure don't know much about it."
7. "Are you really cut out for college?"
8. "You can give advice, but you can't take it."

Effects differ. Just because these comments have certain effects on you does not mean they would have the same effect on others. A lot depends on who makes the comments and in what context. Can you think of other factors that might determine how you would react to them?

communication within the self—as the self is the starting point for all messages we exchange with others. But for the most part, the primary focus of this book will be on communication situations involving two people.

For our purposes, we will think of interpersonal communication as involving no more than two people—a **dyad.** Two is not an arbitrary number. Three—the **triad**—can be considered the smallest of small groups. In the most comprehensive treatment of the nature of triads, Theodore Caplow suggests that "the most significant property of the triad is its tendency to divide a coalition of two members against the third."[3] William Wilmot concludes that "when three people are in a face-to-face transaction, the transaction *at any time* is composed of a primary dyad plus one."[4]

When we define interpersonal communication in terms of the number of people involved, we must remember that interpersonal communication may actually occur between two people who are part of a larger group. Sometimes within a group of people, splinter groups of two or three participants are formed. As groups increase in size, this becomes more likely. When two people in a larger group argue over a point, they are definitely engaged in interpersonal communication. We've all been in discussion groups where two members dominated the conversation until the discussion became simply an exchange of ideas between those two people. This kind of interpersonal communication often occurs in a group setting.

Interpersonal Communication Involves Feedback

When we use the term *interpersonal* we do not include TV newscasters or radio disc jockeys, whose messages go from source to audience but do not return. (See Figure 1.2.) We do not include public-speaking situations either, where the message goes from a speaker to a large audience with only a limited amount of return. (See Figure 1.3.)

Feedback is the message sent by the receiver back to the speaker. Interpersonal communication nearly always involves direct feedback. It is often immediate, obvious, and continuous. (See Figure 1.4.) Note that the figure shows not only an arrow from the source to the receiver but also an equivalent arrow from the receiver to the source. This direct relationship between the source and the receiver is a feature unique to interpersonal communication. I refer to it as *simultaneous message* or *co-stimulation.*

Interpersonal Communication Need Not Be Face-to-Face

Sitting on a bus, you may be affected by a noisy conversation between two people sitting in front of you (even though it does not involve you) and as a result choose to move to another seat. You may speak to a person on the telephone; you may pass nonverbal messages to a friend across the room by using facial expressions or gestures; you could even be in another room and

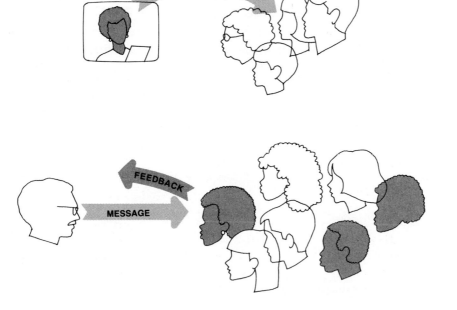

Figure 1.2
A no-feedback situation (mass communication).

Figure 1.3
A limited-feedback situation (public communication).

pass messages to another person by tapping on the wall. You need not be in a face-to-face situation to participate in interpersonal communication.

Although interpersonal communication need not be face-to-face, communication without face-to-face interaction is by no means ideal. Losing direct contact means losing a major factor in feedback. Also, a significant vehicle for conveying emotions is lost. Think about it. When you want to improve the quality of a relationship, how do you communicate this desire without words? Often eye contact, head nods, and smiles are major factors. Eliminating direct contact in interpersonal communication almost has the effect of taking the personal out of interpersonal communication.

In face-to-face situations we receive more information because we can see more of the other person. Communication is likely to be more effective during a face-to-face encounter because we're more apt to catch each other's subtleties, special inflections, and emphases. We can perceive moods more accurately when we are face-to-face, and consequently we have a better chance of getting the whole message.

Interpersonal Communication Need Not Be Intentional

Interpersonal communication is not necessarily deliberate. For example, you might find out through a slip of the tongue that someone has lied to you. You might discover that someone is very nervous around you by the person's constant shifting of weight from one foot to another, continual fumbling over words, or other nervous reactions. You might decide that you do not want to be around a person at all because of a certain abrasiveness or disagreeable manner. The person probably didn't intentionally communicate these things, but they are messages because they are signals that affect you.

Interpersonal Communication Produces Some Effect

To be truly considered interpersonal communication, a message must produce some effect. As we saw earlier, this effect need not be immediately apparent, but it must occur. If you walk along the sidewalk toward a person you don't know, wearing your broadest, warmest, I-want-to-get-to-know-you-better

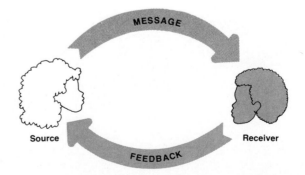

Figure 1.4
A direct-feedback situation (interpersonal or small-group communication).

MESSAGE

Source

Receiver

FEEDBACK

smile, and the other person doesn't see you and walks on by, no interpersonal communication has taken place. A similar situation occurs if you are talking to someone while that person is listening to music on stereo headphones or using a hair dryer and doesn't hear you. These are not interpersonal communications if the messages are not received and have no effect.

Interpersonal Communication Need Not Involve Words

Though I've already mentioned some of the ways we can communicate without words, this characteristic needs emphasis because nonverbal communication is so important. Picture two people secretly in love with each other who are standing on opposite sides of the room at a party. A quick glance between them can reaffirm their whole relationship and love for each other. Often a look or a touch can convey far more than words. Nonverbal messages are a powerful and significant form of interpersonal communication.

A unique aspect of interpersonal communication is its potential to involve a number of senses. People who are engaged in interpersonal communication are, generally, standing or sitting close to one another so they can touch and smell as well as see and hear. The message is intensified because far more stimuli of a personal nature are available to observers.

Interpersonal Communication Is Affected by the Context

When we speak of the **context** of an interpersonal communication we mean all the human and environmental factors that preceeded, will follow, and are at work during the actual exchange of messages. Communication does not occur in a vacuum. There are countless stimuli that affect what is said, what is meant, and what is understood in a message exchange. Obviously, the people involved in interpersonal communication must be in a position to receive cues from each other; however, they could be separated by two inches, two feet, or two miles. The kind of communication that takes place depends heavily on just such factors of circumstance.

Context often determines content. We usually talk about different kinds of things depending on whether we are alone with a friend or surrounded by people who can listen in on our conversation; on whether we're speaking over the phone or talking face-to-face; on whether we're both happy or both depressed. These factors all make up the communication context and have a significant effect on the quality of the communication that takes place.

Interpersonal Communication Is Affected by Noise

In every communication situation noise is a factor. The purpose of communication is to try to make certain that the message you create in your brain is exactly re-created in the brain of the receiver. But this seldom, if ever, happens, There are many reasons for this, all of which can be labeled **noise.** Noise is *any interference in the source, receiver, or environment that reduces the exactness of the message.* Noise exists because we have no way to directly link one brain with another.

Source-generated noise results from a number of different behaviors. Linguistic problems, for example, can cause noise. A speaker may use faulty grammar, improper sentence construction, incorrect word choices, or mispronunciation. When a speaker has an unusual vocal quality, or uses inappropriate pitch or emphasis, or speaks too loudly, too slowly, too fast, or with an unusual rhythm, noise problems can occur. Additional problems may be caused by incongruence (lack of agreement) between the words and the speaker's gestures or facial expressions. Extraverbal behaviors such as incongruent or inappropriate gestures and expressions are a third category of source-generated noise.

Receiver-generated noise also results from a number of different factors. Think, for example, about all the various elements *you* bring to any communication situation: your background and experience, your skills and abilities, your thoughts and feelings. And think how these affect the way you listen to, understand, and integrate what *anyone* says to you. What are your own experiences in communicating? Are you a skilled communicator?

Try This

Using the *last* dyad you were part of as the basis for this analysis, answer the following questions that revolve around the eight characteristics of interpersonal communication just discussed:

1. Who was the other person involved?
2. List the kinds of feedback experienced?
   a. Was it immediate?
   b. Was it obvious?
   c. Was it continuous?
3. To what extent could you (did you) see the other person's face?
4. Was all the communication you experienced intentional?
5. What effects did you detect?
6. How many senses came into play?
   a. Did you *hear* what was being said?
   b. Did you *see* the person as you talked? What did you observe?
   c. Did the sense of *smell* come into play at all?
   d. Did the sense of *touch* come into play?
   e. Did the sense of *taste* come into play?
7. Did the context affect the communication in any way?
8. What kinds of noise affected your communication?

The point of this exercise is to help you become more sensitive to all aspects of your dyadic communication. Obviously, such communication is more than just words being passed between two people.

How do you feel about the other person's communication? What about your reactions to the other person? The level of respect—or distrust—can directly affect your response to the message.

Another important area of receiver-generated noise has to do with feelings about the other's subject matter. What are your own experiences, abilities, or feelings on this topic? Do you have fixed ideas on it, and are your feelings strong? If so, it could be that your mind is somewhat closed to ideas on this subject.

A final area of receiver-generated noise concerns emotional reactions to specific words that are said or things that are done. Some people, for example, stop listening when a speaker uses vulgar language or an obscene gesture. Listening ceases for some when labels that evoke stereotypical (negative) responses, such as dago, polack, women's libber, or male chauvinist pig are used to describe people.

Environmental noise is that which occurs between the source and the receiver. The noise is **acoustic** if it consists of sounds other than those generated by the source or receiver that either block out the message or make hearing difficult. Think, for example, how hard it is to understand conversation at a loud party. Sometimes a message is heard, but heard incorrectly, because of acoustic noise.

Another area of environmental noise is **visual** noise. A lecturer was talking in a large lecture hall when a student came in late at the back of the hall and walked to the very front row of seats before sitting down. All eyes followed the student down the aisle and into the first row—visual noise that blocked the lecturer's message. Have you ever been distracted by something occurring outside the classroom window while a student was giving a speech or a report? Environmental factors can disrupt communication and make the process more difficult.

Ten Principles of Communication

Understanding interpersonal communication involves more than knowing its irreducible elements of people, messages, and effects. When we study this form of communication closely, we will see that there are ten principles that affect every interpersonal communication situation. An understanding of these principles will help us analyze, evaluate, and improve our own communication habits. They provide an important foundation. In the discussion of many of the concepts developed in later chapters, it will be assumed that these ten principles are affecting what takes place in any interpersonal communication situation. These principles are, then, the fundamentals on which other concepts depend.[5]

We Cannot Not Communicate

Think of a time when you sat in a classroom waiting for class to begin, in a rotten mood, not wanting to talk to anybody, staring blankly ahead, and not making a movement or a sound. Anyone coming into the room could see that you didn't want to talk. You may not have wanted to speak but you were communicating. Just as *you* were communicating, so were those people who decided not to speak to you. Communication is more than the exchange of words.

All observable behavior is communication and can be considered a message. No word, gesture, or mannerism is neutral. Even people who dress and speak inconspicuously do so for a reason. The fact that they choose anonymity communicates something about them. Knowing that we cannot *not* communicate should make us more aware of our behavior at all times. In the presence of others, we probably reveal far more about ourselves than we realize.

Communication Can Be Verbal or Nonverbal

When we communicate with others we use either verbal messages, nonverbal messages, or a combination of the two. Verbal messages are either sent or not sent, just as a light switch is either on or off. They have an all-or-nothing feature built in. Nonverbal cues are not as clear-cut.

Nonverbal communication includes such behaviors as facial expressions, posture, and gestures, and *paralanguage*—the vocal but nonverbal aspects of speech. Paralanguage consists of voice qualities such as pitch, rate, and inflection. Just as a dimmer switch on a light can be used to adjust intensity, nonverbal cues often reveal shades or degrees of meaning. You may say, for example, "I am very upset," but *how* upset you are will be conveyed more by your facial expression, gestures, or paralanguage than by the actual words you speak.

Every Communication Contains Information and Defines Relationships

Imagine initiating a conversation with a woman by asking, "How about joining me for a cup of coffee?" The **informational** part of this message, or **content dimension,** refers to what you expect of her—namely, that you want her to join you for coffee. The **relationship** aspect of the message, or **relationship dimension,** is the meaning behind the words that says something about your relationship to her.

The relationship dimension tells her how to deal with the message. She recognizes, for example, that this is not a command, but a friendly invitation that implies no status difference between the two of you. What if she made the same suggestion to you and she happened to be one of your teachers? The relationship aspect of the message would be quite different. Suppose she commanded, "Come, have a cup of coffee with me!" The relationship implied here is one of unequal status, known as a **complementary** relationship. When the status is equal the relationship can be labeled **symmetrical.** But it isn't merely a question of equal versus unequal status that defines relationships. It *is* the kinds of behaviors being exchanged. For example, Jason might talk to his boss in a manner that suggests he is one-up on the boss, and the boss might accept this definition of their relationship. Accordingly, even though their respective statuses may suggest one type of relationship, the way in which they actually communicate defines another. The *behavior* defines the relationship. That is what makes the communicative perspective of relationships more compelling than a primarily sociological or psychological perspective. Also, relationships between people change from complementary to symmetrical and back again depending on the content of the message or the situation.

Try This

"I would really like to get to know you better."

Briefly describe what changes you would make in saying the above phrase if you were speaking to each of the following people:

1. A member of the opposite sex whom you just have met for the first time.
2. The parents of your best friend.
3. One of your teachers.
4. One of the cafeteria (or lunchroom) personnel.
5. A student (same sex) in one of your classes.

Would you make different kinds of changes if the statement were the following, instead of the one above? What kinds?

"You know, you are wrong; I was there and I saw exactly what happened."

The messages "Please, won't you come and have coffee with me?" and "You are going to have coffee with me!" contain the same information but imply a different relationship. The message, "Could I please see your notes from yesterday's lecture?" has essentially the same relationship level as "Please, won't you come and have coffee with me?" but the content is very different. When we have an ongoing relationship with someone, we tend to operate on the same relationship level for all our communication, no matter what information we're exchanging. This relationship level changes only when one of us perceives a change in status in relation to the other.

When you speak to another person you reveal something about how you see the relationship between yourself and that person, not necessarily how that relationship *should* be. In the simple opening comment, "How about joining me for a cup of coffee?" you have offered the woman a definition of your self that implies you are her equal—that you have a symmetrical relationship. She can make any of three general responses:

1. She may **confirm** your definition of self. She might say, "I'd love to," and verify the equality.
2. She may **reject** your view of self by saying, "I'm really not interested." This response implies that her view of the relationship is not the same as yours.
3. She may **disconfirm** by ignoring you—denying your right to definition of self. By ignoring your question, she could be saying she thinks you have no claim to a relationship at all.

True, these responses are extreme. There are many intermediate kinds of responses the woman could make. She could say no without rejecting your view of self by adding, "Could I take a rain check on it?" But clearly, the kind of response she makes has significant implications for the definition of self and the relationship that you have offered. Notice how you can control the relationship dimension by *how* you say something.

Problems in communication most often occur in the relationship dimension rather than in the content dimension. The content dimension involves the information conveyed through word symbols. The relationship dimension involves the feelings conveyed through nonverbal symbols. This distinction between the content and relationship dimensions is simplified here for the purposes of discussion. The distinction is *not* to suggest that people do not discuss relationship issues or express feelings using words, or that specific gestures cannot have clear content-oriented meanings. Obviously, there are crossovers between these dimensions.

Consider a situation in which you have to do a major project and need to use your roommate's desk as well as your own to spread out your materials. You do this without asking permission first. Your roommate returns to find your things spread out all over the room and flies into a rage, saying, "What the hell do you think you're doing?" There is really no issue over the content of that question or how you would answer it on that level: you are doing your project and you are using both desks. But that isn't the real meaning of the question. On the relationship level, what is being said is, "You are taking advantage of me. You are acting as if I didn't matter. You think you are superior to me." To put that response into a communication framework, your roommate could be saying, "I thought we had a symmetrical relationship, but now you have proven that all *you* want is a complementary one." The issue involves feelings, *not* words.

To cope with the situation you need to address the fact that your roommate feels you have threatened the relationship of equality that existed before. Asking permission beforehand would have acknowledged equality; it would have said, "You are a person capable of helping me solve my problem."

The trouble is not that the communication occurs on the relationship level; all messages imply something about a relationship. The problems occur when there is a discrepancy between the content and the relationship conveyed. In the above example, your roommate asks an aggressive question (the literal answer to which is obvious) when the real intention is to reestablish the equal relationship that seems to have been threatened. There is a discrepancy between the content and relationship aspects of the message. The healthier a relationship is, the less discrepancy there is, because we are more likely to say exactly how we feel. And we will be more secure in our status regarding the other person, less likely to feel the balance is being threatened by the smallest word or action. Weak relationships are often characterized by constant struggles over the nature of the relationship.

Try This

In the situations described here, do you see yourself assuming an equal or an unequal relationship with the people indicated?

1. With your best friend: making plans for the weekend.
2. With your parents: deciding what you will do after you graduate.
3. With your roommate: determining when the stereo or television will be on or off.
4. On a date: choosing where the two of you will go.
5. In working with another student on a project: deciding who does what part of the work.

This is not to say that arguments cannot occur over the information dimension of a message. But this kind of conflict tends to be more manageable because the content level of a message generally refers to something external to both parties. The content level refers to something that exists in the real world and can often be verified. An example of an argument on the content level is: "Did the newspaper come this morning?" "No, it didn't." "I thought I heard it hit the door." "Well, I didn't see it when I looked." "But I *heard* it." The content question raised in this argument can be resolved by one or both people looking to see if the paper is actually there. Either it is or it isn't. Relationship questions are not as easily resolved. Often people think they are arguing about content when actually it is the nature of their relationship that they are questioning.

We may find that questions of content can be raised and resolved using a minimum of nonverbal communication. Words and sentences are an effective medium for dealing with informational aspects of messages, both simple and complex. When questions of relationship arise, and particularly when these questions are buried in matter that is supposedly concerned with content, the intricacies of such questions are often better expressed nonverbally. That is, if all we care about is knowing where someone is going, we can simply ask, "Where are you going?" If we want to show what we see as our superiority over that person, we might say very loudly, "Where are *you* going?" with our hands on our hips and exasperation in our voice. We express the relationship aspect of our message nonverbally.

Remember that every communication is a combination of content and relationship factors and is expressed with verbal and nonverbal elements together. If we're unsure about the information someone is trying to pass on to us, we should try not to be distracted by nonverbal messages. If we're trying to understand what that person is saying about the nature of our relationship, nonverbal cues might be more helpful to us.

Communication Relationships Can Be Equal or Unequal

The communication relationships we have with people are all based on whether we see our status as basically equal or basically unequal. This status depends on many factors—circumstance, personality, age, wealth, job position, and so on. We may, at different points in life, feel unequal with our parents, teachers, siblings, or authority figures. These relationships can change at any time. We may find we feel equal or superior to people we once felt inferior to.

When we not only feel, but are, on an equal level with another person, the two of us tend to mirror each other's behavior—sometimes intentionally, sometimes not. We may discover we are depressed at the same time, cheerful at the same time. In relationships based on equality, both people usually try to minimize the differences and emphasize the similarities between them, whether or not they do this on purpose. These are the relationships previously labeled symmetrical.

People involved in an unequal relationship do just the opposite. The relationships are often defined by social or cultural context, such as the relationship between doctor and patient, employer and employee, parent and child. These relationships are labeled complementary.

Complementary relationships also exist in more informal relationships. Two friends may slip into a pattern in which one is the decision maker, the other less decisive; one levelheaded, the other scatterbrained; one the agitator, the other the soother. Sometimes there are more subtle arrangements in which one person is the decision maker on matters of where to eat, but the other is the decision maker on matters of finance. One may be superior in matters of entertaining but the other is superior in matters of car purchase and maintenance. People often work out an equilibrium or balance of complementary relationships. In each case it is important to note the interlocking nature of the roles; the superior behavior of one person often evokes and reinforces complementary behavior from the other person.

There can be problems in both symmetrical and complementary relationships, and one form is not being suggested as better than the other. Some people respond best in symmetrical relationships, others in complementary relationships. Problems can arise in a symmetrical relationship where partners mirror each other's negative behaviors, creating a vicious cycle. Trouble may surface in a complementary relationship when one person's inferior behavior reinforces superiority in the other person to such an extent that the superior person becomes unreasonably rigid or powerful. The nature of our communication relationship depends upon who the other person is, what position he or she holds, what message is being conveyed, and when and where the interaction is occurring.

Communication Relationships Develop over Time

Another dimension of interpersonal communication that relates to relationships is called the developmental perspective.[6] This perspective holds that interpersonal communication emerges—or has the potential of emerging— as relationships progress through time and changes occur in the way the participants perceive each other and in the way they define the rules governing their relationship.

It has been suggested that there are three levels of rules that guide our actions and conduct. **Cultural rules** are those common to all members of a culture. For example, notice the way you, and those around you, smile and nod as you greet each other and say goodbye. You know, as most people in our culture know, that it is appropriate to acknowledge another's presence when you meet. There are cultural rules for greetings and farewells. **Sociological rules** are those shared by specific groups within a culture. Think of the rules that guide the actions and conduct of those in our armed forces, lodge members, fraternity and sorority members, or Girl and Boy Scouts. Have you ever witnessed the exchange of a secret or unique handshake by those members of the same organization, association, or subculture? **Psychological rules** are those worked out by individuals. How do *you* greet your friends? By slapping each other on the shoulder? By hugging? By using joking insults? By complimenting each other? These are the unique things that mark your specific, individual relationship. There are no cultural or sociological rules that specify how *you* should greet your friends—only general guidelines.[7]

The developmental perspective says that when you are in a dyadic relationship, the two of you, working together, create a couple that is unique from other couples: the things the *two* of you talk about, the things the *two* of you like to do together, the kinds of people the *two* of you like to be around. You develop a shared reality. Not only does this make your couple unique, but it means that who you are, in part, depends on the couple you have helped create!

As the unique couple progresses, the interpersonal communication that occurs between the participants becomes similarly unique. They begin to see each other as persons, not as parts of a larger, undefined, mass of people.

As relationship partners begin seeing each other as persons, they begin defining and negotiating their own rules. They develop **relational rules**—a combination of the psychological and sociological levels (you're no longer an individual; and you're not a group!) The relationship partners are no longer being guided entirely by what society says is right or proper. Their behavior is guided by their own rules and what they accept and adopt of society's relational rules. Clearly, if a couple should go too far in creating rules unique to their relationship, society may step in and attempt to change or overcome their divergent rules or punish behavior that is deemed unacceptable.

Relational rules, however, add to the complexity of the communication process. They may determine why a couple decides to dress strangely, engages in anti-social behavior, becomes hermits, or chooses an odd line of work. These examples are extremes, of course; the point is that defining and negotiating are natural parts of relationship (dyadic) progression. It is how the couple puts its unique stamp on the relationship.

Communication becomes more complex simply because a whole new set of rules is operating. When you ask, "Why do Andrew and Carole do what they do?" the answer may not be obvious; in fact, it may never be known. A more important question may be "What is the meaning of Andrew and Carole's behavior?" By itself it may not have any meaning, but when placed in a context—cultural, social, relational, or even psychological— meaning emerges. When relationships progress and relational rules are negotiated within dyads, interpersonal communication takes on an entirely new dimension, and the number of variables involved increases dramatically.

Try This

For this exercise, you will need to use as a reference a relationship you have been in for some time and that has progressed or changed since it first began. With this relationship in mind, answer the following questions:

1. What changes have occurred in the way you view this other person?
2. What changes have occurred in the way you think this other person views you?
3. What changes have occurred in the rules that govern your relationship? Are there rules now that did not exist before? Such rules might include:
   a. Whom you can see and how often.
   b. Whom you can talk to.
   c. The freedom (independence) you have.
   d. What the two of you can do or what each of you can do when separated from the other.
   e. What the two of you can talk about.

Notice from your answers how a different (or deeper) level of interpersonal communication emerges (or has the potential to emerge) as relationships progress and changes occur. Notice too, as the rules that govern your relationship grow in number, how unique that relationship becomes. How similar to or different from other relationships do you think yours is (was)? Did you discover any behaviors for which you could offer no rule? Sometimes, things are the way they are because that is the way they are! Your response may be, "We've always done it this way." It is not a very scientific response, but it is functional!

If you have ever been in a dyad over a long period of time, you will recognize this dimension in operation.

I am *not* suggesting that communication *only* becomes interpersonal once a relationship has developed. All communication has an interpersonal element. Certainly, the clearest instance of interpersonal communication occurs when two people interact personally and directly; however, there are many other interactions that are also interpersonal in nature. The developmental perspective is simply another dimension that needs to be recognized. We will look more closely at the development of relationships in Chapter 12.

The remaining five principles provide additional insight into what is happening in every interpersonal communication situation. Dean Barnlund identifies these principles when he suggests that communication be viewed as (1) a process that is (2) circular, (3) complex, (4) irreversible and unrepeatable, and (5) transactional—involves the total personality.[8]

Communication Is a Process

When we look at communication as a process, we mean that each communication situation is part of an ongoing series of actions. The events and relationships are dynamic, everchanging, and continuous.[9] To fully understand any single communication, you really need to know all that has come before. Our communication experiences are cumulative—each is a result of what has preceded it. And each experience affects all the ones still to come. For example, as you talk with another person, you may discover an attitude or prejudice that you hadn't known about. That new information will change the way you communicate with that person in the future. The present conversation is a point of development for all future conversations with that person. Thus, this event is not static; it is moving. It is in a state of flux. The components of the process interact, each affecting all the others.[10]

Think about the kind of conversation you would have if you, at your present age, could talk to the person you were at sixteen, at thirteen, and at eight. Each "you" would be a completely developed person *for that age,* yet each would be merely a developmental point for the "you" to follow. Communication builds on itself. The process goes on as long as we are alive.

Communication Is Circular

To view each of our interpersonal communication situations as circular means that we are concerned not only with the effect of our initial message on someone else, but also with the effect of his or her response on us. We then respond based on this new message. This process is important to grasp. (See Figure 1.5.) Though it may sound as if we're going in circles, we are not. Both of us are constantly changing and making corrections in our thinking as we interact.

Although a minimum number of stimuli and responses are depicted in Figure 1.5, this figure reveals the cyclical nature of communication triggered by the first stimulus. For example, if your initial stimulus is, "How was the party last night?" I might reply, "Dull!" You might inquire, "Oh, how come?" and I would answer, "Nothing happened." You might follow with, "What do you mean?" and so on. The conversation builds on itself. Each remark makes sense only in terms of what preceded it. Remember that in real conversations, many stimuli can occur and be considered at once. Either person may, at any time, provide a new stimulus that can start off its own chain reaction.

Communication Is Complex

We've already noted some factors that contribute to the complexity of communication. For example, refer back to our discussion of cultural, societal, relational, and psychological rules. Communication also is complex

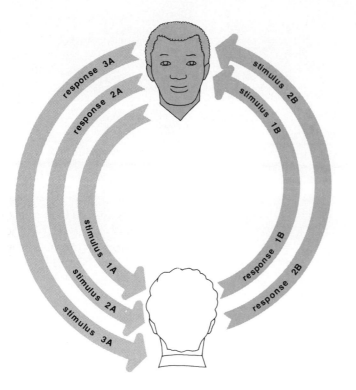

Figure 1.5
*Communication is cir-
cular.*

because of the tremendous number of variables involved. In every interpersonal communication you share with another person, there are at least six "people" involved:

1. The person you think you are,
2. The person your partner thinks you are,
3. The person you believe your partner thinks you are,
4. The person your partner thinks he or she is,
5. The person you think your partner is, and
6. The person your partner believes you think he or she is.[11]

With just four constants, mathematicians must cope with approximately fifty possible relations. When you consider the number of variables involved in each interpersonal situation, you begin to appreciate the "terribly involved, and therefore fascinating puzzle" that is known as human communication.[12] Even the most apparently simple interpersonal encounter is actually quite complicated.

Notice how many variables are operating in the relationship shown in Figure 1.6 when the six "people" are described. When you talk with others, what you say depends on how you perceive each of the variables, just as what others say to you depends on the variables they perceive. The more

Figure 1.6
There are at least six "people" involved in every interpersonal communication.

honestly you talk, the more you can be sure that the variables you perceive are accurate. If the two people in Figure 1.6 take the time to get to know each other, he may discover she's not as self-confident as she first appeared to be, and she may find that his "enthusiasm" is nothing more than undirected nervous energy. She may start to appreciate his sincerity or ambitiousness instead, if those traits seem to apply to him. If your perceptions are not accurate, you correct them. Thus, as open communication proceeds, it becomes better and better because:

1. It becomes grounded on perceptions that are more accurate—perceptions that are tested through actual interaction.
2. It becomes better adapted to the person you're talking to because you have a better idea of where he or she is coming from.
3. It becomes less open to chance. You need to do less guessing about the other person and less guessing about the nature of the message.
4. There is less chance for breakdowns to occur. Breakdowns often involve simple misperceptions and misinterpretations. These can never be avoided completely. But big breakdowns based on gross error become less likely. You know better who and what you are dealing with.

Communication is complex. There is no way to control all the variables involved, but the more accurate our perceptions are, the better chance we will have of minimizing the complexity of the communication.

Try This

Pretend you are doing poorly in a course and decide to go in to see the instructor, who knows you are not doing well. Briefly describe the six "people" who may be revealed at the beginning of your discussion with your instructor.

Communication Is Irreversible and Unrepeatable

Each interpersonal experience is totally unique. It can never occur again in just the same way under any circumstances. Sometimes we wish we *could* take back things we've said. Have you ever said, in the heat of an argument, "You're hopeless! You'll never amount to anything!" or something equally cruel? You can't ever take the sting out of a remark like that, no matter what you say or how you apologize later. The remark cannot be taken back.

It is impossible to re-create a communication situation because the knowledge, feelings, and impressions a person brings to an experience change with time, even within a matter of seconds. Saying "I love you" because you want to in a particular situation is quite different from repeating it because you are asked to, even if the words are the same both times. The communication can never be precisely repeated, no matter how many times you say the very same words, because both people are different as a result of the words' having been said in the first place.

Despite thorough organization and planning, most of what occurs interpersonally is spontaneous—open to chance. Have you ever tried to repeat a funny story or describe a hilarious incident only to have your listeners say, "What's so funny about that?" You end up saying, "I guess you had to be there." It is impossible to reconstruct past communication experiences. Even when we come close, new and different factors over which we have no control arise to change the situation and the communication.

Communication Is Transactional[13]

Our whole being is involved in communication, not just our body or mind, reason or emotion. Just as every message we send reveals, in a way, where we are, how we have developed, right up to that point, so we should look at the messages we receive from others as revealing the same things about them. From the various cues that others give us, we construct a total picture of them. Whether or not the image is accurate does not matter as much as the fact that it is *our* configuration and we use it when we respond to them.[14]

Every time we communicate we define those with whom we communicate just as we unconsciously offer others cues that help them define us. Anything that evokes meaning for others becomes part of our self-definition, whether it be appearance, voice, touch, distance, eye contact, or word choice. We define others and reveal cues for others to define us *every* time we communicate; there are no exceptions.[15]

Transactional communication—or communication as transaction—is the term used to refer to this process.[16] It emphasizes that who people are with reference to others is a result of the communication events—transactions—in which they are involved. Thus, part of what is going on when we communicate with others is this mutual process of defining.[17] You may

wonder why this viewpoint is important. There are several reasons, but the main one is that this view takes into consideration all the preceding characteristics and principles:

1. Communication is *not* linear. From the arrows in the models offered thus far, it appears that interpersonal communication involves looking at one person's choices and then observing the behavior of the other person in response. Although some cause and effect, action and reaction, occurs, the whole process is far more complex than a model can represent.

When you view communication as linear—either one-way from communicator to receiver or two-way (simple cause and effect)—you miss the important dynamics of what occurs between the participants. A transactional viewpoint focuses on the dynamics that occur between communicators.

2. Communication is *not* easily observed. The definitions that communicators construct are likely to be complex images based on a large number of interacting cues. These images are unique psychological experiences, almost totally private, and dependent on complex processes of drawing conclusions—that is, putting seemingly unrelated cues together to make sense of them.

When you take a transactional viewpoint, you recognize that communication is a psychological event and, thus, not easily observed. It involves the minds and behaviors of those involved. All parts of the communication event derive their definition—their very existence and nature—from having been part of the event and perceived by any of the participants.

Consider This

A dictionary of psychological terms defines a transaction as "a psychological event in which all parts or aspects of the concrete event derive their existence and nature from active participation in the event."[18] In other words, a transaction is an event in which *who we are* (our existence and nature) emerges out of the event itself. Human communication is that kind of event. Human communication is transactional. Whenever humans communicate, part of what's going on is that each is defining himself or herself in relation to the other persons involved.

—John Stewart, Ed., *Bridges Not Walls: A Book About Interpersonal Communication,* 4th ed. (New York: Random House, 1986), p. 24.

3. Communication is *not* just people. It is people *meeting.* When you think of a transaction, think of people communicating *with* each other. To look at one person or the other—with no reference to who the others are—is not transactional. We must focus on the meeting between people because who the communicators are at any given moment in a transaction is a result of—or is defined by—both the context and whom they are communicating with and their relationship with those others at any given moment. It is that unique involvement and interaction of the communicators' identities with each other and with the context that gives the transactional viewpoint its distinctiveness and importance.

4. Communication is *not* a result of single forces. It is sometimes easy to think we know why other people acted as they did, yet, in many cases, the underlying reason was not the sole reason or even the principal one. Just as our definitions of others result from numerous cues, our behavior results from a larger number of causes. To view communication as a transaction is to suggest that it involves the total personality. What happens in any one instance is likely to be a result of multiple forces, factors, or causes.

5. Communication is *not* just what is going on *now.* All communications have a past, present, and future. This underscores the process-nature of communication. Every communication is part of an ongoing series of actions. What I think of you right now (present) is likely to be affected by the fight we had last night (past) and is likely to affect my willingness to be open and friendly to you at the party tonight (future). Even if a relationship has no immediate history, it is dependent on all of the past relationships we have had; thus, our experiences provide a past, help determine the present, and often forecast the future.

6. Communication is *not* dependent just on who we are. Who we *really* are is a very private matter! What we share with others are aspects of our

Consider This

When you adopt a transactional point of view . . . you can't help but look at the contact *between* the persons involved. If you focus your attention on just person A, for example, you realize that since person A is who he or she is only in relation to person B, you have to look immediately at what's happening *between* them. The same goes for person B. Since *who the persons are*—their existence and nature—emerges out of their meeting with each other, you can't help but focus on the meeting itself rather than on the individual meeters.

—John Stewart, Ed., *Bridges Not Walls: A Book About Interpersonal Communication,* 4th ed. (New York: Random House, 1986), p. 25.

public selves—the roles we play in relation to others. Some of these roles are established by society, some by individual relationships, and some, too, by whim and fancy (moods). Compare the way you behave in the presence of your father with the way you behave in the presence of your best friend. Have you ever noticed that when you are out with a person of the opposite sex and a group of his or her friends join you, the behavior of this person often changes? Sometimes dramatically! Our behavior is based *not* just on who we are but also on whom we are with.

The transactional viewpoint is essential to a clear understanding of interpersonal communication. It suggests that when you engage another person through communication, you create a relationship that is totally unique, difficult to observe or describe because of its many facets, and, although changeable, likely to endure (and affect future encounters) forever. Relationships seldom cease to exist. They may change in how they are defined, but they do not end.[19] (See Figure 1.7.)

Contexts

Human communication does not occur in a vacuum. It *always* takes place in a series of interacting contexts, and these contexts *always* influence the kind of communication that occurs. Context simply refers to the environment in which communication takes place. Having examined the nature of a transaction, we have been introduced already to one of the most important of these contexts—the psychological. The others are the physical, social, cultural, and temporal. (See Figure 1.8.)

When examining contexts, we are looking at the who, what, when, where, and how of interpersonal communication. These are all important

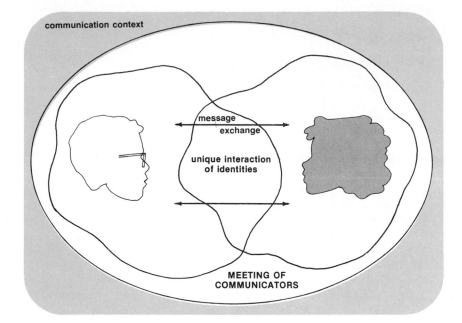

communication context

message exchange

unique interaction of identities

MEETING OF COMMUNICATORS

Figure 1.7
The transactional nature of communication. The amoebalike shape around each person represents both the involvement of the total personality in the communication as well as the changeable nature of the images projected to the other person. It is the meeting of the communicators as a whole as well as the unique interaction of their identities that makes the transactional viewpoint distinctive.

variables. How they interact with each other is also important.[20] Unfortunately, it is impossible to be aware of *all* possible contextual elements, much less the way they affect each other.

Psychological

The **psychological context** consists of aspects that occur in the minds of the participants. Because of the moods or attitudes of the communicators, contexts can be serious or humorous, formal or informal, friendly or unfriendly.

The psychological context is especially important because *we* are the creators of meaning. We create meaning based on what we have learned from our culture and our society. We add to, subtract from, and sometimes distort the information we receive through our senses. Then *our* values, past experiences, needs, cognitive styles (the way we think), and our perceptions of ourselves, other people, and situations help us attach meaning to that information. This is discussed further in Chapter 2.

Physical

The **physical context** is the tangible, concrete environment, part of which is the physical presence and attractiveness of the communicators. Another part of this context is the location. Whether a conversation occurs in a

Figure 1.8
Contexts. All of these contexts affect the communication you engage in with others. Not only does each context have an effect, but there is an interaction effect as well, as each context influences the others.

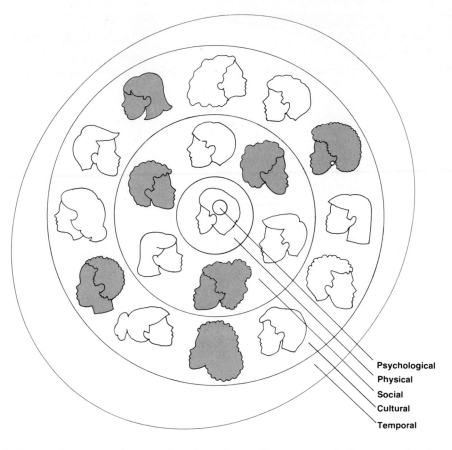

Psychological
Physical
Social
Cultural
Temporal

hallway, classroom, theater, church, or bar will exert some influence on both the content and form of the messages sent. Employers sometimes take employees to a nice restaurant to deliver bad news; the ambience of the restaurant tends to soften the effect of harsh or hostile news.

Social

The **social context** encompasses our relationships with others. Status relationships among the participants are included at this level. Communication is affected by whether we are talking with a peer or a superior, a parent or a child. The groups, organizations, or clubs to which we belong will influence our communication—as discussed previously under sociological rules. Rules, roles (functions you fulfill in relation to others), norms (standards, patterns, or models that have been established for behavior), and games (individual sequences that follow definite patterns) are important factors. There is a close relationship between these; sometimes rules and norms are used

Try This

Think about the last communication you shared with the person you consider your closest friend. What contextual variables affected your communication? How many can you remember? Try to be specific. Here are several variables that may have affected it:

- time of day
- noise or distractions
- how you met (at this time)
- furniture

- weather
- smells
- what you talked about
- what you wore

- touch
- location
- other people present

Explain the significance of each variable and how it affected your communication.

---

synonymously because standards or patterns can become rules, just as a game can become a norm or rule for behavior.

Eric Berne, author of the popular best-seller *Games People Play*, claims that "significant social intercourse [talk] most commonly takes the form of games." The goal of these games, Berne continues, "is to obtain as many satisfactions as possible from his [or her] transactions with others[s] . . ."[21]

Think, for example, of your role as student. As a student, there are certain rules or norms that you follow, such as not sitting in the instructor's chair or at his or her desk. Also, as a student, there are often games that influence behavior—games like "If It Weren't for You" (I'd be a straight-A student), or "Look How Hard I've Tried" (obviously I deserve an A), or "Kick Me" (I'm just a lowly student!).[22] People are experts at creating games—part of their way of dealing with others in the social context.

Cultural

At a still more general level is the **cultural context.** It may be difficult to perceive the influence of this context unless one has experienced other cultures. Traditions, taboos, habits, and customs have powerful influences on the character and personality of people of all cultures; however, many people are ignorant of these influences. When in a culture not our own, we may be unaware of what we are communicating by what we consider to be normal behavior. Cultural influences, however, still get filtered through personal, psychological filters.

Temporal

The **temporal context** is the time at which the communication takes place. The time of the day, day of the week, week of the month, and so on, may have an influence. The time in history may also be important. Some people are "morning" people, others "night" people. This could affect the content or form of the communication they carry on at particular hours of the day. A communication researcher often assesses the importance, impact, or insightfulness of communications in light of the time they took place.

These five contexts interact with each other; they influence each other and are influenced by all the other contexts. It is impossible to isolate these contexts or to plot all the possible interactions between them. What is possible and useful, however, is to become aware of the presence of contexts and to note their potential impact. When we look for causes for certain behaviors, there is often more going on than may be apparent at first. Planning for effective communication can only be done with careful consideration of contexts.

Communication Competence

What is the goal for which you are striving in all this? The goal is to become a *competent* communicator—one who is suitable, fit, or sufficient for the purpose. In this section I will broaden the set of goals communicators should strive for by outlining those characteristics that are perceived to comprise competent communication.[23]

Why be concerned about what other people consider competent

Consider This

Although we all live and learn within cultures and subcultures, each of us is a unique individual. Each of us has a different personal background, a different accumulation of experiences, from the next person's. What our senses tell us about our selves, about each other, and about the world is different for each of us. Members of the same culture or subculture do, however, tend to see the world in ways closer than do persons from different cultures. Further, we hold tightly to our assumptions and expectations.

—Louis Forsdale, *Perspectives on Communication* (Reading, Mass.: Addison-Wesley Publishing Co., 1981), p. 109.

communication? The most important reason is that competent communication has been proven to aid us in gaining success in a wide range of social and occupational situations.[24] **Communication competence** has been defined as "a process through which interpersonal impressions are shaped and satisfactory outcomes are derived from an interaction."[25] This definition shows how closely competence is aligned with success.

If you wanted to attain success in a wide range of social and occupational situations, what characteristics would be necessary? An enormous amount of research has been done in this area. Spitzberg and Hecht, researchers in communication competence, have identified five such characteristics: low anxiety, immediacy, expressiveness, interaction management, and other orientation.[26] To aid in your approach to interpersonal communication, and

to broaden the foundation for all future skills development, each of these characteristics will be briefly examined.

People reveal **social anxiety** when they exhibit such behaviors as excessive perspiration, shakiness, postural rigidity, vocal tremors, and minimal responsiveness to others or to the interpersonal situation.[27] Competent communicators reveal a minimum of social anxiety.

The second of the five characteristics is *immediacy*. People who practice immediacy show interest in other people. They are attentive and engage in the positive reinforcement of others and their ideas. Immediacy is revealed through being physically close to others; having open and direct body postures; showing positive reinforcers such as smiling, nodding, and eye contact; and having effective gestures.[28]

A third area of competent behaviors is described as *expressiveness*. People who reveal expressiveness are perceived to be involved and animated in both their use of words and in their nonverbal behaviors.[29] These people demonstrate appropriate emotion and volume; they laugh and smile; they use appropriate gestures, posture, and facial expressions.[30] When you meet expressive people, you usually are aware of them because of their outgoing, active, and engaging manner.

A fourth characteristic is *interaction management*. The effective management of communication requires order. What do two individuals who are trying to create order in their interactions do? Each is trying to gain the desired response from the other person; thus, each needs to solicit the cooperation of the other person in obtaining this goal—a goal that cannot be attained alone. Often, success in interaction management depends on the setting, the sharing of talk time, and the way the conversations are controlled.

Those who manage their interactions are interested in maintaining some control over their communication. First, they see the relationship between communication and rewards (getting what they want). Second, they monitor their communication in relation to the goals they seek. Third, as they gain new information about how the other person responds to what they say and do, they adjust their communication. At the same time, interaction managers are respectful of others and enable them to achieve their goals, too, where possible, and allow room for their expressive behavior.

Sometimes interaction management is easy. Conversing is comfortable, interruptions feel natural, there are few awkward pauses, and the indications of when to speak are clear.[31] Sometimes it is difficult; conversing is uncomfortable, there are unnatural interruptions, numerous awkward pauses, and you find yourself stepping on the other's lines.

The final characteristic of communication competence is *other orientation*. My wife pointed out an excellent example of other orientation. We were at a large social function, and she mentioned a person with whom she had just talked. Since I had to talk with this person my wife said, "Notice that when she talks with you, she will focus just on you, and she will make you feel while talking with her, that you are *the* most important person in the world." Indeed, that was true. Our ability to be attentive to, adaptive

Consider This

Time is just Nature's way of keeping everything from happening at once.
—Anonymous

toward, and interested in the other(s) during interaction is other orientation. Feingold states it this way:

> *An effective communicator is one who is other oriented by adapting to the needs of their interactional partners, expressing empathy and concern about other's feelings, listening well, and providing relevant feedback to others during conversations.*[32]

These five characteristics provide a fairly broad foundation to guide your progress as you begin to study interpersonal communication in more detail. If you picture these characteristics as the broad, overall goals to be achieved, you will find the skills mentioned in the chapters on perception, self, listening and feedback, language, nonverbal communication, and so on to be some of the specific ways for achieving or moving closer to these broader goals—for establishing a solid and interpersonally competent foundation. The next section introduces a general set of skills to use as a start.

Improving Skills in Interpersonal Communication

The overall goal of this book is to help you understand interpersonal communication and become a more effective sender and receiver of interpersonal messages. Most of the chapters include a final section focusing on specific skills that are tied to the concept developed in that chapter. There are some general skills, too, that relate to interpersonal communication as a whole. Developing these skills will make it easier to master those discussed at the end of a chapter. They are practical and can be started at once.

Broaden your experience. You should actively search out new relationships and not shy away from potential encounters just because they appear to be unlike what you've dealt with before. Interpersonal communication must occur between people—between you and someone else—and often this means reaching out for new relationships.

You can take steps toward forming new associations rather than waiting to let them simply happen to you. Growth will not necessarily be immediate, but there is no doubt that you will open up to many new kinds of experiences. Willingness to reach out requires risk, but exciting relationships are often built on just that kind of risk.

- Plan to attend more activities (parties, athletic events, lectures, socials, movies, and so on).
- Plan to meet more people. Break out of your small group of friends and acquaintances. Make contact with at least one new person a day.
- Eat breakfast, lunch, or dinner with new people. Sit in a different place.
- Join a new club, organization, or program. Look for new ways to use your talents and abilities.

Consider This

Don't accept things on the say-so of established authority: look at the facts, then judge for yourself.
—Bryan Magee, *Man of Ideas* (New York: Viking Press, 1979), p. 222.

Realize that growth takes time. Satisfying relationships don't develop overnight. Like getting to know oneself, really getting to know another person takes time. Give it time. If you know someone in one way only—in the college context, for example—and would like to know more about that person, try interacting in different social settings, talking about different things, and sharing reactions to the new things the two of you have experienced together.

People are often quite different in the context of their own families than they are in the context of college. You may discover a new side of a person by observing him or her in a setting other than the one you're accustomed to. Traveling, shopping, eating, or simply spending time with a person can be very revealing if the two of you usually don't do these things together. Only through time can you become familiar enough with the feelings and motivations of another to really understand the person. The key to relationship building at this stage is simply patience.

- Ask new acquaintances to do things with you.
- Don't push yourself on other people.
- Allow relationships to develop—slowly.
- Begin to spend time with other people.
- Practice being a social animal—feeling the energy that other people transmit and all their unique qualities.
- Decide what you need from other people and what you can give them.
- Let other people know you are ready and open to sharing.

Use existing relationships in new ways. You might try using existing relationships as a testing ground for the information you'll be picking up about interpersonal communication. Try things out with a friend. Practice new patterns of sending and receiving messages. Create hypothetical situations similar to some of the ones described in this chapter and develop other ways of coping with these situations. Allow "communication" to be the subject for conversations and discussions. (Don't give up if this feels strange at first!) Talk about the communication principles discussed in this chapter. Be specific about how to improve skills.

- Begin to talk about your behavior. Share your impressions and be responsive to those of your friends and acquaintances. (Remember that as you encourage feedback, you are likely to get as much negative as positive.)
- Do not refute comments or defend your behavior. It is important to get honest reactions; defensiveness may encourage dishonesty.
- Experiment with things that you are learning about communication. Do some of the "Try This" activities suggested in this book with

your friends. It is better to experiment in a warm, trusting environment first, before taking new behaviors beyond the confines of such security and protectiveness.

- Engage in **metacommunication:** talking about the communication you engage in. Is it effective? Offensive? Can it be strengthened or improved? What can you do better?

Develop openness.

Developing skill in any area begins with an awareness that something can and should be done. You need to be open to change. You can start by simply trying to become more aware of the kinds of things you do, the feelings you have toward yourself and others, the way you view life and what you want your place in it to be. You should learn to monitor your own behavior and feelings as objectively as possible, becoming more open and responsive to your internal experiences.

Openness also means being receptive to all that goes on around you. As you open up to your environment, you will begin to be more sensitive to the small details of things that you may once have overlooked. This sensitivity will increase your ability to re-create situations in your mind to better analyze and dissect their parts. Your new behavior may be more carefully considered than before in light of your past successes and failures. This is growth, change, development—maturity. A lot of people would discover a great deal more if only they would pause and look and feel and care just a bit more than they do.[33]

- Be prepared to find things about yourself that need changing.
- Realize that you are not perfect: there *is* room for improvement.
- Be ready to take action wherever necessary. As you open yourself to discovery, be conscious of those things about which something can be done. Commit yourself to those areas.
- Keep your sights on progress—moving forward in a positive direction. Do not be overly concerned about failures and do not try to anticipate the future; deal with what can be done *now*—in the present.

Improve the exactness of your communication.

We all need to improve the exactness of our communication. It's a great help to be able to convey to others just what you mean to convey and to receive from them just what they mean to send to you. This has been labeled **fidelity.** Improving the exactness of your communication is a skill. If you're aware of the need for fidelity, you will become more sensitive to those situations in which some of the fidelity is lost. You will be better able to detect when meaning is becoming distorted. And, it is hoped, you'll be able to take steps to correct the situation.

- Think about what you intend to say before opening your mouth. Plan it out almost completely.

- Think about ways you can elaborate on or enumerate the things you have to say. Practice the art of skillful repetition; how many different ways can you say the same things?
- Be responsive to the feedback you get and use it to alter your message as necessary. Plan to make changes in your message to ensure that the other person will hear what you intend him or her to hear.

Make a contract with yourself.[34]   Vague, general plans for improvement or change generally do not work. What is needed is an explicit contract that identifies the objectives and enumerates specific measures you can use to achieve them. In this way progress can be charted.

- What changes do you want to make? Be realistic about this. You may want to divide your goal into smaller, more manageable parts. For example, if one of your goals is to make more friends, your first step might be to say hello to four new people each week.
- How will you monitor your progress? Charts and journals may help you keep track. You might also ask your friends to monitor your behavior.
- What rewards will you get for fulfilling each part of your contract? For every new person you say hello to, you might reward yourself with a new magazine or a milkshake. For accomplishing a major step, use a movie or a meal out as a reward. Minor accomplishments deserve small rewards; major ones deserve important rewards. Reinforcement is essential for making the contract work. It helps you meet your own desired standards of performance. Don't be stingy. Self-approval will help you continue with the contract.
- How will you know when you have completed the contract? At the end of two weeks you will have said hello to eight new people and you will be ready to move on to the next step in making friends. Set daily or weekly goals.
- What will you do if you fail to meet the contract? Appropriate punishments can be just as effective as appropriate rewards, provided they are realistic and established in advance of the contract period. But plan to make them stick. Some possibilities are: cleaning out your desk drawers; writing a thank-you note that you've been putting off for months; sorting out that pile of magazines and papers on the floor of your closet.

It is a good idea to put your contract in writing. This makes it more official and increases your likelihood of honoring it. With concentration and practice, many of the goals you set for yourself will soon become second nature to you. You can form a contract around many or all of the skills and activities in this book.

In this chapter we have examined the three basic elements of interpersonal communication: people, messages, and effects. When we are specific in describing the characteristics of any interpersonal encounter, we quickly realize that every communication situation is unique. We have looked at ten principles that operate in every communication situation. The final principle—communication is transactional—is the most important because it is inclusive and because it provides the framework for this book. We have mentioned the five contexts that must be considered whenever we communicate. Finally, we have talked about goals and skills. In the next chapter we will examine perception and creating meaning.

Notes

[1] Beverly Davenport Sypher and Theodore E. Zorn, Jr., "Communication-Related Abilities and Upward Mobility: A Longitudinal Investigation," *Human Communication Research*, *12* (Spring 1986): p. 428.

[2] Sypher and Zorn, "Communication-Related Abilities," p. 428.

[3] Theodore Caplow, *Two Against One: Coalitions in Triads* (Englewood Cliffs, N.J.: Prentice-Hall, 1968), as cited in William W. Wilmot, *Dyadic Communication*, 3rd ed. (New York: Random House, 1987), p. 23.

[4] Wilmot, *Dyadic Communication*, p. 23.

[5] Paul Watzlawick, Janet Helmick Beavin, and Don D. Jackson, *Pragmatics of Human Communication: A Study of Interactional Patterns, Pathologies, and Paradoxes* (New York: W. W. Norton & Co., 1967). See Chapter 2, "Some Tentative Axioms of Communication," pp. 48–71.

[6] Mark L. Knapp and Gerald R. Miller, Eds., *Handbook of Interpersonal Communication* (Beverly Hills, Calif.: Sage Publications, 1985), p. 10.

[7] Gerald R. Miller and Mark Steinberg, *Between People: A New Analysis of Interpersonal Communication* (Chicago, Ill: Science Research Associates, 1975).

[8] From "Toward a Meaning-Centered Philosophy of Communication" by Dean C. Barnlund, *Journal of Communication*, Vol. 12:4 (1962): pp. 202–3. Used by permission.

[9] David K. Berlo, *The Process of Communication* (New York: Holt, Rinehart & Winston, 1960), p. 24.

[10] Berlo, *The Process of Communication*, p. 24.

[11] Barnlund, "Meaning-Centered Philosophy," p. 202.

[12] Barnlund, "Mean-Centered Philosophy," p. 202.

[13] John Stewart, "An Interpersonal Approach to the Basic Course," *The Speech Teacher*, *21* (1972): p. 10.

[14] Dean C. Barnlund, "Communication: The Context of Change," in *Perspectives on Communication*, ed. Carl E. Larson and Frank E. X. Dance (Milwaukee: The Speech Communication Center of the University of Wisconsin, 1968), p. 27.

[15] John Stewart, "Interpersonal Communication: Contact Between Persons," in *Bridges Not Walls: A Book About Interpersonal Communication*, 4th ed., ed. John Stewart (New York: Random House, 1986), pp. 23–24.

[16] Stewart, "An Interpersonal Approach," p. 10.

[17] Stewart, "Interpersonal Communication: Contact Between Persons," pp. 23–24.

[18] Horace B. English and Ava Champney English, *A Comprehensive Dictionary of Psychological and Psychoanalytical Terms* (New York: Longmans, Green, 1958), p. 561.

[19] Stewart, "Interpersonal Communication: Contact Between Persons," p. 28.

[20] See Harold D. Lasswell, "The Structure and Function of Communication in Society," in *The Communication of Ideas*, ed. L. Bryson (New York: Harper & Row, 1948), p. 37.

[21] Eric Berne, *Games People Play: The Psychology of Human Relationships* (New York: Grove Press, 1964), pp. 19, 103.

[22] *Ibid.*, pp. 83, 103, 104.

[23] I am indebted to the work of Brian H. Spitzberg and Michael L. Hecht, "A Component Model of Relational Competence," *Human Communication Research*, *10* (Summer 1984): pp. 575–599 for the ideas in this section. The footnotes that follow are those used by Spitzberg and Hecht to support their findings.

[24] W. H. Fitts, *Interpersonal Competence: The Wheel Model.* Studies on the self-concept and rehabilitation: Research Monography 2. Dede Wallace Center, Nashville, TN: Author, 1970; B. D. Ruben, "Assessing Communication Competency for Intercultural Adaptation," *Group and Organizational Studies*, 1:3 (1976): 334–354; P. Trower, B. Bryant and M. Argyle, *Social Skills and Mental Health*, Pennsylvania: University of Pennsylvania Press, 1978.

[25] Spitzberg and Hecht, p. 576.

[26] D. J. Cegala, "Interaction Involvement: A Cognitive Dimension of Communication Competence." *Communication Education*, *30* (1981): pp. 109–121; B. Farber, "Elements of Competence in Interpersonal Relations: A Factor Analysis," *Sociometry*, *25* (1962): pp. 30–47; D. L. Flint, T. L. Hick, M. D. Horan, D. J. Irvine, and S. E. Kukuk, "Dimensionality of the California Preschool Social Competency Scale," *Applied Psychological Measurement*, *4* (1980): pp. 203–212; P. R. Monge, S. G. Bachman, J. P. Dillard, and E. M. Eisenberg, "Communicator Competence in the Workplace: Model Testing and Scale Development." In M. Burgoon (Ed.) *Communication Yearbook* 5 (New Brunswick, NJ: Transaction Books, 1982), pp. 505–528; J. M. Wiemann, "Explication and Test of a Model of Communicative Competence," *Human Communication Research*, *3* (1977): pp. 195–213.

[27] L. R. Wheeless and B. F. Morganstern, *The Relationship of Perceived Anxiety, Status/Self-Control, and Affective Behaviors to Self-Reported Relational Anxiety and Interpersonal Solidarity.* Paper presented at the Speech Communication Association Convention, Anaheim, CA, 1978; D. C. Zuroff and J. C. Schwarz, "An Instrument for Measuring the Behavioral Dimension of Social Anxiety," *Psychological Reports*, *42* (1978): pp. 371–379.

[28] J. F. Andersen, P. A. Anderson, and A. D. Jensen, *The Measurement of Nonverbal Immediacy.* Paper presented at the Eastern Communication Convention, Philadelphia, PA, 1979; M. L. Patterson, *Toward a General Framework for Nonverbal Exchange.* Paper presented at the American Psychological Association, Montreal, Canada, 1980.

[29] M. L. MacDonald and J. Cohen, "Trees in the Forest: Some Components of Social Skills," *Journal of Clinical Psychology*, *37* (1981): pp. 342–347; Monge, Bachman, Dillard, and Eisenberg, "Communicator Competency in the Workplace," pp. 505–528.

[30] D. H. Barlow, G. G. Able, B. B. Blanchard, A. R. Bristow, and L. D. Young, "A Heterosocial Skills Behavior Checklist for Males," *Behavior Therapy*, 8 (1977): pp. 229–239; D. R. Brandt, "On Linking Social Performance with Social Competence: Some Relations Between Communicative Style and Attributions of Interpersonal Effectiveness," *Human Communication Research*, 5 (1979): pp. 223–237; D. P. Greenwald, "The Behavioral Assessment of Differences in Social Skill and Social Anxiety in Female College Students," *Behavior Therapy*, 8 (1977): pp. 925–937.

[31] H. Arkowitz, E. Lichtenstein, K. McGovern, and P. Hines, "The Behavioral Assessment of Social Competence in Males," *Behavior Therapy*, 6 (1975): pp. 3–13; Barlow, Able, Blanchard, Bristow, and Young, "A Heterosocial Skills Behavior Checklist for Males," pp. 229–239; M. L. McLaughlin and M. J. Cody, "Awkward Silences: Behavioral Antecedents and Consequences of the Conversational Lapse," *Human Communication Research*, 8 (1982): pp. 299–316; Wiemann, "Model of Communicative Competence," pp. 195–213.

[32] P. C. Feingold, "Toward a Paradigm of Effective Communication: An Empirical Study of Perceived Communication Effectiveness" (Doctoral dissertation) *Dissertation Abstracts International*, 37 (1977): pp. 4697A–4698A, 578.

[33] Arthur Gordon, *A Touch of Wonder* (Old Tappan, NJ: Spire Books, 1976), p. 11.

[34] Philip B. Zimbardo, *Shyness* (New York: Jove Publications, 1977), pp. 229–30.

Further Reading

Robert T. Craig and Karen Tracy, eds., *Conversational Coherence: Form, Structure, and Strategy* (Beverly Hills, Calif.: Sage Publications, 1983). Analyzing conversations is an important aspect of understanding interpersonal transactions. This book for the serious student introduces some of the scientific methods scholars use to study conversations. The central issues of this volume include mutual influence, process and organization, multisignal units, cognitive processes, multilevel signals, perception of signals, contexts and situations, and researcher influence.

H. Lloyd Goodall, Jr., *Human Communication: Creating Reality* (Dubuque, Iowa: Wm. C. Brown Company Publishers, 1983). In this fine theoretical textbook, Goodall discusses the theory, process, and practice of human communication. Besides theories and models, he treats inventional aspects and structural, logical, and judgmental considerations. In addition, he looks specifically at interpersonal, group, public, and mass media situations. This is a well-presented, interesting, textbook.

Don E. Hamachek, *Encounters with Others: Interpersonal Relationships and You* (New York: Holt, Rinehart and Winston, 1982). Hamachek focuses on the underlying dynamics of human behavior in an interpersonal context. For example, he discusses how and why self-perceptions are related to perceptions of others, how we form impressions of people, why people are attracted to each other, how self-esteem works, and how we move away from or toward people. This is a well-written, thoroughly referenced textbook that examines important interpersonal underpinnings.

William S. Howell, *The Empathic Communicator* (Belmont, Calif.: Wadsworth Publishing Co., 1982). Howell looks at interpersonal communication as an ever-changing, often unpredictable, joint venture that requires competence in adapting to the flow of events. He claims that, "until a person learns to identify internal monologue and increase control over it, his or her empathic and adjusting competencies show little improvement." This is an excellent, well-written, insightful textbook.

Margaret L. McLaughlin, *Conversation: How Talk Is Organized* (Beverly Hills, Calif.: Sage Publications, 1984). A sophisticated, scholarly book that discusses the rules, maxims, and other lore that conversationalists know, conversational coherence, turn-taking, gaps and overlaps, acts, sequences, preventatives and repairs, and significant issues in research on conversation. A research book for the serious student.

John Powell and Loretta Brady, *Will the Real Me Please Stand Up? (So We Can All Get to Know You!)* (Allen, Texas: Argus Communications, 1985). Although part of the popular, self-help literature, this book relates directly to effective communication. Powell and Brady present twenty-five basic attitudes and practices that help readers move toward effectiveness. Their list includes commitment, self-disclosure, honesty, taking responsibility, empathy, listening, and love. They present interesting and well-written commonsense rules.

Michael E. Roloff and Gerald R. Miller, Eds., *Interpersonal Processes: New Directions in Communication Research* (Newbury Park, Calif.: Sage Publications, 1987). This volume is linked to the 1976 volume, *Explorations in Interpersonal Communication*, which Miller edited. In this volume, there is updated research on uncertainty reduction theory, social exchange theory, and self-disclosure. There is no update here on the rules perspective. In addition, there is information on how selfhood emerges through conversation with significant others, the role of emotion in human communication, compliance-gaining communication, relational control, conversational forms, a formal model of conversation based on the process of information exchange, methods for studying communication, social-penetration theory, and a scathing indictment of past relational research in social psychology. A useful research update.

Susan B. Shimanoff, *Communication Rules: Theory and Research* (Beverly Hills, Calif.: Sage Publications, 1980). In this 300-page volume, Shimanoff constructs a theory of communication based upon rules. To aid in her work, she "considers what a rule is, the relationships between rules and behavior, the best methods by which to approach rules research, and how rules research can contribute to communication theory" (from back cover). The best book on rules and their identification, to date.

Sarah Trenholm, *Human Communication Theory* (Englewood Cliffs, NJ: Prentice-Hall, 1986). Trenholm offers readers a survey of major social scientific theories of communication in the areas of interpersonal, small group, and public communication. In this book, organizational and mass communication contexts are omitted. This is not a research review, rather, she offers interesting examples of different research methodologies. Each chapter contains two or three classic, widely-cited studies that familiarize students with research methods and motivate them to read additional journal articles. A well-written, valuable textbook.

Julia T. Wood, *Human Communication: A Symbolic Interactionist Perspective* (New York: Holt, Rinehart and Winston, 1982). "This book," claims Wood, "reflects my commitment to a perspective which provides an exceptionally rich view of relationships among communication, thought, action, selfhood, and interaction." In this substantive, sophisticated textbook, Wood develops and explains symbolic interactionism as a powerful, comprehensive theory of human communication. She offers an interesting, theoretically coherent approach which incorporates examples that illustrate everyday interactions and concerns.

2

Creating Meaning: Perception

Learning Objectives

When you have finished this chapter you should be able to:
- Define perception and relate it to communication.
- Explain the perception sieve and how you create meaning.
- List factors that affect the reception of stimuli.
- Defend the statement: "Meanings are in us." Why is this statement important?
- Explain the process and importance of construction.
- Distinguish between selecting, organizing, and interpreting, and give a brief example of each.
- Explain the steps of enlarging, simplifying, and closing and know to which of the construction processes they most closely relate.
- List and define forces that may restrict perception: stereotyping, proximity, and role.
- Distinguish between physical and psychological proximity.
- Offer specific skills for improving perception.

Have you ever thought about how people form impressions of others? We do it all the time. But *how* do we form the impressions? Suppose a woman notices a man to whom she is at least superficially attracted. She is aware of his movements, his voice, his clothes. From her observations she draws conclusions about how this man thinks and feels. She may make inferences about his needs, goals, and attitudes. She will guide her

actions toward him and her prediction of future interactions by her perceptions. As she makes judgments about him, he may also make judgments
about her. If the observations and predictions being made are incorrect,
communication between the two may get off to a bad start or may never
start.

This chapter is about perception—how we create meaning. It is divided
into three parts (1) reception, (2) construction, and (3) skills. The first part
will cover how we select, organize, and interpret information. In the second
part I'll discuss some factors that affect construction—such as our tendency
to label things, physical and psychological distance, and the restrictive roles
we sometimes play. Finally, I'll discuss how you can improve your skills in
perception so that genuine, effective interaction is more likely to occur.

As you read this chapter, keep in mind that perception is the basis of
all our knowledge of the world. All the stimuli that affect us in any way
must first be received and perceived. In this chapter, I shall define perception
very broadly, using the definition of Gary Cronkhite, a writer in this area.
He defines it as "the detection, registration, processing, and elaboration of
environmental characteristics."[1] The beauty of this definition is that it includes
all within our environment that we detect, register, process, and elaborate.
Elaboration simply means adding to incoming information everything that
we presently know.

What You Receive Is What You Get: The Reception of Stimuli

You have just come out of a movie with a friend feeling that it was one of
the best you have ever seen. You turn to share your exhilaration and quickly
realize that your friend's reaction was completely different. You saw the
same movie, but your friend says that he was restless and bored, that the
movie was too long and did not have enough action.

You have just completed your third week of the term and are walking
away from class with a classmate who says, "Finally, I understand what is
going on in there!" You look at her, surprised, and reply, "Not me. I have
no idea what's happening. I'm more confused now than on the first day of
class!"

These are normal, everyday occurrences, and they show that perceptions
vary among people. What one person thinks is not necessarily the same as
what another person thinks. Clearly, what each person perceives is a function
of something unique and personal.

Although Cronkhite's definition of perception is a fine one, it can be
further simplified for our purposes. **Perception** is the process of gathering
information and giving it meaning. You see a movie and you give meaning
to it: "It's one of the best I've seen." You come away from class after the
third week and you give meaning to it: "It finally makes sense." We gather

Try This

For just a moment now, exercise your imagination. Listen to the messages being sent from the following environments. What are your perceptions in each case?

1. You see a slum with trash spilling out on the sidewalk. A child is looking down at the concrete from steps going into an apartment. What do you hear?
2. You are in a gray, bleak, and barren ward in a state mental hospital with people sitting on benches. Their drab appearance is heightened by faded, ill-fitting clothes, and there's a smell that is only too common in such a ward. How would you feel in that environment?
3. There is a beautiful, royal-blue ocean with whitecaps breaking against a sparkling, sandy beach. The beach is outlined by palm trees and a few fluffy white clouds. How do you feel about that message?
4. A warm fire is crackling in the fireplace. The lights are dimly lit, and outside the picture window snow is falling quietly. Soft music is playing in the background, and you are there with the person with whom you want to share that environment. What are your feelings now?

—Paraphrased from Ken Olson, *Can You Wait Till Friday?* (Phoenix: O'Sullivan Woodside, 1975), pp. 53–54. Used by permission of the author.

information from what our senses see, hear, touch, taste, and smell, and we give meaning to that information. Although the information may come to us in a variety of forms, it is all processed, or *perceived*, in the mind.

Communication and perception are so closely related that we can't really mention one without the other. To understand interpersonal communication we need some understanding of perception, for it is through perception that we become aware of our surroundings, give meaning to our world, and come to know ourselves and others. Most of he time we engage in the process without paying attention to what we are doing. We rarely think of *how* it is occurring or how we could improve it. Perception is a complex activity, but by understanding the process we can improve our chances for more effective interpersonal communication. We can expand the perimeters of our own personal world.

The Perception Sieve: How You Create Meaning

One way to view the general process of perception is to visualize a large sieve with holes of different shapes and sizes. (See Figure 2.1.) Each hole represents a category we understand or have had some experience with. The largest categories are those areas we're most familiar with or have given preference to—special needs and interests. The number of holes in the sieve changes constantly as we encounter new experiences, just as the size of the holes change according to our changing values—what we consider to be most important.

Our perceptual categories develop as we grow. Our interests, experiences, and knowledge create them. Our culture, parents, religion, education, and peers are probably the strongest influences on how we perceive the world. As our interests change, we drop old categories and form new ones. As a child of six you may have wanted to be a firefighter; as an adolescent you may have wanted to be a veterinarian; as a college student you may want to be a lawyer; as an adult you may choose to become an electronics technician. How many of your other interests have changed over the years? Sometimes we may expand a perceptual category to include a related piece of information; sometimes, when we can't relate the new information to the old, we create a whole new category.

Notice in Figure 2.1 that certain holes are black. There are some areas where we make a determined effort *not* to gain any more information. We may no longer want to hear any more rumors about our roommate. We

Figure 2.1
The perception sieve.

Consider This

These windows of perception appear to open onto opposite worlds.
Looked at fearfully, a person will appear to be motivated quite differently
than he is when looked at with love. Because the world we see reflects
only our choice of what we want to be real, there is no external world.
Truth is not separate from us. When we finally awake there will be no
need for perception because nothing will be separate and at a distance. In
the meantime, the world we see is the best of teaching devices because it
instantly reflects back to us a picture of where we want to be.

—Hugh Prather, *The Quiet Answer* (Garden City, N.Y.: Doubleday & Co., 1982), p.
113.

may no longer want to read science fiction. We may no longer want to taste
any drinks containing rum and coconut milk. These are experiences we
choose to close ourselves off from.

Notice, too, that the sieve holes are irregular in size and shape. If
information comes to us that does not exactly fit one of our present categories,
we may distort that information so that it does fit. One function of our
perceptual filtering process is to protect us from information we dislike or
disagree with. We do not let that information through, or we adjust it as
necessary. For example, if you heard some unflattering remarks about your
roommate but one favorable comment like, "You must admit she has a sense
of humor," you might hear only the compliment and filter out all the other
comments. We tend to hear what we want to hear.

No Two Are Alike

Every person has a unique perceptual filtering system, although there is
some cultural overlap. If we are white, middle-class, urban eighteen-year-
olds, because of our socialization our perceptions are likely to resemble those
of other white, middle-class, urban eighteen-year-olds more than those of
any other group in society. But our own perceptions still won't be exactly
like those of any other person. Each individual's system depends on numerous
elements that either broaden or limit the size of the categories.

Our physiological makeup affects how much information we are able
to gather. The number of visual stimuli we take in is limited, for example,
by how well our eyes work. And although the number of stimuli we ordinarily
sense is impressive, it is small compared with the maximum amount of which
we are capable. Most of us are physiologically able to distinguish 7,500,000
different colors.[2] Our ears can pick up sounds ranging from 20 to 20,000

vibration cycles per second. We can distinguish among 5,000 different smells and 10,000 different tastes. Even our sense of touch is more sensitive than we may have thought. Our fingers can feel the separations between objects as little as 3 to 8 millimeters apart.[3] Our bodies are extremely sensitive instruments for taking in sensory information.

The kind of information we perceive is strongly affected by our expectations, attitudes, values, interests, emotions, needs, language, experience, and knowledge. It is important to realize that the new information we pick up depends on the perceptual categories we have available, and that each of our systems is unique. Although several of our categories may be similar to someone else's, we must never assume that all of ours are like all of his or hers or even that *any* are identical.

Implications

What does this perception-sieve analogy imply? First, that perception is not a passive process. Our perceptions are our own and we have some control over them; we do not have total control because our culture, environment, and upbringing create categories we may not even be aware of. But because

Consider This

Perceptions are what a person actually sees, hears, or otherwise perceives as taking place in a given situation. Whereas assumptions prescribe "the way it *ought to be*," perceptions describe "the way it is *currently* seen as being" for a particular person at a particular point in time. The verb *perceive* comes from the Latin *per* ("thoroughly") and *capere* ("to lay hold of"), combining to mean "to take, receive, to become cognizant of." Thus, perceptions are the way in which we consciously take in what is going on in our lives.

The idea of perception is sometimes difficult to distinguish from the idea of assumption, because almost all assumptions are based on past perceptions. Another difficulty in distinguishing the two is that our assumptions about how things ought to be often influence our perceptions of what we think is taking place. The two folk sayings "You believe what you see" and "You see what you believe" illustrate the close connection between assumptions and perceptions. Generally, a person's prior assumptions and past experience have a very large influence on what that person does or does not see in a given situation.

—Anthony G. Athos and John J. Gabarro, *Interpersonal Behavior: Communication and Understanding in Relationships,* © 1978, pp. 146—47. Reprinted by permission of Prentice-Hall, Inc., Englewood Cliffs, New Jersey.

we have most of the control, we do not record everything our senses take in. Perception is selective. We block out some sights, sounds, and smells. For the most part, we actively apply our perceptual filter to incoming stimuli. Our perceptual system gives us a way of dealing with outside reality in terms of inside reality—our own thoughts, feelings, and attitudes.

Although our perceptions may be well established, they can and do change. The more open we are to new experiences, the more likely it is that our perceptions will change. If we aren't willing to try new things, we may not allow information through that does not correspond with the categories we have consciously or unconsciously established. We may adapt some of the categories to keep up with the times, but we are generally rather inflexible.

We can become less rigid if we realize we have a lot of room for new information and if we are willing to take in information unrelated to what we already know. We might develop conditional categories for information we consider risky, for information we're not sure what we're going to do with yet. We will have a hard time with information totally unrelated to our present knowledge and experience because we have no familiar way of processing it. But knowing that we do have room for new experiences, if we'll only let them in, is a good start toward flexibility. And sometimes just realizing how little we know is an education in itself.

Another implication of the perception-sieve analogy is that we do not accept stimuli just as they are presented. We hear a teacher talking; what is actually being said may *not* be what we hear. Just as we reject some information altogether, we also shape some to make it fit in with our existing perceptions. If we do not understand an assignment, we might make what the teacher says come as close as we can to an assignment we had in the past. We change what the teacher says to make it fit. We place what we take in against what we already know. If we have no history, we try to make the new information fit something we feel is comparable. The more we adapt stimuli to fit in with what we already know, the less likely it is that our views will reflect what actually occurred.

Finally, whatever meaning we are left with is based on *how* we process the information rather than on what actually happened. When a friend says she sat through a doubleheader on a 90° day, what that experience means to us is a result of all our attitudes and feelings about baseball and hot weather. The experience might have meant something quite different to her. (See Figure 2.2.)

Our interpretation of something is just that—an interpretation. Objects, events, and words do not have inherent meanings. Their meanings are in us, in the way we evaluate them. When we talk with someone else, we make up what that person says just as when we see an object, we make up what that object looks like. Our filtering system determines how we view the world. The world exists for us as we perceive it. We cannot "tell it like it is"; we can only "tell it like we perceive it." Understanding this is a big step toward more effective interpersonal communication: it will help us become

Figure 2.2
Our perceptions are based on our own attitudes and experiences.

more sensitive to reactions to experiences, both our own and others', as personal interpretations of events. It's useful to think in terms of how and why we respond to something rather than in terms of the "something" as an experience in itself. Experiences have meaning only as we respond to them. This is the transactional view of communication.

Visual Perception: Coping with Ambiguity

There are some famous drawings that psychologists show their students. Two of these are reproduced in Figure 2.3a. Look at the drawing on the left. Do you see an old witch or a pretty young girl? If you look at the drawing long enough, can you see the other image? (If you have trouble seeing both images in the left-hand figure, look at Figure 2.3b on page 64.) What do you see in the drawing at the right? A vase—or two men facing each other nose to nose? When we see one image in these drawings, we cannot see the other.

Writer Sydney J. Harris has suggested that there is a broader lesson in perception to be learned from looking at these pictures. "What we call our view of life," Harris writes, "is a shifting image, not a continuous reality. Our lives are ambiguous patterns made up of different strands, and at different times we choose one pattern to look at rather than another—but neither is more real than the other." Harris continues:

Figure 2.3a

> *Maintaining one's sanity and sense of balance depends in large part upon acceptance of ambiguity, in recognizing that this is part of the human condition . . . . Reality is not one picture, but two. We cannot see them together, but they are both there. Accepting this fact, and holding them in equilibrium, is more than half the art of coping with ambiguity.*[4]

Since we can never see both images at once, it is important to reserve final judgments and evaluations, remembering that *every* situation is part witch and part pretty girl, part vase and part angry men.

If you wonder how much of perception is a matter of reception and how much must be constructed, the answer is clear. The more information available to us in the environment—that is, the more stimuli presented to our sense organs for reception—the less perception has to be constructed. This is discussed under the "Organizing" step of the construction process because it has to do with enlarging upon and closing in the data we receive.

The Perceiver: The Process of Construction

To develop the concept of perception in greater detail, let's think in terms of construction. The main point of construction is that events do not just present themselves to people; people construct experiences according to the organization of categories they already possess in their minds. Those with a small number of categories reveal *cognitive simplicity* (cognition is the faculty of knowing). Such simplicity leads to stereotyping and nondifferentiation in their perceptions. Those with a large number of categories reveal *cognitive complexity,* which allows a more subtle and sensitive discrimination among perceptions.[5] Reading, traveling, experiencing, and learning contribute positively to our number of available categories.

For the purposes of discussion, let's divide construction into the three steps of *selecting*, *organizing*, and *interpreting* information. These steps occur simultaneously and often instantaneously. The construction process is complicated by the fact that each step depends upon and is affected by countless factors occurring within us and within our environment.

Selecting: Choosing the Pieces of the Puzzle

We perceive selectively. That is, we limit the quantity of stimuli to which we attach meaning. We are selective simply because we are exposed to too many stimuli each day to be able to deal with all of them. Notice, for example, how our selectivity works in reference to advertising messages:

> . . . the average American adult is assaulted by a minimum of 560 advertising messages each day. Of the 560 to which he is exposed, however, he only notices seventy-six. In effect, he blocks out 484 advertising messages a day to preserve his attention for other matters.[6]

We usually choose to focus on those messages we agree with or which are most meaningful to us. During an election campaign, we tend to recall acceptable comments made by the candidate we support and unacceptable comments made by the other person. And we tend to ascribe statements with which we agree to the person we support.[7]

We select what we will perceive on the basis of our experiences. The next time you go to a party, pay attention to what seems most important to the people there. One person may observe the "performance" of the host

Figure 2.3b

Try This

The next time you read a newspaper, be aware of what you decide to read and what you decide not to read. Answer the following questions with respect to your behavior:

1. What section of the newspaper did you turn to first? Why?
2. In what order did you read the remaining sections? Do you know why you chose this order?
3. What sections or articles did you choose not to read at all? Were the reasons the same as in numbers 1 and 2 above?
4. Have you perceived changes in the articles you are interested in reading over the past few months? Over the past few years? Do you expect further changes to occur? Can you predict what they will be?
5. What forces operate in your life that influence you to read certain sections or articles and not others? That is, why are you interested in certain topics and not others?
6. Are there changes in your behavior when you are monitoring or observing what you are doing?

and hostess. Another person might be totally absorbed with what people are wearing. Only the handsome men might catch one person's eye, while somebody else is aware of all the vivacious women present. The pretzels and cheese dip might be the center of attention for a number of people.

Each person chooses what is most meaningful on the basis of his or her experiences. One person may have been brought up to believe that gracious hospitality is an essential element at a party. Another person may have parents who attach great importance to clothes. We will usually select for perception stimuli related to matters we've already given some thought to or had memorable experiences with. The act of selecting stimuli is the first step in the perceptual process. Once we select and receive certain stimuli, what do we do with that information?

Organizing: Putting the Pieces Together

Because information comes to us in a random, unstructured manner, we must do something with it to make sense of it. We must determine relationships: how the new information relates to other information we are receiving and to information we already have. To get an idea of how we need to organize cues, stop reading and look at this page and the marks on it as if there were no structure to it. Look at the room you are sitting in right now as if it contained no structure, as if you didn't know that chairs were for sitting on, floors for walking on, lamps for providing light. How

about the view from the nearest window? Can you look at nature as if there were no structure? Our world, for us to understand it, requires **organization,** and we organize it by perceiving relationships.

If we see a swallow flying by, we know from experience that it is not the only bird in the world. We know there are many swallows like it and many other birds unlike it. We know that birds eat insects or seeds for food, and that birds can be, in turn, eaten by larger forms of life. We know that birds are warm blooded as we are, and feathered as we are not. They walk as we do and fly as we do not. We organize our information about birds by noting relationships between this particular bird and all the other birds in our experience. We organize information more or less consciously, in more or less detail, with all incoming stimuli. We can think of the organizing process as involving three steps—enlarging, simplifying, and closing—that occur simultaneously and instantaneously.

Enlarging.   The information our senses receive is in small pieces. Think of words as tiny pieces of information. In any communication situation, we try to put the words we hear into a larger context so that we can understand them better. We call this **enlarging,** looking for a frame of reference for the message. We might start by observing the whole nonverbal picture—the facial expressions, gestures, and body movements of the person sending the message—and placing the words into that picture. The fewer the pieces received the more enlarging must be done.

Put yourself in a situation where a friend you are waiting for emerges from a classroom banging the door and stamping his feet. These cues, although small, provide the big picture for you. You "enlarge" by framing your friend's behavior as an emotional outburst, and this enlargement allows you to understand your friend's words when he says, "I *hate* that class; I just hate it! I'm never going back in there again." Framing is a process of enlarging because it provides the order or system for what is within the frame. If, later the same day, your friend becomes very short with another friend of yours, you might say, "Oh, Chris is still mad about that history class this morning." Framing suggests the mood into which other behaviors can be classified. In addition to mood, it could be humor, mental constitution, temper, or disposition. When you say that someone is in an unhappy frame of mind, you have organized the perception by enlargement.

Simplifying. Just as we search for a relationship between pieces of information and a larger framework into which we can place those pieces, we also look for ways to **simplify** complex or confusing stimuli. Complex stimuli are those that we have difficulty understanding. We simplify them by finding patterns, an order that will help us make sense of the message.

For example, if you drive into a gas station to get directions, you might hear the attendant say something like, "You go up here to your first stoplight and turn left on Broadview. At your next light turn right. Then just after you pass Wiley High School, turn right; and the street you are looking for will be your next left." As a simplifying response you might reply, "So it's a left, two rights, and a left." We look for order in the stimuli that will help us remember the essential information.

We do the same thing when we hear a teacher explaining an assignment or when we are taking notes in a lecture. We do not need, and we don't have time to record, all the teacher says. We simplify the message so that we have the essentials when it comes time to complete the assignment or to study our notes for a test.

Given a relatively complex perception, we simplify it into some recognizable form. Look at Figure 2.4. We may simplify the five-sided figure in "A" by seeing it as a house, a triangle on top of a square, or an envelope. In "B" we may see a triangle resting on two rectangles (or posts) or even a covered bridge.

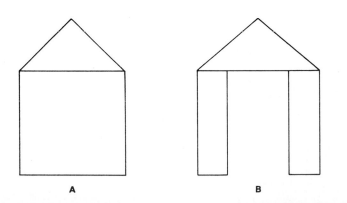

A   B   *Figure 2.4*

Stereotyping and proximity, which will be discussed shortly, are also ways we have for simplifying complex perceptions. We need to be able to make perceptions plain and easy to digest.

Closing.   Because we get information in scraps, we must also fill in gaps. This is the process of **closing.** We tend to think in unified wholes. That is, we tend to see things as complete rather than fragmented. For example, in Figure 2.5 we tend to see a triangle, a square, and a rectangle rather than a series of unconnected, unorganized lines.

We probably engage in closing (or closure) more often than we realize. For example, how often have you completed a sentence for the person you were talking to? The more we get to know people, the better we know how they think, and the more often we will think ahead and close their thoughts. Very close friends can say a great deal to each other with few words; without realizing it, they may depend on closure for their messages to get through. Another example of closing is when you overhear others talking but are able to pick up only fragments of their conversation. From the fragments you fill in the rest of the conversation. Have you ever sat in a bus station or airport and made up stories about the people you observed around you? From a minimum of cues you can put together a fairly complete story, making sense of the available information by closure. Though it may make sense to you, it may not be correct.

Interpreting: Giving the Puzzle Meaning

Not only do we select and organize information, we also interpret it. That is, we assign some meaning to information, making evaluations and drawing conclusions about it so that we can better predict future events and thereby minimize surprise.[8] Most of the **interpreting** we do takes either of two forms: **identification** or **evaluation.** Again, these processes occur rapidly and often simultaneously.

Stop reading for a minute and just listen. Can you label every sound you hear? Most of the sounds that go on around us are common ones and easily identifiable. Sometimes, however, there is a strange one—a scream, a bang, or a sound we've never heard before. After we identify the source of the noise, we evaluate it. Was it startling? Disruptive? Harmful? In identifying, but more significantly, in evaluating information, we bring to bear all of our

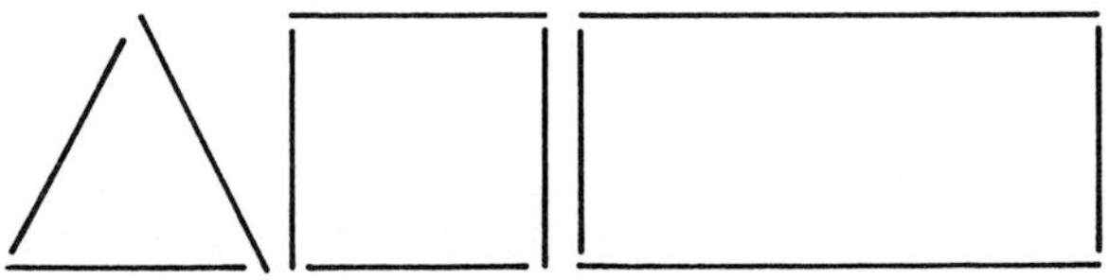

Figure 2.5
We tend to think in unified wholes.

experiences and knowledge. The interpretation of information is a subjective judgment; it is a product of our own creation and it may or may not be valid.

We should realize that in interpreting the information we receive from our senses, we seldom stop with apparent, observable cues. We almost always infer other characteristics. Such things as a person's attitudes, values, beliefs, motives, personality traits, interests, or background are not directly observable. Although identification can be fairly reliable, interpretation is usually open to some question. We need to remember that if appearances are deceiving and untrustworthy, then our own inferences are even more tenuous. They may be little more than guesses.

The Perceived: Other Influences

Although the perceiver has been the main focus of this chapter so far, there are other factors that directly influence our perceptions. In a sense, these factors—stereotyping, proximity, and role[9]—are restricting forces. To understand them will help us detect, analyze, and cope with them as we engage in interpersonal communication.

Stereotyping: Labels Are Restricting

We can usually tell fairly quickly just by looking at another person whether or not we would like to strike up a relationship. How? The person's appearance often provides us with just enough cues to stereotype him or her. **Stereotyping** is the process of assigning fixed labels or categories to things and people we encounter or, the reverse of this, placing things and people we encounter into fixed categories we have already established. When we stereotype a person, we assume things to be true about the individual because that person reminds us of someone else about whom those things may really have been true. We assume that the pattern that applies to one person applies to another, even though the two people may actually have little in common. Stereotyping simplifies the task of making judgments about things and people. It is a commonly used device; all human beings employ it to deal with thc trcmcndous flow of events around them.[10]

It does, however, tend to distort our perceptions. Instead of recognizing what is unique in each person, stereotyping places people into categories, much as mail is pigeonholed according to route. She is a blonde, therefore she must "have more fun" (a category); he has a full beard and glasses, thus he is an "intellectual" (a category); he plays football, thus he is a "jock" (a category). We do this with individuals, events, ideas—anything. To each category we attach an extensive set of corresponding labels, or stereotypes.

Take the man who plays football for example. If we assign him the label of "jock," we may jump to the conclusion that he is insensitive, not

very bright, and a male chauvinist. The man may or may not be any of these things. The point is, we don't know anything about him for certain except that he plays football. Many of our stereotypes are so conditioned into us that it is hard to see that we have them, much less get rid of them.

Besides the fact that stereotyping doesn't take into account the unique qualities of individuals, it also implies that all the people, events, ideas, or things we pigeonhole are static, when in reality they are ever changing. Nobody is witty or bright all the time. Everyone has his or her moments. And yet we tend to attribute static qualities and respond to others as if those qualities were appropriate *all the time*. Think carefully about the last time you made a comment like, "Mark is really the life of *any* party," or "Lisa *always* looks so nice." We use statements like these because they are the best predictors we have of how a person "should" act, if everything we know about the person is right.[11]

Everyone stereotypes, to a degree that varies with the individual and with the groups to which the individual belongs. Take college freshmen as

Consider This

I know many other people who live with their ideas of each other. Not with a real person but with a "really." They doggedly refuse to let the evidence interfere with their opinions. They develop an idea about the other person and spend a lifetime trying to make him or her live up to that idea. A lifetime, too, of disappointments.

As James Taylor sings it:
   "First you make believe
   I believe the things
   that you make believe
   And I'm bound to let you down.

   Then it's I who have been deceiving
   Purposely misleading
   And all along you believed in me."

But when we describe what the other person is really like, I suppose we often picture what we want. We look through the prism of our need.

I know a man who believes that his love is really a very warm woman. The belief keeps him questing for that warmth. I know a woman who is sure that her mate has hidden strength, because she needs him to have it.

Against all evidence, one man believes that his woman is nurturing because he so wants her to be. After 20 years, another woman is still tapping hidden wells of sensuality in her mate which he has, she believes, repressed.

—Ellen Goodman, "People Are What They Seem to Be," *Toledo Blade,* July 3, 1979, p. 12. © 1979. The Boston Globe Newspaper/Washington Post Writers Group, reprinted with permission.

an example of a group. A study was done in which college freshmen, male and female, looked at photographs of men with different amounts of facial hair. The students were to rate the men in the photos on masculinity. The results? The more hair the man had on his face, the more likely the students were to see him as "masculine, mature, good-looking, dominant, self-confident, courageous, liberal, nonconforming, industrious, and older."[12] The students didn't know anything about these men except what they looked like; they formed their judgments on the basis of a stereotype.

Physical attractiveness is another category we use to stereotype people and, unfortunately, we tend to give it disproportionate emphasis as we communicate with them. An attractive appearance creates a "halo effect": this appeal influences all other impressions a person makes on us. For example, research on criminal trials has shown that the defendant received a harsher sentence if either the victim was attractive or the defendant was unattractive.[13] It has been shown, too, that an attractive female has a better chance of changing the attitudes of males than an unattractive one.[14] This is probably not news to anyone. And studies have proved that attractive people, regardless of their sex, will be perceived as having higher credibility.[15] How fair is this? Can you think of any situations where such stereotyping is justified?

Proximity: Distance Distorts

Proximity is simply nearness in place, time, or relationship. It can strongly affect the way we perceive. There are two types of proximity: **physical** and **psychological.**

An example of how physical proximity can influence perception is the experience of sitting near the back of a lecture hall on the first day of class and deciding that your new instructor is quite young. When you go down after class to ask a question, the hair that looked blond from a distance turns out to be gray, and the skin that looked smooth is crossed by age lines. Middle twenties turns out to be late forties. We all make judgments that later prove to be inaccurate because we were either too close to or too far from the object to perceive it accurately.

Psychological proximity may have several effects on our communication. One is that the extent to which our own attitudes are similar to someone else's may determine how well we understand him or her. You must know some people you feel you always have to explain yourself to. You don't have psychological proximity with them—you just don't seem to understand each other. Then there are people with whom you "click." With such people you rarely have to say, "I *meant* that! I was serious," or "I was only kidding." They know without your telling them. Don't you feel you understand this other person? With this person you have achieved psychological proximity.

The second effect is that when we are attitudinally similar to someone, we evaluate this person more positively than if we are not. You probably like teachers you perceive as having tastes similar to yours—teachers who

make a comment you might have made or wear a parka like yours. A research study demonstrated that when teachers are attitudinally similar to their students, the students give them higher ratings on such characteristics as open-mindedness, personal attractiveness, and teaching skills. Attitudinally dissimilar teachers are rated lower.[16]

A third effect of psychological proximity involves our readiness to respond in a specific way. For example, if you witness an automobile accident along with some other people, viewpoints may differ although physical proximity is the same for all of you. A police officer might look at the accident from the point of view of what driving violations took place. A doctor might be most concerned about the injuries sustained by the people involved. A highway worker might notice broken curbs or uprooted sewers. Each person would bring his or her own experiences or psychological set to the accident. Each would be psychologically near to a different aspect of the accident. The testimony of each would be necessary to learn all the important details of the accident. What you bring to an event such as this often influences your perceptions of it more than the actual facts of the event.

Role: A Limiting Point of View

The roles we play affect our perceptions strongly. In relation to your parents, your role is that of a son or daughter. In a classroom, your role is that of student. A **role** is the stance we take or are assigned in a particular situation; the role we play affects our expectations, needs, attitudes, and beliefs about that situation; it restricts how we perceive that situation. There are job roles, family roles, sex roles, friendship roles, and many others.

Try This

What is the first image that comes into your mind when you think of the following people?

1. A gas-station mechanic.
2. Someone who walks with a cane and lives in a rest home.
3. A rock musician.
4. A hairdresser.
5. Someone who sells vacuum cleaners door-to-door.
6. Someone who has five children and is on welfare.
7. A rapist.
8. A business executive for a large corporation.
9. A nurse.
10. Someone who is in the army.

What sex did you think of for each of these people? What age? What ethnic background? What stereotypes are you aware of holding? What do your stereotypes simplify for you? What do they complicate?

Each of us plays roles defined by our culture, by our upbringing, and by how we personally see those roles. We are all familiar with the sex roles that have come to be traditional in our society. Think of how our perceptions are affected by the degree to which we accept these traditional roles. A strong-minded man may be perceived as assertive and a natural leader while an equally strong-minded woman is perceived as pushy and overbearing. How often do we see male children dressed in pink? Our acceptance of traditional sex roles has a direct effect on our perception of the color pink as appropriate or inappropriate in certain situations. A woman wearing an apron at the kitchen sink is a natural and acceptable sight; we have been conditioned to squirm or laugh when we see a man in that same apron at that same sink. Our perceptions are affected.

We have learned to expect to hear a woman's voice in certain situations, a man's in others. Think of telephone operators, airplane pilots, and doctors' receptionists. Listen hard to television commercials. In how many of them is the "voice-over" provided by a man, even in advertising of products intended for use by women? Advertisers are banking on the fact that potential consumers will listen to a persuasive man's voice more closely than to a woman's. They know society has trained us to perceive men's voices as more reliable and more authoritative. How many other instances can you think of in which acceptance of traditional sex roles affects perception in a directly observable way?

Certain roles carry higher prestige or credibility than others. What we see as another person's role will affect our perceptions of that person in certain situations. The role of professor, for example, might carry higher credibility and prestige in a faculty meeting on curriculum than the role of student. On the other hand, any student would probably be better able than a professor to discuss the availability of drugs on campus. In this case, the role of student is perceived as the more reliable source of information. If we see a person in a certain position fulfilling the duties and responsibilities of that job and serving our own best interests, then we are likely to overlook what we see as that person's shortcomings. Our perceptions are affected by the fact that the responsibilities of the position are being satisfied. Other considerations matter less to us in this situation.

Improving Skills in Perception

Because of the broad range of factors affecting our perception and because of the number of ways these factors interact, there are no universal rules that will guarantee improved, accurate perception. But there are several guidelines that might help. Some seem obvious and easy to put into practice; others may require more time to develop and use. All will contribute to the improvement of our perceptual skills. Since our perception influences and directs our reactions to others, improvement becomes crucial to improving our interpersonal communication.

Don't jump to conclusions.   One error we may tend to make that affects the accuracy of our perceptions is generalizing or drawing conclusions based on weak evidence. Just because we see something happen once, we may automatically assume it happens that way regularly.

You may see a bus stopping at a new location and assume that a new route has been established to include that location. You may see a person go into a bar and assume the person drinks heavily. Your perception will improve if you temper your thoughts and comments with conditional statements like, "*I wonder if* the bus route has been changed to include . . . " or "*Maybe* he drinks heavily, because I saw him . . . . " Even better, stick strictly to the simplest facts: "I saw the bus stop at a new location today" or "I saw Ralph going into a bar downtown." If you are not reporting firsthand information, you should identify your source to indicate the potential believability of the observation. That is, if you have heard information from someone else or read it somewhere, you should label what you report: "*Bill says* he saw Jane and Dave together downtown" or "*I read in the paper* that . . . . " This allows those who hear your information to gauge its believability without having your judgment interfere with it.

But often the problem is not in the labeling. Sometimes we believe our own judgments despite weak evidence. We convince ourselves by phrasing the idea in a certain way, stating it to someone else, or repeating it. If we can learn to restrain ourselves—suspend judgment—until we receive more evidence, we will improve the accuracy of our perceptions.

Maintaining a balance between openness and skepticism is difficult in our society. Forced to produce, make decisions, act, and respond quickly, it is hard to stand back and judge the worth of the information we hear daily. The point is not to doubt the validity of everything we hear; the point is to place new evidence into the context of other evidence we already have before drawing conclusions. If no other evidence exists, it is wiser to continue to doubt than to make inferences. If a conclusion is necessary, the cautious skeptic will label the conclusion as a conditional one. We can never anticipate the decisions other people may make based on what we have told them; all we can do is be responsible in reporting what we actually do know. There are other ways, too, that you can avoid jumping to conclusions. Some of these follow:

- Broaden your personal experience. The more experience you have, the better the frame of reference into which new information can be placed.
- Try to find out what other yardsticks can be used to measure the phenomena. Do not depend solely on your own yardsticks.
  —Are you depending on what others have told you?
  —Are you focusing primarily on the situation?
  —Are you looking simply at role relationships?
- Encourage communication. The more people talk the more likely it is that new evidence and impressions will emerge.
- Encourage others to define the langauge they use. Even when two people hear the same cluster of cues and receive similar impressions, the language they use to express those impressions may be so different that one might suspect different perceptions.
- Be on guard for selective perception. Try to deal with contradictory information rather than overlook or deny it.
- Try to assume the role of detached observer—a third person who can be objective about what is being observed.

Give it time. Physical togetherness helps increase the accuracy of our perceptions. We have all had the experience of being impressed by a person from a distance only to change our impression radically upon closer contact. The same phenomenon occurs after knowing people better or working with them.[17] Accurate perceptions of another person do not occur instantaneously like the picture on a solid-state television set. They require both time and spatial closeness. Give yourself time to be with someone. Even so, long-term, face-to-face, physical togetherness only provides the opportunity to understand how another person interprets the world; it does not guarantee that we will understand it.

- Try to reserve judgment. Saying "I need time to think this over" is an easy way to admit this need and make it known to others.

- Be patient. Slow down a little. Let time and experience have an effect. It is amazing how much information can be acquired simply by waiting. Your mind has an opportunity to sift through the relevant material.
- Study the situation. Learn all you can about it. Find out what you need to know to make a decision or identify an impression.
- Use your intelligence to help articulate the impression or perception you wish to convey. Try to reconstruct the cue as accurately as possible and rephrase, in your mind, the response to it until you feel it is accurate.
- Do not use lack of time as an excuse for not responding or for doing nothing.

Make yourself available. It's important to be available to most other people, both physically and psychologically.[18] This means trying to get on another's "wavelength" or "into another person's head." An old Sioux prayer stated it this way: "O Great Spirit! Let me not judge another man without first walking a mile in his moccasins." So often in this hurry-up, get-things-done society, we do not spend much time really making ourselves available to others. Physical togetherness does not necessarily mean psychological availability.

Psychological availability requires an active commitment to openness on our part. We have to make time for other people—time not only to share but also to be aware. To improve the accuracy of our perceptions, we must be willing to go beyond cliché-level exchanges that require little time and demand no commitment from us.

One cautionary note is in order. Availability is not appropriate in every interpersonal-communication setting. Knowing when and where we should make ourselves available to others or strive for peak communication is part of interpersonal competence.

- Strive for "peak communication" based on absolute openness and honesty.[19]
- Whenever possible, move toward complete emotional and personal communion with others. This communion may not be a permanent experience, but a time when you feel almost perfect and mutual empathy.
- Be willing to share your reactions with others. Enjoy sharing in their reactions as well, whether the occasion is one of happiness or grief.

Make a commitment. Any self-improvement requires active commitment, but it is especially important if you truly seek to increase your perceptivity. If you want your perceptions to be accurate, you must make a conscious effort to seek out as much information as possible on any given topic or question before you make a judgment or form an opinion. The more information you have, the more likely it is that your perceptions will be accurate.[20] You should make a real effort to search for possibilities, asking "What if . . . ?" and "What about . . . ?" and "What else . . . ?" at every turn. You cannot hope to have reliable perceptions if you are indifferent and passive about acquiring information.

- Nothing happens unless you want it to. Change your attitude. Decide that change is good.
- Begin now to want to seek new information, knowledge, and experience. Decide that change is beneficial. There are personal benefits to be gained. The more information you have, the more accurate your perceptions are likely to be.
- Life can go by and you may take little part in what happens. On the other hand, you can be a responding, actively immersed participant.
- Remember that the "commitment" is a frame of mind—an attitude— and it can be changed. Notice the people who are having fun, who are getting so much out of life. What do they have? Check it out. Think about it. You only go around once.

Establish the proper climate.   Your perceptivity will improve if you establish a climate conducive to communication. This means maintaining an atmosphere in which self-disclosure is likely to occur. Where open communication can be sustained, the likelihood of accurate perception will increase simply because people will trust each other enough to exchange honest messages. Of course, your behavior should be responsive to the realities of the multiple types of relationships you must manage, but the more you know about the needs and feelings of other people, the more likely it is that your actions toward them will be appropriate and your prediction of future interactions will be accurate. You must establish an environment in which truth is free to surface, so that your perceptions may be based on that truth. Face-to-face encounters where both visual and vocal ingredients are part of the interaction help you gain the information you need.

Part of creating a proper climate also means recognizing that each of us is unique; that is, recognizing that our view of the world is entirely our own. The world does not revolve around us, and if we see that everyone does not share our perceptions of the world, we will have at least acknowledged the need for a proper climate.

- Don't manipulate, dominate, and try to run other people's lives.
- Be authentic. Be yourself, honestly, in your relationship with others.
- Avoid pretense, defenses, and duplicity.
- Don't "play it cool."
- Never use your behavior as a gambit to disarm others—to get them to reveal themselves before you reveal yourself to them.[21]

Be willing to adjust.   Perception involves a perceiver and a context within which the process occurs. These components are so interwoven that they cannot be analyzed apart from each other. Changes in any one affect all others. The most we can do is to recognize that as these components vary, so must our perceptions. The flawless friend of two weeks ago may now be seen as disloyal and hurtful. The arrogant and unfair teacher of yesterday may be the friendly and helpful teacher of today. To be unwilling to change our perceptions, and righteous in our inflexibility, can only cause us perceptual problems. What we need is perceptual sensitivity: full recognition that our perceptions will change as our interests and experiences change. We cannot expect today's perceptions to be accurate if we are basing them on yesterday's attitudes.

- Take a hard look at your spontaneity. Can you open up to something new? Or do you rigidly adhere to your perceptions of what is expected of you?
- Take a hard look at your prejudices. Can you change your impressions of people, ideas, or activities?
- Take a hard look at your life. Are you living according to a rigid, well-defined plan that allows no deviation? There is certainty and security in such a life—but little excitement and growth. Change brings both.[22]

Try This

Extend the normal limits of your senses. Try to answer the following questions:

1. What color is today?
2. What color is the smell of your favorite perfume?
3. How high is the sky? What does the sky sound like?
4. What does your favorite day taste like?
5. What color is a hug?
6. What does a favorite song or work of music smell like? How would you describe its shape?
7. What does yellow taste like?
8. What color is the sound of a parade?
9. How would you describe the texture of your own name?
10. What would your eyes feel like if they could shake hands?
11. What does your favorite season sound and smell like?
12. What is your favorite sense?
13. What smell describes your self-concept?
14. What color is love?
15. Write whatever enters your head (in two or three sentences).

—From *Talk to Yourself* by Genelle Austin-Lett and Jan Sprague. Copyright © 1976 by Houghton Mifflin Company. Used with permission.

Our own interpersonal communications will be a great deal more effective when we realize the role that perception plays. Each of us, in our own unique way, is responsible for our method of arriving at the meaning of things through the processes of reception and construction. Reception involves taking in information through our senses. Construction involves constructing experiences according to the organization of categories we possess.

Construction is a major element of the perceptual process, and it reinforces and underscores the idea of transactional communication developed in the first chapter. The point is that from the cues we receive from others or from the environment, we construct pictures that constitute our reality. No one gives us meaning, and no one can control the meanings we determine for ourselves. It is we who create meaning out of our own experiences.

The more accurate our perceptions, the more likely we are to communicate effectively with others. By acquiring more information, we increase the number of ways we can respond to other people, and we strengthen our ability to grow in a positive direction. And since our first step in communicating with others involves forming some impression of them, how well we form those impressions becomes crucial to interpersonal success. Perception is one method of acquiring information; self-disclosure is another. Disclosing yourself is the key to getting in touch with your self. In the next chapter, we discuss the self and self-disclosure.

Notes

[1] Gary Cronkhite, "Perception and Meanings," in *Handbook of Rhetorical and Communication Theory*, ed. Carroll C. Arnold and John Waite Bowers (Boston: Allyn and Bacon, Inc., 1984), pp. 51–229.

[2] Frank A. Geldard, *The Human Senses* (New York: John Wiley & Sons, 1953), p. 53.

[3] Donald R. Gordon, *The New Literacy* (Toronto: University of Toronto Press, 1971), pp. 25–47.

[4] Sydney J. Harris, *Pieces of Eight* (Boston: Houghton Mifflin Co., 1982), pp. 159–60.

[5] Stephen W. Littlejohn, *Theories of Human Communication*, 3rd ed. (Belmont, Calif.: Wadsworth, 1989), pp. 80–81.

[6] Alvin Toffler, *Future Shock* (New York: Random House, 1970).

[7] Hans Sebald, "Limitations of Communication: Mechanisms of Image Maintenance in Form of Selective Perception, Selective Memory and Selective Distortion," *Journal of Communication* 12 (1962): 142–49.

[8] J. S. Bruner, "Social Psychology and Perception," in *Readings in Social Psychology*, ed. E. Maccoby, T. M. Newcomb, and E. L. Hartley (New York: Holt, Rinehart & Winston, 1958), pp. 85–94.

[9] Richard C. Huseman, James M. Lahiff, and John D. Hatfield, *Interpersonal Communication in Organizations: A Perceptual Approach* (Boston: Holbrook Press, 1976), pp. 28–32.

[10] George J. McCall and J. L. Simmons, *Identities and Interaction: An Examination of Human Association in Everyday Life* (New York: Free Press, 1966), p. 114.

[11] McCall and Simmons, *Identities and Interaction*, p. 115.

[12] Robert J. Pellegrini, "Impressions of the Male Personality as a Function of Beardedness," *Psychology* 10 (February 1973): pp. 29–33.

[13] D. Lancy and E. Aronson, "The Influence of the Character of the Criminal and His Victim on the Decisions of Simulated Jurors," *Journal of Experimental Social Psychology* 5 (1969): pp. 141–52.

[14] J. Mills and E. Aronson, "Opinion Change as a Function of the Communicator's Attractiveness and Desire to Influence," *Journal of Personality and Social Psychology* 1 (1965): pp. 73–77.

[15] R. N. Widgery and B. Webster, "The Effects of Physical Attractiveness upon Perceived Initial Credibility," *Michigan Speech Journal* 4 (1969): pp. 9–15.

[16] Katherine C. Good and Lawrence R. Good, "Attitude Similarity and Attraction to an Instructor," *Psychological Reports* 33 (August 1973): pp. 335–37.

[17] J. W. Shepherd discusses how people's conceptions of each other change as a result of working together. See J. W. Shepherd, "The Effects of Valuations in Evaluations of Traits on the Relation Between Stimulus Affect and Cognitive Complexity," *Journal of Social Psychology* 88 (December 1972): pp. 233–39.

[18] For more on psychological availability, see John Stewart and Gary D'Angelo, *Together: Communicating Interpersonally,* 2d ed. (Reading, Mass.: Addison-Wesley Publishing Co., 1980), pp. 110–12.

[19] John Powell, *Why Am I Afraid to Tell You Who I Am?* (Allen, Texas: Argus Communications, 1969), pp. 61–62.

[20] See Frederick W. Obitz and L. Jerome Oziel, "Varied Information Levels and Accuracy of Person Perception," *Psychological Reports* 31 (October 1972): pp 571–76.

[21] Sidney M. Jourard, *The Transparent Self* (New York: D. Van Nostrand Co., 1971), p. 133.

[22] Wayne W. Dyer, *Your Erroneous Zones* (New York: Avon Books, 1976), pp. 126–31.

Further Reading

Richard Bandler and John Grinder, *Reframing: Neuro-Linguistic Programming and the Transformation of Meaning* (Moab, Utah: Real People Press, 1982). The meaning of any event depends upon the "frame" in which we perceive it. When we reframe an event, we change not only its meaning but also our responses to it. The authors' first book, *Frogs into Princes,* described the basic process of reframing; here they develop the subject further, with several additional models.

Lucia Capacchione, *The Power of Your Other Hand* (North Hollywood, Calif: Newcastle Publishing, 1988). Do you want to change a series of perceptions you may have? Capacchione claims there is an all-pervasive conspiracy against the left hand. What Capacchione does is help readers attack the myths. Through her exercises, she gets them to tap the potential of their little-used right hemisphere and, thus, to talk to their inner child, clarify relationships, unlock creativity, and channel inner wisdom. Insightful, interesting, and informative, this 196-page popular paperback is designed to change perceptions.

Gary Cronkhite, "Perception and Meaning," in Carroll C. Arnold and John Waite Bowers, Eds., *Handbook of Rhetorical and Communication Theory* (Boston: Allyn and Bacon, 1984, pp. 51–229). This is virtually a book in itself. Cronkhite describes the characteristics necessary for accounting for what humans know and the way they perceive meaning. This academic development of the concept is both comprehensive and in-depth. A special strength is the more than 1200 bibliographic sources cited. An excellent reference.

Richard L. Gregory, *Odd Perceptions* (London: Methuen, 1986). Gregory has arranged his topics in a sequence from those that may amuse, to ideas to muse upon, to those you can use. The purpose of this book is to ask questions. Gregory views perception as similar to science in that it generates rich predictive hypotheses from scarcely adequate data. A delightful collection of brief essays on perceptual topics.

Willis Harman and Howard Rheingold, *Higher Creativity: Liberating the Unconscious for Breakthrough Insights* (Los Angeles: Jeremy P. Tarcher, Inc., 1984). Based on contemporary and historical accounts of creative breakthroughs, these authors evolve and describe a simple, reproducible sequence for triggering insights. The chapter on "Opening the Mind's Gate" is especially interesting in this 237-page paperback that seems to bridge the popular- and textbook-market gulf.

John Heil, *Perception and Cognition* (Berkeley: University of California Press, 1983). Heil favors the view that perception is basically a linkage connecting beliefs to ordinary physical objects and events. He includes chapters on "The Senses," "Perceptual Objects," "The Concept of Information," "Seeing is Believing," "Seeing and Conceiving," and "Visual Perception." A readable, understandable approach to perception.

Claire F. Michaels and Claudia Carello, *Direct Perception* (Englewood Cliffs, NJ: Prentice-Hall, 1981). These authors present a short, understandable explanation of the ecological approach, which holds that perception is of *events*—not of objects isolated in time and space. They emphasize the importance of time and space, and that perception is an ongoing activity of knowing the environment. An excellent 200-page explanation.

Theron Raines, *The Singing: A Fable About What Makes Us Human* (New York: The Atlantic Monthly Press, 1988). The last book of this kind I read was Saint-Exupery's *The Little Prince*. This is an imaginative, fascinating love story that emphasizes throughout what it is that makes us human. More importantly, for our purposes, are the perceptions of Forrest, a visitor from Mars, about Earth and the contradictory ways of humans. His perceptions may cause you to wonder why we act as we do! An interesting, moving book.

Irvin Rock, *The Logic of Perception* (Cambridge, Mass: The MIT Press, 1983). In this textbook, Rock avoids technical language, defines terms when necessary, and explains experiments clearly. Rock takes us through twelve chapters, from characteristics and theories of perception to criticisms, clarifications, and conclusions. A well-illustrated, thorough examination of the concept.

John M. Wilding, *Perception: From Sense to Object* (New York: St. Martin's Press, 1983). This is not a standard textbook on perception. Wilding provides a framework within which knowledge about perception can be organized and answers the question, "What are the methods of researchers trying to fill the gaps in our knowledge?" The focusing question of the book is, "How can we know what this thing is?" Wilding leaves readers in awe of the sophisticated and highly efficient mechanisms we have evolved to cope with our environment—and our enormous ignorance about how these mechanisms work.

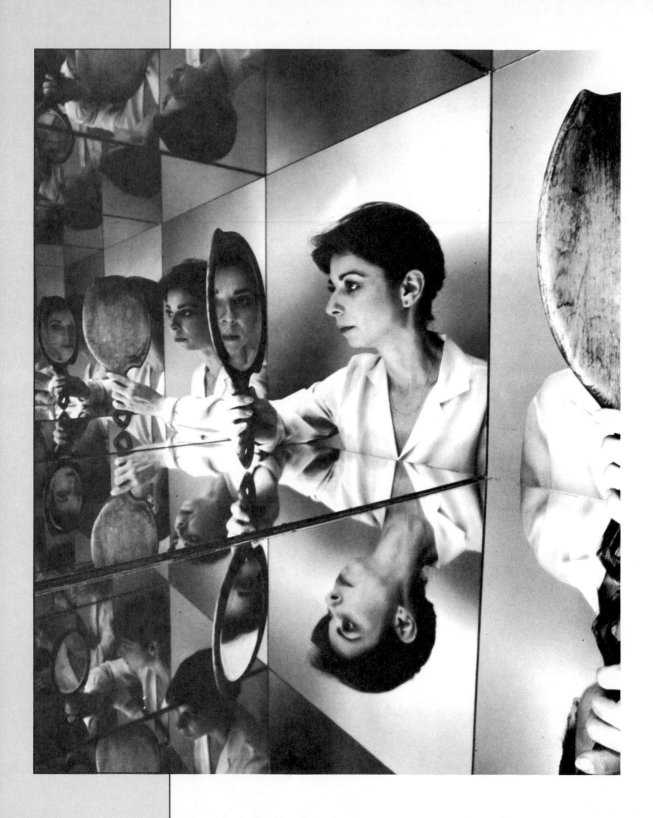

3

Getting in Touch: The Self and Self-Disclosure

Learning Objectives

When you have finished this chapter you should be able to:

- Explain the importance of a realistic perception of self in interpersonal communication.
- Describe the importance of the role of the media in the development of self-concept.
- Explain five ways we have for getting in touch with the self.
- Explain the forces that affect positive self-concepts.
- List and explain some of the obstacles to your accepting yourself.
- Mention at least four things that can be done to improve your attitude toward yourself.
- Characterize the self-actualizing person. How would you know if you met one?
- Describe what happens in self-disclosure.
- Distinguish the panes of the Johari Window and describe their relationship to self-disclosure.
- Describe the skills that will further self-disclosure and how trust—an essential element in the process—is built.

We will begin the discussion of how we can improve our skills in communicating with others by discussing how we communicate with ourselves. This may sound contradictory, but to be in touch with someone else, we must first be in touch with ourselves. This process of communicating with ourselves is called **intrapersonal** communication. It is interesting that the way we learn most about ourselves is through communicating with others. Let's look at an example of how this works.

If you grew up with strong-minded parents or siblings who made all the decisions, and if the only interpersonal contacts you ever had were with your own family, you could end up thinking of yourself as an indecisive person. But you also interact with your friends, and among them you may be very opinionated and action-oriented. Your friends may look to you for leadership and decisions. Conceivably, other communication contexts could bring out even more strongly the bully or the shrinking violet in you. You may be more or less decisive depending on whether you're talking to a small child or to a salesclerk or to a police officer. The point is, your principal ways of evaluating your decision-making ability are the communication contacts you have with other people.

Your Self-Concept

The starting point for all your interpersonal communication is your concept of self. After discussing the development of self-concept and the importance of disclosing that self to others, I will outline the skills necessary for improving your ability to self-disclose. This ability is the key to discovering the self and continuing to grow.

Who Are You?

If you had to use *one* word to characterize yourself, what would that one word be? Shy? Enthusiastic? Loving? Confident? Your characterization of yourself will probably involve more than one word. You may think of yourself as interesting and friendly once people get to know you; you may think you are intelligent, attractive, and generally concerned about other people and what happens in the world. Whatever words you select, this idea of yourself—your **self-concept**—is directly related to how you behave. It works both ways. If you've always had the knack for making new friends, you've probably come to think of yourself as friendly and outgoing. And if you think of yourself as basically outgoing, it can actually make meeting other people and making new friends easier. Your behavior reflects the opinion you have of yourself.

Your success in college and in life may depend more on *how* you feel about yourself and your abilities than on your actual talents. And your self-concept will affect your skill in dealing with other people. You can see how your communications with people could go haywire if you think of yourself as a friendly, warm person and people around you see you as a loud, offensive boor. What you consider a concerned inquiry into a friend's health could be perceived by that person as nosy, prying into something that is none of your business. Interpersonal communication, to be effective, depends upon a realistic perception of self.[1]

How Did You Get to Be This Way?

The background for, development of, and influences on our self-concept are numerous. What makes it even more difficult to discover the roots of our self-concept is that all of the causes interact with one another in unpredictable ways. And even the ways we respond to various influences differ. We are born with different patterns of reaction. My wife and I have noticed, for example, that one of our four children has been independent and self-determined from birth, another has been timid and shy, a third has been affectionate and dependent, and a fourth has been extroverted and assertive. All were raised in the same environment, yet all grew up differently— different from birth. Children are not blank slates to be written on by family and fate. Imagine the possible effect on a child when parents who wanted a docile "doll" receive a tough kid!

There is no doubt that parents serve as a shaping force in a child's upbringing. Their influence can be direct and specific. Consider how much you may have been influenced by the family you were born into, the religion they followed, the ethnic culture they supported, the socioeconomic group with which they identified, and the national society of which they were a part.

Direct and specific influence also includes the respect you were shown. How did your parents treat your actions, feelings, and statements? Did your parents act as if you were worthwhile and valued? The respect they showed you probably had a major influence on your self-concept, one with a lasting effect as well.

Another direct and specific influence was the standards your parents set for you. Did your parents ever say, "You should be a professional," or "You should be a parent," or "You are good for nothing"? These early

Consider This

In rearing children, we know that the kind of praise or encouragement they get—in short, the environment they are raised in—often determines the path in life they will follow. A home with good books and good music and good talk is far more likely to produce a creative and valuably contributing adult.

—From "Strictly Personal" by Sydney J. Harris, *Toledo Blade*, September 16, 1985. By permission of NAL, Inc.

goals—or nongoals—became part of your self-concept. What's more, they created the potential for fulfillment, disappointment, or failure. Think, for example, of the child who never reaches an assigned goal and feels like a failure despite other worthwhile achievements. Or, what about the child who achieves the goal and discovers he or she is not comfortable with it?

Self-concept can be formed, too, in the struggle against parents. Excessive parental pressure can cause grief. Some parents don't want their kids to grow up. Some expect perfection or skill beyond the realm of reality. Some want their kids to follow exactly in their footsteps. One student developed ulcers because he could not produce the grades his father desired.

Some people, on the other hand, received no direct guidance. They didn't ever have anything to struggle against! Lack of parental direction can lead to an unclear self-concept. Without such direction, some people have problems meeting their needs and being self-assertive. Frequently, these people work for the benefit of others and fail to pay sufficient attention to the kind of person they are and what is best for them. Sometimes it is useful for children to have parents who make suggestions and propose goals.

I am not trying to suggest that parents are the only influence on our self-concept. That is far from true. People whom we admire as we grow up influence us; so do our friends, the parents of our friends, religious leaders and teachers, our schoolteachers, and even the environment in which we grow up. Molding of self-concepts can result from contact with classmates, lovers, spouses, and even media personalities. Cathcart and Gumpert, writers in the area of self development, claim that our self-concept is dependent in large part on the media.[2] Motion pictures and television, they say, play a significant part in the role-taking function that is necessary to maintaining a self-image. They write:

> Role-taking is the process of taking on the role of another person in order to be seen as others see that person. To take a role we must not only be able to observe that role over time but also establish enough distance between the "I" [the portion of the self that initiates acts and represents all the possible behavior choices available to the person (p. 92)] and the "me" [the social self and its awareness of cultural mores, social norms, attitudes, and values (p. 92)] to be aware of the role we are enacting as compared to the role to be assumed. Thus, role-taking feeds the internal dialogue between the "I" and the "me" which enables a person to form a self image.
>
> Role-taking begins early, usually in the childhood play stage, and goes on throughout life. . . . (p. 99)

Although their position on the influence of the media is speculative, Cathcart and Gumpert offer food for thought as we try to determine how we got to be the way we are. The statistics regarding how much time the television set is on in the average home, and the informal surveys I have

taken in my interpersonal-communication classes regarding how many college students of *both* sexes watch soap operas, lead me to believe that the media can play a major role in self development.

In discovering where our self-concepts came from, it probably makes sense to look less at specific experiences and more at the conclusions we drew from those experiences. People get different information from the same stimulus. This is why a "lecture" from a father could serve as an instructional lesson for one child, a joke to another, a cause for rebellion in a third, and a "putdown" or reprimand to a fourth.

From this discussion, then, it becomes clear that our self-concept is a picture of ourselves based on earlier experiences. It has been shaped by how people have treated us and what they have expected of us, as well as our own emotional reactions to and conclusions from these and other experiences.

Now, think back to the word or words you used to describe yourself a bit ago. Chances are you arrived at that self-concept ("I'm popular") by the reactions other people have to you ("Glad to see you!"). But then you had to think about those reactions and decide what they meant to you ("They like to have me around. They appreciate my sense of humor"). In other words, your self-concept is created through both interpersonal and intrapersonal communication. Much of this occurs without your being really conscious of it. There are four processes we all more or less unconsciously engage in as we build our self-concepts. By becoming more aware of the processes and by working at them, we will gradually be more in touch with our true selves. Those processes are: (1) *self-awareness*, (2) *self-acceptance*, (3) *self-actualizing*, and (4) *self-disclosure*.

Self-Awareness

You have some understanding of yourself—how attractive, intelligent, influential, and successful you are. These understandings of yourself constitute your **self-awareness.** You derive these perceptions from experiences and interactions with others. (See Figure 3.1.) Not all your beliefs about yourself are realistic—some are beliefs about what you would *like* to be rather than what you are.

For example, if you would like to be chosen as the leader of a certain organization, you may behave the way you feel will get you the leadership role. What you would *like* to be—a leader—makes you more careful about your clothes, your speech, your associates. Both the roles you play and, perhaps, the roles you would like to play are important ingredients in your identity. Self-awareness involves comprehending the sum total of beliefs you have about yourself.

As another example, a woman who thinks of herself as fragile, elegant, and sophisticated may avoid anything that does not match her self-concept. She may avoid activities that require physical effort, like a touch-football game or backpacking. Getting dirty or hurting herself wouldn't fit her self-image. Activities more satisfactory to her might be going to the theater, belonging to social organizations, or playing bridge.

Different experiences have different impacts on her self-image. She can accept experiences consistent with her values more easily; she will probably reject those that don't fit well. We all do this. Some experiences may be rationalized to fit our needs if they are inconsistent with our perceptions of ourselves. For example, if at a meeting the woman is asked to do something she considers inappropriate, like sitting on the floor, she may do it because she needs to be accepted by the members of this group. She may rationalize the activity as one that is novel or amusing—even though it is inconsistent with her self-image.

Getting in Touch with the Self

Speech is central to human communication *and* to self development. In this brief section (brief, simply because I am unable to consider *all* the possible factors in this space), I want to show how speech (whether internal or external) can be used to get in touch with the self. This can be accomplished through self-talk, decentering, role-playing, visualization, and communion.

Self-talk is one way of getting in touch with the self. Think about it. How often do you talk to yourself? When you're driving? When getting ready for a date? When you've been in an argument, and you're telling yourself to "Stay calm now! Don't lose control!" When you're pondering a difficult problem? Chances are you talk to yourself quite often. You've probably seen professional athletes on television who, during pressure-packed moments, talk to themselves about the situation. John Modaff and Robert Hopper, writing about why speech is basic, claim that "Speech is a good

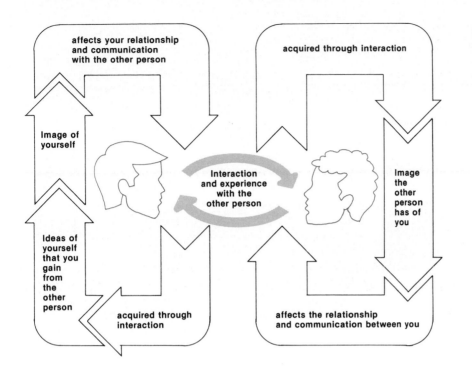

Figure 3.1
We derive information about ourselves from our interactions with others.

behavior-regulator. If you want to do something well, tell yourself how. It is often best if you tell yourself out loud."[3] Whether the speech is internal or external, talking to yourself is one way to get in touch with yourself.

A second way is *decentering.* According to Carol Zak-Dance, a researcher on self-concept development, decentering is the ability to move from an egocentric or self-centered point of view to an awareness of yourself from the viewpoint of others. With the internalization of speech communication, we can think about things not perceptually present. We can decenter ourselves from specific, concrete situations and begin to see ourselves as objects—from outside ourselves (p. 4).[4] With this objectivity we can begin to comment on, respond to, and perhaps even judge what we see about ourselves or what we see ourselves doing, with the goal of improvement, change, and growth.

Picture yourself driving along the expressway; suddenly another car nips your fender. You and the other driver pull over to the shoulder to investigate the damage. Now, objectively watch yourself "perform" in this situation. What was the first thing *you* did? Did you get out and approach the other driver with words like, "You idiot! Where did you get your license, from a breakfast-cereal box?" Watching yourself perform—as an object—is the process of decentering. The goal, in this example, is to become more humane. Thus, you decide that your first consideration should be the welfare of the occupants of the other vehicle. Now, picture yourself going over to the other car and saying, "Is everyone here all right?" By decentering you

have moved from an egocentric stance (blaming the other for damage to you) to a stance that involves awareness of others. Decentering is the process or tool used to achieve this new awareness.

Role playing is a third way of getting in touch with the self. It utilizes both self-talk and decentering techniques because it can involve both overt verbalization and objective observation of the self. Walter Ong writes that if we place ourselves in a specific setting, create the actors, create the dialogue, and then let the scene evolve, we can become actor *and* observer as our self unfolds. We then have a vehicle for experimenting and replaying scenes that will aid in self testing and development.[5]

The difference between decentering and role playing is primarily a difference of emphasis. The focus in decentering is awareness of ourselves from the viewpoint of others. In role playing, the emphasis is on the scene as a whole and on acting out our role in reference to everything else that is occurring. If you picture yourself discussing a grade with an instructor, and you try to see yourself performing or acting in that scene, it is decentering. If you substitute different dialogue or different alternative outcomes, it is more likely to be role playing. Role playing gives us a chance to set up scenes with a boss, friend, or loved one before they occur, or to reestablish them after they have occurred: "If I had only remembered to say . . ." Decentering is viewing our self in the scene objectively—from outside our self; role playing is acting out our role in the scene.

Closely tied to self-talk, decentering, and role playing is the concept of *visualization* or imaging—the creation of mental pictures. Hazel Markus, a psychologist, and her colleagues have discovered that the *possible selves* we envision can help us cope.[6] Markus defines possible selves as "components of the self-concept that have to do with what I can be, what I would like to be and, very importantly, what I am afraid of becoming." Hoped-for selves might include the thin, rich, motivated, attractive, and successful self. Those we fear becoming could include the lonely, alcoholic, unpopular, weak, unemployed, or unimportant self. From their study, Markus concludes that "possible selves are powerful motivators and are effective in guiding action."

Coping well—that is, having positive, hoped-for selves—helps us create new worlds and new ideas for ourselves. Even that feared self, especially if it is powerful enough, can create positive change: "I feared failing that class so much that I studied harder for *that* exam than I ever studied for an exam before." Markus recommends:

> *. . . trying to elaborate the self that you want to become, make it as vivid and specific as you possibly can. Imagine how you will look, how you will feel. But at the same time try to create the feared self—what could happen if you don't succeed.*

How does visualization differ from decentering and role playing? It doesn't. Any time we are involved in creating mental pictures—daydreams, fantasies, dreams, and nightmares are a few examples—we are visualizing. We probably cannot decenter or role-play without visualizing, but we can engage in self-talk with or without the mental picture. It is the mental *picture*, however, that makes it visualization. Some people use visualization more easily than others. It is, however, an easy technique that can be used at any time and in any place.

The fifth way we have for getting in touch with the self is *communion*. This does not refer to religious communion, but rather to the process of becoming involved and integrated with others.[7] Speech is the primary means by which this link to society, which is essential to our self-development, is forged.[8] Studies of children completely cut off from human companionship, such as the "Wild Boy" discovered living in the woods of Aveyron, France, in 1799 or children raised in total isolation, have inevitably shown mental retardation and incomplete physical development of the brain.[9]

The point is that the self-concept cannot be developed in isolation; we need others. The concept of communion represents the need for that link with others. We learn about our capabilities and limitations, our thoughts and feelings, and our distinctions and uniqueness through our interactions with others. The five methods discussed for getting in touch with ourselves are closely intertwined. Certainly, our communion with others provides the reference for, if not part of the content of, self-talk, decentering, role playing, and visualization.

Consider This

. . . it is enough to arrive at the conviction—no matter whether it is in some sense objectively justified or quite absurd—that others are whispering behind our backs and secretly, ridiculing us. Faced with these "facts," our common sense will suggest that it would be foolish to trust these people. And since all of their actions take place under a rather flimsy veil of secrecy, it makes good sense to be on guard and pay attention to even the most minute details. It is then only a question of time until we do catch them in the act of whispering, secretly giggling, and exchanging conspiratorial winks and nods. The prophecy has fulfilled itself.

—Paul Watzlawick, *The Situation Is Hopeless, But Not Serious [The Pursuit of Unhappiness]* (New York: W. W. Norton, 1983), p. 61.

The Self-Fulfilling Prophecy: Like a Dream Come True

Once we get in touch with ourselves, it is more likely that our behaviors will begin to reflect how we truly feel. If, for example, we feel strong, self-confident, and assertive, we may ask for what we want in an unquestioning, clear, and articulate manner. Because of our manner, it may be that the person we are asking responds to us as a strong, self-confident, and assertive individual. This would confirm our feelings about ourselves—especially if this happened a number of times. This is what is called a **self-fulfilling prophecy:** your behavior reflects feelings you hold about yourself, others respond to your behavior, and the original feelings are confirmed.

Now, think what might happen to a woman if everyone she met thought of her as tough, vulgar, and simple, and she thought of herself as fragile and sophisticated. Her self-image would be compromised or threatened. She might react in any of several ways: she might change her self-image; she might reject the people who provided negative feedback; or she might seek out people who give her only positive reinforcement. Faced with a similar situation, most of us would be unlikely to change our self-image. More probably, we would seek confirmation by associating with people who reinforce our own feelings about ourselves and by avoiding people who give us messages that contradict our self-image.

Your self-concept develops over a long period of time. Periodic and regular reinforcement from others is necessary to help confirm your feelings about yourself. Problems arise if you have negative feelings about yourself, because the self-fulfilling prophecy can strengthen a negative self-concept as easily as a positive one. If you want to change some quality in yourself, the best way to begin is by believing in the characteristic you want to possess. For example, if you want to be considered dependable, begin by thinking that you *are* dependable.[10]

   This may sound easy, but it isn't. You might need to get rid of some self-defeating ideas you didn't even know you had. This kind of change requires hard work.

Negative Self-Concepts: The Power of Negative Thinking

What happens when your feelings about yourself are weak or negative? Since you tend to act consistently with the feelings you have about yourself, this can be a damaging or destructive situation. For example, what if you perceive yourself as a failure in school? This attitude may be a result of something as insignificant as misunderstanding directions for an assignment, or it may have developed over a long period of time: having to compete with a very successful brother or sister, having a string of unsympathetic teachers, or not gaining enough positive reinforcement at home for schoolwork. Whatever the cause, it is likely that once you start thinking of yourself as a failure, you will begin to act the part. Because of poor study habits, inadequate reading, and lack of participation in class, a poor grade may result, reinforcing your feeling. Such negative feelings feed upon themselves and become a vicious cycle, a cycle that will begin to encompass all your thoughts, actions, and relationships. (See Figure 3.2.)

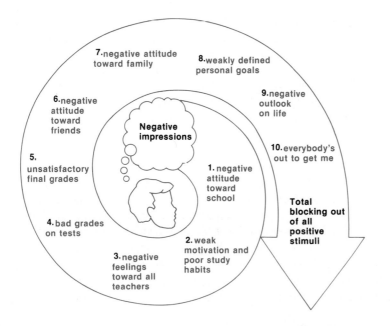

Figure 3.2
A negative cycle.

You may know people whose **negative cycle** is already well developed. It may be the person, for example, who can't accept criticism or who is overresponsive to praise. It may be someone who complains constantly, or someone who withdraws into self-imposed isolation. We all know people who couldn't think of a self-promoting thing to say if their lives depended on it. Why a person behaves this way, or how the feeling came about, is too complex a topic for our purposes. We are concerned with changing negative self-concepts to positive ones because of the effect such a change can have an interpersonal communication.[11]

Positive Self-Concepts: You Can Do It

We all know people who are confident about their ability to deal with problems. Given a difficult situation, they seek ways of approaching it. They feel equal to other people and have self-respect. These people accept praise simply and graciously. They can admit to a wide range of feelings, behaviors, and desires, some of which are socially approved and others of which are not. They are realistic in their assessment of self.

People with a positive self-concept can accept their negative feelings, behaviors, and desires if these are balanced and kept in perspective. They recognize that nobody is all good. Finally, these people are also capable of self-improvement. When they see they have an unlikable or negative quality, they find ways to change it.[12] And they are *likely* to discover personal faults because they are open and responsive to the way they behave and do not expect perfection. A positive self-concept creates a framework that is stable and well balanced so mistakes and failures can be successfully integrated into the behavior pattern without a shattering effect.

Few of us have entirely negative or entirely positive self-concepts. Either would be unrealistic and difficult to maintain. You probably fall into some middle-ground position. It would be healthy for all of us if we could be aware of our negative self-concepts and move away from them as well as we are able. Our self-concept affects how we view life, how we want to be viewed, how we view others, and how we interpret messages. Our self-concept holds a controlling influence on our life.

How you view life.   Do you see the world as generally threatening and unfriendly? Or does it seem basically a friendly place where you feel at home? Your images of yourself, whether positive or negative, form the framework for your intrapersonal and interpersonal communication. If you have a positive self-concept and rewarding and enjoyable relationships with others, you probably will hold a generally positive overall view of life. You'll be able to sort out what is important and what is irrelevant to you. A warm and open relationship with even one other person often makes you look on *all* others with a more positive outlook.[13]

How you want to be viewed.   If you think of yourself as a "super salesperson" or as a "terrific storyteller," then you want that view confirmed by others. You'll try to live up to the label, whether you chose it yourself or someone else chose it for you. Labels can be limiting if you don't think beyond them. It's not a good idea to let labels come to *define* who you are and what you want to be. But on the other hand labels can be useful for providing direction, for helping you make choices.[14] If you decide to aim for the label of "popular," you will behave in such a way that certain people will admire you. If the people whose esteem you're after—referred to as significant others—insist on a neat and fashionable appearance, nonstop smiles, and sociability, then you will choose to comb your hair carefully, wear stylish clothes, smile a great deal, and seek the company of others. Your self-concept determines how you wish to be responded to and will encourage you to seek that response.[15]

How you view others.   Your view of other people also will be affected by how you label yourself. If you chose the label "popular," you might suddenly become very aware of the relative popularity of other people. You'll be more eager to keep as friends those people who are generally considered popular. You'll be more likely to avoid people who seem to be unpopular. Because the label is important to you, you'll see other people in terms of it. If you view yourself as reliable, you are likely to judge others according to how reliable or unreliable they are. If you're very conscious of how well dressed you are, you'll become especially aware of how other people dress. How you view others often results from how you view and label yourself.[16]

How you interpret messages.   Your self-concept also affects the kinds of messages you accept and the way you interpret them. If you see yourself as "popular," you are likely to see people around you in terms of how they respond to your label. You'll probably keep as friends those people who accept you on your own terms. If it's popularity you're after, then your friends will be not only friends but also admirers. You're likely to see people you don't get along with as nonadmirers—they do not help you cultivate your "popular" self-image. You accept messages that confirm your popularity. You might distort, misinterpret, or ignore messages that don't confirm your popularity in order to protect your self-image.

We have examined self-awareness at length here because if we want to be more effective in our communication, we must come to grips with a realistic view of ourselves. We've seen the influence our self-image has on our intrapersonal and interpersonal communication; this image must be realistic. We've seen how the self-fulfilling prophecy works, and the importance of having it work for us rather than against us. It makes sense to be careful about the labels we assign ourselves because we're probably going to

Try This

How aware are you of yourself? Write ten statements that begin with the words "I am." We'll get back to your statements later in this chapter.

live up to them sooner or later. This might sound like a warning to you, but think of it as encouragement. We all face similar problems in this respect. Realistic self-awareness is difficult to achieve, but it is crucial if we want our communication to be effective.

Self-Acceptance

You begin by being aware of yourself, but you must also be satisfied with yourself. You must accept yourself. By this I do not mean you are smug or uncritical of negative qualities, but rather that you see your shortcomings for what they are, making neither too much nor too little of them. **Self-acceptance** means seeing how your positive and negative qualities are equally valid, equally *you*, equally normal to have. It means building on those qualities you're satisfied with and working to change the ones you're not happy with.

Like self-awareness, self-acceptance doesn't come easily. It isn't easy to accept yourself when you are constantly being measured by other people's standards. There are the standards of your parents ("Your friend Jimmy Bentley has been accepted by both Harvard and Yale. Have you heard from any schools yet?"); your teachers ("If you don't love *Moby Dick* you might just as well give up on American literature because you'll never understand it"); and even of advertisers ("Use Whammo lemon-herbal-avocado shampoo

Consider This

To achieve the good life, said Socrates, there is one paramount rule: *Know thyself.* This is not an easy thing to do. Knowing oneself, deeply and fully, also means *facing* oneself, squarely and honestly. This means looking beyond and through the emotional costuming, the sham, and the pretense in order to more clearly see ourselves as we actually are and not just the image of what we want to be. It means reconciling in a realistic way the discrepancies between our hopes and our accomplishments and making our peace with the differences that may exist between our ambitions and our talents. It means accepting, in a deep and final way, a simple psychological truth: The self is not something we find, but something we create. Becoming an emotionally healthy, happy person, or a self-actualized, fully functioning individual, or whatever you care to call your version of someone who has it all together, is not something found by accident or coded in the genes. Rather, it is an emotional position built over time and constructed by blending reasonable, reachable goals with hard work, some sacrifice, and a willingness to take some risks now and then.

—Don E. Hamachek, *Encounters with the Self,* 2d ed. (New York: Holt, Rinehart & Winston, 1978), pp. 242–43.

and get out there and have fun like you're supposed to"). If you are unsure of yourself and doubtful about how acceptable you are to others, if you cannot accept yourself much of the time, your communication will suffer. Accepting your feelings, beliefs, goals, and relationships with others provides the base for a healthy, integrated self. What are some of the things that stand in the way of your self-acceptance?

Living Up to an Image

If you are always trying to live up to the image of a perfect or straight-A student that your parents expect, you may have difficulty with your self-concept. Whenever someone else tries to impose an image on you, it may be an unrealistic one or one that demands qualities that simply are not important to you. In much the same way, setting your own goals too high may cause you to have a negative self-concept if you can't achieve fulfillment or satisfaction.

Teachers sometimes have a habit of setting students' goals for them. Have you ever been told, "You know, you're not working up to your potential"? With little or no positive reward, or with little or no definition about specific expectations, students often feel frustrated, confused, or depressed, which may result in low self-esteem. Parents, teachers, employers, and friends all seem to have goals for you—standards they want you to meet or think you should meet. Trying to live up to someone else's goals or image of you will make self-acceptance more difficult.

Living Without Answers

Add to these pressures the ones imposed upon you because of your age, your family situation, the decade, the place you live. There are pressures on you to make personal decisions, many of which seem to conflict with each other. These conflicts can make it difficult to accept yourself.

At probably no other time in life will you be faced with so many momentous decisions about who you are, what to do with your life, what to believe, what principles to value highly, what standards to follow. Increasingly, most of us have to face and answer these questions without the answers family, school, and church once provided. Such a barrage of questions can make decisions, interaction, and life itself difficult.

Living with Constant Change

In addition to having to cope with the high expectations of others and the struggle to find answers to important personal questions, you also live in a society where a great deal of rapid technological and social change is occurring. This makes self-acceptance difficult. How do you relate to conditions that are always changing? How can you accept yourself when your own standards—and society's—change constantly?

Consider This

To venture causes anxiety, but not to venture is to lose one's self. . . . And to venture in the highest sense is precisely to become conscious of one's self.

—Soren Kierkegaard

Try This

Work toward independence in your life. That is, make a habit of setting and working toward your own standards. Some things you can do to establish adaptability—and independence at the same time—would be to:

1. Be more independent. Listen when others tell you, "You can do it. You know what to do."
2. Act rather than react. When you make a decision, carry it out. Do not make excuses or rationalize about why you could not do it.
3. Rather than say, "I have to . . . ," say, "I've decided to. . . ." Take responsibility for your life.
4. Set your own standards. Stop looking over your shoulder for other significant standard setters.
5. Listen to praise and compliments. People are telling you that you are capable.
6. Learn to say "no" and really mean it.
7. Take chances. Test what happens when you let your desires be known.
8. Explore freedom—freedom to be yourself, to love and to be loved on our own merits.

—From *Your Personality and How to Live with It* by Dr. Gregory Young. Copyright © 1978 by Gregory Young, M. D. Reprinted with permission of Atheneum Publishers, an imprint of Macmillan Publishing Company.

Rapid change affects the level of self-acceptance we are able to achieve. Change in the environment affects the work we do. Are you preparing for an occupation that will be obsolete ten years from now? Change will affect your friendships. What kind of permanent relationship can you establish with someone you may never see again after two or three years? Change will affect your family. Will the ties in the family you form be the same as those in the family in which you were raised? What are the forces that cause a splintering of the family? Change will affect your religion. Do you want rigid dogma or a philosophy that is adaptable to you and to a changing world? Change affects your sexual relationships. How much stability do you want or need in your intimate associations? With all these changes, it's easy to become disoriented. How can you accept or measure the person you are when the measuring rod is different from one day to the next?

If these pressures and influences worry or upset you or make you uncertain, then you are normal. The adjustments you need to make to cope with the pressures of life do change your life and your concept of who you are. Self-acceptance will always be a problem when we are not certain of who we are. But actively working to accept ourselves is an important step toward healthy interpersonal communication.

Putting It All Together

If we construct our self-concept mainly from our interaction with the people and world around us, and if those people and that world are constantly changing, then you can see how difficult it is to get in touch with your self and feel confident in accepting it. It is very important to recognize the significance of change and its effect on your self-concept.

The more realistic your self-concept is, the more value it will have for you. To make it realistic means to consider the expectations that others have of you, to answer or at least confront the most important personal questions you face, and to fit your self-concept with your current environment, not the world you grew up in. The expectations others have of you, the questions you must answer, and the demands of your environment are continually shifting, and if your responses do not change accordingly, you may develop an unrealistic picture of the world and of your relationship to it.

The part of your self-concept that evaluates your self is called **self-esteem.** The closer your real self is to your ideal self, the higher your level of self-esteem. Your real self is the self you reveal as you function in daily life; your ideal self is the self you want to be. The greater the distance between ideal and real, the lower the self-esteem. This is nothing new—we all know we're much prouder of ourselves when we act according to our best impulses than when our hopes lie in one direction and our behavior in another. (See Figure 3.3.)

How closely do you measure up to the standards you've set for yourself as ideal? The closer you come, the more likely you are to respect yourself.[17]

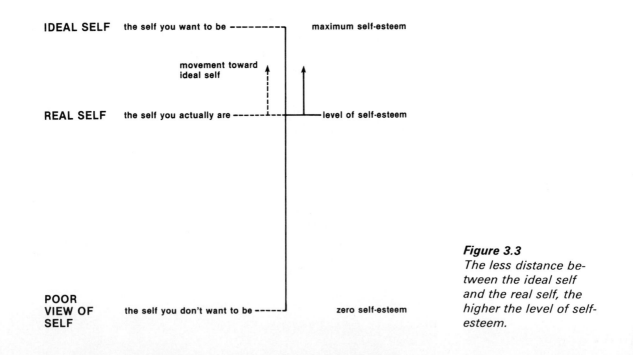

Figure 3.3
The less distance between the ideal self and the real self, the higher the level of self-esteem.

Self-confidence, self-respect, self-esteem—those words all have the same general meaning. If your self-esteem is high, your behavior will reflect that.

Whether or not you can accept yourself and feel that you are worthwhile may depend on your beliefs about who you are. Go back and briefly review your responses to the "I am" phrases you listed earlier. Having completed those statements, put each into one of the following categories:

1. Your *physical attributes*—such bodily characteristics as age, height, and weight;
2. Your *emotional attributes*—your basic temperament: timid, optimistic, gloomy, cynical, cheerful, etc.;
3. Your *mental attributes*—your intellectual characteristics: smart, average, or below average;
4. Your *roles*—functions you fulfill in relation to others: your class level in school, whether you are single or married, your major, your profession, and so on;
5. Your *relationships with others*—the characteristic stance you take toward others, such as whether you are accessible and open, closed and withdrawn, or neutral and moderate.[18]

You may find you tend to describe yourself more in one way than in another. One person may be very role conscious ("I am a son." "I am an account executive." "I am a sophomore.") while another is more aware of emotional traits ("I am often depressed." "I am sensitive to criticism." "I am generally optimistic."). While you should not take a listing of only ten such statements too seriously, what you've said about yourself can give you a rough idea of what's important to you. You're likely to have listed personal attributes that you've given some thought to, possibly had doubts about, or tried to improve. If you've been honest in your responses, they can give you an approximate profile of what we've been calling your real self.

The next step is to evaluate your responses either positively or negatively. Chances are you listed some characteristics you feel good about having and some you feel bad about having. Put a plus (+) or a minus (−) next to each statement. The statements you've marked with a minus are probably areas where you feel you don't come up to your own standards, where you are less than your ideal self. If you've marked mostly minuses, it could be a sign of low self-esteem, at least in those areas. Bear in mind that this exercise is only a very crude measuring tool, and that the person who can label every response with a plus is rare indeed.

Check your statements once again for accuracy. Have you been unduly modest? Underestimating yourself is just as dishonest and useless as being arrogant. To the extent that you have made an accurate assessment, you probably have a realistic self-concept. And only if you have a realistic self-concept can you fairly measure where you are in relation to your ideal self, and, consequently, your level of self-esteem.[19]

What happens if your self-esteem turns out to be low? A related question could be, how can I increase my self-esteem—although it is already quite good—beyond what it is now? First you must realize that self-esteem *is* shaped and molded. That is, you *do* have control over it. You can increase your liking for yourself. When you experience yourself positively, you have high self-esteem. Second, the primary difference between those with low self-esteem and those with high self-esteem is attitude. What can you do to improve your attitude toward yourself?[20]

- Accept yourself totally and unconditionally, starting now! Since *you* control this, *you* can start now by believing that you are worthy and that you are someone to be valued.
- Begin saying positive things about yourself. Stop cutting yourself down. When you feed positive thoughts and evaluations about yourself into your mind, you will begin to believe those things. Positive evaluations are something your self-esteem can grow on. This does not mean that you ignore criticisms from others but simply that you break the habit of devaluing yourself.
- Go to work on the things that you need to, and can, change. Don't allow yourself to become hooked on "That's the way I am, I can't change!" Such a statement discourages further effort at self-understanding. The case is *not* closed. "That's the way I am . . ." is likely to be an old decision, made without adequate data. A new decision is needed.
- Adopt a positive mental attitude and seek out positive people. It is possible to act your way into thinking positively. When you discover people with a positive attitude and spend your time with them, you will quickly discover that others do affect your outlook. Spend time with those from whom you can draw strength.
- Be self-reliant and helpful to others. It need not be one *or* the other. Self-reliance means learning to stand on your own two feet—but

Consider This

Your self-acceptance is built by knowing that others are accepting you. If they think you are worthwhile, then you think you are worthwhile. The acceptance of you by others plays a critical role in increasing your self-acceptance. This is especially true for those you care about and respect. One of the ways in which you become more self-accepting is to believe that other people whom you like and respect accept and value you.

—David W. Johnson, *Reaching Out: Interpersonal Effectiveness and Self-Actualization* (Englewood Cliffs, N.J.: Prentice-Hall, 1981), p. 173.

not to the extent of saying, "It's every man for himself." You need to control your own life as well as reach out to help others. You will find that this combination of control and help makes you feel better about yourself.

- Cultivate strong relationships. A friend has been described as someone who knows all about you—and loves you anyway. Friends rejoice when you are happy, and they stick by you when the going gets tough. But realize, too, that some friends do not want to see change in you! They like what is predictable and known—the *old* you. Thus, sometimes your desire to change can best be accomplished by discussing it first with your current friends, so they know what's going on. The other alternative is to seek new supportive friends. We all need friends with whom we can share our misery as well as our victories. But we draw strength best from those who help us build our own self-esteem. One person said, "My friends didn't believe that I could become a successful writer. So I did something about it. I went out and found some new friends."

People with low self-esteem need relationships that will bolster their self-confidence, relationships with people who expect the best from them and will urge them to become all they can be. Just people with low self-esteem? Don't we all need these kinds of relationships?

Self-acceptance is always a difficult process, but it need not be painful. It's valuable for all of us to become conscious of and sensitive to the pressures that stand in the way of self-acceptance—the pressures of living up to an image, coping with environmental factors, and living with constant change. Acquiring such sensitivity is an important first step, but it is not enough. Learning to accept yourself is an ongoing, lifelong process. It involves continuous awareness and evaluation of yourself. Your standards and values are probably quite different from what they were five years ago. Five years from now they'll be even more different. As you continue to reevaluate your own standards honestly, you'll probably find some things you want to change.

Implied in the information in this section is a quest for a "true," "real," or "ideal" self. Such a pursuit can cause frustration and disappointment for some. It can result in people searching their whole lives and developing a reluctance to commit themselves to *any* less-than-perfect image of themselves or to relationships that appear to promise less-than-ideal results. Certainly, some consideration for realism (realistic goals and expectations) and propriety is essential to finding happiness and a sense of well-being.

Self-awareness and self-acceptance are pretty much internal changes. Self-actualizing is a term for the change that comes when you really work at getting in touch with yourself. This kind of change requires real commitment.

Try This

1. Make a list of ten positive characteristics you possess. Be generous but honest.
2. Make a list (any length) of things you don't like about yourself. Be honest. Place a check by the things you can change. Now, write two brief paragraphs: Make the first an acceptance speech acknowledging the things you don't like but can't change. Make the other a pledge to change all the things you can.
3. Write a short personality profile describing the person you have identified yourself to be. Give full attention to both your strengths and limitations.
4. Write a short speech accepting the gift of yourself.

—Adapted from Nido R. Qubein, *Get the Best from Yourself* (Englewood Cliffs, N.J.: Prentice-Hall, 1983), p. 42. Copyright © 1983 by Prentice-Hall, Inc. Used by permission.

Self-Actualizing

Self-awareness on some level and then self-acceptance are necessary prerequisites for self-actualizing—a very important idea in interpersonal communication. To actualize means simply to make something (in this case, the self) *actual*, to develop it fully. **Self-actualizing** involves growth that is motivated from within. It means willingness to pursue your ideal self on your own—to grow and change because *you* think it is important. I have used the term self-actualizing rather than self-actualization because it is a process: a never-ending process of movement and growth.

The self-actualizing person is one who has taken steps to make things happen. Such people know their potential and actively strive to realize it. The question is, of course, how do you know what your potential is? The preceding discussions on self-awareness and self-acceptance should give you some clues. What it amounts to, again, is being completely honest about your real self, your real abilities. The real self is not a fantasized version—positive *or* negative—of yourself, but a real picture of the you other people see, the you that functions in the real world, the you that has been proven by experience to be your true self.

People who have a good idea of their potential are likely to act in ways they know are right for them, to establish and maintain personal standards, to become open to new experiences, and to trust themselves. That is, they have fairly assessed their own personal characteristics and have come to

Try This

Have you ever recorded some of your personal goals so that you have a specific set of guidelines, a direction in which you want to move? Write down five of your most important personal goals—things *you* want to achieve and things *you* want to accomplish. Be as idealistic as you like. How do you want to accomplish these goals? For each of them, write three things you can do that will help you reach them. Be as concrete and practical as you can. Setting goals is one thing; working toward them is another. Are your methods realistic?

accept and believe in the self they discover. And, most important, such people are able to act on that belief. They tend to realize the importance of change in their lives, and they are willing to be forever in the process of "becoming."[21]

How might the behavior of a self-actualizing student be different from that of one who is not self-actualizing? Such a student is aware and accepting of his or her self. If this person consistently gets A's and B's it is likely to be more out of a belief in the value of learning than out of a desire to play the role of perfect student for parents, peers, or professors. Such a student will work chemistry problems and write English papers without constant reinforcement or prodding or praise from other people. This student does not panic when a course in economics turns out to be tougher than expected, or a grade lower than hoped for. The self-actualizing student interacts on an equal basis with the people he or she lives with and socializes with. This person might really enjoy belonging to a choir, working on the yearbook, and being on an athletic team all at the same time, getting satisfaction from each activity. Such a student enjoys searching, seeking, and pursuing. This person might decide that after graduation he or she will live in California and work for a film-production company, selecting college courses accordingly, at the same time remaining open to the possibility of living somewhere else and doing some other kind of work.[22]

You probably already know some people who seem to have it all together, the kind of people who know who they are and act on that knowledge. You may even know some for whom the whole process is pretty much unconscious, people who may have never even heard or considered the term *self-actualizing*.

There are certain characteristics that identify the self-actualizing person. If you are self-actualizing, you:

1. Are willing to stand on your own two feet. This simply means that you appreciate and try to capitalize on your own strengths and abilities.
2. Trust yourself. You are willing to make decisions for yourself, and you trust that those decisions will serve your own (and others') best interests.
3. Are flexible. Flexibility is the willingness to broaden your own interests by experiencing as much as possible. It is also the willingness to change when you see that certain decisions or alternatives are wrong.

An additional note of balance is needed. The assumption of constant growth of self and of one's relationships with others is implicit in the information in this section. But, not every person is destined to become a self-actualizing person. No doubt you have observed stable and, perhaps, fulfilling relationships that, given their specific contexts, are stagnant. Once again—just as in our quest for an "ideal" self—the expectation of constant growth can, for some, lead to frustration and disappointment. It is important to maintain realistic goals and expectations.

© 1970 United Feature Syndicate, Inc.

Try This

Develop a skill or become an authority on something that you would be able to share with others in a social setting. Develop some attribute that others will enjoy, profit from, be entertained by, or be wiser for.

 Some of the following suggestions might be helpful to you in your quest:

1. Learn to play an instrument (guitar, harmonica, or piano).
2. Learn to tell jokes well.
3. Learn to do magic tricks.
4. Learn how to dance well.
5. Be up-to-date on current events.
6. Specialize in some particular world issue of importance (overpopulation, hunger, ecology, the decline of heroes in our culture, etc.).
7. Read and be able to discuss some good books (from both the fiction and the general best-seller lists).*

The purpose of this exercise is to become a more social being. To succeed in social situations is positive reinforcement for further development of one's self—further self-actualizing.

*From Philip Zimbardo, *Shyness,* © 1977, Addison-Wesley Publishing Company, Inc., Reading, Mass., p. 165. Reprinted with permission.

Making What You Have Count

The phase of personal development called self-actualizing is important to an understanding of interpersonal communication because the self-actualizing person is usually more capable of using interpersonal communication skills in an effective, healthy way. As I have said, the self is at the heart of intrapersonal communication, and it is also at the heart of interpersonal communication. How well you'll be able to apply the concepts treated in the following chapters of this book depends on how realistic and well defined your self-concept is. It will be to your benefit if you know yourself well and are able to act on what you know.

 Most of us are painfully aware of our shortcomings and failures. We can learn to be equally *realistically* aware of our strengths. To do this, first find qualities you already possess that you can emphasize. These can be very simple qualities. You might begin with: I am a good tennis player. I can make people laugh. I like animals. Make what you already have a starting place upon which you can build.

 Then think about how often you act on your own likes and strengths. Do you play tennis often? Do you always wait for someone else to ask you to play? Try initiating a game with someone the next time *you* feel like playing. Do all your friends think you have a good sense of humor or is it something you reserve for a few select people? Maybe you're holding back without knowing it. Do you own a pet? If you do, find out as much as you can about how to care for it. If you don't or can't have a pet, join an animal welfare society. Make a small donation to a zoo. Pursue your own interests! It makes sense. It can lead you to new, deeper interests and relationships. And it's the beginning of self-actualizing.

Self-Disclosure

Think of the last interpersonal communication you had with someone in which you exchanged ideas and information freely and came away feeling the relationship had been strengthened, or at least better defined. What are the ingredients that cause one encounter to be memorable and another to be meaningless and forgotten? Perhaps one ingredient was the amount of self-disclosing that occurred. **Self-disclosure** simply means disclosing or revealing yourself, showing what you know about yourself. Isn't it true that when somebody reveals private, personal information you could acquire from no other source except him or her, the quality of communication increases?

What probably made your encounter significant was that both of you shared information. It did not come from just one of you. In addition, the information probably concerned your feelings about each other, the social situation, or about other people in your social situation. For example, maybe you said, "I feel great just knowing you" or "I'm glad I could do this with you" or "Can you imagine what Mike would say if he could see us now?" You were revealing personal feelings that resulted from your interaction with the other person. These are potentially high-disclosure messages; that is, they say something particular about the circumstances of your relationship. Such messages need not be intimate exchanges, but they can be. They can also be quite simple. But they do depend for their complete meaning on your having shared certain experiences with the other person.

Potentially low-disclosure messages might concern situations that the two of you do not share. For example, to mention the name of a book you just read, or the fact that you did not like the eggs you had for breakfast, or that your roommate has a cold, is to share low-disclosure messages. They may, however, pave the way for high-disclosure messages. Self-disclosing is important because you need to know yourself in order to do it, and because by disclosing yourself you come to define your feelings toward yourself more clearly.[23]

It's likely that the last significant interaction you thought of involved a friend. It is in such close relationships that most self-disclosure occurs because revealing yourself involves risk, and we are not as likely to take a risk with a new acquaintance. We usually do not want to share feelings with

Consider This

In every sort of interpersonal relationship, from business partnerships to love affairs, the exchange of self-disclosure plays an important role.

—Z. Rubin, *Liking and Loving* (New York: Henry Holt and Company, 1973), p. 168.

a person we have not yet learned to trust. It's interesting, however, that we cannot create trust in a relationship, and thus diminish the amount of risk in that relationship, without self-disclosure. And the more we trust another person, the more likely it is that we will self-disclose. Self-disclosure creates trust, and trust encourages self-disclosure. As in so much of what we talk about in interpersonal communication, a positive interacting cycle creates growth.

What Happens in Self-Disclosure?

Before any further explanation of self-disclosure, we might consider some of the benefits to be gained. What happens when you self-disclose? One of the first things you might notice happening is *increasing accuracy in communication.* Because self-disclosure involves the expression of personal feelings, you not only pass along information ("Your philodendron died while you were gone") but you can also say how you feel about delivering that message ("I'm sorry to have to tell you your philodendron died while you were gone. I know how diligently you cared for it"). Otherwise, the other person would have to guess how you feel from your behavior. Feelings are often interpreted from behavior, and we hope that others interpret our feelings correctly. But we know from experience that other people do not always guess correctly how we feel unless we tell them. The first benefit of self-disclosure, then, is that it ensures a certain level of accuracy in communication.

Another benefit of self-disclosure has to do with *getting to know others better.* Interpersonal relationships are built upon self-disclosure. If you want to deepen your friendships, discover more about how others think and feel, and increase the intensity of your associations, self-disclosure provides one means. Think of the person you consider your closest friend. Chances are more mutual self-disclosure has taken place with this person than with anyone else you know.

Self-disclosure also is a way of *increasing your number of contacts and enlarging your group of friends.* Getting to know a larger number of people can add knowledge, interest, and a degree of excitement to your present life. It might provide opportunities for you to experiment—to try out new attitudes, to experience new behaviors, and to encounter new relationships. It is not necessarily dishonest in your interpersonal encounters to be one thing to one person, something a little different to another. You have many sides. You are not composed of a single set of attitudes, behaviors, or relationships, but often routine, habits, or laziness can prevent you from sharing certain aspects of yourself. In every situation the self you reveal should be an honest one, but it need not always be the same one exposed to everyone, and it certainly can change.

Perhaps the most important personal benefit to result from self-disclosure is *gaining increased personal insight.* Self-disclosure opens the window through which you see yourself. This is not to suggest that you

will discover, nurture, or gain insight into a single "real" you. There are several (perhaps many) selves, all equally valid. The "ideal" or "real" self is neither achievable nor desirable. But through self-disclosure you are more likely to discover attributes, uniquenesses, and peculiarities that you may not have been aware of. Exposing these new facets is part of gaining increased personal insight.

The Johari Window: Here's Looking at You

Joseph Luft and Harrington Ingham created a diagram that looks at the self-disclosure process as a means of expanding what you know of yourself. They called it the Johari Window (Joseph + Harrington).[24] (See Figure 3.4.)

The **Johari Window** identifies four kinds of information about yourself that affect your communication. Think of the whole diagram as representing your total self as you relate to other human beings. Remember that for every person you relate with, a new window can be drawn. The panes of the window change in size according to your awareness, and the awareness of others, of your behavior, feelings, and motivations. The size will also vary for different people because your behavior, feelings, and motivations are actually different with them. Every relationship you have can be described by a Johari Window, and no two would be alike.

The open pane.   The size of the *open* pane reveals the amount of risk you take in relationships. As relationships become deeper, the open pane gets bigger, reflecting your willingness to be known. This pane comprises all aspects of yourself known to you *and* others. It includes such things as your sex, the color of your eyes, and whether you are standing up or sitting

Figure 3.4
The Johari Window identifies different kinds of information about ourselves.

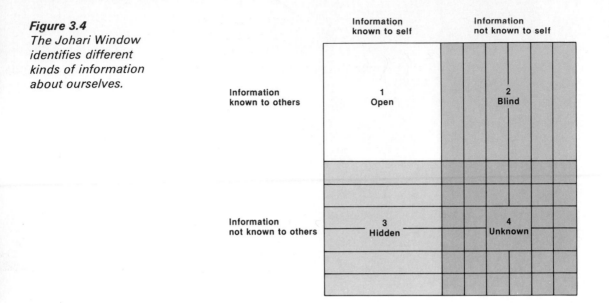

down at the moment. It may also include things you know and don't mind admitting about yourself, such as the fact that you are married or a teacher or happy or depressed. Information included in this pane provides the substance for the biggest part of your communications with others.

The blind pane. The *blind* pane consists of all the things about yourself that other people perceive but that are not known to you. For example, you may see yourself as open and friendly, but you may come across to others as reserved and somewhat cold. You may think of yourself as genuinely humorous; others may think your humor has an acid bite. On the other hand, the blind pane may contain some good qualities you don't realize you have. For example, you may be very aware of your own insecurities; others may see you as confident and self-assured. The more you learn about the qualities in your blind pane, the more you will be able to control the impressions you make on others, understand their reactions to you, and learn to grow beyond them. Growth requires such discovery of things unknown to you, but known to others.

The hidden pane. In the *hidden* pane, you are the one who exercises control. This pane is made up of all those behaviors, feelings, and motivations that you prefer not to disclose to someone else. These things could be events that occurred during your childhood that you do not want known. They could include the fact that you failed biology in high school, that you like soap operas, that you eat peanut butter at every meal. They could concern other people besides you, and need not be things you are ashamed of or

Try This

Plot a Johari Window for the following encounters in your life—as specifically as you can:

1. your roommate (if you have one)
2. your best friend
3. someone you recently met for the first time
4. the teacher of this course
5. one of your parents
6. someone you know who does not know you (and has not spoken to you)

Note that a Johari Window represents a relationship between you and this other person. The relative size of the various panes of the window depends on the amount of self-disclosure that has occurred between you.

think are wrong. Everyone is entitled to some secrets. There are certain things that can remain private and personal and need never be disclosed. These things remain in the hidden pane: things unknown to others but known to you.

The unknown pane. The *unknown* pane is made up of everything unknown to you and to others. No matter how much you grow and discover and learn about yourself, thus shrinking the size of this pane, it can never completely disappear. You can never know all there is to know about yourself. This pane represents everything about yourself that you and other people have never explored. This pane includes all your untapped resources and potentials, everything that currently lies dormant. It is through interpersonal communication that you can reduce the size of this pane; without communicating with others, much of your potential will remain unrealized.

The interdependence of the panes. The four panes of the Johari Window are interdependent: that is, a change in the size of one pane will affect all the others. For example, if through talking with a friend you discover something about yourself you never knew before (something that existed in the blind pane), this would enlarge the open pane and reduce the size of the blind one. Your discovery could be of something insignificant, like the fact that your socks don't match, or it could be something crucial to your relationship, like the fact that Sam doesn't care about you as much as you thought he did.

It can be rewarding and satisfying to add to your open pane, whether by revealing or by discovering things about yourself. It can also be painful;

enlarging the open pane involves some risk. You need to use discretion here, as inappropriate disclosure can be damaging whether you are giving it or receiving it. Be sure you are ready to cope with the consequences before you try to empty your hidden and blind panes into your open pane.

Generally, though, the more you reveal yourself to others so that they can know you better, the more you will learn about yourself. And the more truth about yourself you are willing to accept from others, the more accurate your self-concept will be. This increased knowledge of self can result in greater self-acceptance. After all, if your friend is not shocked by your C average, perhaps you can accept it too. A Johari Window representing a close relationship between two people in which there is a great deal of free and honest exchange has a very large open pane. (See Figure 3.5.)

Sidney Jourard, a researcher, has concluded that humans spend an incredible amount of energy trying to avoid becoming known by other human beings. Jourard contends that when we permit ourselves to be known, we expose ourselves to a lover's balm, but also to a hater's bombs! When haters know you, they know just where to plant their bombs for maximum effect. But acts of avoidance keep us from healthy human relationships. According to Jourard, allowing yourself to be known to at least one other person who is important to you and whose opinions and judgment you value and respect highly is one characteristic of a healthy personality. It is risky, but it is important, as Joseph Luft, co-creator of the Johari Window, points out in the "Consider This" at the top of the next page.

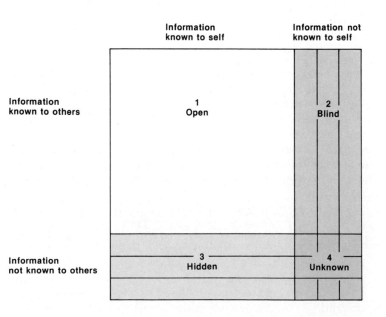

Figure 3.5

This window describes a relationship with a great deal of free and honest exchange.

Consider This

. . . the risks of being more open and more transparent must be borne not only for the satisfactions and enjoyment of people and of self, but for increased realization of self. Lest that last phrase slip by as just another platitude, I'd like to rephrase it something like this. Your talent and your potentials have a better chance of being developed if you as a person have access to your own feelings, your imagination, and your fantasy. If you can be open and free even with but one other person there is greater likelihood that you can be in touch with self.

—Joseph Luft, *Of Human Interaction* (Palo Alto, Calif.: National Press Books, 1969), p. 129.

What Are You Afraid Of?

Why are we afraid to reveal ourselves to others? Why is it easier to hold back than to express our real being? In *Why Am I Afraid to Tell You Who I Am?* John Powell suggests that each of us thinks, "If I tell you who I am, you may not like who I am, and it is all that I have."[25] We fear rejection. We fear discovering that we might not be totally acceptable to others or that we are unworthy. Another reason is that we feel we may not get reinforcement. What if I open myself to you and you offer no support or positive feedback? Even the possibility of some slight negative reaction scares us. Or we may be afraid of hurting another person or making him or her angry. You may have wanted for a long time to tell someone that if she continues to treat her boyfriend callously she will lose him. Your fear of angering her may have kept you from telling her.

Researchers have found that whether or not people disclose themselves to others depends on a number of different factors:[26]

- The nature of the other person or people.
- The relationship between the discloser and the recipient.
- The kind of information to be disclosed.
- The degree of liking that exists between the people (particularly for women).
- The degree of trust that exists between the people (particularly for men).
- The perceived appropriateness (particularly on the part of recipients of disclosure).
- The degree of self-esteem on the part of both discloser and recipient.
- The willingness to risk.

Studies also indicate that the primary reason people avoid self-disclosure is that they feel that if they disclose themselves they might project an image they do not want to project. Research shows, further, that beyond protecting their image, males and females avoid self-disclosure for different reasons. Males, for example, do not want to give information that might make them appear inconsistent. They also do not want to lose control over other people, nor do they want to threaten relationships they have with others. For males, the predominant concern is to maintain control.[27]

For females, research shows that they do not want to give other people information that might be used against them. Also, females feel that self-disclosure is a sign of emotional disturbance. Further, they do not want to hurt a relationship. Their object, according to the research, is to avoid personal hurt and problems with a relationship that might result from self-disclosure.[28]

We may avoid self-disclosure if we believe that no one else is interested in our thoughts, feelings, or view of the world.[29] Or we simply may not know how to self-disclose constructively. Since this disclosure is the primary channel for gaining information about ourselves, some of the basic skills for successful, constructive self-disclosure will be outlined next.

Improving Skills in Self-Disclosure

Before discussing the skills that will improve self-disclosure, several comments need to be made. First, a high degree of self-disclosure is *not* always preferred. That is, there is some research that suggests that some people prefer low-

Consider This

Our feelings about ourselves are *learned* responses. Sometimes bad feelings have to be unlearned and new feelings acquired. This is not always easy, but it is possible. Sometimes this means "taking stock" of oneself—a kind of personal inventory. Or it may mean baring one's self to another person—a friend or therapist—so that the possibility for honest evaluation and feedback is more probable. And for certain, it means changing those things which one can and accepting those which one cannot.

For most persons, a positive, healthy self-image is quite within reach if they are willing to accept the risks and responsibilities for mature living and if they know how to go about it.

—Don E. Hamachek, *Encounters with the Self,* 2d ed. (New York: Holt, Rinehart & Winston, CBS College Publishing, 1978), p. 271.

disclosing others.[30] This research highlights the importance of "testing the waters" before engaging in disclosure, especially if one's goal is to impress the recipient. Testing might include starting with some low-risk, low-disclosure messages. Testing might also include patience—just waiting until the relationship develops a bit before engaging in disclosure.

Second, there are norms that govern self-disclosure. According to Shirley Gilbert, a researcher in this area, these norms "exert powerful influences to regulate times when it is socially acceptable and rewarding to divulge personal information about oneself to another."[31] Research done by P. M. Blau shows that in an initial encounter, disclosing negative aspects of oneself is considered inappropriate.[32] C. Arthur Vanlear warns that it is socially inappropriate and interpersonally inept to offer private-personal disclosures too early in a relationship.[33] Such norms are likely to vary from situation to situation.

Third, research suggests that the disclosure must be perceived as a social reward in order to produce a positive effect. Think about it: this other person has chosen *you* to disclose with; this makes you special. Think about how you would feel if you discovered that this discloser had shared this same information with others. *You* are no longer special! Perhaps you would feel betrayed. The social reward has been removed.

Fourth, as we learned in Chapter 1, the greatest depth one is likely to achieve in self-disclosure—especially depth over a prolonged period—is in intimate relationships. In intimate relationships one has a great deal more to lose and much more to protect! Remembering that the transactional perspective emphasizes that who we *are*, with reference to our intimate other, is a result of the transactions we engage in with that person, Gilbert explains the transactional forces that operate in self-disclosure:

. . . it may be argued that the impact of disclosure in intimate relationships may be understood not by simply focusing on the effects of the disclosure on the other, as has most frequently been the case in the past, but by focusing on the effects that the response of the other has on the person engaging in the disclosure. Thus, the first condition which may allow the pursuit of optimum levels of disclosure is a healthy 'self,' capable of accommodating to and ameliorating [helping to make better] the consequences of one's disclosures for the other.[34]

Jourard claims that healthy self-love may be *the* catalyst in establishing and maintaining intimate relationships.[35] Thus, the extent to which participants feel that a transaction has been established—that there is some *positive* response to us by the other—influences self-disclosure. Research suggests that there must be an affective response of acceptance and commitment before self-disclosure can take place.[36]

Finally, self-disclosure with another guarantees nothing. If we engage in it with the intention of establishing openness, closeness, friendship, or intimacy, we may be disappointed. Although it may be an index of the depth of our communication with another, there are no guaranteed outcomes.

This information is *not* designed to discourage you from self-disclosing; rather, it is to guide you in situations where self-disclosure is appropriate. My advice on self-disclosing in ambiguous situations is this: (1) Do it cautiously, watching for *any* kind of response and (2) Go slowly. Taking it slow and easy helps reduce some of the risk involved. Remember, there is a great deal of evidence to support the conclusion that self-disclosure is a critical ingredient in the development of relationships.[37]

Improvement in self-disclosure generally begins with attitudes. With the proper attitude, our skills in self-disclosure will improve.

Commit yourself to growth. If you have no desire to grow or change, no commitment to improve your relationship with another person, you are not likely to self-disclose. You have to care about another person before taking the risk necessary to build a trusting relationship. The fact you acknowledge the value of a relationship shows the other person your level of commitment and makes the self-disclosure even more useful.

It takes courage to let another person know he or she means something special to you. To say, "It has been fun talking to you" sounds superficial, but it may be enough to trigger further interaction. So, feeling a commitment to a relationship is part of it, but you also need to disclose that commitment to the other person. How often do you tell other people that you need them or appreciate them?

- Cultivate the ability to see—and enjoy—people as individuals. Look for the qualities in others that make them unique.
- Learn to enjoy life more. Take time to savor the things you do. Get involved in the world around you. Look for good experiences, expect them to happen, celebrate them when they do.

Try This

Write down some of your positive traits, characteristics, abilities, and accomplishments. What is there about yourself that you would like to emphasize? For example:

Are you in good health?
Are you comfortable meeting new people?
Are you good at math problems and puzzles?
Do you have a good memory?

List as many things as you can think of—they don't have to be earth-shaking skills or accomplishments. Then, for each skill, write down the last time you can think of when you acted on that preference or ability. If it's been so long that you can't remember, list concrete steps you can take to revive that particular skill. This can be as simple as talking to someone, writing away for information, looking something up in the library, or joining a club or musical group. As you discover new preferences and skills, add to your list.

- Avoid cynicism. Cynics feel that everyone is out for his or her own personal gain. No one is genuine or generous; everyone wants to get something from others—this is the cynic's view. Allow yourself to act as if you expect the best from others.
- Try to be more positive. Do not blame others for your troubles or trace your unwise choices to their advice or example. Take responsibility for your behavior, ideas, and decisions.

Build trust. Trust grows when you begin to risk with others and confirm them as human beings. For example, if you disclose a thought, feeling, or reaction to someone else, and he or she responds with acceptance, support, and cooperation, a risk has been taken and confirmation has followed. *Trust* is simply your reliance on the character, ability, strength, or truth of others—you place your confidence in them. To build trust you must:

- Openly accept others. To demonstrate this you must reveal favorable responses to them.
- Demonstrate support and concern. Avoid making fun of others.
- Show respect. Let others know you regard them or admire them. Help them to understand how worthy they are of esteem.
- Be understanding. Evaluative responses convey rejection as readily as moralizing responses or silence (no response at all). To react to others with rejection, ridicule, or disrespect destroys trust.
- Reciprocate the self-disclosure of others. To be closed or unresponsive is a sign of rejection. Responding with an adequate (near equal)

amount of self-disclosure of your own keeps others from feeling overexposed or vulnerable.

- Reveal your thoughts, feelings, and reactions if the other person has indicated considerable acceptance, support, and cooperativeness.
- Express warmth. Say it. Act it out. Smile. Use nonverbal behavior to express your sensations, feelings, and intentions. Eye contact, a touch, or a wink might express warmth. Verbal responses also work: saying, "I feel very good right now," or "I like you" are two possibilities.
- Communicate accurate understanding. Restate the content, feelings, or meaning of others' disclosure in your own words.
- Indicate cooperative intentions. Show that you are willing to work with others toward a common goal—getting to know them better, deepening a relationship, finding out what something means (together).

Share your feelings.   Beyond sharing with another person what you consider the value of the relationship, it helps if you both agree to share feelings and awarenesses. This sharing often occurs naturally when the relationship is already comfortable and mutually supportive. Other times it might help if you simply make a comment like "I hope we can be honest with each other. I know I'm going to try." Self-disclosure operates best in a situation where both people know the value of sharing. Each should be willing to share feelings about the other person's actions, being careful not to confuse honest communication with thoughtless or cruel remarks.

We all need some reinforcement in our communications. Have you ever come out of a movie really excited and wanting to share your enthusiasm, only to have your companions say nothing at all? You don't know if they agree with you or don't agree with you or are simply thinking about something else! Sharing is a two-way process. Without give *and* take, one person might stop giving anything at all. To be ready and willing to share means each partner views the relationship from nearly the same viewpoint, lessening the feeling of risk.

- Cultivate the ability to empathize—the ability to feel and to care about other people's experiences. This not only makes your own life richer, it connects your life to that of others and makes you more likable as well. To develop empathy, study your own experiences; remember the way you felt—or imagine the way you might feel— in similar situations; relate your feelings—or probable feelings—to the other person.
- Encourage other people to talk about their feelings and their lives. Try to remember what they say and to get a sense of what their experiences feel like.
- Be ready to confront people when you disagree with them about a matter that is important to you. This helps give you purpose and

identity. It also lets others know you are capable of strong beliefs and feelings.

- Cheer for your friends. Can you rejoice at other people's successes? Not being able to—because of envy or fear—makes you less a friend and less confident and secure in your own life.

Take a chance. You must be willing to take chances in self-disclosure. There is no guarantee that you will not get hurt or that you will not be rejected. If a relationship is important, it is worth risking being honest so that both people can learn and grow. You may become angry or defensive at something the other person says, but if you aren't willing to express your real feelings, the result is superficiality and facade building.

If it bothers you that a friend always dominates conversations by griping about her parents, you might say, "Let's make any discussion of parents off-limits for tonight." This takes some courage, but it allows your real feelings to show. And your friend may not even have been aware that she was dominating the conversation. It's worth taking the chance of telling her how you feel as long as you have her best interests at heart and care about preserving an honest relationship with her. The habit of honesty in all matters, no matter how small, makes it easier to be honest in more difficult, personal areas. For example, to tell a friend that he seems to be feeling sorry for himself takes a lot of courage. But taking such a chance is often worth the risk. The other person may value you even more because of your honesty.

- Don't suppress strong emotions—especially anger. If, for example, you feel you have more than fulfilled the instructor's requirements for a project or paper and yet you receive a low grade, tell the teacher that you are annoyed. Don't just let it go by saying, "It's no big thing." It *is* a big thing. Resigning yourself to mistreatment makes you believe that you *deserve* mistreatment.

- Meet all the challenges you possibly can. Decide for yourself—honestly—what you can and cannot do with respect to each one. Even if you know others will excuse you, do not excuse yourself from challenges you *can* meet with an effort.
- Act ethically toward others. How you treat others *does* matter—even in small things. Remember to thank people for small favors as well as great ones.
- Force yourself to do things you've never done before—talk to people you've never spoken to, engage in activities you haven't tried. Taking chances in some areas of your life makes it more likely that you will take chances in other areas.
- Snatch at all fleeting moments of intense feeling. Avoid the repetitive and automatic. Look for opportunities to inject freshness and emotionality into your experiences and your relationships.

Don't manipulate.   The best self-disclosure occurs when neither person tries to change or manipulate the other person. Despite the intense emotions that may surface, conversation should never turn to who is at fault but, rather, focus on making the relationship more satisfying and productive for both parties. For example, if your friend seems to be indulging in self-pity, it would be more helpful to point this out than to tell him or her to stop it. Stopping or not stopping is your friend's choice to make. Any change that occurs in a relationship should result from one person acting freely in response to information provided or acquired. This nonmanipulative atmosphere is created when you truly care for and accept the other person.

- Do not tell other people how they feel: "I'm sure you don't like this." "I know how uncomfortable Sue makes you feel, so I won't invite her." People's feelings change. Ask others how they feel, but don't tell them.
- Do not tell other people what they should do: "You should never be angry." "You should control your temper." Let the other person decide what is or is not appropriate behavior.
- Do not always try to be the powerful one in your relationships. You may be forceful, but not dominating. Listen, and be aware of your own weaknesses.
- Don't be passive and let others control your life. Do not feign helplessness and stupidity. Learn to be willing to express your own convictions strongly.

Watch your timing.   Whenever possible, express your feelings and reactions at the time you actually feel them. Both parties must realize what behavior caused a particular reaction. Parents usually find a reprimand means more to a small child if they say "No!" just as the child is about to do something wrong than if the incident goes undiscovered for an hour and the "No!" comes too late. This is true for adult interactions, too. Even disturbing reactions should be discussed at once. Sometimes feelings are accumulated and then dropped on the other person; this hinders healthy self-disclosure. Of course there are times when immediate expression of your reaction may be inappropriate. For example, you would not want to share highly personal reactions with a friend in a crowded elevator. It's generally better to wait until no one else is around.

- When someone asks you how you feel about something, answer as quickly as possible. Don't censor your response. You have the right to any reaction you feel. A quick answer is often more authentic and accurate than a delayed one.
- Make your comments to the people you think are affecting you and to no one else.
- Do not object to another person's behavior in front of others. Objections often are interpreted as personal attacks. Unless waiting would be costly, waiting until you are alone reveals your concern for fairness to the other person and your consideration for his or her feelings.
- Avoid comparisons. Nobody likes being described as inferior to someone else. Comparisons may predispose others not to listen to what you have to say.
- Make your comments as soon as you can. Speaking up becomes more difficult the longer you postpone it. Also, if the comments are tied to a strong emotional reaction, like anger, waiting allows the reaction to build with the possibility that irrelevant comments will be added. If you comment on things that happened a long time ago, too, you will look as if you have been holding a grudge.
- Try to make only one comment at a time. Too many comments—especially criticisms—might demoralize the other person and may obscure and detract from the major point.

Clarify, clarify. If you're not sure you understand what another person means, you should try restating his or her comments. If you offer a paraphrase of the other person's remarks before supplying your own response, there's less chance of your misunderstanding each other. (Ralph: "I'm sick of taking this bus with you every day." Mike: "I hear you saying you're sick of riding to work with me. Is that right?" Ralph: "No, I just meant I'm sick of this bus. I wish we had a car.") Make sure the other person understands your comments in the way you mean them.

As you respond to another person, you can try to eliminate any kind of personal judgments ("Don't you *ever* listen?"), name-calling ("You really are a hypocrite"), accusations ("You love walking all over people, don't you?"), commands or orders ("Stop running his life"), or sarcasm ("You really want to get to the top," when the other person just flunked an exam).

Instead, talk about things the other person did—actual, accurate descriptions of the action that took place. You can try to describe your own feelings, letting the other person see them as temporary rather than absolute. Instead of saying "I hate sitting next to you in class," you might try "I can't stand it when you crack your knuckles."

According to research, the clearest self-disclosure messages are:

- mutually relevant. That is, they are based on the immediate situation—the here and now, not something which is past or unrelated to the present situation.
- personally owned. To say "I feel" is much more exact than the more general "People feel."
- source specific. Saying "I feel anxiety toward you, Allen" rather than "I feel anxious around people."
- based on a clear causal connection with your feeling or perception. Try to use the word *because* rather than omitting a reason or alluding to the cause indirectly by saying something like "There may be a reason."
- behavior specific. Rather than saying that someone is irresponsible or can't be counted on, it is better to say, "You were late for our appointment."

Your success in college and, indeed, in life, will depend on *how* you feel about yourself and your abilities. Your self-concept is a product of intrapersonal and interpersonal communication. What you think about yourself affects your behavior toward others. And it is what other people say about you and to you that is the information you use in thinking about yourself. Thus, intrapersonal communication and interpersonal communication are intricately entwined. We see this especially in the process of self-disclosure. Disclosing yourself is the key to discovering yourself, but productive, worthwhile self-disclosure requires interaction with other people. Self-disclosure is an important method of acquiring information. Other practical methods of acquiring new information are listening and feedback. These subjects are treated in the next chapter.

Notes

[1] Donald Washburn, "Intrapersonal Communication in a Jungian Perspective," *Journal of Communication*, 14 (September 1964): pp. 131–35.

[2] Robert Cathcart and Gary Gumpert, "I Am a Camera: The Mediated Self," *Communication Quarterly*, 34 (1986): pp. 89–102.

[3] John Modaff and Robert Hopper, "Why Speech Is 'Basic.'" *Communication Education*, 33 (1984): pp. 37–42.

[4] Carol Zak-Dance, *Research Outcomes of a Functional Perspective in the Context of Self-Concept Development.* Paper presented at the 1982 Central States Speech Association Convention.

[5] Walter Ong, "Voice as Summons for Belief: Literature, Faith and the Divided Self," *Thought*, 33 (1958): p. 49.

[6] As cited in Pamela Adelmann, "Possibly Yours," *Psychology Today*, 22:4 (April 1988): pp. 8, 10.

[7] Abraham Kaplan, "The Life of Dialogue," *Communication: A Discussion at the Nobel Conference*, ed. John D. Rolansky (London: North Holland Publishing Co., 1969), as reprinted in *Wisconsin Communication Association Journal*, 3:2 (1973): p. 58.

[8] James L. McFarland, "The Role of Speech in Self Development, Self-Concept, and Decentration," *Communication Education*, 33 (1984): pp. 231–35.

[9] J. A. L. Singh and Robert M. Zingg, *Wolf Children and Feral Man* (New York: Harper and Row, 1934), p. 132.

[10] It is unclear at times whether thinking precedes or follows the action. It could be that the sufficient cause of the change in self-concept is an action not a thought process.

[11] Paul Watzlawick, Janet Helmick Beavin, and Don D. Jackson, *Pragmatics of Human Communication: A Study of Interactional Patterns, Pathologies, and Paradoxes* (New York: W. W. Norton & Co., 1967), pp. 98–99.

[12] Don E. Hamachek, *Encounters with the Self*, 2d ed. (New York: Holt, Rinehart & Winston, 1978).

[13] Charles T. Brown and Paul W. Keller, *Monologue to Dialogue: An Exploration of Interpersonal Communication*, 2d ed. (Englewood Cliffs, N.J.: Prentice-Hall, 1979), pp. 82–105.

[14] John C. Condon, Jr., *Semantics and Communication* (New York: Macmillan Co., 1966), p. 60.

[15] The following writers maintain that the self-concept is a direct result of the reactions of "significant others": Harry Stack Sullivan, *The Interpersonal Theory of Psychiatry* (New York: W. W. Norton & Co., 1953); John J. Sherwood, "Self Identity and Referent Others," *Sociometry*, 28 (1965): pp. 66–81; and Carl Backman, Paul Secord, and Jerry Pierce, "Resistance to Change in the Self-Concept as a Function of Consensus Among Significant Others," in *Problems in Social Psychology*, eds. Carl Backman and Paul Secord (New York: McGraw-Hill, 1969), pp. 462–67.

[16] Experiments by Robert Rosenthal have confirmed that labels become self-fulfilling prophecies. See Robert Rosenthal, "Self-Fulfilling Prophecy," in *Readings in Psychology Today* (Del Mar, Calif.: CRM Books, 1967), pp. 466–71.

[17] Nathaniel Branden, *The Psychology of Self-Esteem* (Los Angeles: Nash, 1969), p. 103.

[18] From *Personal and Interpersonal Communication: Dialogue with the Self and with Others* by John J. Makay and Beverly A. Gaw, p. 28. Copyright © 1975 by Bell & Howell. Used by permission of the authors.

[19] Makay and Gaw, *Personal and Interpersonal Communication*, p. 28.

[20] Nido R. Qubein, *Get the Best from Yourself* (Englewood Cliffs, N.J.: Prentice-Hall, 1983), pp. 41–50.

[21] Earl C. Kelly, *Perceiving, Behaving, Becoming: A New Focus on Education*, 1962 Yearbook (Washington, D.C.: Association for Supervision and Curriculum Development, 1962), pp. 9–20.

[22] From *Encounters with the Self* by Don E. Hamachek. Copyright © 1971 by Holt, Rinehart & Winston. Adapted by permission of Holt, Rinehart & Winston.

[23] Sidney M. Jourard, *The Transparent Self* (New York: D. Van Nostrand Co., 1971), p. 6.

[24] Adapted from *Group Processes: An Introduction to Group Dynamics* by Joseph Luft, by permission of Mayfield Publishing Co. Copyright © 1984, 1970,

and 1963 by Joseph Luft. See also Luft, *Of Human Interaction* (Palo Alto, Calif.: National Press Books, 1969).

[25] John Powell, *Why Am I Afraid to Tell You Who I Am?* (Chicago: Argus Communications, 1969), p. 27.

[26] Shirley J. Gilbert, "Empirical and Theoretical Extensions of Self-Disclosure," in *Explorations in Interpersonal Communication*, ed. Gerald R. Miller (Beverly Hills: Sage, 1976), p. 200. This is Volume V in the Sage annual review of communication research. For a review of the literature on self-disclosure, see P. W. Cozby, "Self Disclosure: A Literature Review," *Psychological Bulletin*, 79 (1973): pp. 73–91.

[27] Lawrence B. Rosenfeld, "Self-Disclosure Avoidance: Why I Am Afraid to Tell You Who I Am," *Communication Monographs*, 46 (1979): pp. 72–73.

[28] Rosenfeld, "Self-Disclosure Avoidance," p. 73.

[29] Jourard, *The Transparent Self*, p. 193.

[30] S. A. Culbert, "Trainer Self-Disclosure and Member Growth in T-Groups," *Journal of Applied Behavioral Science*, 4 (1968): pp. 47–73; R. G. Weigel, N. Dinges, R. Dyer, and A. A. Straumfjord, "Perceived Self-Disclosure, Mental Health, and Who Is Liked in Group Treatment," *Journal of Counseling Psychology*, 19 (1972): pp. 47–52.

[31] Gilbert, "Empirical and Theoretical Extensions," p. 202.

[32] P. M. Blau, *Exchange and Power in Social Life* (New York: Wiley, 1964), p. 49.

[33] C. Arthur Vanlear, Jr., "The Formation of Social Relationships: A Longitudinal Study of Social Penetration," *Human Communication Research*, 13 (1987): p. 314.

[34] Gilbert, "Empirical and Theoretical Extensions," p. 211.

[35] Sidney Jourard, "Healthy Personality and Self-Disclosure," pp. 123–34 in C. Gordon and K. Gergen (eds.) *The Self in Social Interaction* (New York: Wiley, 1968).

[36] Gilbert, "Empirical and Theoretical Extensions," p. 212.

[37] I. Altman and D. A. Taylor, *Social Penetration: The Development and Dissolution of Interpersonal Relationships* (New York: Holt, Rinehart, and Winston, 1973); C. R. Berger and R. J. Calabrese, "Some Explorations in Initial Interaction and Beyond: Toward a Developmental Theory of Interpersonal Communication," *Human Communication Research*, 1 (1975): pp. 99–112. As cited in Rebecca J. Cline and Karen E. Musolf, "Disclosure as Social Exchange: Anticipated Length of Relationship, Sex Roles, and Disclosure Intimacy," *The Western Journal of Speech Communication*, 49 (1985): pp. 43–56.

Further Reading

William Glasser, *Control Theory: A New Explanation of How We Control Our Lives* (New York: Harper & Row, 1984). Glasser claims that everything we do, think, and feel comes from inside us. Our behavior is our best attempt to control the world to bring it as close as possible to the pictures in our heads of what we would like it to be. Glasser analyzes how the pictures got there and what can be done about them, and cites examples and case histories.

Don E. Hamachek, *Encounters with the Self*, 2d ed. (New York: Holt, Rinehart & Winston, 1978). A book about the self-concept—how the self grows, changes, and expresses itself in behavior. A very thorough, well-documented book that offers a great deal of information. The final chapter on developing a healthy self-image is especially worthwhile.

Shad Helmstetter, *What to Say When You Talk to Yourself* (New York: Pocket Books, 1986) and *The Self-Talk Solution* (New York: Pocket Books, 1987). Books on self-talk. If you have ever wondered *what* to say to optimize your outlook, focus your plans, and keep you in touch, Helmstetter provides the phrases. These are popular self-help books with hundreds of self-talk suggestions. The second book has more than 2,500 self-talk messages. Useful, interesting resources.

David W. Johnson, *Reaching Out: Interpersonal Effectiveness and Self-Actualization*, 3rd ed. (Englewood Cliffs, N.J.: Prentice-Hall, 1986). Johnson's chapters on self-disclosure and developing and maintaining trust are both specific and practical. The exercises included in these chapters and throughout the book are interesting, challenging, and enlightening. A great resource book for those involved in human-relations training.

Sidney M. Jourard, *The Transparent Self* (New York: D. Van Nostrand Co., 1971). This has become a classic! Jourard describes how people can gain health and full personal development once they have the courage to be themselves. A lively, straightforward, relevant, and readable book on the self and self-disclosure.

Sheldon Kopp, *Even a Stone Can Be a Teacher: Learning and Growing from the Experiences of Everyday Life* (Los Angeles, Calif.: Jeremy P. Tarcher, 1985). Kopp shows how many experiences of daily life contain overlooked opportunities for self-development and growth. He offers a perspective for shunning pretensions, facades, and empty routines so that we can be genuine and awake to the wonders in everyday experience. An inspiring, exciting book.

Joseph Luft, *Of Human Interaction* (Palo Alto, Calif.: National Press Books, 1969). This is a classic. Luft writes about human interaction from the point of view of the Johari awareness model. In separate chapters, he explains the four quadrants of the Johari Window and then discusses group interaction, interaction and influence, and interaction values. A useful book for explaining human behavior in the context of ties between people.

John R. Noe, *Peak Performance Principles for High Achievers* (New York: Frederick Fell Publishers, 1984). Noe uses his mountain-climbing adventures as an allegory for the challenge of goal-setting and the thrill of high achievement. Noe shows how to choose accurate goals, how to reach them, and how to remain committed to the accomplishment of those goals. An exciting and challenging book.

Kay Porter and Judy Foster, *The Mental Athlete: Inner Training for Peak Performance* (New York: Ballantine Books, 1986). This book is a training manual for learning how to draw on your mental power to build self-confidence, self-control, and an effective inner game. It is a "how-to" book on identifying negative thought patterns, thinking positively, learning to relax, mastering visual imagery skills, achieving concentration, psyching yourself up, and handling pressure and stress. Interesting and enjoyable.

Charles V. Roberts and Kitty W. Watson, eds., *Intrapersonal Communication Processes: Original Essays* (New Orleans, La.: SPECTRA Inc., Publishers, 1989). This is an excellent 580-page, comprehensive textbook that discusses all the communication processes that take place within us as we create and assign meanings for stimuli. The editors cover models and definitions, cognitive approaches, psychophysiological approaches, characteristics and causes of affected states, nonconscious and conscious processes, the nexus of communication, and listening as intrapersonal processing. A readable, rewarding work useful to anyone interested in intrapersonal communication.

4

Responding to Others: Listening and Feedback

Learning Objectives

When you have finished this chapter you should be able to:

- Explain the importance of listening in your daily life.
- List and explain the steps in the listening process.
- Identify the influences that affect your listening.
- Describe the four phases of the empathic process and explain why we do not often listen empathically.
- Describe some of the results of effective listening.
- Explain how to improve your skills in listening.
- Explain the three-part feedback process and the need for receiving and giving it.
- List and explain the six major kinds of response styles for giving feedback to others.
- Outline the benefits of the paraphrasing—understanding—response.
- Describe how to improve your skills in feedback.

You have just spent five minutes explaining to a friend the time and place of a birthday party and as you turn to go he asks you, "Oh, yes, where are we meeting and what time did you say?" You know he hasn't listened. And you know how it feels when someone hasn't listened to you.

Do I listen well? Chances are this is a question we never ask ourselves. After all, listening is something we have done all our lives with no special training. We take it for granted. Everything in this book about successful interpersonal communication describes it as a circular give-and-take situation in which we really tune in to the other person. An essential part of that give-and-take is listening. This does not mean simply putting on

Consider This

The most significant differences between good and poor listeners, when they had no unusual motivation to listen because of test awareness, were that good listeners were more adventurous (receptive to new ideas), (emotionally) stable, mature, and sophisticated. Although the other six differences . . . were not statistically significant, it is interesting to note that all were in the same direction, with the good listeners being more emotionally mature: outgoing, bright, dominant, enthusiastic, trustful and controlled. The opposite ends of the personality scales, describing the poor listeners in the surprise listening test, were: aloof, dull, emotional, submissive, glum, timid, suspecting, simple, lax, and tense.

—Charles M. Kelly, "Empathic Listening," in *Readings in Speech Communication,* ed. Richard L. Weaver II (Dubuque, Iowa: Kendall/Hunt Publishing Co., 1985), p. 37. Reprinted by permission of Charles M. Kelly, Charlotte, N.C. 28210.

a "listening" expression and nodding and grunting agreement now and then while mentally planning our evening; it means listening with full and active attention—listening empathically, as though we are in the other person's place. We can never take this kind of listening for granted. It requires skill and constant practice, but the reward is greatly improved communication.

This chapter is about the importance of listening empathically and giving appropriate feedback. I'll first discuss the importance of listening and describe the difference between empathic and deliberative listening. The process of listening will then be explained, and you will discover that it is, essentially, the same as the process of perceiving. In the next section I identify the factors that influence listening. And since empathic listening is so central to effective interpersonal communication, I include a section on some of the barriers to empathic listening. A brief discussion of the results of effective listening and improving skills in listening concludes the first part of this chapter.

Feedback is closely related to listening, and in brief sections I discuss receiving it, giving it, and its effects. Withdrawing, judging, analyzing, questioning, reassuring, and paraphrasing as styles of feedback are also covered. The chapter concludes with a section on improving feedback skills.

The Importance of Listening

When we think of ourselves in communication situations, we usually think more about getting our ideas to others than about receiving ideas from them. This is normal. We've come to think the word *communication* means a process that flows out from us rather than one in which we are the receiver. But communicating orally involves far more than just talking to another person. It involves sharing ideas, trying to exchange meaning with each other as perfectly as possible. In most interpersonal situations, we spend just as much time listening and responding to the other person as we do talking. Considering all the communication activities of a normal day—talking, listening, reading, writing—we spend, on the average, more time listening than in any of the other activities. (See Figure 4.1.[1]) In our daily lives, listening is the most important form of verbal communication response.[2]

Most of us take listening for granted until someone does not listen to us. We *do* get a great deal of experience in it. Think of all the things and people we listen to in an ordinary day: a clock radio to wake up by, family or friends at meals, teachers and other students in classes, piped-in music in stores, radios and tape players in cars, television and stereo at home.

Because we spend so much of every day listening we may think it takes little effort. Not true. Listening is not the same as hearing. Hearing is done with the ears and, unless our hearing is impaired, goes on virtually all the time. We have no mechanism in our bodies that lets us shut our ears as we shut our eyes. If we want to improve our listening we need to monitor our own listening habits and then actively work to improve them. The kind of practice we get is important if we really want to get rid of bad habits.

The kind of listening we are concentrating on here is empathic listening. We cannot and need not listen empathically to every gas station attendant or bank teller with whom we exchange a few words during the course of a day.[3] There are situations that require only the simple exchange of information and small talk. But empathic listening is quite different.

Empathic listening involves integrating physical, emotional, and intellectual inputs in a search for meaning and understanding. It is an active,

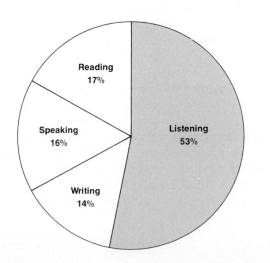

Figure 4.1
Percentage of time used in various communication skills.

© 1980 United Feature Syndicate, Inc.

not a passive, process. We cannot just make sure that our ears are alert or open and let the rest come naturally. Because empathic listening involves both emotional and intellectual inputs, it does not just happen. We have to make it happen and that's not easy. It takes energy and commitment. We have a lot going against us—there are many influences that combine to make us poor listeners. Some of them we can control, some we cannot.

Perhaps it will be easier to understand the nature and function of empathic listening if we contrast it to **deliberative listening.**[4] When we make a definite, "deliberate" attempt to hear information, analyze it, recall it at a later time, and draw conclusions from it, we are listening deliberatively. This is the way most of us listen because this is the way we have been trained. This type of listening is appropriate in a lecture-based education system where the first priority is to critically analyze the speaker's content.

In empathic listening the objective is also understanding, but the first priority is different. Because empathic listening is transactional, the listener's first priority is to understand the communicator. Empathic listening means listening to the whole person. We listen to what is being communicated not just by the words but by the other person's facial expressions, tone of voice, gestures, posture, and body motion. It is the integration of these functional units—their combination—that tells us what we want to know. We seek maximum understanding of the communicator's comments from his or her point of view. Deliberative listeners listen with a view to criticizing, summarizing, concluding, and agreeing or disagreeing.[5] To be an empathic listener, we must not limit our concentration and focus to words alone. That kind of listening restricts the amount of information available to us and inhibits our behavior because we base our behavior on insufficient information. That is why empathic listening—the most effective kind of listening—means responding to the *gestalt*: the totality that is the other person.

The Process of Listening

The process of listening is identical to the process of perceiving. The first step is **receiving.** Most of us think of the ears as the primary receiver of information in listening, and yet we listen with our whole bodies to the whole (gestalt) that others present. Although we may think we are only hearing, our reaction to stimuli is likely to be based on a combination of variables, not just on what we hear. If I hear someone say, "Get out of there," I may not be prompted to move as quickly as when I simultaneously see that the phrase is being uttered by a 250-pound man with his fist raised and moving rapidly in my direction!

When we attend to particular stimuli in listening we are involved in **selecting**—listening selectively. We may even have to concentrate very hard to select just those cues we need or want. Think about how effectively—selectively—you listened at a party when the group of people standing behind you began discussing your best friend!

Once we have received the stimuli and selected them, we **organize** the information. To do this we must assign meaning to what we have perceived. At this moment, our mind is actively carrying out an array of processes. Data is identified, registered, and analyzed. This is the time when we enlarge,

Consider This

What you do when you listen goes like this:

1. From the very beginning of the utterance you hear, you start generating in your own mind a set of possible meanings to match the meaning the speaker is trying to express. You do this by using your knowledge of the language, of the speaker, of the particular situation, and of the real world.
2. The instant you have what you perceive as a meaning match, you move on to the next sequence being spoken. Only if you suddenly discover that you have what can only be a serious *mis*match do you slow down and consider each and every word separately—and you do that only until you are satisfied that you have eliminated the problem.

Notice that this is *not* a passive process! This is an *active* process, in which you use your own language skills to create meanings that are syntonic [matching] with the meanings intended.

—From *The Last Word on the Gentle Art of Verbal Self-Defense* by Suzette Haden Elgin. Reprinted by permission of the author.

simplify, and close the information we have received and selected. It is all part of this near-instantaneous process of getting material into order.

Just as in the perception process, the final step in listening is **interpreting**. We relate the information received, selected, and organized to past experiences or future expectations. To be able to respond as a result of our listening, we must interpret what we have taken in. If we do not understand it, we may interpret the data as "confusing." That could prompt the response, "What do you mean by that?" or "Could you explain that to me?"

Because these steps occur spontaneously (when we have chosen to listen) and with amazing speed, they often overlap or occur out of sequence. For example, you might wonder how people can organize data without interpreting it first; no doubt these processes interact closely, just as the reception, selection, organization, and interpretation of data interact. The ears provide one input; our other four senses offer four others. Thus, listening is just part of the whole perceiving process.

What Influences Your Listening?

Being aware of the factors that affect listening not only will help us improve our own listening skills but also will help us become more considerate of people who listen to us. Knowing what factors operate increases our understanding of the entire communication process and can help explain why breakdowns and confusion sometimes result. Following are some of the factors that influence how well we listen.

Physiological Differences Affect What You Hear

Because listening is part of the perceiving process, its effectiveness is limited by the mechanics of the physical process of hearing—to be able to select from aural stimuli we must first be able to hear them. People differ from each other **physiologically,** in the makeup and responsiveness of their organs, tissues, and cells. If we are hard-of-hearing our listening will be affected simply because we won't have as many stimuli to choose from, to organize, and to interpret as someone who hears well.

You Process Words Faster Than They Can Be Spoken

The average person speaks at a rate of 125 to 150 words per minute. But as listeners, we can easily process 500 words per minute.[6] Though our minds can absorb words very rapidly, in our ordinary listening we are rarely challenged to process them as efficiently as we can. Even the most skilled speaker pauses and stumbles occasionally; even the most polished speech contains words that are not essential to the message. These hesitations and extraneous elements add up to many precious seconds of wasted time *within* a message. What do we, as listeners, do with this time? We let our minds wander, mostly. Unless we purposefully make use of that time to concentrate on the speaker's message, we are easily distracted.

Effective Listening Requires Active Commitment

If we believe that listening is a passive process in which we simply monitor what we hear, we may misinterpret information or overlook important cues. We'll hear only what we want to hear or what grabs our attention. Productive listening involves real work. It takes emotional and intellectual commitment. It's possible that our TV-watching habits contribute to our tendency to listen passively. For example, often we simply hear the TV in the background while our thoughts are elsewhere; this is especially true during commercial breaks. We don't have to respond to commercials, we just let them happen. But in interpersonal communication, if we listen halfheartedly and passively we get only part of the message.

Consider This

In his autobiography, Lee Iacocca discusses the importance of listening and the active commitment that it not only requires but inspires in others:

> I only wish I could find an institute that teaches people how to listen. After all, a good manager needs to listen at least as much as he needs to talk. Too many people fail to realize that real communication goes in both directions.
>
> In corporate life, you have to encourage all your people to make a contribution to the common good and to come up with better ways of doing things. You don't have to accept every single suggestion, but if you don't get back to the guy and say, "Hey, that idea was terrific," and pat him on the back, he'll never give you another one. That kind of communication lets people know they really count.
>
> You have to be able to listen well if you're going to motivate the people who work for you. Right there, that's the difference between a mediocre company and a great company. The most fulfilling thing for me as a manager is to watch someone the system has labeled as just average or mediocre really come into his own, all because someone has listened to his problems and helped him solve them.

—From Lee Iacocca (with William Novak), *Iacocca: An Autobiography* (New York: Bantam Books, 1984), pp. 54–55.

Those Hidden Messages . . .

Effective listening means listening with a third ear. By this I mean trying to listen for the meanings behind the words and not just to the words alone. The way words are spoken—loud, soft, fast, slow, strong, hesitating—is very important. There are messages buried in all the cues that surround words.[7] If a mother says, "Come *in* now" in a soft, gentle voice, it may mean the kids have a few more minutes. If she says, "Come in NOW" there is no question about the meaning of the command. To listen effectively we have to pay attention to facial expressions and eye contact, gestures and body movement, posture and dress, as well as to the quality of the other person's voice, vocabulary, rhythm, rate, tone, and volume. These nonverbal cues are a vital part of any message. Listening with our third ear helps us understand the whole message.

The ability to expand on the obvious—to listen beyond words—allows us to really "see into" another person. People who seek help and sympathy bear two messages—the one they speak and the one beneath the surface. To help them we need to "see through" what they say. You may know a person to whom everyone goes with problems, a person other people seek out for counsel or just to share ideas. This person is probably an effective listener, someone who listens with the third ear.

Effective Listening Requires Empathy[8]

What is it that we derive from empathy? It helps us in two ways. First, it helps us understand another person from within. With empathy, we communicate on a deeper level and actually share the other person's feelings. This kind of communication often results in our acceptance of the other person and our entering into a relationship with him or her of appreciation and sympathy. Second, it becomes a source of personal reassurance. Empathy often evokes empathy. We are reassured when we feel others really understand our state of mind. We enjoy the satisfaction of being accepted and understood. When others fail to empathize we feel disappointed and rejected. We look for a feeling response just as others do, and when that is lacking, we often feel something is wrong with the relationship. Empathy, then, helps us achieve a correspondence of mood.

However similar human beings may be, there is something distinctive and unique about each. If we are to communicate effectively, our goal must be to understand what is individual and distinctive in others. To achieve this goal, empathic methods are essential.

There appear to be four phases of the empathic process. The most characteristic and fundamental of the sequence is **identification.** Through imitation and the relaxation of our conscious controls, we absorb ourselves in, consider, and even engulf others and their experiences. This is more than conscious and deliberate intellectual effort. The identification in empathy

means becoming engrossed in the personality of another and losing con-sciousness of self. Our entire consciousness is projected into others so that the feelings that inhere in others act upon us.

Incorporation, the second phase, *means the act of taking the experience of the other person into ourselves.* Essential to an understanding of empathy is that it is the experience of others that we take in, rather than an experience of our own that we project onto others. Through incorporation, then, we introduce into our consciousness something partly alien and foreign to us. In this way, we reduce the social distance between ourselves and others.

Reverberation is the third phase. It is not enough just to take in the experience of another or just to feel what the other person is experiencing. We must take another step. Reverberation *consists of our interaction with the experience of others.* It underscores Friedrich Schiller's comment, "If thou wouldst understand others, look into thine own heart!" We don't need to experience the actual event ourselves; we can imagine it and anticipate what our response might be. Sharing a common emotional endowment with others, we can, solely from within ourselves, understand what the meaning of an experience might be for them.

Detachment, the final phase of empathic understanding, *occurs when we withdraw from our subjective involvement and use reason and scrutiny.* This is where we consciously break our identification and deliberately move away to gain both social and psychic distance. Our goal in this phase is objective analysis. We try to place our understanding in perspective.

To understand what another person is feeling requires a broader base than most of us are accustomed to using. Using the four phases of empathy—which may not occur exactly in the order listed—is a well-established means for obtaining that more comprehensive framework: the total image that is the other person.

Why Don't We Always Listen Empathically?

If it is so helpful, you might wonder why more people are not empathic listeners. Actually, there are three reasons—all of them directly interrelated. First, listening empathically is not easy. It is far more difficult than simply taking note of actual words spoken and responding to them literally. Second, empathic listening requires that we get outside ourselves by trying to share in the meaning, spirit, and feelings of another person. We're not always willing to do this. Our egos get tied up in our communication; we get involved in our own thoughts and problems. The next time you are involved in an interpersonal encounter, notice how hard it is to concentrate on what the other person is saying if you are preoccupied with your own next remark. Do you begin to plan what you are going to say before the other person even has a chance to stop talking? Instead of listening, you may find you are figuring out how to impress him or her with your next comment.[9]

The third reason we may not listen empathically is because of ingrained listening habits. We may listen too literally or too judgmentally by habit. We may habitually think of communication as a talking medium rather than a listening medium. The following sections discuss some other habits we may have that hinder effective listening.

Tuning out.   Habit may cause us to tune out much of the talk we hear. Our society is talk-oriented. We tune out to avoid listening, to protect ourselves from the communication babble that sometimes seems to surround us. We may tune out for physical and emotional preservation as well. It is necessary to tune out some things. We must be selective or we would be inundated. But we cannot listen empathically if habit has caused us to avoid the very basics of the process—tuning *in!*

This does not mean we need to tune in to everything we hear. But good listeners do tend to discover interesting elements in almost all communications. They are able to cope with the bombardment of stimuli. Whereas poor listeners tend to find all topics uniformly dry and boring, effective listeners concentrate their attention well and learn efficiently through listening.

We can't expect to be fascinated by every subject. But if we too often find ourselves bored by the communication in a certain situation—eating lunch with the same people every day, for example—we might ask ourselves, "What were my reasons for going to lunch with these people in the first place? Do those reasons still hold?" Perhaps we started eating with these people because they are politically active and we wanted to discuss politics with them. If we still feel the same way, remembering the original motive can help us focus our listening in this group's communications. We may be able to pick out useful bits of information from conversations that would otherwise seem pointless.

Wanting to be entertained.   Another habit that can affect our listening might be labeled the "Scsame Street Syndrome." We want to be entertained. We may mentally challenge a speaker: "Excite me or I won't listen." If we think ahead of time that the message we're going to hear will be dull, we're not likely to listen well. And if we expect to be bored, there's a good chance we will be. We generally prefer a lively, entertaining presentation to a straight, unembellished delivery. Think of the way local television news programs present the news. You may notice a real difference from one station to another in how many program elements are included mainly for their entertainment value.

Avoiding the difficult.   Another version of the "Sesame Street Syndrome" is that we tend to stay away from difficult listening. That is, given a choice, we are likely to avoid listening that requires mental exertion. Any kind of communication that deals with unfamiliar subjects can seem tough to follow, especially if the speaker moves quickly from one point to the next. If we're not used to a speaker's reasoning, we may give up on the message rather than try to follow his or her thought processes. Editorial comments on TV, panel discussions, and some lectures can be hard to follow if we're not used to really concentrating.

Criticizing the superficial.   Think about a recent interpersonal encounter you had with people you do not know well. Can you remember what they looked like? What they were wearing? What they said? We often let externals distract us from what the other person is saying.

If we don't know someone well, we're more likely to be diverted by that person's lisp or hairstyle or purple sweater. We may find ourselves criticizing some unimportant characteristic of the person instead of listening to what he or she is saying. Think of how you size up a political candidate. Do you notice the candidate's hairstyle? Smile? Clothing? These nonverbal cues are important, but they shouldn't distract us from really listening to what the person is saying.

Letting emotions take over.   Finally, we may habitually either (1) block things out; (2) distort things; or (3) agree too readily to everything. When we hear things that don't fit in with our own beliefs, we often put up a mental block so we don't get frightened or angry. Sometimes we hear just what we want to hear. We may have a conviction so strong that we

Try This

Next time you catch yourself being distracted by another person's clothes, mannerisms, or looks, *stop* and try to:

1. *Refocus* your attention on the message.
2. *Paraphrase* what is being said.
3. *Review* the important elements of what has been communicated.

The idea is to redirect your attention to the message and away from distracting elements.

twist whatever we hear to conform. Some words (*mother, I love you*) may appeal to our emotions to such an extent that we agree with anything that follows. If we loved every minute we spent at Barnwood High School, meeting someone else from old Barnwood automatically produces a favorable emotional climate for our conversation.

Our emotions may be triggered by a single word or phrase that seems to leap out. Suppose we meet a woman at a party who says, "I just got back from Colorado." Some emotional reactions we may have are "I never get to go anywhere" or "Colorado is overrun by crazy outdoor types. I wouldn't go there if you paid me" or "Colorado! I love Colorado! Mountains! Fresh air! Good times!" Any of these thoughts will color how we hear the rest of what the woman says to us. Once we hear that trigger-word (*Colorado*), we listen to nothing else. Instead we plan a defense, rebuttal, supportive example, argument, or other way to involve our ego. Effective listening means controlling emotional responses—trying to break old habits.

Results of Effective Listening

Animated, cooperative, and responsive listeners help the person they are talking to because their reactions produce an immediate effect. They can influence what the other person will say next. And the listener will benefit from the improved communication that results. (See Figure 4.2.)

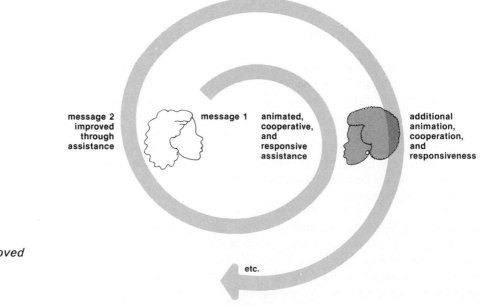

message 2 improved through assistance

message 1

animated, cooperative, and responsive assistance

additional animation, cooperation, and responsiveness

etc.

Figure 4.2
The cycle of improved communication through effective listening.

Specifically, what are the rewards of effective listening? The first is that we will get a more stimulating and meaningful message—the other person may subconsciously adapt the message specifically to our knowledge and background. The more closely we listen to a person and indicate what we do and don't understand, the more likely we are to receive a message that makes sense. And we're more likely to remember it. By improving our listening habits we should be able to recall more than 50 percent of the information we hear, rather than forget it.[10]

For example, if you respond to a friend's description of a recent trip with partial or complete silence, your friend will probably cut the description short. But if you ask such questions as "Where did you go?" or "What did you do?" or "Was it fun?" or "Who did you see?" he or she will be more interested in providing the details. Your understanding of your friend's experience will be far more complete. Of course, we can purposely cut short a conversation by showing no interest or involvement. But we might miss out on a stimulating and meaningful message.

The second reward of effective listening is improvement in our own communication techniques. By paying closer attention to the communication of others and by observing their methods, we will be able to analyze our own efforts more completely.

For example, we may notice that a friend ends every other sentence with the words *you know*. If this interferes with our listening, we'll be more alert to certain phrases or words that *we* overuse ourselves. Once we see how distracting such things are, we'll be more inclined to ask a friend to point out mannerisms we have that we are not aware of.

Consider This

At any point, each person is both reacting to and causing a reaction in others. Most of us tend to see ourselves as responding to what others say, without realizing that what they are saying may be a reaction to us. We are keenly aware that we said what we did because of what she said, but it may not occur to us that she said what she did because of what we said—just before, yesterday, or last year. Communication is a continuous stream in which everything is simultaneously a reaction and an instigation, an instigation and a reaction. We keep moving in a complex dance that is always different but made up of familiar steps.

—From Deborah Tannen, *That's Not What I Meant! How Conversational Style Makes or Breaks Your Relations With Others* (New York: William Morrow and Company, Inc., 1986), p. 99.

We may find that another reward of effective listening is an enlarged circle of friends. Good listeners are in great demand. People have an emotional need to be heard; the person who is willing to take the time to listen is often sought out.

Finally, in becoming effective listeners we are likely to become more open and involved human beings. The ultimate reward is more meaningful interpersonal relationships. Effective listening habits will increase our capacity to meet the demands of modern life. It is one of the most important communication skills needed for human interaction.

Improving Skills in Listening

As I said earlier, improving listening skills requires time and energy. The suggestions that follow may seem to be based on ordinary common sense. Some may seem obvious. Even so, the most commonsensical ideas are often not put into practice. If you simply read these and do not incorporate them into your own listening behavior, they will serve little purpose. Perhaps these suggestions will also bring to mind other practical ideas you can put to use in listening settings.

Prepare to listen.   In many cases you do not listen well because you are not physically or mentally prepared. Your attention span is directly related to your physical and mental condition. This is obvious if you recall that listening involves an integration of physical, emotional, and intellectual elements. Think how impatient or short-tempered you become when you are mentally run-down, or physically tired. You stayed up all night studying for an exam and now everyone around you pays for it! You do not want to listen to anyone!

Control or eliminate distractions.   Anticipating situations where you might have to listen helps prepare you for the experience. There may be something you can do to improve the situation: turning off a television, closing a door, asking the other person to speak louder, or moving to a less distracting location. If you can't eliminate distractions, you'll have to concentrate with greater effort.

Anticipate the subject.   Whenever possible, think ahead about the topics or ideas that might be discussed. The more familiar you are with the subject matter, the more likely you will learn, and the more interested you will be. Also, thinking ahead may prompt questions to ask. Becoming actively involved in interpersonal situations makes them more memorable and meaningful.

Anticipate the speaker.   Anticipating the speaker means adjusting in advance (or being prepared to adjust) to the other person. You cannot control how the speaker will look or talk, but you can make sure, in advance, that distracting appearance or faulty delivery does not dominate your attention. Your aim should be to try to find out what the other person is saying. You should try not to be bothered by peculiarities or eccentricities. If you are always ready to adjust, you will find it becomes a natural part of your behavior when you *must* adjust.

Create a need to listen.   We do not enjoy listening to some people as much as to others. We do not listen as well to some topics as we do to others. We often know in advance that we may not listen as well as we

Try This

As you are listening to someone or just after a conversation, ask yourself the following questions:

1. What did the other person do—as far as effective communication goes—that was particularly strong? What aspects of the other person's presentation were especially powerful or convincing?
2. What did the person do that was especially weak? What would you change in his or her presentation?

The purpose here is growth and change. Try to learn something from each communication experience that will help you improve your own communication patterns and behaviors.

might in a certain situation. To try to counteract this situation, become a "selfish listener."[11] What can the speaker do for *you?* The key to being interested in another person or in a topic is making it relevant or useful to ourselves.

Try to discover if the message has any personal benefits for you. Can it provide personal satisfaction? Does it stimulate new interests or insights? Good listeners are interested in what they are listening to, whereas poor listeners find all people and all topics dry and boring. True, some topics are dull, but we often decide this in advance and don't give the speaker a chance.

If the speaker or the material does not satisfy a need, ask yourself, "Why am I here?" Try to remember what caused you to be there and see if the motive is still active. You might also try to discover a reward—some immediate way to use the material that will make the experience personally profitable.

Monitor the way you listen.   Even if you are prepared to listen and need to listen, your listening will not necessarily be effective. You need to check occasionally to make sure your thoughts are not wandering and that you are keeping an open mind to the other person's ideas. Because of the difference between speaking and listening rates, you need to use wisely the spare time that results.

Concentrate on the message. To keep your mind on the message, try to review what the speaker has already said so that you can keep ideas together and remember them. Listen for the main ideas. Try to go "between" the words. Listen with your third ear. Listen for words that may have more than one meaning and discover, if possible, how the other person is using the word. Try to anticipate what the speaker will say next and compare this with what he or she actually says. This keeps your mind focused on the message.[12] Concentrate on the message, not on the speaker's blue eyes or Hawaiian shirt.

Suspend judgment. Some words, phrases, or ideas evoke an automatic reaction. You may overreact to bad grammar, ethnic slurs, or vulgarity. You must learn not to get too excited about certain words until you have the whole context. Suspend judgment until you thoroughly understand where the speaker is coming from.

Think about those words you react strongly to. Why do they affect you like that? Sharing your reactions with others will often help you see that your reactions are entirely personal. Finally, try to reduce the intensity of your reaction by convincing yourself that the reaction is extreme and unnecessary, that the word does not merit such a reaction.[13] Our listening will always be affected when certain words touch our deepest prejudices or most profound values. Knowing that such reactions can occur is the first step toward overcoming them.

Consider This

Good conversation is equally divided between talking and listening. If you regularly bemoan the fact that you never know what to say, you could solve a good part of your problem by learning to listen. When you're too frightened to open your mouth, chances are you're not listening to anyone else, you're listening to yourself—your thumping heart and the little voice inside your head telling you: <u>I don't have anything to say. I'll make a fool of</u> myself. If you can learn to listen to other people, you won't be able to hear those self-centered and self-defeating sounds.

—From *What to Say When You Don't Know What to Say* by Alice Fleming. Copyright © 1982 by Alice Fleming. Reprinted with permission of Charles Scribner's Sons, an imprint of Macmillan Publishing Company.

Consider This

In every language interaction, the adjustments you make in your language behavior should always be . . . based on the information you get from your listener's reaction to what you say. There are few communication strategies more guaranteed to fail than making such adjustments based upon nothing but your personal determination to talk in a particular way *no matter what happens.* That's like deciding in advance when you reach for an object that you will always reach exactly the same distance, with exactly the same amount of effort, *no matter what happens.* If your language habits have become so fixed and rigid that you follow them without paying any attention to the situation, then the part of your language behavior they cover is not a feedback system. When the furnace in your house comes on because a thermostat has registered a drop in air temperature below its setting, that's a feedback system; if you rig your furnace to come on every three hours no matter what the temperature is, that's not feedback, but an *arbitrary* system. It is not likely to make an efficient or satisfactory use of your energy resources. An arbitrary system for communication is just as wasteful, and just as unsatisfactory.

—From *The Last Word on The Gentle Art of Verbal Self-Defense* by Suzette Haden Elgin. Reprinted by permission of the author.

Empathize. Try to see the other person's ideas from his or her perspective. If Sam is telling you how angry he is with his brother, try to discover why he says what he does. Listen for his reasons, his views, and his arguments. You needn't agree with him. Sam's brother may be a friend of yours. But just because Sam's feelings differ from yours does not mean they aren't valid. Since you differ from Sam as a result of different past experiences, search for the message he is *really* trying to communicate. Look for elements he may have left out. What is he basing his evidence on? How did he come by his opinion? Through personal experience? Other people's observations? Guesswork? You should try to see the problem through Sam's eyes.

The Importance of Feedback

The benefits of good listening occur only when the cues we give back to a speaker allow that person to know how we receive the message, permitting the speaker to adjust the message as needed.[14] This important process is known as *feedback*. Feedback is not a simple, one-step process. First, it involves **monitoring** the impact or the influence of our messages on the other person. Second, it involves **evaluating** why the reaction or response occurred as it did. Third and finally, it involves **adjustment** or modification. The adjustment of our future messages reveals the process-oriented nature of communication, and, too, the impact the receiver has on the communication cycle. Feedback can provide reinforcement for the speaker if it shows that he or she is being clear, accepted, or understood.

The heart of this feedback process is the adjustment or corrective function. Feedback can be words ("Yes, I get it") or physical messages (a smile) or responses that show the other person that we are, indeed, sharing in the spirit of what he or she is saying. It can also show if we do *not* understand or agree. Just as we know, by the response we get, whether or not we are being listened to, the other person is in the same situation. We recognize that mutual understanding has or hasn't occurred through feedback. An atmosphere that promotes honest feedback is a necessary condition for understanding and for being understood.

In any communication setting, each of us is both a source of messages and a receiver of messages simultaneously. This means that we are at all times responding and being responded to. Feedback exists when each person affects the other—each is a cause and an effect.[15] Just as we cannot *not* communicate, we cannot *not* send some kind of feedback. We send messages even when we do not speak.

Try This

Next time you are in a conversation with someone, listen with the goal of finding out as much as you possibly can. Plan to ask the other person a series of probing questions to gain the necessary information. Some sample questions might be:

1. How did you discover that?
2. What else happened?
3. Why do you suppose that is so?
4. What was the outcome?
5. Would you do the same again?
6. Do you think it could happen again?
7. What do you think you gained from this experience?

Do not interrupt the other person with your probes. Listen closely so that your questions will be relevant to what is being said. Maintain a positive, supportive spirit of inquiry.

Wouldn't it be fascinating if we had more time to do this on a regular basis? We would become not only better listeners, but more retentive learners as well.

Receiving Feedback

Imagine yourself, for a moment, as only a source of messages; you gain no feedback to any message you send out. You say hello and nobody answers. You say, "It sure is a beautiful day" and nobody reinforces or acknowledges what you've said. You have no way of knowing if you were heard or understood. You have no way to gauge your effectiveness. It's understandable that someone in this hypothetical one-way-communication situation could become frustrated, feeling unacceptable and unloved.[16] What's the use in talking if there is no one to respond? Receiving feedback is one of the best ways we have of modifying our behavior. Monitoring feedback is our way of assuring that the message we intended is as closely related as possible to the message received.

Think of some people with whom you enjoy communicating. Do these people provide you with honest feedback as you speak? Their feedback affects not only *how* you communicate with them, but *why* you express yourself as you do and why you treat them as you do. The cues we receive may cause us to keep talking, restate our ideas, begin to stumble or stammer, or become silent. Whatever the case, we need feedback to gain insight into our own communication and to help us understand the communication behavior of others.

Giving Feedback

Just as we need to receive feedback, we also need to give it. Listening attentively and giving appropriate feedback show that we are attempting to cope successfully with our environment; we are active participants, not passive observers, able to act in direct response to a specific stimulus.[17] The feedback we give people can make them feel unique and worthwhile and heighten their sense of well-being—it's personally rewarding to know that our reactions matter.

Communication does not continue for long when the direction of flow is one-way. A person who receives no feedback, whose feelings are not encouraged and reinforced, will look somewhere else for support. Effective communication assumes a two-way flow of information.

The Effects of Feedback

If you ever think that your feedback is insignificant and makes no difference, remember that in a two-person interpersonal situation, you are the *only* source of reactions for the other person. If you do not provide feedback, the other person can't know how well he or she is getting through. It's up to you to help the other person make the message as accurate as possible. How much feedback you give is also important.

In a landmark study, researchers investigated the role of feedback in message transmission in a classroom setting.[18] The students participating in the study were divided into four groups, each with an instructor. They were all to draw geometric patterns according to oral instructions given them by the instructor. In one group the students could hear the directions but could not see the instructor; no feedback of any sort was permitted. In a second group, the students and the instructor could see each other but could not ask or answer questions. In a third group, the students could answer yes or no questions from the instructor. In a fourth group, students could ask any questions and get information—a free-feedback situation. The researchers discovered that as the amount of allowed feedback increased, it took students longer to complete their tasks but they also drew their geometric figures more accurately. And they felt far more confident about their success in drawing the figures when free feedback was permitted. We can conclude from this that feedback in an interpersonal communication encounter takes extra time but results in more accurate message transmission and more confidence in the message-transmission process.

Styles of Feedback

Feedback begins within us. **Internal feedback** takes place all the time as we communicate with others.[19] As we speak, we anticipate certain responses from the other person. As we receive feedback from the other person, we adapt and correct our own message; the process of adapting and correcting depends on internal feedback.

Giving feedback to the other person also begins with our own internal feedback. If we want to give someone feedback as he or she speaks, we must first be very attentive to that person's communications. We can't give helpful feedback if we aren't listening effectively to start with. To be ready to respond appropriately we must be alert to the other person's overall message, trying hard to see where he or she is coming from so that our feedback is not insensitive or confusing.

Thomas Gordon, in *Parent Effectiveness Training*, suggests that there are twelve kinds of response styles for giving feedback.[20] Other authors list only five.[21] The following scheme describes six typical ways of responding—withdrawing, judging, analyzing, questioning, reassuring, and paraphrasing. Paraphrasing is the one that I feel leads to the most successful interaction.

Withdrawing. The **withdrawing response** essentially ignores what the other person has said. "Just forget about it" or "Let's not talk about it now" are common examples of this style. Withdrawing can also take the form of distracting. For example, when a friend comes to you with a problem about one of her professors, you might ask her, "Say, how is your boyfriend? I haven't heard much about him lately." If that appears too obvious a change

Try This

In your next conversations with people, notice the feedback you receive as you talk:

1. How extensive is it?
2. What are the primary cues that provide the feedback (eyes, face, gestures, posture, body movement, tone of voice)?
3. Do different people use different kinds of feedback? Do they depend on different cues?
4. Does the amount of feedback differ between friends and strangers? Does it depend on the nature of the message or situation?
5. How much do you depend on the feedback you get from others?
6. Do you find yourself adjusting your message when you receive feedback? In what ways?

If nothing else, this exercise should encourage you to become more conscious of feedback in any communication situation. As you grow more sensitive to it, your messages can become more exact and specific.

of subject, you might ease into the distraction with the question, "That's the professor you liked so much last week?"

Withdrawing responses are weak because they do not address the problem at hand. Responding in this way *can* spring from a sincere wish to take the other person's mind off a problem, but it is likely to come across as lack of concern, poor listening, or callousness on the part of the listener. With so many other possible responses available, withdrawing is not considered a positive method for successful interaction.

Judging.   The **judging response** is one of the most common responses. It is very easy to give advice or make a judgment. By telling people that their idea or behavior is good or bad, appropriate or inappropriate, effective or ineffective, right or wrong, we imply that we know how they can solve their problem or how they ought to behave. Judging responses often begin with "If I were you, I would . . . ," "You know you should . . . ," or "The thing you might consider doing is . . . ."

One reason a judging response can hinder a relationship is that it can appear threatening. What is your immediate reaction when someone tells you that something you did, or an idea that you have, is wrong? You probably get defensive; defensiveness causes closed-mindedness, rejection, and resistance. You want to stop exploring, to change the subject, to retreat or escape. When people judge, they imply that their evaluation is superior to someone else's. Someone with a problem or with specific feelings about something that has happened does not want to feel inferior.

Further, judging responses are quick ways to deal with others' problems or feelings. They do not necessarily reveal genuine concern. If others perceive that you are trying to deal with them in a quick or easy way, rejection is likely to follow. Nobody wants to be brushed off.

Also, when you give advice often you encourage others not to take responsibility for their own problems. You provide an escape route—an "easy out." If others can ask for and get advice whenever they are face-to-face with problems, why should they bother to take responsibility for or solve their own problems? In addition, if you give advice they could blame you when your evaluation or suggestion does not work out. You set yourself up as a convenient scapegoat.

Finally, a judging response can limit communication. By making a judgment, the responder takes over the communication and cuts things off before real communication can take place. The judging responder may not seem to be really interested in hearing the whole story, and the person who receives the judgment may feel there is no point in continuing the discussion.

Analyzing. If you rephrase your response above so that it explains the other's action or dissects it, you are **analyzing**—and the situation is not greatly improved. "You know, the reason you are disturbed is . . ." or "Your situation is simply . . ." are likely to be analyzing responses. In these cases you end up trying to instruct others or to tell them what their problems or feelings mean. It is as if you have assumed the role of psychiatrist: "Your problem implies (or indicates) that . . . ." The difference between judging and analyzing responses is small. When analyzing others' problems we imply what they ought to think. We are supplying the motives, justifications, or rationale for their behavior—once again, giving them a convenient "out."

Consider This

If the other person yawns while you're talking with him, does that allow you to infer that he's not interested in what you're saying? Maybe it means he didn't sleep well last night. If he leans forward with a pained expression, can you infer that he's really sharing your tale of woe? Or is it a sign of gastritis? Inference from observed behavior is subject to inaccuracy because such inference assumes that only one reality exists: yours. Remember that you will not see the same event in precisely the same way as anyone else.

—Thomas G. Banville, *How to Listen—How to Be Heard: A Guide to Successful Relationships Through Effective Listening* (Chicago: Nelson-Hall, 1978), p. 161.

The drawbacks, too, are similar to those for the judging response. Analyzing the behavior of others can make them defensive and less likely to reveal thoughts and feelings, thus preventing them from engaging in further interpretation or analysis. Although analyzing takes longer than judging, it still can seem to "brush others off" because with a single analysis, we may explain their behavior. It may encourage others *not* to take responsibility for their own problems; analyzing supplies answers that keep them from thinking through and trying to solve their own problems. Also, it can convey superiority: "I know more about what makes you tick than you do."

Questioning. A **questioning response** may draw out other people. The purpose of questioning feedback is to get other people to discuss their feelings. A questioning response is a good beginning, because it gives us information about the nature of the situation and provides an emotional release for other persons at the same time. This response takes the form of a question: "What makes this situation so upsetting to you?" or "What do you suppose caused this to happen?"

In questioning, we don't want to be threatening or accusatory. Phrasing our questions carelessly can cause more problems than we solve. For example, we would probably not ask, "How did you ever get into this mess?" because that puts a value judgment on the experience and changes the response to a judging one. Questions like, "Didn't you know that was wrong?" or "You really weren't thinking, were you?" are also judging. Again, we don't want to imply what that person should have done or ought to do.

In using the questioning response, communicators should avoid questions beginning with *why*. *Why* questions create defensiveness. When asked, "Why did you do that?" our immediate impulse is to defend ourselves. It automatically indicates disapproval: "You shouldn't have done that." Criticism and advice tend to be threatening. *What, where, when, how,* and *who* questions are more helpful in opening others up. They encourage specificity, precision, and more self-disclosure.

Reassuring. If a friend comes to us upset, we probably want to reassure him or her that all is not lost. Pointing out alternative ways for perceiving the situation that he or she may not have thought of would be **reassuring.** Our response should be calming, to reduce the intensity of our friend's feeling. Initially, our reassurance may be no more specific than a look or a touch that says, "I'm on your side." A reassuring response may reveal agreement. Once a friend knows that we are empathic, we can discuss actions, alternatives, or other choices.

To provide reassurance we should first reduce the intensity of the feeling. A comment like, "That is a serious situation, and I can see why you are upset . . ." is a good beginning. Reassurance means acknowledging the seriousness of the other person's feelings. It does not need to reveal agreement, but we don't want to argue or suggest that these emotions are inappropriate.

Although reassuring responses may be stronger than many of the preceding styles, they can come across negatively, too. If by tone of voice or phrasing we imply that others should not feel the way they do, once again we have turned our response into a judging one, and the weaknesses of the judging response become operative.

Paraphrasing. Our first comment to our friend could be, "I can see you're very upset about this. It must mean a great deal to you." In **paraphrasing** the other person's remarks we show that we understand. Thus, paraphrasing can show that we care about correctly understanding our friend's situation. When we reinforce our remarks with nonverbal cues—eye contact, facial expressions of sincerity, touching, tone of voice—this response is very supportive.

You might ask, why **paraphrase?** Why restate in your own words what others have just said? First, paraphrasing helps make certain that you have understood what others are saying. In a sense, it gives you a second chance to make sure you are understanding them. Second, it can begin a clarifying process—drawing others out, gaining more information, and talking things out more extensively. Both talk and time allow communicators opportunities to gain clearer understanding of themselves and the implications of their feelings and thoughts. Third, paraphrasing can serve as a summarizing process—covering the main points of a situation more concisely, or trying to add things up—as others reflect and review. Fourth, it assures others that you did, indeed, hear what they said. You are alert, responsive—involved. And finally it shows others that you are trying to understand their thoughts and feelings. It helps legitimize your efforts as a concerned, caring person.

In positive response styles we avoid judging the other person and the situation. Our **intentional communication,** our choice of words, for example, is not as crucial as is our **unintentional communication,** our nonverbal cues that reveal our honest effort to understand the other person's problem or feelings. The idea is to indicate acceptance and respect for the other person. As these feelings are reflected back to us, an atmosphere of mutual respect, support, and trust develops. And our interpersonal relationships are likely to become more satisfying.

Improving Skills in Feedback

Effective feedback is as important as good listening. As listeners, we have a duty to respond, to complete the communication cycle. Although we can't avoid giving some feedback even if we don't say a word, there are ways we can improve our conscious feedback.

Be prepared to give feedback.   Feedback can be verbal, nonverbal, or both. Nonverbal feedback usually can say more about your sincerity than words alone. Your verbal feedback is more likely to be believed if you support it with appropriate gestures, direct eye contact, and possibly touching.

Try This

To practice your response styles, think of one response of each kind for each of the following situations:

1. Your best friend tells you: "I just flunked my second exam in my psychology course. It's all over. I just don't care about anything any more . . ."
2. Your roommate says: "Someone stole my books and notebooks. I left them on a table in the cafeteria and when I came back they were gone . . ."
3. A friend down the hall laments: "Oh, I can't stand it, I can't stand it any more! My roommate leaves the room in a mess, plays the stereo at full volume, and sleeps only during the day. It's driving me out of my mind and . . ."

Try This

The next time you are communicating interpersonally, do not respond to what the other person says until you do three things:

1. Wait until the other person <u>finishes</u> what he or she has to say.
2. Fully <u>paraphrase</u> what he or she has said.
3. Receive an <u>affirmative response</u> to the question, "Is that what you mean?" directly following your paraphrase.

Following an affirmative response, you may make any appropriate comment you wish to keep the conversation going. If the other person says your paraphrase was inaccurate, keep trying until you get it right.

Although in many situations we don't need to wait until the other person finishes talking before we respond, forcing yourself to wait will indicate how often you do <u>not</u> wait. Does this kind of communication seem awkward or labored to you? Do you think it is a good way to get at the other person's meaning?

Be certain that you are close enough to the other person—face-to-face if possible—for your feedback to be perceived. We will discuss nonverbal communication in more detail in a later chapter.

Although you must be prepared to give feedback, you shouldn't enter a situation with your specific reactions already planned. Spontaneity is important. The best feedback arises naturally as a result of an immediate and specific stimulus. But being prepared to give feedback does not preclude being spontaneous; it simply means that you are alert and sensitive to the need for feedback and are ready to give it.

Make your feedback prompt.   Your response to the other person should be clear and prompt. The more closely tied feedback is to the original message, the less ambiguous it will be. The longer the delay between message and feedback, the more likely you are to confuse the other person.

Make your feedback accurate.   Accuracy means making feedback specific to a single message and not general to the whole conversation. You probably know people who continually nod and smile the entire time you're talking to them. In addition to being distracting, this also appears insincere. It makes you want to ask, "All right, what exactly do you agree with? How will I know when you disagree?" Try to provide only necessary feedback.

React to the message, not the speaker.   Your accuracy in giving feedback also will improve if you remember to direct it to the message and

Try This

Next time you have a long, chatty telephone conversation with someone, see how the communication is affected when you do the following things:

1. Let the other person talk for a while with limited verbal or vocal feedback from you.
2. See what kind of feedback works best to encourage the other person to talk:
   No feedback
   "Ummm," "Uh-huh," "Oh," "Ah"
   Questions
   Comments
   Paraphrasing (restating the other person's words in your own words)
3. Instead of silence, engage in parallel talking: you talk on a subject parallel to your telephone partner's but with no response to his or her communication; if he or she is telling you about a movie, you talk about your plans for the weekend.
4. Try to provide <u>vocal</u> responses only with no words. How many meanings can you provide without using words?
5. Try to affect the context of the message by your responses to your telephone partner's responses. Can you change business to pleasure? Can you change a serious message to a humorous one? Can you take the initiative in directing the conversation if your partner originally assumed it?

not to the person communicating. In addition to being distracting, personal comments may create hostility or frustration and a breakdown in communication.

Oddly, both complimentary and critical feedback may be better received if you phrase your responses in a slightly impersonal way. If you wish to praise someone for playing a piano sonata well, saying "I've never heard that piece done so beautifully. I really heard it in a new way" may make the performer less uncomfortable than "Sarah, you really did that well. I didn't know you were that good." Such personal comments can imply, however subtly, "That was good, for *you*" when what you mean is "That was good." Effective feedback is message-oriented.[22]

Monitor your own feedback. If your feedback is not interpreted by the other person as you mean it, it serves no purpose. Check the effect you're making. You might have to repeat or clarify a feedback response. If Louise says, "I can never think of what to say to Alvin," and your response is "I know," it can either mean, "I know. I've noticed you never have anything to say" or it can mean, "I know. Alvin is hard to talk to." You must monitor your feedback to make sure you're being understood. Like any message, feedback can be blocked or distorted.

Concentrate on exchanging meaning. Finally, your feedback will be perceived more accurately and sent more accurately if both parties are committed to the honest exchange of meaning. Think about how to help the other person express ideas more effectively. You are more likely to provide constructive feedback if you are motivated by a sincere desire to enhance communication.

Effective communicators respond to others through listening and feedback. We should work to increase listening and feedback skills. Make your feedback supportive. Try to develop sensitivity to the feedback and listening of others. We will be using our listening and feedback skills to learn more about the process of communication; applying what we learn to our own behavior will help us grow. Just as listening and feedback are essential in human communication, so are the words that make up a good part of the message. The words—verbal communication—are the subject of the next chapter.

Notes

[1] Adapted from Lyman K. Steil, Larry L. Barker, and Kittie W. Watson, *Effective Listening: Key to Your Success* (New York: Random House, 1983), p. 3. Copyright © 1983 Random House, Inc. Used by permission.

[2] Andrew D. Wolvin and Carolyn Gwynn Coakley, *Listening* (Dubuque, Iowa: Wm. C. Brown Co., 1982), p. 4.

[3] Charles M. Kelly, "Empathic Listening," in *Readings in Speech Communication*, ed. Richard L. Weaver II (Dubuque, Iowa: Kendall/Hunt, 1985), pp. 33–39.

[4] Kelly, "Empathic Listening," pp. 33–35.

[5] Kelly, "Empathic Listening," p. 34.

[6] Wolvin and Coakley, *Listening*, p. 88.

[7] G. Egan, *Encounter: Group Processes for Interpersonal Growth* (Belmont, Calif.: Brooks/Cole, 1970), p. 248.

[8] Based on Robert L. Katz, *Empathy: Its Nature and Uses* (London: Collier-Macmillan Ltd., 1963), pp. 7–8. Katz's development of the four phases of the empathic process follows the outline provided by Theodor Reik, *Listening with the Third Ear* (New York: Farrar, Straus & Co., 1979).

[9] This phenomenon is called "EgoSpeak." Edmond G. Addeo and Robert E. Burger, *EgoSpeak* (New York: Bantam Books, 1973), p. xiii.

[10] The retention rate of orally communicated messages is approximately 50% immediately after the message is communicated and only 25% two months later. Ralph G. Nichols, "Do We Know How to Listen?" in *Communication: Concepts and Processes*, ed. Joseph A. DeVito (Englewood Cliffs, N.J.: Prentice-Hall, 1971), pp. 207–8.

[11] Larry L. Barker, *Listening Behavior* (Englewood Cliffs, N.J.: Prentice-Hall, 1971), p. 74.

[12] Barker, *Listening Behavior*, pp. 75–76.

[13] Barker, *Listening Behavior*, pp. 76–77.

[14] Norbert Wiener, one of the first persons to be concerned with feedback, defined it as "the property of being able to adjust future conduct by past experience." Norbert Wiener, *Cybernetics* (New York: John Wiley & Sons, 1948), p. 33, and Norbert Wiener, *The Human Use of Human Beings: Cybernetics and Society* (Boston: Houghton Mifflin, 1950). Also see discussion of the monitoring function of feedback in David K. Berlo, *The Process of Communication* (New York: Holt, Rinehart & Winston, 1960), p. 111.

[15] Arnold Tustin, "Feedback," in *Communication and Culture*, ed. Alfred G. Smith (New York: Holt, Rinehart & Winston, 1966), p. 325.

[16] Warren G. Bennis, et al., eds., *Interpersonal Dynamics: Essays and Readings on Human Interaction* (Homewood, Ill.: Dorsey Press, 1968), p. 214.

[17] William C. Schutz, *The Interpersonal Underworld* (Palo Alto, Calif.: Science and Behavior Books, 1966), p. 13.

[18] Harold J. Leavitt and Ronald A. H. Mueller, "Some Effects of Feedback on Communication," in *Interpersonal Communication: Survey and Studies*, ed. Dean Barnlund (Boston: Houghton Mifflin, 1968), pp. 251–59.

[19] See Wendell Johnson, *Your Most Enchanted Listener* (New York: Harper & Row, 1956), p. 174.

[20] See Thomas Gordon, *P.E.T.—Parent Effectiveness Training: The Tested New Way to Raise Responsible Children* (New York: New American Library, 1975), pp. 41–44.

[21] David W. Johnson, *Reaching Out: Interpersonal Effectiveness and Self-Actualization*, 2d ed. (Englewood Cliffs, N.J.: Prentice-Hall, 1981), pp. 150–55. These styles are also discussed in Thomas G. Banville, *How to Listen—How to Be Heard* (Chicago: Nelson-Hall, 1978), pp. 166–77.

[22] Barker, *Listening Behavior*, p. 124.

Further Reading

Mortimer J. Adler, *How to Speak; How to Listen* (New York: Macmillan Co., 1983). Adler includes several chapters that have direct relevance to this chapter. The first, "With the Mind's Ear," provides some rules for deliberative listening. In the second, "Writing While and After Listening," Adler makes numerous suggestions for effective listening. In addition, his chapters on "How to Make Conversation Profitable and Pleasurable" and "The Meeting of Minds" make valuable contributions. Useful and instructive information.

Madelyn Burley-Allen, *Listening: The Forgotten Skill* (New York: John Wiley & Sons, 1982). The author shows how effective listening can aid in professional and personal growth. Using examples, exercises, and drawings, she takes you step by step through a twelve-point program to acquire active, productive listening skills.

Suzette Haden Elgin, *The Last Word on the Gentle Art of Verbal Self-Defense* (New York: Prentice-Hall Press, 1987). A well-written trade book on language behavior. Elgin explains *syntonics*—"a system for putting human beings in tune with one another linguistically . . ."; Syntonics depends heavily on both effective listening and feedback, which she also discusses. A terrific book—just like her two preceding books on the same subject!

Ralph G. Nichols and Leonard A. Stevens, *Are You Listening?* (New York: McGraw-Hill Book Co., 1957). This is a classic, the first book devoted to "the science of listening." The authors show how inefficient listening is usually the result of poor habits of concentration; and how good listening habits, resulting in greater comprehension and retention, can be achieved with the aid of the simple exercises included in this book. A provocative, challenging book—even after 30 years!

Jerry Richardson and Joel Margulis, *The Magic of Rapport: How You Can Gain Personal Power in Any Situation* (San Francisco: Harbor Publishing, 1981). The authors treat four major elements: (1) rapport, (2) communication, (3) persuasion, and (4) resistance. They show how to pace other people and how to use the power of suggestion in Part One. Parts Two and Three are traditional. In Four, they offer ideas on how to prevent or contain resistance. This is a communication book for the lay person.

Lyman K. Steil, Larry L. Barker, and Kittie W. Watson, *Effective Listening: Key to Your Success* (Reading, Mass: Addison-Wesley Publishing Co., 1983). The authors offer a guide for improving knowledge, attitudes, and skills in the art of listening. They answer questions such as "What is the importance of listening?"; "What are the different purposes of listening?"; and "What are the various steps involved?" This is a complete, detailed treatment of the subject.

Lyman K. Steil, Joanne Summerfield, and George de Mare, *Listening—It Can Change Your Life: A Handbook for Scientists and Engineers* (New York: McGraw-Hill Book Co., 1983). The strength of this book is in the examples cited and "The Voices of Listeners" section at the back of the book based on interviews with eminent people. The authors deal with myths about listening, keys to effective listening, and habits of good listeners.

Carl H. Weaver, *Human Listening; Processes and Behavior* (Indianapolis: Bobbs-Merrill Co., 1972). This textbook proves that listening is a type of behavior difficult both to understand and to change. By doing the exercises provided, one can learn how to improve listening skills.

Florence I. Wolff, Nadine C. Marsnik, William S. Tacey, and Ralph G. Nichols, *Perceptive Listening* (New York: Holt, Rinehart & Winston, 1983). This is a comprehensive textbook on listening. The authors combine an explanation of current theory about the listening process with numerous research-based principles designed to guide the reader toward improvement. They emphasize both economy and enjoyment. A useful, practical, readable approach.

Andrew D. Wolvin and Carolyn Gwynn Coakley, *Listening* (Dubuque, Iowa: Wm. C. Brown Co., 1982). After treating the need for and the process of listening, the authors give individual treatment to appreciative, discriminative, comprehensive, therapeutic, and critical listening. This is a thorough, well-researched, well-documented—but readable—textbook. Each chapter begins with concepts and skills and ends with activities and extensive notes.

5

Creating Messages: Verbal Communication

Learning Objectives

When you have finished this chapter you should be able to:

- Explain the process of making and using words. How does it relate to the process of perception?
- List and explain the three energy transformations that occur when we use language.
- Describe the process of abstracting and the reasons we do it.
- Explain how words function as symbols. Be able to define these words or concepts: denotation, connotation, and levels of abstraction.
- Explain how levels of abstraction and the abstraction ladder relate to interpersonal communication.
- Describe the essential characteristics of powerful talk. Be able to list and explain the characteristics that identify communicators as powerless.
- Describe how gender influences language use. Explain why it is important to be cautious in applying generalizations about gender differences.
- Explain the purpose of fine tuning our language behavior. Show how the word *syntonics* relates to definitions of rhetoric.
- Understand the key to fine tuning messages. Explain what a perfectly fine-tuned message is like.
- Describe how you can improve your skills in language usage.

Words, words, words! We live in a sea of words. If we are not talking, we are reading or writing or listening to others talk.[1] So many words—so much talk—it's no wonder we take most of it for granted. From birth we are confronted with people making noises at us trying to get us to do this, believe that, buy this, or think about that. Even so, sometimes we feel that not much is being communicated. We rarely give the words themselves much thought.

Have you ever said something to someone and, in return, gotten an odd answer or no answer at all? You may have wondered, "What's wrong with me?" Words can be strange or, at least, can appear to be strange, but can you imagine a civilization without them? Their role and function in interpersonal communication are crucial. Understanding how language works will help us make sure we come across just the way we want to.

Think about the transactional nature of communication. In any communication transaction we are involved in constructing a mental image of the other person, just as he or she is constructing a mental image of us. We base all future communication with each other on these mental images. Our use of language, and especially the way we view each other's use of language, will affect how we construct these mental images. The more closely we can make the other person's mental image of us conform to the one we have of ourselves, the more effective our interpersonal communication will be. We use words to communicate ideas and describe feelings. We use them to reason and to transform experience into ideas and ideas into experience. Knowing how to use them well will increase our effectiveness in interpersonal communication.

In this chapter I will discuss language from the perspective of you, the language user. After a brief section on the process of producing words, I will discuss what words can and cannot do. Since the problem of abstract language is major, I will spend some time talking about how we can modify our use of words for more precise meaning. I will explore powerful and powerless talk and male/female language differences. Before suggesting specific things we can do to improve our language skills, I will discuss the need for fine tuning our language behavior.

Consider This

... Human language use will best be understood if viewed in its natural context as one of a set of channels available to humans to transmit and receive information.

—From *The Psychology of Language and Communication* by Andrew Ellis and Geoffrey Beattie, p. vii. Reprinted by permission of The Guilford Press.

Language: The Process of Producing Words

The process of producing words is a personal matter, just as the way we perceive is a personal matter. These processes help define the transactional nature of communication. That is, how we construct an image of the person with whom we are communicating depends on our perceptions of that person and also on the words we choose to use as we label and mentally describe that person. Through our perceptions and our choice of words, we create our own personal reality. Each of us does it differently because no two of us are alike.

The process of producing words goes on in our nervous system. It involves three types of energy transformations: (1) sensory input, (2) filtering, and (3) symbolic output, in that order.[2] (See Figure 5.1.) We can think of these in terms of the three processes of receiving, evaluating, and speaking.

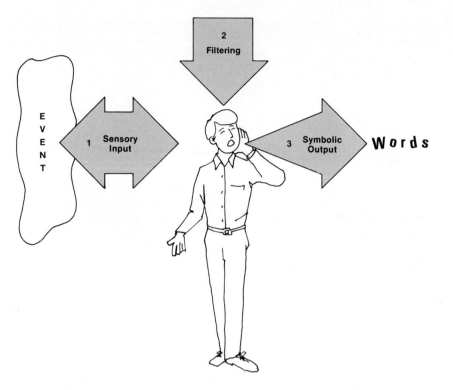

Figure 5.1
The process of produc-ing words.

The first energy transformation occurs at the point of contact between our sensory receptors (sight, sound, smell, taste, or touch) and an outside event. This contact may be made by our senses unaided; that is, by the naked eye, the naked ear, or the naked nose. It may be made by the senses aided; that is, by the eye aided by the lens or the ear aided by the sound amplifier.

The second energy transformation is in our nervous system. Here, we filter the sensory input. Some of the ways that information can be filtered were mentioned in our discussion of the perception sieve in Chapter 2. At this point we join the sensory input with whatever is going on in the nervous system at the time and anything else that is available to us to help us select, organize, and evaluate that input. This is a preverbal state of affairs.

In the third transformation we manage to symbolize (put into symbols) this preverbal state of affairs. We deliver this preverbal state of affairs in the form of a symbol. If language is the symbol system we're using, we use words.

But look what else is going on at each energy transformation point. Because we are affected by a broad barrage of stimuli, at each transformation point we must select details to pass on. We abstract (abridge or summarize) at each point so that fewer details are passed on than were taken in. Abstracting involves three processes: (1) *ignoring* many of the stimuli that

"*Verbally speaking . . .*"

Drawing by Frascino; © 1985 The New Yorker Magazine, Inc.

might be perceived, (2) *focusing* on a limited number of stimuli, and (3) *combining* and *rearranging* what is perceived into a meaningful pattern.[3] The sensory input is an abstraction of the event. The preverbal state of affairs is an abstraction of the sensory input. The symbol is an abstraction of the preverbal state of affairs.

Why do we abstract? At the point of contact between our sensory receptors and the event, we abstract because that is the way our receptors are constructed. Our eyes react only to a small part of the light spectrum just as our ears react only to a small part of the sound spectrum. In addition, there can be some impairment of the sensory functions which would cause greater abstraction.

There is another reason for abstracting, however. We have no choice! Even if we have all our sensory marbles and a powerful lens through which to view stimuli, our fate is that we sense the world only by the weak signal that comes to us through a tiny antenna atop a very small and insignificant tower. Of all the information that is available, we get but a small fraction. We can know our world only in part; thus, we come to know only an abstraction of it.

As if this first abstraction were not limited enough, we limit it further by filtering. How many filters we have, what kind they are, and how they are arranged vary from person to person. No two people have the same filtering system. We have mood filters, family filters, economic filters, doctrinal filters, ethnic filters, geographic filters—and the list goes on.

Take the mood filter, for example. Two people are watching a sunset. One has just learned that his mother is gravely ill. The other has just received a phone call from his girlfriend saying that she will marry him after all. Imagine the different perspectives each one will have on this sunset. The reports are likely to be dramatically different based on the mood filter alone.

Consider doctrinal filters. There are states' rights filters, local option filters, civil rights filters, citizenship responsibility filters, activist filters, Communist filters, Republican filters, Democratic filters, Buddhist filters, Baptist filters, atheist filters, black magic filters, optimistic filters, and pessimistic filters, and so on. People with different doctrines will make different reports of the same event. It isn't that some people lie and others tell the truth, although this certainly occurs; it is that people process sensory input through different filters.

When we reach the third transformation, where we symbolize the filtered preverbal state of affairs, we are dealing with a third-level abstraction. The sensory input was an abstract of the event, to begin with. The preverbal state of affairs was an abstract of that abstract. Now symbolizing is a third level of abstracting.

Words are *symbols:* they *stand for something other than what they are.* No symbol exactly or completely duplicates that which is being symbolized. It takes the place of or serves instead of that other level of experience—that which is being symbolized. And so the word is not the thing. A word is an abstraction of the thing. Thus, words—our verbal output—are incomplete because they are abstractions.

Have you ever tried to explain something to someone and realized that you could go on forever and still never completely describe it? You could talk about an experience all day, all week, all your life—and still find something that you hadn't already said about it. There is no one-to-one relationship between your words and what you use them to describe. A picture is said to be worth a thousand words. An experience may be worth a million!

Here is the point: When we talk, we are talking mainly about ourselves. Because of filtering and abstracting, it is our background of experience, our ignorance or knowledge, our anxieties and exasperations, our likes and dislikes, and our purposes and interests that come into play. No matter what else we may be talking about, we also are talking about ourselves. There is a good deal of us in whatever we say.

Not only are we giving others a highly personal account of reality, but our account is very incomplete as well. Physically, we are able to sense only part of what there is to sense. Perceptually, we are able to perceive only part

Consider This

Confucius told us long ago that the good society must begin with "the rectification of words." This has nothing to do with grammar, and everything to do with using the specific, concrete, accurate word to describe and define the tangible object, no more and no less. And we can only aim at this goal, but never achieve it, for no word fully expresses its referent.

—From "Strictly Personal" by Sydney J. Harris, *Toledo Blade*, December 9, 1983. By permission of NAL, Inc.

of what there is to perceive. And we filter and symbolize the part that remains in a system both limited in scope and faulty in structure. Thus, it is essential to be aware that our use of language is always personal, partial, and tentative—and always subject to revision.

There are several essential skills implicit in these observations. When we realize how restricted and inhibited we are in our use of symbols, we can:

- Make our observations as carefully as we can.
- Report our observations as carefully as we can.
- Discipline our generalizations as much as we can.
- Realize how much we don't know.
- Recognize that inner and outer space are different and are not to be confused.

When we recognize the problems we have with perception and the problems we have with language, it becomes clear that the transactional-communication process—dependent for accuracy on both perception and language use—is fraught with problems: basically, inaccuracies and incompleteness. We must be cautious, tentative, and careful as we construct our images of those with whom we communicate.

What Words Can and Cannot Do

If we see a series of stones lying across a stream, we know they will help us get to the other side. But our experience with such stones tells us that some of the stones may be loose or covered with slime and could cause us to slip. Like these stones, words can help us to reach our goals, or they can cause us to stumble and fall. Let's look at some characteristics of language that affect our interpersonal communication.[4]

When we talk to people we often assume too quickly that we are being understood. If we tell people we are going to put on some music, we probably don't think about whether they are expecting to hear the kind of music we intend to play—we just turn it on. But think about the word *music* and how many different interpretations there are of it. (See Figure 5.2.)

We depend on context and on nonverbal cues to give us the meaning of words. If we say we are going to put on some music, our friends may be able to predict from knowing our taste and from nonverbal cues (our mood) what we might play. But they have a good chance of being wrong. In our daily conversation we use about 2000 words. Of those 2000, the 500 we use most often have more than 14,000 dictionary definitions.[5] Think of the possiblities for confusion! The problem of figuring out what a person means

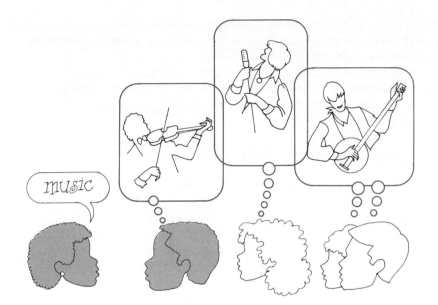

Figure 5.2
One word may have many different interpretations.

by a certain word is compounded by the fact that even dictionary meanings change, and new words are constantly being added to the language.

Denotative meanings.   The denotative meaning of a word is its dictionary definition. Dictionaries provide alternatives; we still must choose from those alternatives. The choice of what is "appropriate" or "inappropriate" is left to the user.

Some words have relatively stable meanings. If several people were to define a particular word special to their discipline, they would probably use about the same definition—an agreed-upon interpretation. To lawyers, the word *estoppel* has one precise, *denotative* meaning. Doctors would probably agree upon the definition of *myocardial infarction*. People in many disciplines depend on certain words having precise, unchanging meanings in order to carry on their work. There is little likelihood of confusion with denotative meanings because there is a direct relationship between the word and what it describes. Connotative meanings, on the other hand, depend a lot more than denotative meanings on our subjective thought processes.[6] (See Figure 5.3.)

Connotative meanings.   Dictionary definitions would probably not help our friends predict the kind of music we would play or what we mean by "music." But their experience with us and with music will give them a clue as to what we mean. If "music" connotes the same thing to us and to our friends, there's less chance of misunderstanding.

When we hear a word, the thoughts and feelings we have about that word and about the person using it determine what that word ultimately

Consider This

The belief that sitting down and talking will ensure mutual understanding and solve problems is based on the assumption that we can say what we mean, and that what we say will be understood as we mean it.

—Deborah Tannen, *That's Not What I Meant!* (New York: William Morrow & Co., 1986), p. 124.

means to us. This is the word's *connotative* meaning. Connotative meanings change with our experience. Just as we experience something different in every second of life that we live, so does everyone else. And no two of these experiences are identical! It's no wonder there are infinitely many connotations for every word we use. Figure 5.3 illustrates the process through which words may accumulate their connotative meanings.

If a word creates pretty much the same reaction in a majority of people, the word is said to have a general connotation. Actually, the more general the connotation of a word, the more likely that meaning will become the dictionary meaning, because most people will agree on what that word represents. The more general the connotation of a word, the less likely people are to misunderstand it.

Problems in interpersonal communication increase as we use words with many connotative meanings. Because these meanings are so tied to the particular feelings, thoughts, and ideas of other people, we have a bigger chance of being misunderstood when we use them. On the other hand,

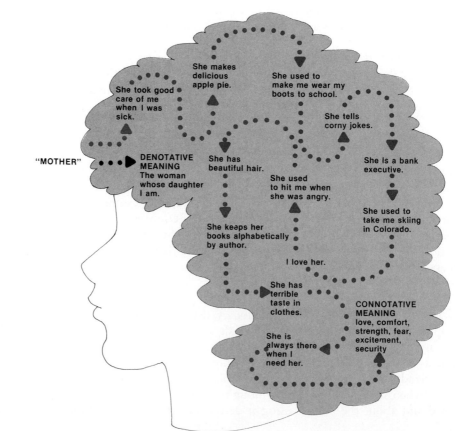

Figure 5.3
Connotative meanings may depend a great deal on the perceiver's experience.

richly connotative words give our language power. Note, for example, the differences between the following lists of words:

freedom	book
justice	piano
love	tree
liberty	teacher
music	fire

The words in the left column have many connotations; the words in the right column are more strictly denotative. "The teacher put the book on the piano" is an unambiguous statement. The sentence, "The love of freedom burns like a white flame in all of us" can be interpreted numerous ways.

What does all this have to do with our use of words? First, we should recognize that words evoke sometimes unpredictable reactions in others. We should try to anticipate the reactions of others to our words as much as we can. For example, if we are talking to an art major we may cause confusion or even produce a hostile response if we use the psychology-major jargon we have picked up. If we anticipate this negative reaction, we'll leave the jargon in the psychology classroom.

Second, most words have both denotative and connotative meanings, and we should recognize that these meanings vary from person to person. People will react to words according to the meaning *they* give them. An effective communicator tries to recognize different reactions and to adapt to them. Remember as you communicate that meanings do *not* reside in the words themselves. Meanings are in the minds of the people who use and hear the words. That is the essence of the transactional view of communication.

Consider This

Simplification is in! There is a growing need to simplify and clarify speech. Notice the following humorous directive on simplification:

Please be so kind as to proceed with previously agreed upon actions designated for simplification and normalization of communications. All further correspondence is to be, as herein outlined, constructed in a straightforward and demystified manner. The target goal of clear and unambiguous information transfer can only be ultimately achieved by embracing of terse, goal-oriented thinking with the fundamental precept of reducing excess verbiage. Compliance with this directive is to be construed as mandatory and it is to be punctually incorporated into your daily usage.

—Tal D. Bonham, "Growth-A-Gram," *Ohio Baptist Messenger*, August 9, 1984. Reprinted by permission.

Coping with Levels of Abstraction

In this section, the words we use will be examined specifically. This is the third energy transformation, that of symbolic output. Words, you will recall, are an abstraction of the things they represent. Also, words vary in their degree of abstraction.[7] (See Figure 5.4.) The word *cow* means different things to different people. Think of experiences you have had with cows. It is considered a low level of abstraction when we perceive not the word *cow*

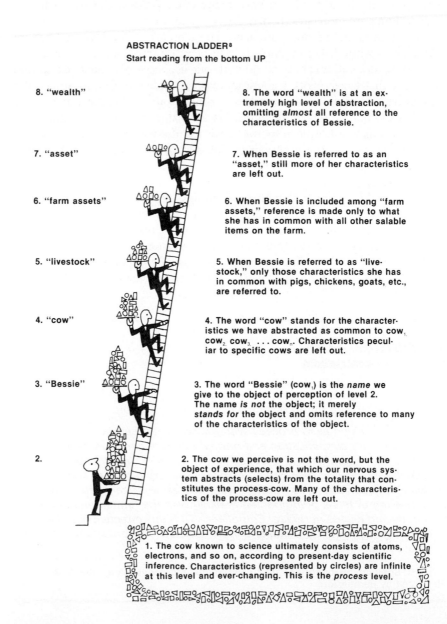

ABSTRACTION LADDER[8]
Start reading from the bottom UP

8. "wealth"

8. The word "wealth" is at an extremely high level of abstraction, omitting *almost* all reference to the characteristics of Bessie.

7. "asset"

7. When Bessie is referred to as an "asset," still more of her characteristics are left out.

6. "farm assets"

6. When Bessie is included among "farm assets," reference is made only to what she has in common with all other salable items on the farm.

5. "livestock"

5. When Bessie is referred to as "livestock," only those characteristics she has in common with pigs, chickens, goats, etc., are referred to.

4. "cow"

4. The word "cow" stands for the characteristics we have abstracted as common to cow_1, cow_2, cow_3, ... cow_n. Characteristics peculiar to specific cows are left out.

3. "Bessie"

3. The word "Bessie" (cow_1) is the *name* we give to the object of perception of level 2. The name *is not* the object; it merely *stands for* the object and omits reference to many of the characteristics of the object.

2.

2. The cow we perceive is not the word, but the object of experience, that which our nervous system abstracts (selects) from the totality that constitutes the process-cow. Many of the characteristics of the process-cow are left out.

1. The cow known to science ultimately consists of atoms, electrons, and so on, according to present-day scientific inference. Characteristics (represented by circles) are infinite at this level and ever-changing. This is the *process* level.

Figure 5.4

but the cow itself as an object of our experiences. If we think of *Bessie*, a particular cow, the name of this cow stands for one cow and no other. Or we may think of cows in general, all the animals that have the characteristics common to cows. This is a higher level of abstraction. At a higher level yet, we might think of *cow* as part of the broader category of *livestock*. Going higher up the abstraction ladder, Bessie may be thought of as a *farm asset*, as an *asset*, or as *wealth*.

You can see how these references to the word *cow* have become more and more abstract. At each higher level of abstraction, more items could be included in the category. The more that can be included in a category, the less possible it is for someone to know exactly what we are talking about.

We may have been in conversations where different levels of abstraction were at work without our being aware of it. We can see from the abstraction ladder how easy it would be, when dealing with something specific, to jump to a higher level and avoid answering or responding to the specific issue. If someone asked us, "What do you think of Dr. Smith as a lecturer?" we could say, "I do not like Dr. Smith's lecturing," which would be answering at the same level of abstraction. But if we think such a commitment is risky, we might say, "Lecturers just do not seem to care about the students in their audiences." By doing that, we move to a higher level of abstraction. If we say, "Teachers at this institution just do not care any more," we go to a higher level. Saying "Education has sure gone to pot" is even more abstract.

Consider This

Notice how this "thing" is symbolized and regarded at several different levels of abstraction in this illustration by the poet e.e. cummings.

Here is a thing.

To one somebody, this 'thing' is a totally flourishing universal joyous particular happening deep amazing miraculous indivisible being.

To another somebody, this 'same thing' means something which, if sawed in two at the base, will tell you how old it is.

To somebody else, this 'selfsame' thing doesn't exist because there isn't a thunderstorm, but if there were a thunderstorm, this 'selfsame thing' would merely exist as something to be especially avoided.

For a fourth somebody, this 'very selfsame' thing, properly maltreated, represents something called 'lumber,' which, improperly maltreated, represents something else called 'money,' which represents something else called (more likely than not) 'dear.'

—From George G. Firmage, ed. *e.e. cummings: A Miscellany* (Cambridge, Mass.: Harvard University Press, 1957), p. 12. Reprinted by permission of Harvard University Press.

Consider This

Educational Jargon Phrase Indicator

1	2	3
perceptual	maturation	concept
professional	guidance	process
environmental	creative	articulation
instructional	relationship	philosophy
homogeneous	motoric	activity
developmental	culture	resource
sequential	orientation	curriculum
individualized	cognitive	approach
exceptional	accelerated	adjustment
socialized	motivation	interface

To use the indicator I selected at random one word from the first list, one from the second, and one from the third. This produced as many phrases as I needed. By sprinkling a few common Anglo-Saxon words among these phrases I was able to quickly compose answers to questions, speeches, letters to government agencies, and so forth.

—Excerpt from p. 129 in *The Peter Prescription* by Laurence J. Peter. Copyright © 1972 by Laurence J. Peter. By permission of William Morrow and Company, Inc.

Teachers and politicians often try to avoid difficult questions by escaping to a higher level of abstraction when pressed on a specific issue.

As we escape to a higher level, we depend more on the connotative meanings of words than on the denotative meanings. Moving up the abstraction ladder causes the meanings of words to be less directly related to the thing they represent and more dependent on the perceiver of the word. If we actively work to keep our language at a low level of abstraction, there's much less chance for ambiguity and misunderstanding.

There are always some teachers who deal only in principles and theories and do not tie these abstractions to concrete reality. When we ask, "What does that have to do with me?" or "How can I apply that in my life?" we are asking to have the level of meaning brought down the abstraction ladder. We are asking for concrete particulars so that we can make sense out of the abstract principles.

Usually when we talk to people we go continually up and down the abstraction ladder. We adapt our words to each other's experiences. Knowing that certain words are more abstract than others will help us stay flexible. Words like *love* and *beauty* and *truth* are highly abstract and open to the possibility of confusion and error.

Giving Power to Your Words[9]

Powerful talk is straightforward and to the point. It causes people to perceive communicators as having high power and dominance. Powerless talk is tentative and uncertain, characterizing communicators as powerless and submissive. It is important to understand these differences when you want your interpersonal communication to have impact. Powerful talk has been shown to benefit communicators in such widely varying situations as a job interview,[10] a courtroom witness box,[11] a small group,[12] and a crisis intervention dialogue.[13] One would expect powerful talk to make a difference whenever one wanted to reveal assertiveness, take a stand on an issue, or gain compliance (persuade others to do what you request). Because researchers have devoted their attention to defining the types and effects of powerless talk, more powerless forms have been identified. It is useful to know that communicators are often perceived as powerful or powerless solely on the basis of their language choices.[14] Thus, knowing which features to *avoid* will help give power to your speech. According to recent speech-communication research, the following characteristics type communicators as powerless:[15]

- hedges/qualifiers. Hedges such as "kinda," "I think," and "I guess" qualify statements by detracting from their certainty and weakening their impact.
- hesitation forms. When communicators use "uh," "ah," "well," and "um" (all but "well" are called vocalized pauses), they are not being straightforward and direct.[16]

- "you knows." Heard often in informal conversation, this expression is often used for emphasis, and yet, similar to the hesitation forms, "you knows" contribute to perceptions of powerlessness.[17]
- tag questions. Tag questions make declarative sentences less forceful. "Sure is cold in here, isn't it?" has less impact than "It sure is cold in here."[18]
- deictic phrases. (Deictic means pointing out or proving by showing.) "Over here" and "over there" are deictic phrases. "That woman over there looks like a teacher of mine."[19] These expressions are rated as powerless because they have been linked to perceptions of low status in courtroom situations.[20]
- disclaimers. Disclaimers are "introductory expressions that excuse, explain, or request understanding or forbearance."[21] "Don't get me wrong, but . . ." is one form and "I know this sounds crazy, but . . ." is another. Such phrases indicate uncertainty and lack of commitment to a position.[22]

Powerless talk may have direct, negative effects of which the communicator is completely unaware. It is important to recognize the features that characterize talk as powerless and to eliminate them from our communications because powerless communicators have lower credibility, appear less attractive, and may be less persuasive.[23]

Since meanings are in people's heads and *not* in words, you need to monitor your language so that the impressions others have of you are exactly the impressions *you* desire them to have. Powerless talk may be appropriate in some situations; however, if you are trying to have a positive impact, you need to be aware of your language usage. Awareness and monitoring are often the first steps toward control and increased effectiveness.

Try This

Begin monitoring your communication behavior. How often do *you* use powerless talk in your communications? Is it a natural part of your communication habits? The questions that follow are based on the characteristics of powerless talk:

1. Do you use hedges/qualifiers?
2. How often do you use hesitation forms?
3. Do you incorporate "you know" into your talk?
4. How often do you use tag questions?
5. Do you use deictic phrases?
6. What kind of disclaimers do you use as introductory expressions?

Understanding Gender Differences in Language Use

The study of male/female differences in language use is relatively new. One of the first studies in the area—just over 30 years ago—discovered differences in the way males and females spontaneously described interesting or dramatic life experiences.[24] Since then a number of researchers have demonstrated that gender differences exist in a variety of communication forms. These include spoken monologues[25] and written essays,[26] as well as dyadic and small-group interactions.[27] In addition, a number of researchers have shown that differences in language use between boys and girls appear as early as age 4.[28]

    Why is it important to be aware of these differences? There are several answers.

Why Look at the Differences?

First, it probably confirms something that you may have suspected all along. You communicate differently than do members of the opposite sex!

    Second, knowing that your language and that of most members of the opposite sex differ significantly, is one more piece of information that helps you understand others. It's like having one more piece of the puzzle! Language is one means of sharing your perceptions with others as well as giving them an impression of yourself. Thus, the language choices you make are likely to affect how other people perceive you and your world. Knowing that certain differences exist simply because you are male or female can add to your understanding of how and why people make the language choices they do.

    Third, increased understanding is likely to bring increased empathy. If I know, for example, that friends or relationship partners are expressing themselves the way they are *because* that is the way many men or women do, it is easier for me to be supportive and accepting rather than defensive or unaccepting. We often tend to be quick to criticize someone who doesn't do—or say—something the way we would have.

    Fourth, with greater understanding and empathy, communication is likely to improve. No, there is no guarantee that communication will improve if understanding and empathy increase, but it appears likely!

    When you read the sections that follow, notice how males and females tend to complement each other's behavior. That is, one supplies a quality or feature that is not available through the other. I have found this an especially interesting and valuable feature of married life. My wife and I tend to approach situations, people, and events in a slightly different manner. Each of us provides a perspective that, taken together, offers a more complete picture of what is under consideration. Thus, when we are communicating we are being nourished and enriched in unique ways.

What Are the Distinguishing Language Features?

Language features that tend to distinguish the discourse of male communicators suggest "a relatively egocentric orientation (use of *first person singular pronouns*), a focus on the present as opposed to the past or the future (*present tense verbs, progressive verbs*), an active posture (*active voice verbs*), a low level of concern with formal linguistic standards (*grammatical errors*), and a high level of concern with holding the floor . . . while planning utterances (*vocalized pauses*)."[29]

Language features that tend to distinguish female communicators suggest "a style that might be described as relatively complex (*mean length of sentence, prepositional phrases*) and literate or formal (*adverbials beginning sentence, rhetorical questions*). Their frequent use of fillers (which some investigators have labeled *hedges* . . .) and *prepositions* indicate a relatively high degree of tentativeness or uncertainty, although the latter variable could also be used out of politeness or interpersonal sensitivity. . . . Their relatively frequent use of *negations*, or statements of what something is not rather than what it is . . . similarly indicates a less assertive stance. Their comparatively large number of *references to emotion* suggests an affective orientation that is stereotypically female,[30] and their frequent use of *intensive adverbs* may connote relatively low social power."[31]

Linguist Robin Lakoff of the University of California, Berkeley, along with other researchers, has pointed out some of the distinctive characteristics of women's speech.[32] Notice, here, the similarities between "women talk" and "powerless talk." This could be because women have traditionally occupied subordinate positions in our society. Suzette Haden Elgin, in her book on *The Last Word on the Gentle Art of Verbal Self-Defense* (see pages 17–20), says "So many women are subordinate in so many situations that women spend a great deal of their time following the rules for the subordinate, while men spend most of *their* time following the rules for the dominant."

Consider This

Linguist Sally McConnell-Ginet of Cornell University urges women to adopt a conversational style that doesn't sacrifice sensitivity but "nevertheless doesn't make you sound as if you have less commitment to your beliefs than you have." The issue, she adds, is not just how women should change the way they speak, but how men should change the way they listen.

—From "Girl Talk, Guy Talk" by Alfie Kohn in *Psychology Today, 22* (February 1988): 66. Copyright © 1988 by Alfie Kohn. Reprinted by permission of the author.

Lakoff states that women ask more questions, make statements in a questioning tone ("I was walking near that, um, new construction site?"); use more tag questions (adding a brief question at the end of a sentence like "don't you think?"); use more lead-off questions ("Hey, y'know what?") to ensure listeners' attention; and use more hedges or qualifiers ("kinda") and intensifiers ("really") to add double force to make sure listeners understand what they mean.

Why Be Cautious in Applying These Generalizations?

Several cautions need to be expressed with reference to the differences in male and female language. First, gender differences in language use vary with time and place. Some features that distinguish male from female communicators in one study do not distinguish them in another study. This suggests that caution needs to be exercised in making generalizations.

Second, it seems likely that culture is a general determinant of the nature and amount of fluctuation in the distinctions between male and female talk. That is, in some communities there is more separation of the genders; in others there is less. Even this, however, is a complex issue. One might think, for example, that "modernity" would be a factor. That is, "modern" males and females would show less distinctions in their language. But "modern" males and females in one study "were perfectly distinguishable on the basis of their language"![33]

A third factor likely to affect the language differentiating males from females is individual differences. Just because one group of males or females reveals these differences does not mean that all males or females from that group do. It is easy to get caught in the trap of generalizing from the group to the individual.

A fourth factor is the context in which the differences occur. Some contexts promote group differences whereas others minimize them. Situations, for example, in which one sex may be operating in a context that is usually or predominantly occupied by the other sex may promote the differences. It could occur over lunch when a group of truck drivers, only one of whom is female, are conversing; or in a hospital hallway where a group of nurses, only one of whom is male, are discussing various duties. In groups where the mix of males and females is more equal, or where both sexes are normally represented equally, language differences may be less likely to occur.

Fifth, it should be pointed out that the differences outlined here represent generalizations. All are not true for everyone; but even more important, just because one difference occurs, or is true, does not mean the others necessarily occur, or are true.

Finally, no value judgment is intended. That is, one set of language choices is not necessarily better than another. (It sometimes is for a specific individual operating in a specific context!) But a group of characteristics is just that: a group of characteristics. They are presented here for the purpose of enhancing understanding, fostering empathy, and improving communication.

Fine Tuning Our Language Behavior

We've looked at the process of producing words; we've looked at what words can and cannot do; we've looked at powerful and powerless talk; and we've looked at male/female language differences. It seems clear that using language effectively presents difficulties and challenges. The way we meet these difficulties and challenges is likely to determine others' impressions of us, and yet it is likely to be personal and unique as well. Although there are specific suggestions for improving our skills in language in the next section, I first want to discuss a framework for implementing verbal skills. This framework involves the need for and process of "fine tuning" and making adjustments to our conversational partners. Elgin calls this process *syntonics*, an idea that gains its strength from its reliance on the transactional-communication perspective.

Syntonics, according to Elgin, is "a system for putting human beings in tune with one another linguistically [through their language usage] so that they are able to communicate with maximum efficiency and effectiveness and satisfaction."[34] Indeed, this definition resembles one of the broadest definitions of rhetoric, as the art by which a discourse is adapted to its end. Marie Hochmuth Nichols, a writer on rhetoric, sharpened this definition somewhat when she wrote that rhetoric is "a means of so ordering discourse as to produce an effect on the listener or reader." Kenneth Burke, one of our discipline's legends in rhetoric, defined it as "the use of language as a symbolic means of inducing cooperation in beings that by nature respond

to symbols." Aristotle's definition of rhetoric focuses most sharply on the specific kind of verbal activity that Elgin is talking about: "the faculty of discovering all the available means of persuasion in any given situation."[35] The field of speech communication has a rich heritage of writers and researchers who have addressed the need for communicators to fine tune their messages for particular listeners.

The key to fine tuning a message is adjustment: the willingness of both parties to make every effort to adjust to the other to maximize their communication. Obviously, this requires *both* effective listening and feedback—making adjustments based on the information we get and our reactions to that information.

One way to think of "adjustment" would be to think of a perfectly tuned situation. Pretend you want to tune the A string on your guitar to the A of a pitch pipe. You pluck the guitar string and listen, then you blow into the A slot of the pitch pipe and listen. You compare the two. If the pitch pipe sounds higher, you tighten the A string; if it sounds lower, you loosen the string. You continue this until you hear no difference between the two sounds. This is perfect tuning because you have an exact target to match. It is exact because it can be measured by scientific instruments. If it vibrates at 440 cycles per second, it is correct.

The goal in the situation just described is to detect the match between the pitch pipe and the string. One task humans are good at is comparing things, detecting similarities and differences, and making adjustments until they are perceived the same. But can we compare this situation with one in which the two items being compared are people using language? After all, language transactions:

- cannot be measured scientifically.
- do not follow orderly steps.
- reveal little or no control over the responses of the other.
- allow little or no control over the number of chances you have to speak.
- give little or no control over the number of opportunities you have to observe the other's behavior.
- do not guarantee predictable responses.
- are a two-way process in which both people are adjusting to each other.

But do not be deterred. People are *not* at the mercy of totally random, unstructured, unpredictable events and occurrences. You *can* detect a mismatch between your language behavior and that of another person. Rapport, symmetry, synchrony, agreement, harmony, and congruence—all synonyms for success—*can* be achieved.

The basic concept of fine tuning involves an overall change in focus. When we listen to someone else, we often ask ourselves, "What's in this for *me?*" "What am I going to say when he/she stops talking?" or "When will he/she give me a chance to say something?" This self-centered approach

Consider This

When two radio sets are so well adjusted with respect to each other that they can be used to transmit information effectively and efficiently, they are said to be *syntonic.* The word comes from ancient music theory, and it has to do with being in tune. The first syllable, *syn-,* specifies that it means not just "in tune" but "in tune *with.*" And that's very important, because it isn't possible for something to be syntonic in isolation. Even if one of a pair of shortwave radios is taken as the base, and all adjustments are made to the other set, you can't find out if either one is syntonic without turning on both and trying to use them together. *Being syntonic is an interactive matter.*

—From *The Last Word on the Gentle Art of Verbal Self-Defense* by Suzette Haden Elgin. Reprinted by permission of the author.

distracts us from concentrating on *what* the other person is saying. Fine tuning requires understanding *what* the other person is saying. This can be accomplished in a two-fold approach: (1) you assume that what is being said is true, and (2) you try to imagine and discover what it is true of.[36] You may not like the reality in which the statements are true, but nothing obliges you to live in that reality. This is simply a framework for getting yourself in tune with the signal provided by your listener's reactions.

Fine tuning does *not* mean accepting or believing the content. It means trying to avoid a negative reaction to yourself as a communicator in order to avoid a negative reaction to your message.[37] This is why adjustment is so important. Think of it this way: if *we* are rejected, whatever we are saying becomes superfluous and meaningless.

Fine tuning and adjustment provide both a framework and a goal. The framework is transactional communication: people communicating *with* each other. But fine tuning is a goal as well because we know that a perfect match can never be achieved. The better the tuning that takes place, however, the more likely the communication will be efficient, effective, and satisfying. Keep the concept of fine tuning in mind as you consider the following skills for improving your language use.

Improving Skills in Language

A word is simply a vehicle we use to produce a certain response in another person. If our words do not accomplish their mission, we say there is a breakdown in communication. There is no guarantee that our language will produce the responses we want even if we apply all the suggestions given here. Interpersonal communication can never be perfect. But learning language skills can help us move closer to the goal of effective, efficient communication. It will increase the chances for our success as communicators.

Make the Message Complete

Because there are so many ways for words to be misinterpreted, you must try to give listeners as much information as possible about your ideas, experiences, feelings, and perceptions. There should be enough information so the other person can understand your frame of reference. But don't go too far! Too much information can create a negative effect. You are very likely to bore or overwhelm your listener if you give more details than are necessary or manageable.

Your message will be more complete if you repeat the message with some variation; that is, if you add details to the original message that make it more accurate. If the listener does not "get it" one way, he or she will have another chance the second time with the added information. To simply restate a misunderstood word or phrase in precisely the same way does not serve the listener's purposes and perpetuates confusion. What you want to make sure of is that your message is as complete and "on the mark" as possible.

Remember that Meanings Are in People

If you're going to use abstract language, it's important to monitor the reception of your messages to see that they are getting through. It often helps to move to a lower level of abstraction. Remember that as you talk you tend to project meanings into words just as much as your listener does. These projections are the result of your own experiences. The higher the level of abstraction, the more you must deal with your own and your listeners' connotations. If you remember that meanings are in people, not in words, you'll have a better chance of avoiding error and confusion. What someone brings to a word is usually more important than the word itself.

Stereotyping can also create breakdowns. Developing a sensitivity to labeling will help you avoid some of it. More important, it will help you to be conscious of labels used by others. You can't control what other people think when they either use stereotypes themselves or hear yours. But rather than take a chance that you hold the same stereotypes, you should try to avoid generalizations. Be specific and concrete instead.

It is impossible to know everything about anything. The mental picture we get of this world is incomplete; no matter how we describe the world, there will be distortion. To say that we "know all that" or that we "understand completely" is not recognizing that our picture of reality is partial. Too often we operate as if we know all the facts, and what's more, as if others see the facts as we do.

Talk the Same Language

If you can comfortably and naturally use words, including slang and jargon, that your listener understands, so much the better. If you adapt your language to the listener, very specifically, you show concern for him or her—an attempt at genuine communication to reach honest understanding. It is helpful to remember that fine tuning is a two-way process of accommodation and adjustment. To litter your speech with fancy words, "cute" phrases, or inappropriate slang will do little to help create understanding (and can make you look ridiculous and phony).

There is nothing "wrong" with any word that you have in your vocabulary or that appears in any dictionary. *Words are wrong only if they are used inappropriately.* You might not talk to your roommate as you do to your parents; the language you use with your roommate may be inappropriate for your parents. You may have all kinds of names and profanities to describe a teacher who seems to be doing you in, but you use them with your friends or classmates, not with the teacher. It would serve a negative purpose to use abusive language with the teacher; it would be "wrong" in that context.

To use different language in different contexts and with different people is not necessarily deceptive or hypocritical. Some language may be appropriate for a casual party with a group of friends, other language is better suited for dinner with one's future mother-in-law. Hypocrisy and deceit *do* result from using language that is not our own, language that reflects character or beliefs and principles that we do not really possess. We are being hypocritical when we try to appear as we are not or try to present a facade, when we are no longer adapting our language to the context in an honest manner. It is deceptive to manipulate others by using language that misrepresents who we really are.

Be Flexible

Stereotyping paints an unrealistically black-or-white world because things either fit our categories or they do not. If you say, "Teachers are too tough," meaning *all* teachers are too tough, you haven't allowed for variations among teachers. If you think in terms of what is unique to a person or a situation, your language will become more accurate and flexible.

You increase your flexibility if you avoid extreme language. If you say, "I am totally happy," you allow no room for increased happiness. Happiness is seldom total, just as success and failure most often occur in degrees. Saying "I am a complete failure" is a rigid, inflexible response.

True, some things *are* either-or, such as whether a person is employed or not, whether we are here or somewhere else, or whether or not there is another person in the room with us right now. We can describe these things in definite terms. But generally we tend to be too rigid rather than too flexible in our use of language. Rigidity makes adjustment difficult.

It's a good idea to think in terms of *sometimes, possibly, normally,* and *now and then.* Such words as *always, never, all,* and *none* can cause problems. "Allness" language makes us tend to think in set, rigid patterns. And in doing so, not only do we fail to distinguish what is unique in each case, but we do not allow for change.

Get Others Involved

If you assume that your communication has a good chance of being *un*successful and if you accept the fact that misunderstanding is *likely* to occur, you will be more cautious in your use of words. It will help if you can get others to share in your frame of reference. It is very easy to overwhelm another person with a verbal barrage and not realize you have caused that person to withdraw or become defensive. Saying "Do you understand?" or "You *do* see what I mean?" can seem accusatory or severe. But asking "Am I making sense?" or, simply, "What do you think?" involves the listener and can help you find out whether you really have been understood.

Tie Your Impressions Down

You have probably met people who are immune to new information. They continue to vote by party label, view all "baseball players" or "Harvard graduates" as exactly alike, and regard all "mothers" as sacred. You may have a friend like one of mine. Once, simply to be polite, I said something nice about a piece of music he was playing. Now, despite all my negative comments since then about that kind of music, he still plays it whenever I'm around. Can I convince him that I really don't like it at all? Never!

But how do *you* prevent yourself from getting in such intellectual blind alleys? Or, when you discover you are already in one, how do you get out?

First, specifically what is the blind alley? It occurs when you refer to one particular situation as if it represents *all* such situations. Hayakawa gives examples such as "Business is business," "Boys will be boys," and "Republicans are Republicans" to show this kind of thinking.[38] How might this look in the context of college life?

"I don't think you need to go in to talk to Professor Jones. He won't remember that he said it anyway."

"Yeah, I suppose not. Just another absent-minded professor."

The final assertion, "Just another absent-minded professor," may look like a simple statement of fact, but it is not. It is a directive. In effect, it says, "Let us treat this transaction with complete disregard for Professor Jones's personal qualities as a human being." Statements like "Blondes have more fun," "Athletes are dumb," and "Used-car salespeople are fast-talking crooks" do the same thing. They are directives that tell us to classify a person in a given way so that we feel or act toward the person or event in the way suggested by the terms of the classification.

The simple technique for preventing such directives from having a harmful effect on our thinking is **indexing** or **dating.** Korzybski suggested the idea of indexing.[39] He said we should add "index numbers" to our terms; for example, cow_1, cow_2, cow_3, . . . The terms of classification, like *cow*, tell us what the individuals of the class have in common; the index numbers remind us of the characteristics left out. The rule that follows is that cow_1 is not cow_2; boy_1 is not boy_2; and $professor_1$ is not $professor_2$.

Dates can be substituted for index numbers as a reminder that no word ever has exactly the same meaning twice. Then Professor $Jones_{1987}$ is not Professor $Jones_{1988}$, and Professor $Jones_{1988}$ is not Professor $Jones_{1989}$. The point of all this is to help you remember to consider the facts of each particular thing, person, or place. If you leap to conclusions which you might later have cause to regret, just remember cow_1 is not cow_2; and cow_2 is not cow_3.[40]

Consider This

Semanticists [specialists in the study of meaning in language] are sometimes thought to desire complete honesty of expression, directness, and "no beating around the bush." An understanding of the many purposes of communication should dispel that view. We use language for too many purposes and find ourselves forced to make some comment in too many difficult situations to hold such a view. Simple friendship, not to mention diplomacy and tact, prohibits us from always saying what we are thinking.

—John C. Condon, Jr., *Semantics and Communication,* 3d ed. (New York: Macmillan Publishing Company, 1985), pp. 163–64.

Using words well is not simple. Trying to put our finger on the problems of using words is hard because so much depends on the users of the words and the contexts in which they are used. And we have to use words even to describe the problems of using words! There's no way around it. Even if we understood all about users and contexts, we wouldn't have all the answers, because things would change. Words, we have seen, are flexible in meaning. Our effectiveness in using them depends upon understanding how they can vary depending on different communication contexts. In this chapter I have tried to make it clear that as humans we belong to a peculiarly symbol-making, symbol-using, symbol-misusing species.

Verbal communication has a tremendous impact on interpersonal relationships. Verbalizing our feelings can help us feel better about ourselves and can strengthen our interpersonal interactions. Although verbal communication is important, it makes up only a fraction of our total communication with others. We communicate at least as much through nonverbal means as through verbal means, as we will see in the next chapter.

Notes

[1] Stuart Chase, *The Power of Words* (New York: Harcourt Brace Jovanovich, 1954), p. 3.

[2] Based on Wendell Johnson and Dorothy Moeller, *Living with Change: The Semantics of Coping* (New York: Harper & Row, 1972), pp. 74–79.

[3] John C. Condon, Jr., *Semantics and Communication*, 3d ed. (New York: Macmillan Publishing Co., 1985), p. 25.

[4] For their ideas on characteristics of language, see Kim Giffin and Bobby R. Patton, *Fundamentals of Interpersonal Communication*, 2d ed. (New York: Harper & Row, 1976), pp. 161–72.

[5] Giffin and Patton, *Fundamentals*, p. 161.

[6] C. K. Ogden and I. A. Richards, *The Meaning of Meaning* (New York: Harcourt Brace Jovanovich, 1953).

[7] For the discussion on levels of abstraction I am indebted to S. I. Hayakawa, *Language in Thought and Action*, 4th ed. (New York: Harcourt Brace Jovanovich, 1978), pp. 153–66.

[8] From *Language in Thought and Action*, 4th ed., by S. I. Hayakawa, copyright © 1978 by Harcourt Brace Jovanovich, Inc. Reproduced by permission of the publisher. This "Abstraction Ladder" is based on a diagram originated by Alfred Korzybski to explain the process of abstracting. See Alfred Korzybski, *Science and Sanity: An Introduction to Non-Aristotelian Systems and General Semantics* (Lancaster, Pa.: Science Press Printing Co., 1933), especially Chapter 25.

[9] For the discussion of powerful and powerless talk I am indebted to Craig E. Johnson, "An Introduction to Powerful and Powerless Talk in the Classroom," *Communication Education*, 36 (April 1987): pp. 167–72.

[10] J. Bradac and A. Mulac, "A Molecular View of Powerful and Powerless Speech Styles: Attributional Consequences of Specific Language Features and Communicator Intentions," *Communication Monographs*, 51 (1984): pp. 307–19.

[11] B. Erickson, E. Lind, A. Johnson, and W. O'Barr, "Speech Style and Impression Formation in a Court Setting: The Effects of 'Powerful' and 'Powerless' Speech,"

Journal of Experimental Social Psychology, 14 (1978): pp. 266–79; J. Conley, W. O'Barr, and E. A. Lind, "The Power of Language: Presentational Styles in the Courtroom," *Duke Law Journal* (1978): pp. 1375–99; E. A. Lind and W. O'Barr, "The Social Significance of Speech in the Courtroom." In H. Giles and R. St. Clair (eds.), *Language and Social Psychology* (College Park, Md: University of Maryland Press, 1979), pp. 66–87; W. M. O'Barr, *Linguistic Evidence: Language, Power, and Strategy in the Courtroom* (New York: Academic Press, 1982).

[12] P. H. Bradley, "The Folk-Linguistics of Women's Speech: An Empirical Examination," *Communication Monographs*, 48 (1981): pp. 73–90.

[13] J. Bradac and A. Mulac, "Attributional Consequences of Powerful and Powerless Speech Styles in a Crisis-Intervention Context," *Journal of Language and Social Psychology*, 3 (1984): pp. 1-19.

[14] Bradac and Mulac, "A Molecular View," pp. 307–19.

[15] These features are based on Johnson's review of the powerful-powerless talk literature. See Craig E. Johnson, "An Introduction," pp. 167–72.

[16] Bradac and Mulac, "A Molecular View," pp. 307–19; Erickson, Lind, Johnson, and O'Barr, "Impression Formation in a Court Setting," pp. 266–79; A. Siegman and B. Pope, "Effects of Question Specificity and Anxiety-Producing Messages on Verbal Fluency in the Initial Interview," *Journal of Personality and Social Psychology*, 2 (1965): pp. 522–30.

[17] S. L. Ragan, "A Conversational Analysis of Alignment Talk in Job Interviews." In R. Bostrom (ed.), *Communication Yearbook*, 7 (Beverly Hills, Calif.: Sage, 1983) pp. 502–16; C. Johnson, "Powerful and Powerless Forms of Talk, Status, Credibility, and Financial Awards" (Doctoral Dissertation, University of Denver). *Dissertation Abstracts International.* In publication.

[18] See C. L. Berryman and J. R. Wilcox, "Attitudes Toward Male and Female Speech: Experiments of the Effects of Sex-Typical Language," *Western Journal of Speech Communication*, 44 (1980): pp. 50–59; N. Newcombe and D. B. Arnkoff, "Effects of Speech Style and Sex of Speaker on Person Perception," *Journal of Personality and Social Psychology*, 37 (1979): pp. 1293–1303; D. Siegler and R. Siegler, "Stereotypes of Males' and Females' Speech," *Psychological Reports*, 39 (1976): pp. 167–70.

[19] Bradac and Mulac, "A Molecular View," p. 310; Erickson, Lind, Johnson, and O'Barr, "Impression Formation in a Court Setting," pp. 266–79.

[20] Erickson, Lind, Johnson, and O'Barr, "Impression Formation in a Court Setting," pp. 266–79.

[21] Bradley, "Folk-Linguistics," pp. 73–90; B. W. Eakins and R. G. Eakins, *Sex Differences in Human Communication* (Boston: Houghton Mifflin, 1978), p. 45; J. P. Hewitt and R. Stokes, "Disclaimers," *American Sociological Review*, 40 (1975): pp. 1–11; K. Warfel, "Gender Schemas and Perceptions of Speech Style," *Communication Monographs*, 51 (1984): pp. 253–67.

[22] Warfel, "Gender Schemas," pp. 253–67; Bradley, "Folk-Linguistics," pp. 73–90.

[23] C. Johnson, "An Introduction," p. 169.

[24] G. C. Gleser, L. A. Gottschalk, and W. John, "The Relationship of Sex and Intelligence to Choice of Words: A Normative Study of Verbal Behavior," *Journal of Clinical Psychology*, 15 (1959): pp. 182–91.

[25] See, for example, A. Mulac and T. L. Lundell, "Linguistic Determinants of the Gender-Linked Language Effect." Paper presented at the annual meeting of the

International Communication Association, Boston, Mass., 1982; M. Swacker, "The Sex of the Speaker as a Sociolinguistic Variable." In B. Thorne and N. Henley (eds.), *Language and Sex: Difference and Dominance* (Rowley, Mass.: Newbury House Publishers, 1966), pp. 76–83; M. M. Wood, "The Influence of Sex and Knowledge of Communication Effectiveness on Spontaneous Speech," *Word*, 22 (1966): pp. 112–37.

[26] See, for example, H. Gilley and C. Summers, "Sex Differences in the Use of Hostile Verbs," *Journal of Psychology*, 76 (1970): pp. 33–37; A. Mulac, S. Blau, and L. Bauquier, "Gender-Linked Language Differences and Their Effects in Male and Female Students' Impromptu Essays." Paper presented at the annual meeting of the Speech Communication Association, Washington, D.C.; D. W. Warshay, "Sex Differences in Language Style." In C. Safilios-Rothschild (ed.), *Toward A Sociology of Women* (Lexington, Mass.: Xerox College Publishers, 1972), pp. 3–9; R. Westmoreland, D. P. Starr, K. Shelton, and Y. Pasadeos, "News Writing Styles of Male and Female Students," *Journalism Quarterly*, 54 (1977): pp. 599–601.

[27] See, for example, N. Barron, "Sex-Typed Language: The Production of Grammatical Cases," *Acta Sociologica*, 14 (1971): pp. 24–72; Fr. Crosby and L. Nyquist, "The Female Register: An Empirical Study of Lakoff's Hypotheses," *Language in Society*, 6 (1979): pp. 519–35; R. A. Koenigsknecht and P. Friedman, "Syntax Development in Boys and Girls," *Child Development*, 47 (1976): pp. 1109–15; J. R. McMillan, A. K. Clifton, D. McGrath, and W. S. Gale, "Women's Language: Uncertainty or Interpersonal Sensitivity and Emotionality?", *Sex Roles*, 3 (1977): pp. 49–67; E. F. Sause, "Computer Content Analysis of Sex Differences in the Language of Children," *Journal of Psycholinguistic Research*, 5 (1976): pp. 311–24.

[28] E. S. Andersen, "The Acquisition of Sociolinguistic Knowledge: Some Evidence from Children's Verbal Role-Play," *Western Journal of Speech Communication*, 48 (1984): pp. 125–44; Koenigsknecht and Friedman, "Syntax Development in Boys and Girls," pp. 1109–15; C. M. Staley, "Sex-Related Differences in the Style of Children's Language," *Journal of Psycholinguistic Research*, 11 (1982): pp. 141–58.

[29] Anthony Mulac, Torborg Louisa Lundell, and James J. Bradac, "Male/Female Language Differences and Attributional Consequences in a Public Speaking Situation: Toward an Explanation of the Gender-Linked Language Effect," *Communication Monographs*, 53 (1986): p. 125. These were differences perceived in a public context. The researchers suggest that when these results are compared with male-female communication in other settings, there is "fluctuating overlap"—the features vary with time and place.

[30] McMillan, Clifton, McGrath, and Gale, "Women's Language: Uncertainty or Interpersonal Sensitivity and Emotionality?" pp. 545–59.

[31] W. M. O'Barr, *Linguistic Evidence: Language, Power, and Strategy in the Courtroom* (New York: Academic Press, 1982).

[32] Robin Lakoff, *Language and Women's Place* (New York: Harper & Row, 1975).

[33] Mulac, Lundell, and Bradac, "Male/Female Language Differences," p. 125.

[34] Suzette Haden Elgin, *The Last Word on the Gentle Art of Verbal Self-Defense* (New York: Prentice Hall Press, 1987).

[35] Edward P. J. Corbett, *Classical Rhetoric for the Modern Student* (New York: Oxford University Press, 1965), p. 6.

[36] Elgin attributes this to George Miller. See "Giving Away Psychology in the 80's: George Miller Interviewed by Elizabeth Hall," *Psychology Today*, 14 (January 1980): p. 46.

[37] Elgin, *Gentle Art of Verbal Self-Defense*, p. 211.

[38] See S. I. Hayakawa, *Language in Thought and Action*, p. 204.

[39] Alfred Korzybski, *Science and Sanity: An Introduction to Non-Aristotelian Systems and General Semantics* (Lancaster, Pa.: Science Press Printing Co., 1933).

[40] Hayakawa, *Language in Thought and Action*, p. 205.

Further Reading

Charles R. Berger and James J. Bradac, *Language and Social Knowledge: Uncertainty in Interpersonal Relations* (London: Edward Arnold, 1982). The specific focus of this book is on the relationships among language, social cognition, and the process involved in the development of interpersonal relationships. The authors' purpose is to show how language and the ways in which we think about ourselves and others influence the ways in which we develop relationships. They discuss language and impression formation, social interaction, relational development, and social knowledge. A sophisticated book for the serious student.

Deborah Borisoff and Lisa Merrill, *The Power to Communicate: Gender Differences As Barriers* (Prospect Heights, Ill.: Waveland Press, Inc., 1985). In this 100-page paperback, the authors define the "gender gap" then proceed to discuss five topics: (1) The Stereotype, (2) Vocal, Verbal, and Nonverbal Behavior, (3) Professional Image, (4) Male Dominance as a Barrier to Change, and (5) Effective Change: Expanding Human Potential. The unique value of this book is the strategies and techniques they recommend for dealing with persistent traditional attitudes. A well-written and documented book packed full of practical information.

John C. Condon, Jr., *Semantics and Communication*, 3d ed. (New York: Macmillan Publishing Company, 1985). Condon illustrates the many ways in which words influence behavior, some of the problems we create through language along with appropriate warnings and suggestions, and the three considerations necessary for understanding interpersonal communication (semantics, pragmatics, and syntactics). This is an excellent book on the relation of language and communication.

Suzette Haden Elgin, *The Gentle Art of Verbal Self-Defense* (1980), *More on the Gentle Art of Verbal Self-Defense* (1983), and *The Last Word on the Gentle Art of Verbal Self-Defense* (1987) (New York: Prentice Hall Press). The first book is an emergency first-aid manual that tells what to do when under verbal attack. The second extends the system developed in the first book beyond one-to-one interaction to other language situations. The third brings in a new set of verbal skills and offers ways to improve the entire language environment so that verbal abuse is abolished.

Andrew Ellis and Geoffrey Beattie, *The Psychology of Language and Communication* (New York: The Guilford Press, 1986). These authors cover the mainstream concerns of psycholinguistics such as speech production, speech perception and comprehension, language acquisition, and the psychological reality of linguistic theories. They also treat gestural and facial communication, conversational management, social class influences on language, animal communication, neuropsychology, and other topics. A broad-ranging textbook that provides a view of human language in its natural context.

S. Morris Engel, *The Language Trap or How to Defend Yourself Against the Tyranny of Words* (Englewood Cliffs, N.J.: Prentice-Hall, 1984). This is an amazingly in-depth look at words, the maze of intellectualism, and the lure of authoritarianism. It is a manual of verbal self-defense—defense against the deceptions we practice on ourselves and the deceptions others try to practice, either unwittingly or deliberately. A fine, readable, thorough treatment for the serious student of language.

S. I. Hayakawa, *Language in Thought and Action*, 4th ed. (New York: Harcourt Brace Jovanovich, 1978). A classic book. Semantics is the study of human interaction through communication. This is a study of semantics based on the assumption that cooperation is preferable to conflict. The principles explained here relate to thinking, speaking, writing, and behavior. Challenges are provided for undertaking actual semantic investigations and exercises.

Judy Cornelia Pearson, *Gender and Communication* (Dubuque, Iowa: Wm. C. Brown Publishers, 1985). This is an academic textbook designed to synthesize the research findings on this topic into a single, manageable source. Pearson includes hundreds of citations to suggest the breadth of research in the area. Both theory and practice are represented here. The book is divided into "considerations," "components," "codes," and "contexts." Numerous exercises are included throughout.

Lea P. Stewart, Pamela J. Cooper, and Sheryl A. Friedley, *Communication Between the Sexes: Sex Differences and Sex-Role Stereotypes* (Scottsdale, Ariz.: Gorsuch Scarisbrick, Publishers, 1986). This book is an introduction to the major differences in the ways men and women communicate. The authors explain how these differences influence our communication with each other. Also, they suggest some strategies readers might use to change their communication behaviors. The authors include numerous further readings and a comprehensive set of references. Excellent reading.

Deborah Tannen, *That's Not What I Meant! How Conversational Style Makes or Breaks Your Relations with Others* (New York: William Morrow and Company, Inc., 1986). Tannen suggests that such ingrained conversational habits as the use of questions and stories, voice level, choice of words, or how much or how little we talk, differ from culture to culture and from person to person. When others misread us, it may be annoying, inconvenient, or, if it is someone we love, may shake the foundation of our lives. Tannen offers a unique and important way of looking at the way language works. An interesting, important book.

6

Communicating Without Words: Nonverbal Communication

Learning Objectives

When you have finished this chapter you should be able to:

- Explain the importance of nonverbal communication.
- Explain the value of congruency in checking your interpretation of others' nonverbal messages.
- Describe the three major forms of nonverbal communication.
- List and describe the various types of nonverbal cues.
- Distinguish between intimate, personal, social, and public distances.
- Explain why body movement is considered the heart of human nonverbal communication.
- Describe the various things that vocal cues can reflect.
- List and explain the three primary emotional dimensions that are involved in nonverbal behavior.
- Explain what limits you in reading the nonverbal cues that others send.
- Describe how to improve your skills in nonverbal communication.

Have you ever been in a public place and discovered someone was staring at you? You look away, but just to test your perception of the situation you look back at the person. "I wonder why he's staring at me," you think. You look away again, hoping that his gaze will shift. This time

Consider This

The most intelligible part of language is not the words, but the tone, force, modulation, tempo in which a group of words are spoken—that is, the music behind the words, the emotion behind the music; everything that cannot be written down.

—Friedrich Nietzsche

when you look back at him, you do it quickly. If the person continues to stare, you might become uncomfortable, angry, or even alarmed. In our society, the direct, unwavering stare is perceived as a form of threat.[1] What does it mean to "give someone the eye"? Americans often interpret prolonged eye contact as an indication of sexual attraction, depending, in part, on the accompanying facial expression. You may have noticed a man give a woman a steady, challenging stare, with that stare followed by the woman lowering her eyes.[2] A great deal has been communicated without a word being spoken.

Communicating without words is the subject of this chapter. I'll examine the many different ways we send messages without using words. I'll discuss how our nonverbal communication conveys certain messages better than verbal communication can, sometimes revealing more about ourselves than we want to! "Body language" is part of this nonverbal communication. Vocal cues and spatial cues are just as important. Nonverbal language is not a precise language; in our eagerness to understand why a person nods that way or stands so close to us we may misinterpret nonverbal signals.

There is a lot of research and popular psychology about nonverbal communication. It has become faddish to "read people like a book." Because nonverbal communication is not precise, there can be as many reasons for a nonverbal cue occurring as there are interpretations of that cue. We *do* have certain "textbook" agreement about verbal symbols, but that has *not* occurred to a significant extent with nonverbal symbols. Thus, it is wise to exercise caution in our interpretation of nonverbal symbols. But even though we're not dealing with an exact science, we can learn to send and interpret nonverbal messages in a way that enhances the total meaning exchanged in any communication.

The Rules of the Game

The long stare is quite unusual in our society because of the connotations attached to it and because it is contrary to the kind of behavior we have been socialized to accept. In the prior example, the accepted cultural rules usually dictate that the woman look away or lower her eyes. If she aggressively stares back or smiles or winks, the man might be pleased or uncomfortable, but he would definitely know the usual rules were not in effect.

To be stared at is an invasion of privacy and can make us very uncomfortable. To be caught staring is an embarrassment. We've probably all been caught staring, and quickly looked away and pretended to be studying the clock or the wall just above the person's head. Erving Goffman, a sociologist who investigated the behavior of people in public places, stated that Americans meet one another with "civil inattention." Goffman meant that we take enough visual notice of others to let them know that we know they are there, but not enough notice to seem curious or to intrude.[3]

You may be disturbed by the idea that we are "socialized to accept" certain types of behavior; we don't like to think our responses are predictable. But our culture programs us from childhood, teaching us what to do with our eyes and what to expect of other people. Think of what happens when we shift our eyes to look away from another person's gaze. If that person is a friend, the response may range from anger to hurt to puzzlement or frustration, but it will fall within a culturally defined range of expected and acceptable behavior. In either case, the response we call forth is out of all proportion to the small muscular effort made.[4]

Do you recall one of your parents or teachers admonishing you to "take that look off your face"? The slightest suggestion of a smile at an inappropriate time can draw a lot of attention! The same is true of eye movements and touching and other forms of nonverbal communication. We all know what it is to share an inside joke with a friend and to express our understanding of the joke with a timely nudge when other kinds of communication would be out of place. That nudge can say a great deal, considering how little effort we put into it. Nonverbal messages are like that; they can pack a lot of meaning into otherwise small looks and gestures.

All nonverbal communication is influenced by a variety of factors—our personality, the situations we are in, the attitudes we hold toward people, the pecking order we maintain with others, and our cultural upbringing. Nonverbal components almost always operate in conjunction with one another. At the same time we are establishing eye contact, for example, we are also dealing with the nonverbal variables of facial expressions, gestures, and larger movements. We draw conclusions from numerous nonverbal signals simultaneously and we do it very quickly. Whether the conclusions are accurate or inaccurate, we seldom have time to check. We respond, hoping that we have perceived accurately and hoping, too, that we'll get further cues.

Consider This

Fellow I know says he went AWOL from the U.S. Navy in Japan shortly after World War II. He didn't speak a word of Japanese. He met no one who spoke English during his two weeks' absence. Yet with facial expressions, hand waving, body language he was able to get food, drink, places to sleep, everything he wanted. His point: You can conduct countless transactions without saying anything. Quite on. Scientists have listed 700,000 different combinations of face and body movements that people use to convey meaning.

—L. M. Boyd, "Checking Up," *Toledo Blade,* April 19, 1980. Reprinted by permission of L. M. Boyd, Crown Syndicate, Inc.

The Importance of Nonverbal Communication

Communication researchers have shown that words by themselves carry only a small part of the information exchanged between people when they talk. Ray Birdwhistell, a noted authority on nonverbal communication, estimates that, on the average, people speak words for only 10 to 11 minutes daily. The standard spoken sentence takes 2.5 seconds. Also, Birdwhistell notes, in normal two-person conversations, verbal components carry less than 35 percent of the social meaning; all the rest, 65 percent, is carried by nonverbal components.[5] It is easy to slip into the error of thinking that *all* communication must be verbal. But even when we think we are not consciously sending or receiving nonverbal messages, their influence is present and it is significant.

Nonverbal Communication Is Continuous

The more we think about nonverbal communication, the more we see how true it is that we cannot *not* communicate. Words come one at a time, but nonverbal cues come continuously. Several, even many, may exist and are

Consider This

There are three well-tested assumptions (basic assumptions) that underlie any theory or set of theories about nonverbal communication:

One is that individuals develop expectations about the nonverbal behavior of others. These expectancies arise from social norms and one's prior knowledge of a communicator's idiosyncrasies. (In the case of interactions with strangers, only the social norms dictate expectancies.) A second assumption is that communication behaviors have evaluations attached to them. Whether a specific behavior or collection of behaviors is placed within the positive or negative end of the evaluative continuum depends on the social community's values or standards and on individual preferences. For example, fluent speaking is positively valued in the U.S. culture, whereas frequent touching from strangers is not. The evaluation of a behavior may be a function of what meanings are attached to it (e.g., frequent touching expresses high intimacy, which is inappropriate coming from a stranger). This ties into the third assumption that nonverbal behaviors have meanings. Some behaviors may have unitary and unambiguous meaning, and others may have multiple and possibly conflicting meanings, but it is assumed that the array of possible meanings is recognized within a social community (e.g., a caress may convey sympathy, comfort, dominance, affection, attraction, or lust).

—From "Communicative Effects of Gaze Behavior: A Test of Two Contrasting Explanations" by Judee K. Burgoon, Deborah A. Coker, and Ray A. Coker in *Human Communication Research,* 12 (Summer 1986), p. 497. Reprinted by permission of the International Communication Association and the authors.

perceived at the same time. All these nonverbal signals are used as a foundation for understanding the words. Words become distorted if spoken too slowly or too rapidly, but nonverbal cues can be sent slowly or quickly. We send *and* receive nonverbal messages in an uninterrupted, persistent flow. And while we are observing someone else's gestures and mannerisms, that person may also be observing ours.

Nonverbal Communication Conveys Emotions

When you think of it, objects and actions can generate more emotion than words because objects and actions are less abstract than words. Words usually exert more of an intellectual appeal. To hear that someone cried or was injured is not nearly as powerful as seeing that person cry or get hurt. If we want to convey sincerity, our facial and bodily gestures can probably do it more effectively than our words, although words *reinforced* by nonverbal cues will convey the most unmistakable message.

Since nonverbal cues are so closely tied to the emotions, how well we understand nonverbal messages depends on how empathic we are. Everything I have said earlier about empathic listening applies here as well. The empathic, alert perceiver is very likely to understand (or at least be aware of) nonverbal cues. Understanding verbal expression requires more skill. Nonverbal expression, learned much earlier and often closely tied to universal human emotions, is sometimes easier to attach meaning to, even though that meaning may be less than perfectly accurate.

Nonverbal Communication Is Rich in Meaning

Think of the last time you went to the doctor when you had certain symptoms but did not know what your illness was. You probably listened as the doctor mystified and, perhaps, terrified you by using polysyllabic technical terms to describe your disorder. But what did you do? You watched the doctor's face very carefully to see if you could detect how sick you really were. How did the doctor *say* the words? What kinds of sounds like "Hmm-m-m" or "Aha!" could you detect? In such situations, we look for even the most minute nonverbal signs to interpret—especially when we cannot understand the verbal signs. There is even a field known as *iatrogenics*, which is, in part, "the study of how doctor-talk can intensify and even induce illness."[6]

Consider how the slightest sound or the most delicate movement can be fraught with meaning. Put these sounds and movements together into the larger context in which they occur and you realize how rich nonverbal communication can be. A raised eyebrow, a sly smile, a touch of the hand can all say a lot in the right circumstances. Such nonverbal cues are especially useful when for some reason oral or written communication is inappropriate— during a concert or a lecture, perhaps, or even a movie. Nonverbal communication can be rich with meaning.

Nonverbal Communication Can Be Confusing

Although nonverbal communication may be rich with meaning, it can also be confusing. Certain cues may mean something entirely different from what we imagine. A man may be sitting on a sofa next to a woman with his legs crossed away from the woman. "Aha, obviously he has no interest in her, since his legs are crossed away from her," the enthusiastic reader of body language might think; "he is excluding her." Not necessarily. Some people *always* cross their legs right over left, no matter what. It's their habit, it's comfortable, and it doesn't mean a thing as far as nonverbal communication goes (except perhaps to show that they feel at ease in the situation).

We can't assume that a woman with her arms folded in front of her is close-minded and rigid—she may simply feel cold! We must be careful in interpreting nonverbal cues. We do not always have enough information to make a judgment, and our guesses may be far from accurate.

Do Your Actions Match Your Words?

One of the best and most logical ways to check your interpretation of somebody's nonverbal message is through that person's words. He or she might say, "I like you" or "You are a wonderful person to be with," confirming this compliment with affectionate eye contact. But it's rare for

Consider This

Common sense suggests that our impressions of people are shaped more by how they act than by what they say about themselves. But Brandeis University psychologist Teresa M. Amabile and her student Loren G. Kabat tested this idea by videotaping women while they deliberately acted either introverted or extroverted in conversations and while they described themselves as having one or the other personality trait.

Then, 160 students watched the videotapes and evaluated how "outgoing," "friendly," "shy," or "withdrawn" the women were. When the women's self-descriptions and actual behavior conflicted, the students usually gave more credence to behavior. In general, the students' judgments were influenced about 20 times more strongly by what the women did than by what they said about themselves.

—From "You Know What They Say . . ." by Alfie Kohn in *Psychology Today,* 22 (April 1988): 39. Copyright © 1988 by Alfie Kohn. Reprinted by permission of the author.

people to come right out and express their feelings so directly. Usually you have to pay attention to more subtle verbal cues. What you should watch for is whether the words and the actions are congruent. When there is congruency, you can be surer of your interpretations. When there is incongruency, we either try to get more information, we suspend judgment, or we tend to believe either what we hear *or* what we see.

Nonverbal and verbal communication usually work together, even if incongruently.[7] A nonverbal message may *repeat* what we say, reinforcing it. For example, our message is reinforced when we wave and say "good-bye" at the same time. Nonverbal *replaces* verbal when we wave without saying "good-bye" or when we nod in agreement to indicate "yes." Nonverbal communication may *underscore* the verbal portion of a message the way italics strengthen the written word; leaning toward another person with concern reinforces "Tell me about it."

Nonverbal behavior may *regulate* behavior, too. We can often tell when it is our turn to speak in a conversation through a nonverbal cue—for example, a questioning look from the other person. Finally, a nonverbal message can *contradict* the verbal message. We rarely send this kind of contradictory communication on purpose. Perhaps the most common example is when someone sees us looking "down in the dumps," asks us what's wrong, and we reply, "Nothing." Albert Mehrabian suggests that when a person's actions and words contradict each other, we rely more on his or her actions to reveal true feelings.[8]

Forms of Nonverbal Communication

Nonverbal elements sometimes work separately from verbal communication; that is, we may receive a nonverbal message without any words whatsoever. The nonverbal component, in this case, is the entire message. But usually the nonverbal domain provides a framework for the words we use. If we think of nonverbal communication as including all forms of message transmission *not* represented by word symbols, we can divide it into five broad categories: emblems, illustrators, affect displays, regulators, and adaptors.[9]

In their early work in this area, Jurgen Ruesch and Weldon Kees outlined just three categories: sign, action, and object language.[10] **Sign language** includes gestures used in the place of words, numbers, or punctuation. When an athlete raises his index finger to show his team is "Number One," he is using sign language. **Action language** includes all those nonverbal movements *not* intended as signs. Your way of walking, sitting, or eating may serve your personal needs, but they also make statements to those who see them. **Object language** includes both the intentional and unintentional display of material things. Your hairstyle, glasses, and jewelry reveal things about you, as do the books you carry, the car you drive, or the clothes you wear.[11]

These early categories have been subsumed in the new classification system. The advantage of the new classification system is that it permits further divisions and, thus, more accurate classification of nonverbal behavior. Also, it reflects the writing and research that has been done since Ruesch and Kees—much of it generated from the base they provided.

Emblems

Emblems are similar to Ruesch and Kees's sign language. They have a direct verbal translation, usually a word or a phrase.[12] Many of these are culture-specific; that is, they are known or recognized by members of a particular culture or historical period only. Hand gestures indicating "A-OK" or "Victory" (popularized by Winston Churchill during World War II) are examples of emblems. Although most emblems are produced with the hands, a facial expression such as a nose-wrinkle that says "I'm disgusted" or "It stinks!" also qualifies as an emblem. Shaking the head might represent "No more!" or "No, thank you." Slouched posture could represent "I'm not interested" or "Count me out." Think of the emblems you use to indicate "Okay," "It's hot," "Tastes good," "Whoopee," "Gossip," or "I don't know."

Try This

Classify each of the following into sign, action, or object language:

1. You jump out of bed in the morning.
2. You put on your best sweater.
3. You smile because you feel good and this promises to be a good day.
4. You shake your head because your roommate borrowed the shoes that you wanted to wear today.
5. You storm out of the room slamming the door furiously.
6. You see your roommate in the cafeteria and shake your fist in anger.
7. You turn away just as your roommate is going to say something.
8. You grab your books, walk slowly out of the building drooping with frustration.

Based on your own experience, is any one of these types of nonverbal communication more effective than any other in expressing how you really feel?

Now, reclassify each into emblems, illustrators, affect displays, regulators, and adaptors.

Consider This

Here, "Miss Manners" writes about emblems. Notice that "The Look" to which she refers is a nonverbal cue that has a direct verbal translation known by both partners in the relationship.

The most useful code [performed in public to avert disaster] is The Look—that facial expression, undecipherable to any outsider, that means, "Watch out, something is very, very wrong."

Let us say, for example, that one person wants to go home from a gathering, while the other would prefer to stay longer.

The first says, pleasantly enough, "I'm afraid it's late, darling," or "This is such fun, but I have to get up early."

The second counters with a jovial, "Oh, let's just have one more drink," or "But tomorrow's Saturday."

As stated, this is a tossup. But if the first statement is accompanied by The Look, it means "I can't stand this one more minute, get me out of here before I scream," while the second, with The Look added, is transformed into "Hold off, I'm closing an important deal." It should be a rule of marriage [or relationships] that the person with The Look should be obeyed, with any disagreement to be conducted afterwards.*

*From Judith Martin, "'The Look' Is the Most Useful Communication Between Spouses," *Toledo Blade,* April 14, 1985, Section F, p. 8. Reprinted by permission of United Feature Syndicate, Inc.

Illustrators

Illustrators are similar to Ruesch and Kees's action language. Illustrators are nonverbal cues directly tied to speech. They serve to illustrate what is being said in words. Think of all the movements you use to accent, emphasize, or reinforce your conversations: gestures, bodily action, even emblems. Used in context, these emblems are illustrators because their primary intention is to reinforce (not substitute for) verbal communication. Jerry slammed his fist against the table when he said, "I think that is wrong!" Barbara paused, then said very slowly, "But Al, I just don't want a serious relationship at this time." Tim is one of those people who talks with his hands. Someone once said of him, "If you tied Tim's hands behind him, he'd fall silent."

Affect Displays

Affect displays are all those nonverbal cues that reveal our affective—or feeling—state. These are primarily facial cues since the main way we reveal our feelings to others is through facial expressions. Anne's smile turned sour when she actually saw the grade she received on her exam. Wendy knew her evening was going to be rough when she saw Mike's face. Mike had gone for a job interview earlier in the day, and Wendy knew by looking at his face that it hadn't gone well. The students sensed it was going to be a long class period when their normally jovial instructor came into class looking serious and determined. However, we may reveal affect displays with other parts of the body, too. The face may give the first sign of sadness, but a drooping, slouched posture may confirm it.

Affect displays can be illustrators when they are tied to our speech. For example, when they are used to repeat or augment our conversation, they are illustrators. They can have the opposite effect, too, when they contradict or are unrelated to our verbal statements.

Regulators

Regulators are nonverbal cues that regulate the give-and-take of speaking and listening. The most commonly used regulators are those that occur in normal conversations. These regulators are associated with turn-taking.[13] When you are talking to others, you use specific cues to let them know you want to talk, to keep them from talking, or to show them you are finished talking. Most of these are nonverbal cues such as head nods, eye behavior, and inflection. In talking with Ron, you find that he gets his comments into the conversation by raising his voice slightly. Shirley dips her head and looks directly at the other person when it's that person's time to talk. Ed raises his voice at the end of his last sentence when the other person is supposed to talk. Jean uses rapid head nods to indicate "Hurry up." Lou's head nods are slow and deliberate and emphasize others' points as they are presented, thus conveying, "I like what you're saying."

Adaptors

Adaptors are related to Ruesch and Kees's object language. When objects like pencils, cigarettes, and glasses are manipulated for a purpose, they become adaptors. Other objects we exert control over include our clothing, hairstyle, and, to a certain degree, our body shape. Patrick normally dresses very casually, but today he is wearing a three-piece suit, manipulating the clothing he is wearing to make a good impression on the company representatives who are conducting employment interviews. Anyone who knows Charlotte knows that whenever she gets nervous or upset she lights a cigarette. Jim controls his mood by the way he dresses. On days when he feels down, he can improve his mood by dressing up, getting somewhat the same feeling a soldier or a police officer may get when he or she puts on a uniform.

But adaptors include more than the manipulation of objects. Ekman and Friesen have also identified self- and alter-directed adaptors. Self-adaptors refer to manipulation of your own body by scratching, rubbing, pinching, picking, holding, squeezing, and touching. Alter-adaptors are used in interpersonal situations as we engage in giving and taking from others, attacking and protecting, establishing closeness and withdrawing. Think, for example, of how you indicate to others that you disagree with an idea that has been mentioned, that you want to terminate a conversation, or that you are interested in pursuing a more intimate relationship.[14]

Types of Nonverbal Cues

Let's look more closely at these cues that tell others about us or that tell us about them. Our own self-awareness and empathic skills will increase as we become more sensitive to different kinds of nonverbal cues. The broader our base of understanding, the more likely we are to be able to interpret the cues we perceive. But we know that nonverbal communication can be ambiguous, and we must be careful not to overgeneralize from the behavior we observe. We may feel hurt by the listless "Hi" we receive from a good friend unless we remember that that listlessness could have been brought on by a headache, lack of sleep, preoccupation, or some other factor we don't know about. We would be unwise to assume we are being personally rejected if this friend doesn't smile and stop to talk with us every single morning.

We should always be alert to *all* cues and try to get as much information as possible on which to base our conclusions. One way to organize our thinking about nonverbal communication is to think in terms of spatial cues, visual cues, and vocal cues. In considering each of these, we should not overlook the fact that any communication occurs in a specific environmental setting. This setting will influence much of the nonverbal interaction that takes place. The weather can affect how we behave just as much as the actual setting—cafeteria, classroom, car, park bench, or wherever.

Spatial Cues

Spatial cues are the distances we choose to stand or sit from others. Each of us carries with us something called "informal space." We might think of this as a bubble; we occupy the center of the bubble. This bubble expands or contracts depending on varying conditions and circumstances such as the:

- age and sex of those involved.
- cultural and ethnic background of the participants.
- topic or subject matter.
- setting for the interaction.
- physical characteristics of the participants (size or shape).
- attitudinal and emotional orientation of partners.
- characteristics of the interpersonal relationship (like friendship).
- personality characteristics of those involved.[15]

In his book *The Silent Language*, Edward T. Hall, a cultural anthropologist, identifies the distances that we assume when we talk with others. He calls these distances intimate, personal, social, and public.[16] In many cases, the adjustments that occur in these distances result from some of the factors listed above.

Intimate distance.   At an *intimate distance* (0 to 18 inches), we often use a soft or barely audible whisper to share intimate or confidential information. Physical contact becomes easy at this distance. This is the distance we use for physical comforting, lovemaking, and physical fighting, among other things.

Personal distance.   Hall identified the range of 18 inches to 4 feet as *personal distance*. When we disclose ourselves to someone, we are likely to do it within this distance. The topics we discuss at this range may be somewhat confidential, and usually are personal and mutually involving. At personal distance we are still able to touch each other if we want to. This is likely to be the distance between people conversing at a party, between classmates in a casual conversation, or within many work relationships. This distance assumes a well-established acquaintanceship. This is probably the most comfortable distance for free exchange of feedback.

Social distance.   When we are talking at a normal level with another person, sharing concerns that are not of a personal nature, we usually use the *social distance* (4 to 12 feet). Many of our on-the-job conversations take place at this distance. Seating arrangements in living rooms may be based on "conversation groups" of chairs placed at a distance of 4 to 7 feet from each other. Hall calls 4 to 7 feet the close phase of social distance; from 7 to 12 feet is the far phase of social distance.

Try This

Would you like to know the size of "bubble" that a friend of yours carries around as his or her personal space? The next time you are involved in a conversation with your friend, get into a position where you are directly facing each other and there is nothing behind him or her. Then, as you talk, *slowly* inch closer and closer. As you infringe on the "bubble," your friend may begin to move backward. As the movement just begins, notice the size of the personal space that your friend is protecting. To test your perception of the size of the "bubble," *slowly* move closer yet. What distance did you find most comfortable for a casual conversation?

The greater the distance, the more formal the business or social discourse conducted is likely to be. Often, the desks of important people are broad enough to hold visitors at a distance of 7 to 12 feet. Eye contact at this distance becomes more important to the flow of communication; without visual contact one party is likely to feel shut out and the conversation may come to a halt.

Public distance.   *Public distance* (12 feet and farther) is well outside the range for close involvement with another person. It is impractical for interpersonal communication. We are limited to what we can see and hear at that distance; topics for conversation are relatively impersonal and formal; and most of the communication that occurs is in the public-speaking style, with subjects planned in advance and limited opportunities for feedback.

Hall points out that his distances are based on his own observations of middle-class people native to the northeastern United States and employed in business and professional occupations. We should be cautious about extending his generalizations to other regional, social, vocational, and ethnic groups.

The important point about intimate, personal, social, and public distance is that space communicates. Our sense of what distance is natural for us for a specific kind of interaction is deeply ingrained in us by our culture. We automatically make spatial adjustments and interpret spatial cues. Can you imagine, for example, talking to one of your professors at the intimate distance? What would your most intimate friend say if you maintained the social distance for an entire evening? Try talking to people you interact with daily at a public distance. Becoming aware of how we and other people use space will improve our communication.

Let's look briefly at some of the factors that may affect how close you sit or stand to someone. The distance is likely to be dependent on both social norms and the idiosyncratic (unique) patterns of those interacting.[17] You are likely to stand closer to a member of the opposite sex than to one of the same sex.[18] There may be distance shifts during an encounter, too, because of topic changes or beginnings and endings.[19] How pleasant, neutral, or unpleasant the topic being discussed is to the participants may also affect distance.[20] When a topic is pleasant, people stand or sit closer together. Also, one research study indicates that close distances may decrease the amount of talking between the partners.[21] There is little doubt that social setting can make a great deal of difference in the spatial relationships, too. The amount of space available may be a factor, as well as the light, noise, and temperature. Physical characteristics of the people involved may cause changes in distance; for example, a short person and the captain of the basketball team will not have a very comfortable conversation if they stand too close to each other. Attitudinal and emotional orientations also have an important effect on distance. Wouldn't you choose to stand closer to someone you thought was friendly and farther from one you were told was unfriendly?

When we see a group of people standing close together as they talk, we perceive them as being warmer, more empathic and understanding, and liking one another more.[22] It follows, then, that we interact more closely with friends than with acquaintances, and more closely with acquaintances than with strangers.[23] Closer distances are perceived, too, when people have a high self-concept and high affiliative needs (needs to associate with others), are low on authoritarianism, and are self-directed.[24]

Visual Cues

Greater visibility increases our potential for communicating because the more we see and the more we can be seen, the more information we can send and receive. Mehrabian found that the more we direct our face toward the person we're talking to, the more we convey a positive feeling to this person.[25] Another researcher has confirmed something most of us discovered long ago, that looking directly at a person, smiling, and leaning toward him or her conveys a feeling of warmth.[26]

Facial expression.   The face is probably the most expressive part of the human body. It can reveal complex and often confusing kinds of information. It commands attention because it is visible and omnipresent. It can move from signs of ecstasy to signs of despair in less than a second. Research results suggest that there are ten basic classes of meaning that can be communicated facially: happiness, surprise, fear, anger, sadness, disgust, contempt, interest, bewilderment, and determination.[27] Research also has shown that the face may communicate information other than the emotional state of the person—it may reveal the thought processes as well.[28] In addition, it has been shown that we are capable of facially conveying not just a single emotional state but multiple emotions at the same time.[29]

The face can communicate more emotional meanings more accurately than any other factor in our interpersonal communication. Dale G. Leathers has determined that the face:

Try This

Do you have a characteristic style of facial expression? Answer the following questions under each category honestly to see if you can detect any regular pattern of behavior in your nonverbal facial expressions.

- *Withholder:* Do your facial expressions show how you feel? Are you a person who shows very little expressiveness? Are you aware that you are not expressive?
- *Revealer:* Do you tell all with your face? Are you very expressive? Can other people tell whether or not you like a present, or some food, just by the expression on your face?
- *Unwitting Expressor:* Do you show emotion without realizing it? Do you ever say, "How did you know I was angry (or upset)?"
- *Blanked Expressor:* Do you think you are showing an emotion when in fact you show little if any expression at all? Do you have a neutral look on your face at all times?
- *Frozen-affect Expressor:* Do you constantly show one emotion (such as happiness) even when you are not experiencing that emotion at all?
- *Substitute Expressor:* Do you feel one emotion, think you are expressing it, but have others tell you that some other emotion was being expressed? Have you ever felt angry but looked sad, for example?
- *Ever-ready Expressor:* Do you almost instinctively show the same emotion as your first response to any new event? For example, do you express surprise as a first response to good news, bad news, an announcement that you have been fired?
- *Flooded-affect Expressor:* Do you frequently display more than one emotion? Is one of these emotions characteristic of you (like the Frozen-affect Expressor) and the other emotion, when felt, is mixed with the old, characteristic expression? For example, have you ever looked fearful but showed both fear and anger when you were angry?

—From *Unmasking the Face* by Paul Ekman and Wallace Friesen, pp. 155–57. Reprinted by permission of the authors.

1. Communicates *evaluative* judgments through pleasant and unpleasant expressions;
2. Reveals level of *interest* or lack of interest in others and in the environment;
3. Can exhibit level of *intensity* and thus show how involved we are in a situation;
4. Communicates the amount of *control* we have over our own expressions; and
5. Shows whether we *understand* something or not.[30]

Because faces are so visible and so sensitive, we pay more attention to people's faces than to any other nonverbal feature. The face is an efficient and high-speed means of conveying meaning. Gestures, posture, and larger body movements require some time to change in response to a changing stimulus, whereas facial expressions can change instantly, sometimes even at a rate imperceptible to the human eye. As an instantaneous response mechanism, it is *the* most effective way to provide feedback to an ongoing message. This is the process of using the face as a regulator.

People seem to judge facial expressions along these dimensions: pleasant/ unpleasant, active/passive, and intense/controlled. It has also been shown that no single area of the face is best for revealing emotions. For any particular emotion, certain areas of the face, however, may carry important

Consider This

Where in the brain does [nonverbal recognition] take place? There is much evidence to suggest that facial identity and facial expression are processed better by the right hemisphere than by the left. Similarly, recent evidence strongly suggests that emotional tone and voice identity are also processed by the right hemisphere, despite being interwoven in spoken language.

For more than a century, it was held that the left hemisphere was the sole arbiter of communication through the medium of speech and language. The right, 'nondominant' hemisphere was thought to be superfluous to human communicative abilities. But the findings in familiar-voice recognition, in the prosody [the nonverbal information in speech] of emotions and in facial-emotional perception suggest that although the left hemisphere knows best what is being said, the right hemisphere figures out how it is meant and who is saying it.

—From "Old Familiar Voices" by Diana Van Lancker in *Psychology Today,* 21 (November 1987): 13. Copyright © 1987 (PT Partners, L. P.) Reprinted by permission.

Consider This

Most of our facial signals occur in the area of the eyes, and each signal may possess a number of subtly varying meanings, depending upon the context (language, accompanying signals) in which it is used. Even without special training, instinctively we all know the meanings of many of these signals. Blinking, for example, may indicate either surprise or attention; winking, confidentiality or flirtation. Widened eyes may signal amazement or appetite, while closed eyes may be a sign of anything from sorrow to simple concentration. Consider the range of possible meanings in a stare: a dull gaze of apathy or boredom; a brightly transfixed look of fascination or wonder; a clouded gaze of incomprehension or disbelief; cold eyes of aggression; bold eyes of sexual attraction. Eyes that shift sideways may signal deception or doubt; lowered eyes, guilt, embarrassment, modesty, or obedience. And a gesture as simple as lowering the eyelids has proven as powerful as any lover's magic.

—Evan Marshall, *Eye Language: Understanding the Eloquent Eye* (New York: Dodd, Mead & Co., 1983), pp. 11–12.

information. For example, the nose-cheek-mouth area is crucial for conveying disgust, the eyes and eyelids for fear, the brows-forehead and eyes-eyelids for sadness, and the cheeks-mouth and brows-forehead for happiness. Surprise, it has been shown, can be seen in any of these areas.[31] The research has also confirmed that judgments of emotion from facial behavior are more accurate.[32]

But, often, more than just facial expressions must be seen or known to make judgments of emotions. Some of these factors include the prior expectations of the person doing the observing. We often see what we want to see. Also, our familiarity with a person and prior exposure to his or her face will make a difference in the accuracy of our judgment. When we have seen someone express other emotions, we will identify more precisely an emotion we have not seen before. Information about the context may also affect our judgments. How long we can see the face and how clearly we can see it also may make a difference in our perceptions.[33] Finally, the words, too, are factors. The words used are an indicator of what is being thought; the nonverbal signals are an indicator of the emotional response to what is being thought.

Eye contact.   A great deal can be conveyed through the eyes. If we seek feedback from another person, we usually maintain strong eye contact. We can open and close communication channels with our eyes as well. Think of a conversation involving more than two people. When we are interested in a certain person's opinion, we will look him or her in the eye, opening the channel for communication. If we are having difficulty finding the right words to say, we may break eye contact. We not only signal our degree of involvement or arousal through eye contact, but we use eye contact to check on how other people are responding. Have they completed a thought unit? Are they attentive? What are their reactions?

Eye contact may be hard to maintain if we are too close to someone. We can use our eyes to create anxiety in another person. Eye contact also can show whether we feel rewarded by what we see, whether we are in competition with another person, or whether we have something to hide. Our eye-contact habits may differ depending on the sex and the status of the person we're talking to. We will look at sex and status influences in a moment. In addition, if we are extroverted, our eye behavior is likely to be different than if we are introverted.[34]

Of all facial cues, eye contact is perhaps the single most important one. The fact that our culture has imposed so many rules regarding its use shows its significance. Think about your own patterns of eye contact. What rules do you follow? Until a certain age, children are rarely uncomfortable staring or being stared at. How long can you maintain eye contact with someone before it starts to feel awkward to you? It has been observed that as two people who do not wish to speak to each other approach, they will cast their eyes downward when they are about 8 feet apart so that they don't have to look at each other as they pass. Goffman calls this "dimming your lights."[35] Eye contact can have a major impact on both the quality and quantity of interpersonal communication.[36]

Try This

In your next conversations with others, keep track of your eye contact. Which of the following motives for eye contact are you most aware of using? Does it depend on the other person? Does it depend on what you are talking about? Does it depend on the context? What other factors about the communication situation affect the kind of eye contact you use?

- monitoring the feedback
- regulating the flow of the communication
- expressing your emotions
- communicating the nature of the interpersonal relationship

Do you usually combine these as you talk? Are they ever used independently of each other?

Try This

Try an experiment. Assume various body postures. How do you feel when you assume each one? Does each position allow you to experience different emotions? Can you assume a body posture that makes you feel confident? Insecure? Elated? Depressed? Emotional change involves the body. When you assume a new attitude, the new attitude brings on new perceptions, new feelings, and new muscular patterns. There is a close link between the body and the mind.

Eye contact often indicates the nature of the relationship between two people. One research study showed that eye contact is moderate when one is addressing a very high-status person, maximized when addressing a moderately high-status person, and only minimal when talking to a low-status person.[37] There are also predictable differences in eye contact when one person likes another or when there may be rewards involved.

Increased eye contact is also associated with increased liking between the people who are communicating. In an interview, for example, you are likely to make judgments about the interviewer's friendliness according to the amount of eye contact shown. The less eye contact, the less friendliness.[38] In a courtship relationship, more eye contact can be observed among those seeking to develop a more intimate relationship.[39] One research study suggests that the intimacy is a function of the amount of eye gazing, physical proximity, intimacy of topic, and amount of smiling.[40] This model best relates to established relationships. It could also include body orientation, forms of address, tone of voice, facial expression, or other factors.[41] All the factors interact; a change in one causes changes in the others.

The body.   The body reinforces facial communication. But gestures, postures, and other body movements can also communicate attitudes. They can reveal differences in status, and they can also indicate the presence of deception. With respect to attitudes, as noted previously, body movements also reveal feelings of liking between people.[42]

According to some investigators, a person who wants to be perceived as warm should shift his or her posture toward the other person, smile, maintain direct eye contact, and keep the hands still. People who are cold tend to look around, slump, drum their fingers, and, generally, refrain from smiling.

When a male or female in our society engages in courtship, he or she reveals this attitude, according to one researcher, through a category of behaviors. The first stage is *courtship readiness.* This stage is characterized by high muscle tone, reduced eye bagginess and jowl sag, lessening of slouch and shoulder hunching, and decreasing belly sag. The second stage is *preening behavior.* At this stage males and females will stroke their hair, rearrange makeup, glance in the mirror, rearrange clothes, leave buttons open, adjust suit coats, tug at socks, and readjust knots. The third stage involves *positional cues* such as sitting in a way that prevents third parties from joining the conversation, or moving arms, legs, or torsos to inhibit others from interfering. The final stage, labeled *actions of appeal,* includes flirtatious glancing, gaze holding, and moving the body in a sexually suggestive way.[43]

Body movement can also reflect status differences between people. Mark Knapp, a researcher and writer on nonverbal communication, summarized Albert Mehrabian's findings on nonverbal indicators of status and power as follows:

High-status persons are associated with less eye gaze, postural relaxation, greater voice loudness, more frequent use of arms-akimbo [hands on hips], dress ornamentation with power symbols, greater territorial access, more expansive movements and postures, greater height, and more distance.[44]

Consider This

According to the research of Paul Ekman, a psychologist at the University of California at San Francisco, there is no foolproof method of lie detection yet. However, clues that may signal someone is trying to deceive you include the following:

- Hesitation in answering a question that should elicit an immediate response. "If you asked someone 'Who'd you have lunch with today?,' no thought should be required to remember or answer that question."
- Signs of having to think about an answer—and perhaps make one up. These include "looking away while talking" and pausing between sentences. Other clues are "repetitious speech" and "lack of animation in the face, body and voice while speaking."
- Tightening the lips.
- Raising the tone of voice. A voice "being a little higher in tone than usual" is one clue to fear in an inexperienced liar.
- Appearance of "micro-expressions"—flashes of expression that betray what a person is really feeling.
- A smile that doesn't use any of the muscles around the eyes, or a look of sadness that fails to show any expression in the forehead.
- Lengthy facial expressions—expressions that last five to ten seconds or more. "Unless someone is having a peak experience, at the height of ecstasy, in a roaring rage or at the bottom of depression, genuine emotional expressions don't remain on the face for more than a few seconds."
- A crooked expression that is "slightly stronger on one side of the face than the other may signal a deceptive emotion, which may indicate lying."

A lie catcher should never rely upon one clue to deceit. There must be many. The facial clues should be confirmed by clues from voice, words, or body.

—From "These Are the Clues That May Signal Someone Is Trying to Deceive You," the *Washington Post.* As reprinted in the *Toronto Star,* June 28, 1985, Section F2. Used by permission.

These characteristics are in contrast to the behavior of the low-status person. Lower-status people communicating with higher-status people tend to be more formal, more rigid, and less adaptable.[45]

Deception has been associated with a variety of nonverbal body behaviors. Research on lying indicates that liars will have:

1. Higher voice pitch,
2. Less enthusiastic gestures,
3. Slower speaking rate,
4. Less immediacy (closeness) to others in body position,
5. Less eye contact,
6. More uncertainty in gestures,
7. More speech errors, and
8. Less nodding.[46]

Cues that cause another person to notice or to become aware of deception are called leakage clues. Leakage clues associated with the face might be smiles that are drawn out too long or frowns that are too severe. But other kinds of clues are numerous and include gestures as well as body movement—for example, digging hands into cheek, tearing at fingernails, aggressive foot kicks, etc.[47]

Personal appearance. Even if we believe the cliché that beauty is only skin-deep, we must recognize that not only does our personal appearance have a profound effect on our self-image, but it also affects our behavior and the behavior of people around us. Our physical appearance provides a basis for first and sometimes long-lasting impressions. It also affects who we talk to, date, or marry, how socially and sexually successful we will be, and even our potential for vocational success. This is unfair, but it's true.

The billion-dollar cosmetics industry testifies to the fact that people care about physical appearance and firmly believe it makes a difference. We apply all kinds of creams, lotions, and colorings to our skin. We may adorn our bodies with glasses, tinted contact lenses, ribbons, beards, hair ornaments, jewelry, and clothes. Body adornments are a big part of what Ruesch called object language.

Clothing is another communication medium over which we exert special control. Clothing reflects the way we choose to package ourselves. Researchers have determined that our clothes provide three different kinds of information about us.[48]

1. Clothes reveal something about the *emotions* we are experiencing. This works both ways: how we feel affects what we wear and what we wear affects how we feel. We'll put on our most comfortable clothes in the morning if comfort is going to be our most important consideration that day. If we're going to speak as a student representative at a meeting of the board of regents of our college, chances are we'll choose our clothes less for

comfort and more for the feeling we hope to convey at the meeting—confidence or maturity or whatever. In these cases we are dressing both for how we feel and how we intend to feel later on. We've all had the experience of feeling inappropriately dressed, either too formally or too informally, on some occasions, and we know how our clothes affect how we feel about those occasions.

2. Our clothes may disclose something about our *behavior*. If you have ever worn a uniform of any kind, you know how clothes can transform you and change your behavior. If we get dressed up for a job interview, we feel important; in our own mind our actions also take on importance. Because this occurs in our mind, it is also very likely to affect our behavior. We will be more calculated, purposeful, and dynamic. We may stand erect rather than slouch. We may tend to lower our voice, slow our rate of speaking, and use fewer nonfluencies ("uh's" and "um's"). Just as dress affects us, we are also likely to judge other people's behavior by the way *they* dress. What expectations do you have for a person dressed as a police officer, judge, nurse, or priest?

3. Our clothes function to *differentiate* us from other people. Twenty-year-old college students dress differently than twenty-year-olds with jobs in the business world. Clothing also differs between age groups. For example, one group of researchers determined that a single man of 20-25 spends twice

MISS PEACH, Courtesy of Mell Lazarus. © 1990, Mell Lazarus.

as much on clothes as a man of 45-50 and three times as much as a man of 65-70.[49] Clothing may also be used by people to raise themselves from a subordinate position, to raise self-esteem and apparent status.[50] Clothes serve to differentiate, too, between people who wish to be perceived as fashionable and those who don't care about fashion, between the formal and the informal, and between people with different social roles.

Personal appearance also relates to our body type. That is, our particular body configuration (fat, thin, or athletic) affects the way we are perceived and responded to by others, and even what they expect of us. In research studies, body types have been labeled endomorph (fat), ectomorph (thin), and mesomorph (athletic). (See Figure 6.1.) People who were shown silhouette drawings of such body types in males were asked to respond on a variety of scales. Knapp summarizes the findings of these tests:

> *Their results show that (1) the endomorph was rated as fatter, older, shorter (silhouettes were the same height), more old-fashioned, less strong physically, less good-looking, more talkative, more warmhearted and sympathetic, more good-natured and agreeable, more dependent on others, and more trusting of others; (2) the mesomorph was rated as stronger, more masculine, better-looking, more adventurous, younger, taller, more mature in behavior, and more self-reliant; (3) the ectomorph was rated thinner, younger, more ambitious, taller, more suspicious of others, more tense and nervous, less masculine, more stubborn and inclined to be difficult, more pessimistic, and quieter.*[51]

Although space does not allow a complete presentation of research findings in all areas of personal appearance, it should be noted that some of the other cues that may affect interpersonal responses are height, body color, body smell, body hair, and other body-related cues (freckles, moles, acne, and beauty marks). Even our own perception of our personal appearance—our self-image—will affect our interpersonal communication. It is the basic kernel from which our communication behavior grows and flourishes.

1 ENDOMORPHIC	2 MESOMORPHIC	3 ECTOMORPHIC
◯	▽	‖
dependent	dominant	detached
calm	cheerful	tense
relaxed	confident	anxious
complacent	energetic	reticent
contented	impetuous	self-conscious
sluggish	efficient	meticulous
placid	enthusiastic	reflective
leisurely	competitive	precise
cooperative	determined	thoughtful
affable	outgoing	considerate
tolerant	argumentative	shy
affected	talkative	awkward
warm	active	cool
forgiving	domineering	suspicious
sympathetic	courageous	instrospective
soft-hearted	enterprising	serious
generous	adventurous	cautious
affectionate	reckless	tactful
kind	assertive	sensitive
sociable	optimistic	withdrawn
soft-tempered	hot-tempered	gentle-tempered

Figure 6.1
Characteristics associated with particular body configurations.

From CORTES, J. B. and GATTI, F. M., "Physique and Self-Description of Temperament," *Journal of Consulting Psychology*, 1965, 29, 432-439. Copyright © 1965 by the American Psychological Association. Adapted by permission of the publisher and author.

Vocal Cues

Vocal cues are all those attributes of sound that can convey meaning. Sounds (not words) are considered nonverbal communication. This includes how loudly or quickly we speak, how much we hesitate, how many nonfluencies we use. These vocal cues can convey our emotional state.

As we well know, all we have to do to reveal anger is change the way we talk: we may talk louder, faster, and more articulately than usual. We may use our silences more pointedly. We can say exactly the same thing in a fit of anger as in a state of delight and change our meaning by how we say it. We can say "I hate you" to sound angry, teasing, or cruel. Vocal cues are what is lost when our words are written down. The term often used to refer to this quality—what occurs beyond or in addition to the words we speak—is **paralanguage.**[52]

If you don't think paralanguage is very important, think of the impression made in a job interview by an applicant who mispronounces words or speaks too loudly or too fast or with too many hesitations. Such a person might find it hard to get employment in some prestigious business firms or to penetrate the upper strata of society. Although a person's social or business acceptance will probably never depend *only* on vocal cues, there are times when it helps to have correct pronunciation and articulation as part of our credentials.

Try This

Read the following sentence aloud seven times, each time emphasizing a different word in the sentence: I hit him in the eye yesterday.
Notice how the meaning changes as you change your emphasis. You can get seven more variations by reading the sentence as a question instead of a statement.

Consider This

The voice does help to express and to identify emotions, whether or not content is an available cue. Furthermore, people who monitor their own emotions efficiently are especially capable of expressing their feelings intentionally and of judging others' emotions correctly.

—Loretta A. Malandro and Larry Barker, *Nonverbal Communication* (Reading, Mass.: Addison-Wesley Publishing Co., 1983), p. 281.

It has been observed that if we use great variety in pitch (high or low), we are likely to be perceived as dynamic and extroverted. Males who vary their speaking rate are viewed as extroverted and animated. Interestingly, females demonstrating the same variety in rate are perceived as extroverted, but also high-strung, inartistic, and uncooperative. If our voice is flat, we may be thought of as sluggish, cold, and withdrawn. A person with a nasal voice is often perceived as unattractive, lethargic, and foolish.[53] Whether these perceptions are accurate or not, it's useful for us to know how we are likely to be perceived if we speak a certain way.

Certain vocal characteristics are perceived as revealing interpersonal trust, confidence, and sincerity: when trust or confidence is in jeopardy, excessive pauses and hesitations tend to increase. Also, the number of nonfluencies we use—stuttering, repetitions, slips of the tongue, incoherences—increases in situations where we are nervous or ill at ease.

It should be clear that vocal cues do not just refer to *how* something is said. Frequently they *are* what is being said. Vocal cues, then, can reflect attitudes, emotions, control, personality traits, background, or physical features.[54]

There are also vocal stereotypes that relate vocal characteristics to one's occupation, sociability, race, degree of introversion, and body type, among other characteristics.

Although different times, situations, and causes may result in different ways of expressing emotion, it is true that people use vocal cues to judge emotions and feelings. Our total reaction to others may be colored by our reaction to their vocal cues.

Reading Nonverbal Messages

One purpose of learning about nonverbal communication is to increase our understanding of our own actions and reduce the chances of someone misinterpreting us. It's easy to accidentally convey an attitude that may be misleading, inappropriate, or damaging to an interpersonal encounter.

Emotional Dimensions of Nonverbal Behavior

According to Albert Mehrabian, there are "only three primary feeling dimensions that are involved in nonverbal behavior": *immediacy* or *liking*, *dominance* or *power*, and *change* or *responsiveness*.[55] This method of classifying nonverbal communication can be useful in understanding our own nonverbal behavior and the nonverbal behavior of others. In the following discussion, nonverbal behavior is categorized by emotional intent. That is, to understand nonverbal communication, we must consider the emotions from which certain behaviors spring.

Immediacy or liking.   Mehrabian suggested that one of the main determinants of our nonverbal behavior is our tendency to get involved with things we like and to avoid things we don't like. Touching, eye contact, and physical closeness characterize a feeling of immediacy with someone or something; distance, lack of eye contact, and absence of physical contact characterize dislike.

Dominance or power.   According to Mehrabian, another factor at work in our nonverbal communications is our feeling of power or subordination in relation to a particular person or situation. If we feel dominant, we are likely to make large, expansive gestures, stand tall, and move in a relaxed way; we demonstrate submissiveness by avoiding eye contact, maintaining a rigid, erect posture, and making small, tense movements.

Change or responsiveness.   A third factor Mehrabian identified as crucial to our nonverbal expressions is our responsiveness to our environment. We respond either positively or negatively to all the stimuli we encounter— the weather, the food we eat, the people we run into, circumstances, events, and so on. In every waking moment we are reacting to our environment in some way; our nonverbal behavior reflects these reactions.

Try This

Next time you get a telephone call, make some judgments about what you heard. Which of the following vocal cues* did you perceive?

breathiness	throatiness
thinness	orotundity
flatness	increased rate
nasality	increased pitch variety
tenseness	

Now determine which of the following feelings were being conveyed:

affection	impatience
anger	joy
boredom	sadness
cheerfulness	satisfaction

Was there any relationship between vocal quality and the feeling being expressed? Could you find reasons or justifications for what you heard?

*For descriptions of these cues, see P. Heinberg, *Voice Training for Speaking and Reading Aloud* (New York: Ronald Press, 1964), pp. 152–81. Copyright © 1964 by John Wiley & Sons, Inc. Used by permission.

There Are Limits

In reading the nonverbal cues that others send, we are automatically limited: our eyes can handle about five million bits of information per second, but our brain can process only about 500 bits per second.[56] We must be selective. We are also limited by what we decide to look at, and by what we can understand. If we can attach no meaning to cues we observe, we are obviously limited in those areas.

Once you understand the importance of nonverbal communication, its major forms, the various types of nonverbal cues, and its function with respect to spacial distances, body movement, vocal cues, and emotion (the different codes), you should be better able to read nonverbal cues. Reading some of the research (it is extensive) on the various nonverbal codes and how they function together can provide additional insight. Perhaps the best thing you can do, however, to improve your ability to read nonverbal messages, is to become a better observer of the ways nonverbal codes are used to convey meanings. How do people emphasize one code (vocal tone, for example, or facial expression) to communicate their meaning?

It is important, however, *not* to fall into the simplistic "how-to-read-a-person-like-a-book" approach that would have you believe that each nonverbal cue has a particular meaning. It does not work that way. The power of nonverbal communication is in its combined effect, which produces the same message in a variety of ways. Because of this clustering effect, nonverbal communication can be easily misinterpreted. Misinterpretation can occur, too, because individuals have unique nonverbal styles.

Nonverbal communication may vary dramatically among individuals. Therefore, it is important to try to get to know and understand the repertoires and habits of those who are close to us, or those with whom we interact frequently.

As our knowledge and understanding of these people increase, so will the accuracy of our interpretations.

Our success in reading nonverbal messages depends on several factors. First, how interested are we in doing it? The more value we ascribe to developing and using our nonverbal skills, the more likely we are to study and improve. Second, what is our attitude toward communication situations as learning environments? If our attitude is, "I want to learn; this looks like fun," it is likely we will find the learning process productive and worthwhile. Third, are we willing to enlarge the scope of our nonverbal knowledge? To develop a skill requires basic understandings; to perfect that skill we must use and expand it by careful observation and conscientious study. Finally, are we actively seeking out opportunities to practice? There is no substitute for experience. The greater the variety, the better chance for improvement, growth, and change.[57]

Improving Skills in Nonverbal Communication

As we try to improve our nonverbal communication skills there are three important ideas to keep in mind:

1. Nonverbal communication always occurs in a context. The meanings conveyed are intimately and directly tied to that context. If a man at a party stands with his hips thrust forward slightly, his legs apart, his thumbs locked in his belt, and his fingers pointing down toward his genitals, it may be considered a sexually provocative pose in that context.[58] If he stands the same way as he waits in line for a hamburger with his family, his pose probably does not carry the same message.

Consider This

Do males and females differ in their ability to read nonverbal signals? According to the research, the answer is yes.

> Just as tiny infant girls respond more readily to human faces, female toddlers learn much faster than males how to pick up nonverbal cues from others. And grown women are far more adept than men at interpreting facial expressions. A recent study by University of Pennsylvania brain researcher Ruben Gur showed that they easily read emotions such as anger, sadness, and fear. The only such emotion men could pick up was disgust.

—From "Attitude: In Politics and Management, the 'Gender Gap' is Real," by Merrill McLoughlin, Tracy L. Shryer, Erica E. Goode, and Kathleen McAuliffe in *U.S. News & World Report,* August 8, 1988, p. 56. Reprinted by permission.

2. No nonverbal cue should be viewed in isolation. Cues must be observed as they interact with each other. In the instance just cited, it was not the man's posture alone that was suggestive, but that cue in combination with the position of his legs, thumbs, and fingers. Cues must be viewed in combination.

3. Although we can learn a great deal from observing nonverbal communication, our conclusions should always be tentative rather than final. Every individual is unique. There is always the possibility of actions occurring that are exceptions to any rule. We should view each behavior as existing at this time only, not assume it exists permanently or always.

Some people have mannerisms that are habitual and are not meant to convey any special meaning. We must be careful not to read too much into the behavior of people we don't know well and can only guess about. A person's eye may twitch when he or she is nervous; the twitch could be interpreted by a stranger as an enticing wink. We don't have to refrain from making *any* observations, but it is good to be cautious. Remember, whatever meaning we assign to what we see is a meaning that exists *for us*. Meaning is not in the nonverbal cues we observe; meaning is *in us*. Because it is in us, it will differ from the meaning other people assign.

Work on your self-awareness.   The more you are able to express yourself clearly and accurately and the more in touch you are with your own feelings, the more likely you are to understand the nonverbal communication of others.[59] Your knowledge of yourself can be increased through self-disclosure and feedback. To open up, share, and request feedback from

Consider This

To achieve control and charisma, executives must develop "a physical game plan," according to [management consultant Debra] Benton. Says she: "Walk slowly and purposefully. Plant some pauses along the way." Good posture is also important. "A modified West Point cadet look is critical for business," says Benton. Copying gestures is a fine idea: "When talking to Mr. Big, try to copy whatever he does. It's instant rapport." Use hand gestures: "You will appear more charismatic." When walking downstairs, look not down but straight ahead to project the image of being levelheaded. Of course, this could also be an instruction for falling down.

—"Body Language: Teaching the Right Strut," *Time,* April 30, 1984, p. 54. Copyright © 1984 Time Inc. All rights reserved. Reprinted by permission from TIME.

people you trust increases personal sensitivity. Opening channels for healthy, honest, open feedback can be of mutual benefit for you and for your friends. Your effectiveness in receiving nonverbal cues will be increased through self-awareness.

Monitor your own behavior. It's helpful to review your own communication experiences, whether positive or negative, to become aware of what you are doing. If you discover something you think might be important, you could solicit the help of friends to verify or deny your observations. You should think more about what you do. It is not easy to see yourself as others see you, but difficult or not, it is useful and worthwhile. It would be ideal if you could watch a videotape of your interactions with others over a period of twenty-four hours or so. Since this is not likely, what you *can* do is enlist the cooperation of close friends to help you identify your nonverbal cues that are disruptive to communication.

Experiment with your behaviors. There are two reasons for trying out different behavior: to improve communication and to break some of your routine, habitual ways of interacting. When you discover you have certain ineffective or distracting mannerisms, you should try to alter them in a meaningful way to increase your interpersonal effectiveness. If you force yourself to try new approaches, you'll increase the number of alternatives you have for behaving. You can "try on" new behaviors to see how they fit. This is part of the process of growing, changing, and becoming. If you find it very hard to break away from your usual routine, you can at least observe how other people handle themselves in similar circumstances to get a framework for monitoring your own behavior in the future.

Respond empathically. Your sensitivity to nonverbal communication will increase as you train yourself to be empathic. Try to understand how the other person feels. Try to get "the big picture." You should always imagine how you would feel if you experienced the same thing. If you are the twentieth applicant for a job to be interviewed on a certain day and you see a tired, expressionless face on the interviewer, you should try to understand how you would feel if you had just been through a day of interviews. Again, this means trying to see where the other person is coming from. It can explain a lot when you're trying to understand what a certain twitch or posture might signify. Your success in reading nonverbal messages will increase if you try to be *empathic.*

Look for patterns. The behavior you observe in others is usually reflected in their whole body and not just in their face or hands. You can usually recognize trembling hands as a sign of nervousness, but nervousness may be shown in other ways as well. Nervous people may bite their lips, speak too quickly, squirm in their chairs, always be ready to leave, avoid

Try This

Watch parts of TV programs with the sound turned way down. Notice how skilled certain actors or entertainers are in enhancing their messages with nonverbal activity. Notice specifically if they:

1. Use exaggerated facial expressions;
2. Touch other people in some way;
3. Make special use of hand gestures;
4. Use the space in which they are communicating (moving closer to or away from other people);
5. Seem to move naturally and comfortably, like "real" people.

You may find that some performers you thought were quite skilled turn out to depend almost entirely on their verbal messages to make a point. In which kinds of programs did you find the performers most adept at nonverbal communication—comedy? drama? action programs? news presentations? commercials?

direct eye contact, or play with paper clips while talking. Too often you draw conclusions from too little evidence. The face and the hands are obvious and easy to observe, but you must also notice posture, body movement, dress, and speech, and try to see patterns of behavior as they relate to different social settings.

Check your perceptions.   If you feel that someone's nonverbal behavior is influencing your reaction to that person, it may be wise to find out whether you have correctly understood the behavior. Just because people close their eyes does not mean they are not paying attention. Some people close their eyes to concentrate better on the message by blocking out distractions. If you are talking to Jennifer and she keeps looking beyond, you could ask, "Do you care about this?" or "Are you listening to me?" Something may be occurring behind you that you should see too!

Express your feelings.   The cultural norm that says people should not openly express their feelings is powerfully restricting. How can you accurately read other people's nonverbal cues if they are feeling one thing and trying to show something else? All you can do is try to watch for congruency or noncongruency in the total communication. Some people smile constantly; a pleasant expression has become such a habit with them that they cannot clear their faces of pleasantness even when they are feeling frustration or despair. To understand a person's total message you need to put together the whole communication puzzle—including all verbal and nonverbal elements—and notice which pieces fit together and which don't.

Likewise, you must strive for congruency in your own communication. If you concentrate on not hiding what you feel, it will be much easier to make your nonverbal messages congruent with your verbal messages. In fact, if you are being perfectly honest, you shouldn't have to worry about sending consistent signals—they will take care of themselves. You must discover the potential of your body; what messages does it want to send? Many of us tend to be too restrictive, too closed, and too inhibited in bodily expression. It's healthy to open the channels for sending honest messages.

People are often influenced more by our nonverbal messages than by our words. We tend to believe what we see and the tone of what we hear far more than the words we hear, and rightly so. People generally have more control over their verbal messages than over their nonverbal ones. True feelings, as revealed through nonverbal cues, are difficult to disguise. Becoming aware of our nonverbal communication habits will help us become more expressive. It will also increase our sensitivity to others.

Notes

[1] Flora Davis, *Inside Intuition: What We Know About Nonverbal Communication* (New York: New American Library, 1973), p. 55. The direct, unwavering stare is also a threat to some animals. See George Schallar, *The Year of the Gorilla* (Chicago: University of Chicago Press, 1964).

[2] Davis, *Inside Intuition*, p. 58.

[3] Erving Goffman, *Behavior in Public Places* (New York: Free Press, 1963), pp. 83–88.

[4] Davis, *Inside Intuition*, p. 61.

[5] As cited in Mark L. Knapp, *Essentials of Nonverbal Communication* (New York: Holt, Rinehart & Winston, 1980), p. 15.

[6] Neil Postman, *Crazy Talk, Stupid Talk: How We Defeat Ourselves by the Way We Talk—and What to Do About It* (New York: Delacorte Press, 1976), p. 228.

[7] P. Ekman and W. V. Friesen, "Nonverbal Leakage and Clues to Deception," *Psychiatry*, 32 (1969): pp. 88–106. Also see P. Ekman and W. V. Friesen, "The Repertoire of Nonverbal Behavior: Categories, Origins, Usage and Coding," *Semiotica*, 1 (1969): pp. 49–98.

[8] Albert Mehrabian, *Silent Messages* (Belmont, Calif.: Wadsworth Publishing Co., 1981), p. 88. See especially Chapter 5, "The Double-Edged Message," pp. 73–88.

[9] Eckman and Friesen developed this system. See Paul Ekman and Wallace V. Friesen, "The Repertoire of Nonverbal Behavior: Categories, Origins, Usage, and Coding," *Semiotica*, 1 (1969): pp. 49–98. Also see updated reports of their research: Paul Ekman and Wallace V. Friesen, "Hand Movements," *Journal of Communication*, 22 (1972): pp. 353–74, and Paul Ekman and Wallace V. Friesen, "Nonverbal Behavior and Psychopathology," in *The Psychology of Depression: Contemporary Theory and Research*, eds. R. J. Friedman and M. M. Katz (Washington: Winston & Sons, 1974).

[10] See Jurgen Ruesch and Weldon Kees, *Nonverbal Communication: Notes on*

the Visual Perception of Human Relations (Berkeley and Los Angeles: University of California Press, 1956), p. 189.

[11] I am indebted to Mark L. Knapp for his "Perspectives on Classifying Nonverbal Behavior." See Mark L. Knapp, *Nonverbal Communication in Human Interaction*, 2d ed. (New York: Holt, Rinehart & Winston, 1978), pp. 12–18.

[12] See Paul Ekman, "Movements with Precise Meanings," *Journal of Communication*, 26 (1976): pp. 14–26.

[13] For more information on these regulators, see John M. Wiemann and Mark L. Knapp, "Turn-Taking in Conversations," *Journal of Communication*, 25 (1975): pp. 75–92.

[14] Knapp, *Nonverbal Communication in Human Interaction*, 2d ed., pp. 12–18.

[15] Knapp, *Nonverbal Communication in Human Interaction*, pp. 125–31.

[16] Edward T. Hall, *The Silent Language* (Greenwich, Conn.: Fawcett Publications, 1959), pp. 163–64. He expands upon these classifications in his second book, *The Hidden Dimension* (Garden City, N.Y.: Doubleday & Company, 1966), pp. 114–29.

[17] J. K. Burgoon and S. B. Jones, "Toward a Theory of Personal Space Expectations and Their Violations," *Human Communication Research*, 2 (1976): pp. 131–46.

[18] F. N. Willis, "Initial Speaking Distance as a Function of the Speaker's Relationship," *Psychonomic Science*, 5 (1966): pp. 221–22.

[19] F. Erickson, "One Function of Proxemic Shifts in Face-to-Face Interaction," in *Organization of Behavior in Face-to-Face Interactions*, eds. A. Kendon, R. M. Harris, and M. R. Key (Chicago: Aldine, 1975), pp. 175–87.

[20] W. E. Leipold, "Psychological Distance in a Dyadic Interview" (Ph.D. diss., University of North Dakota, 1963); and K. B. Little, "Cultural Variations in Social Schemata," *Journal of Personality and Social Psychology*, 10 (1968): pp. 1–7.

[21] R. Schulz and J. Barefoot, "Non-verbal Responses and Affiliative Conflict Theory," *British Journal of Social and Clinical Psychology*, 13 (1974): pp. 237–43.

[22] M. Patterson, "Spatial Factors in Social Interaction," *Human Relations*, 21 (1968): pp. 351–61.

[23] Willis, "Initial Speaking Distance," pp. 221–22.

[24] For an excellent discussion of the factors that affect spatial distance, see Knapp, *Essentials*, pp. 81–87.

[25] Albert Mehrabian, "Orientation Behaviors and Nonverbal Attitude Communication," *Journal of Communication*, 17 (1967): pp. 324–32.

[26] Michael Reece and Robert N. Whitman, "Expressive Movements, Warmth, and Verbal Reinforcement," *Journal of Abnormal and Social Psychology*, 64 (1962): p. 250.

[27] P. Ekman, W. V. Friesen, and P. Ellsworth, *Emotion in the Human Face: Guidelines for Research and an Integration of the Findings* (Elmsford, N.Y.: Pergamon Press, 1972), pp. 57–65. These authors suggest eight categories. Dale G. Leathers adds the last two in *Nonverbal Communication Systems* (Boston: Allyn & Bacon, 1976), p. 24.

[28] C. E. Izard, *The Face of Emotion* (New York: Appleton-Century-Crofts, 1971), p. 216.

[29] Ekman and Friesen, "The Repertoire of Nonverbal Behavior," p. 75.

[30] Dale G. Leathers, *Nonverbal Communication Systems* (Boston: Allyn & Bacon, 1976), p. 34.

[31] Knapp, *Essentials*, p. 167.

[32] Ekman, Friesen, and Ellsworth, *Emotion in the Human Face*, p. 107.

[33] Knapp, *Essentials*, pp. 168–77.

[34] Mark L. Knapp, *Nonverbal Communication*, 2d ed., p. 305.

[35] Goffman, *Behavior in Public Places*, p. 84.

[36] See A. Kendon, "Some Functions of Gaze Direction in Social Interaction," *Acta Psychologica*, 26 (1967): p. 46.

[37] G. Hearn, "Leadership and the Spatial Factor in Small Groups," *Journal of Abnormal and Social Psychology*, 54 (1957): pp. 269–72. As cited in Knapp, *Essentials*, pp. 188–89.

[38] J. M. Wiemann, "An Experimental Study of Visual Attention in Dyads: The Effects of Four Gaze Conditions on Evaluations by Applicants in Employment Interviews," paper presented to the Speech Communication Association, Chicago, 1974.

[39] Z. Rubin, "The Measurement of Romantic Love," *Journal of Personality and Social Psychology*, 16 (1970): pp. 265–73.

[40] M. Argyle and J. Dean, "Eye Contact, Distance, and Affiliation," *Sociometry* 28 (1965): pp. 269–304.

[41] From *Essentials of Nonverbal Communication*, 2d ed., p. 190, by Mark L. Knapp. Copyright © 1980 by Holt, Rinehart & Winston. Reprinted by permission of CBS College Publishing. Permission also covers material cited in notes 44, 46, and 51.

[42] A. Mehrabian, *Nonverbal Communication* (Chicago: Aldine, 1972). This source includes a summary of his work. As cited in Knapp, *Essentials*, p. 135.

[43] A. E. Scheflen, "Quasi-Courtship Behavior in Psychotherapy," *Psychiatry*, 28 (1965): pp. 245–57. As cited in Knapp, *Essentials*, pp. 136–37.

[44] Knapp, *Essentials*, p. 138. See note 41.

[45] Knapp, *Essentials*, p. 138. See note 41.

[46] Knapp, *Essentials*, p. 140. See note 41.

[47] Knapp, *Essentials*, p. 141.

[48] Mary Kefgen and Phyllis Touchie-Specht, *Individuality in Clothing Selection and Personal Appearance: A Guide for the Consumer* (New York: Macmillan Co., 1971), pp. 12–14.

[49] F. Zweig, "Clothing Standards and Habits," in *Dress, Adornment and the Social Order*, eds. M. E. Roach and J. B. Eicher (New York: John Wiley & Sons, 1965), p. 164.

[50] J. Schwartz, "Men's Clothing and the Negro," *Phylon*, 24 (1963): p. 164.

[51] Knapp, *Essentials*, p. 106 (see note 41). From W. Wells and B. Siegel, "Stereotyped Somatypes," *Psychological Reports*, 8 (1961): pp. 77–78; and K. T. Strongman and C. J. Hart, "Stereotyped Reactions to Body Build," *Psychological Reports*, 23 (1968): pp. 1175–78.

[52] See George L. Trager, "Paralanguage: A First Approximation," *Studies in Linguistics*, 13 (1958): pp. 1–12.

[53] D. W. Addington, "The Relationship of Certain Vocal Characteristics with Perceived Speaker Characteristics" (Ph.D. diss., University of Iowa, 1963), pp. 157–58. Also see D. W. Addington, "The Relationship of Selected Vocal Characteristics to Personality Perception," *Speech Monographs*, 35 (1968): pp. 492–503.

[54] See Addington, "The Relationship of Selected Vocal Characteristics to Personality Perception," pp. 492–503. As reported in Knapp, *Essentials*, p. 208.

[55] From *Silent Messages*, pp. 113–18, by Albert Mehrabian. © 1971 by Wadsworth Publishing Company, Inc. Used by permission of the publisher.

[56] W. V. Haney, *Communication and Organization Behavior* (Homewood, Ill.: Richard D. Irwin, 1967), p. 53.

[57] Knapp, *Essentials*, p. 232.

[58] Julius Fast, *Body Language* (New York: Pocket Books, 1971), p. 85.

[59] J. R. Davitz, *The Communication of Emotional Meaning* (New York: McGraw-Hill Book Co., 1964).

Further Reading

Flora Davis, *Inside Intuition* (New York: New American Library, 1973). Davis provides a comprehensive examination of nonverbal communication. This is a good starting point for learning about this important kind of communication.

Julius Fast, *Body Language* (New York: Pocket Books, 1971). This is the book that first created widespread popular interest in nonverbal communication. Fast briefly discusses the major areas of the field and gives a rather superficial glimpse of what it is all about. Easy to read and full of examples.

Edward T. Hall, *The Hidden Dimension* (New York: Anchor Books, 1969). In this book Hall focuses on people's use of space—that invisible bubble that constitutes personal territory. He demonstrates how the use of space can affect personal and business relations. This is a well-written, entertaining book full of examples and illustrations.

Edward T. Hall, *The Silent Language* (New York: Premier Books, 1959). Behind the mystery, confusion, and disorganization of life, there is order. Hall urges a reexamination of much that passes as ordinary, acceptable behavior.

Mark L. Hickson III and Don W. Stacks, *NVC—Nonverbal Communication: Studies and Applications*, 2d ed. (Dubuque, Iowa: Wm. C. Brown Publishers, 1989). In this book, the authors emphasize the interaction between biological functions and sociopsychological functions. A well-presented textbook, it is divided into three sections: The first explains the terminology, the second reviews the literature, and the third, a unique section, shows how the research can be applied to real-life situations.

Mark L. Knapp, *Essentials of Nonverbal Communication* (New York: Holt, Rinehart & Winston, 1980). This textbook is well written and comprehensive despite its brevity. The research base is thorough. For an extended version, see Knapp's *Nonverbal Communication in Human Interaction*, 2d ed. (New York: Holt, Rinehart & Winston, 1978).

Dale G. Leathers, *Successful Nonverbal Communication: Principles and Applications* (New York: Macmillan Co., 1986). Written for the introductory course in nonverbal communication, Leathers's book demonstrates how knowledge of the informational potential of nonverbal cues can be used to communicate successfully in the real world. The real strength of this book is its emphasis on applications.

Loretta A. Malandro and Larry L. Barker, *Nonverbal Communication* (Reading, Mass.: Addison-Wesley Publishing Co., 1983). This is a textbook that is enjoyable to read. It includes examples, applications, research findings, a historical perspective, and contemporary information, as well as a complete reference list with both traditional and nontraditional books and articles. The book is both intellectually and emotionally stimulating.

Virginia P. Richmond, James C. McCroskey, and Steven K. Payne, *Nonverbal Behavior in Interpersonal Relations* (Englewood Cliffs, N.J.: Prentice-Hall, Inc., 1987). The authors have approached nonverbal communication from a blend of social, scientific, and humanistic perspectives. In this textbook, the authors provide an overview, then examine in detail the major categories of behavior, and, finally, discuss four important relationship contexts: female/male, superior/subordinate, teacher/student, and intercultural.

Shirley Weitz, *Nonverbal Communication: Readings with Commentary*, 2d ed. (New York: Oxford University Press, 1979). Biological rhythms in paralanguage and psychopathology, environmental psychology, touch, and smell are some of the topics touched on in this volume. Designed for a more serious examination of the topic.

7 *Influencing Others: Interpersonal Persuasion*

Learning Objectives

When you have finished this chapter you should be able to:

- Relate communication to attitudes and values.
- Recognize the difference between attitudes and values.
- Explain the difference between instrumental and terminal values.
- Describe the components of attitudes.
- Discuss Fritz Heider's balance theory as a model of attitude change and point out some of the limitations of Heider's model.
- Explain how people resolve imbalances.
- Explain some of the variables that determine which persuasive strategy is selected and describe the relationship of power to interpersonal influence.
- Define compliance-gaining strategies and give an example.
- Give an example of a compliance-resisting strategy.
- Discuss ways to improve your skills in influencing others.

A classmate closely follows you out of the classroom and in the hallway asks to borrow your notes to study for an upcoming exam. Since this classmate is someone you would like to know better, since you were not planning to review your notes tonight, and since, at least from all outward appearances, you think you can trust this person, you comply with the request saying, "All right, but please bring them back to class tomorrow so I can use them tomorrow night."

You are seated in the no-smoking section of a restaurant. The section is clearly marked. At the table next to you a man and woman sit down to talk. Both proceed to light up cigarettes. You try to make eye contact so you can point out the "No Smoking" sign, but you are unable to do so. You gather up your courage, go find the manager, and explain the problem. The manager approaches their table, points to the "No Smoking" sign, and asks the couple to move. They comply.

A member of your work team is loafing, goofing off, and not doing his fair share of the work. All other members of the team recognize the problem but do not confront the person. They do his share of the work so the team can continue. Because much of the additional work has fallen on your shoulders, you decide to speak to this member. When alone with him, after some informal talk and an explanation of how important the team's project is to everyone, you say, "Will you please do the task you were assigned?" He responds, "Oh, I plan to. I just haven't had time yet." So you say, "We need the help *now,* not later. Could you help us out *now?*" He says that he will try to rearrange his work schedule to accommodate the group.

Edwin Weinstein, a writer on interpersonal competence, has said that the communicative ability to get others to do what we want them to do is likely to be the single most essential skill for participating in society.[1] The process of attempting to bring about changes in other people's attitudes or behavior is known as persuasion. *Compliance gaining*—that is, getting another person to think or act in a specific way, is one form of persuasion. Researchers note that people "do not seem to possess this skill in equal measure. Some do it very well; others, terribly. Unfortunately," they add, "the consequences of not performing this communicative act successfully may be severe."[2] What it boils down to is that inappropriate behavior in making requests of others or in responding to such requests (known as compliance-resisting) may be attributed to incompetence[3]. Since you are likely to be judged—in *any* interpersonal situation—on your ability to make requests of others and to respond to them appropriately, it is important to develop and improve your skills in persuasion.

In this chapter, I will first discuss the relationship of communication to attitudes and values. Why should we study attitudes and values in the first place? Then I will examine attitudes and values specifically. What are they, and how do they relate to each other? In the third section, I will offer an explanation of balance theory as a model of attitude change. How are attitudes changed? I will then look at the positive and negative aspects of attitude change. This section includes information on the duration of attitude change, the process of selecting strategies for attitude change, and the ethics of interpersonal influence. Compliance gaining and compliance resisting are discussed, as well as the variables that affect our choice of compliance strategy. Finally, I'll discuss improving skills in influencing others.

Communication and Attitudes and Values

What have attitudes and values to do with interpersonal communication? First, speech communication is a form of behavior. Studying attitudes and values gives us insight into the *why* of human behavior. We can look at *what* is said by examining verbal communication, and we can study *how* it is being said by analyzing nonverbal components. Remember from the preceding chapter that the words we use are an indicator of what we are thinking; the nonverbals are an indicator of our emotional response to what we are thinking. But a deeper, more essential question is *why* is it being said? And the answer to this question ties into the whole web of human experience that makes each of us unique.

Second, the roots for what people say lie in their attitudes and values. Thus, if we wish to touch people directly and deeply, we must do so by touching these roots. True, we cannot always know the exact nature of the roots. But, knowing that there *are* roots and that the more we understand those roots the better we will be equipped to deal with them, will help us communicate with others in a direct and profound manner.

Third, such knowledge can aid us in interpersonal communication because it can guide us in probing for the roots. Suppose one day you hear a friend make a seemingly frivolous remark that expresses a positive attitude toward suicide. You know that your friend has been depressed, and has suffered some small failures and rejections lately, so you have reason for concern. You may not want to pursue this attitude immediately, but you might start probing subtly. Has your friend had any direct experience involving suicide? The suicide of a friend or family member can have a powerful, lasting effect. How much does she value life? Does she value her own life? Does it appear that she has concrete reasons for living?

If you discover she has a weak value system supporting living, this is where you could concentrate future communications: show her how valuable she is to you and to others. Emphasize the contribution she has to make, or how much others have to gain from her knowledge or expertise. What you want to do is, in a sense, offer a positive value system to supplant her negative one.

What if your probing does not reveal a negative value system after all? What's left? You might find out if her remark was primarily an emotional response to a particular frustration. A low grade on a paper, a brush off by an old friend, or being jilted by a relationship partner.

As you probe the emotional basis, you may discover a value system operating that you did not know about. The depression you detected at the outset is real, and your friend is experiencing an emotional response to a trying, complicated situation over which she has no control. Her father and mother are in the process of getting a divorce, and this situation is tearing your friend apart emotionally. At the moment she feels as though her only outlet is suicide; it is apparent that she needs serious counseling.

The value system operating here can be expressed succinctly: Your friend values family security (marriage, the traditional family). When these roots (values) are disturbed, attitude changes are likely to occur, or at least, attitudinal fluctuations.

What your probing has determined, then, is that your friend's emotional response (the attitude) is a result of values about her parents and her family (the value system). At that point, you can make your communication with her more specific and purposeful: try to show her that her parents' divorce need not destroy her, to let her know that she has a large group of concerned friends, and to encourage her to see a professional counselor.

Although the example is extended, it demonstrates how understanding these roots can make our communication more precise and purposeful. It adds a "depth" dimension to our communication that allows us to go beyond superficial, everyday interaction.

Attitudes and Values

What exactly is an "attitude"? Attitudes are intangible concepts. They are generally referred to as general tendencies of people to act in a certain way under certain conditions.[4] The tendency to feel despondent after getting back a paper with a low grade, the tendency to be concerned about your appearance when around members of the opposite sex, or the tendency to feel as though you are getting a bargain regardless of the type of product you buy during a sale would all be attitudes under this definition. More specifically, however, the word attitude is taken to mean a tendency to evaluate a person, thing, or idea either favorably or unfavorably.[5] The objects of your attitudes could be inanimate objects, living things, experiences, ideas, or events.

Sometimes people's attitudes are deduced from their behavior. For example, from the previous examples we might deduce that you have an unfavorable attitude toward getting low grades, feel favorably about looking good for members of the opposite sex, or feel favorably about getting bargains. Our behavior and communication habits are based, to a large extent, on our attitudes. But to properly understand and discuss attitudes, we must know about values because attitudes and values are closely inter-related. Because our real interest here is on attitudes and how attitudes can be changed, we will return to a fuller discussion of attitudes after an introduction to values.

Values

There are about as many definitions of values as there are writers on the subject. One helpful approach defines them as matters of importance, as distinct from matters of fact.[6] As matters of importance, values provide enduring standards or yardsticks that guide our actions, attitudes, comparisons, evaluations, and even our justification of self and others.[7] Because they *guide* our attitudes, they need to be considered first. It is their basic or fundamental nature that closely aligns them with our self-concept and puts them at the center of our personality structure. They form the roots for such strongly held beliefs as life, liberty, and the pursuit of happiness. And values most likely determine which clubs, groups, organizations, and associations we join: because they support the same values as we do.

Values can be organizing systems for attitudes. If we value honesty, for example, this value may provide guidelines for forming and developing attitudes. We may have favorable attitudes toward the police, controlling plagiarism, telling the truth, obeying traffic signs, following directions, and so on. Values are usually enduring because they relate to the way we conduct our lives; they provide us with guidelines for our behavior. They influence our behavior—our communication—so that it is consistent with the achievement of our goals. The relationship of values and attitudes is shown in Figure 7.1.

Values can be classified as **instrumental** or **terminal.** According to Milton Rokeach, a well-known scholar of human values, *instrumental values* are those that influence our daily decisions—such as being ambitious, cheerful, honest, and polite. They provide the standards that we use on a daily basis. *Terminal values* are goals that we strive for. For example, we desire happiness, mature love, security, self-respect, and wisdom. Rokeach's list of instrumental and terminal values is provided in Table 7.1.[8]

One thing may have become obvious to you: We are likely to have a small number of values whereas the number of attitudes we hold is many. Rokeach claims that the human values he lists are universal. Of course, the priority we give to any single value depends on our society and on the individual. But these are *the* values that serve as standards for behavior and judgment.

Attitudes

Attitudes exist internally. We derive them from different sources and hold them with different degrees of strength. Attitudes relate to things, people, and concepts. In general, we acquire them as a result of our experiences: we

Figure 7.1
The relationship of values (left) and attitudes (right).

Table 7.1
Rokeach's instrumental and terminal values.

Instrumental Values	Terminal Values
Ambitious	A comfortable life
Broadminded	An exciting life
Capable	A sense of accomplishment
Cheerful	A world at peace
Clean	A world of beauty
Courageous	Equality
Forgiving	Family security
Helpful	Freedom
Honest	Happiness
Imaginative	Inner harmony
Independent	Mature love
Intellectual	National security
Logical	Pleasure
Loving	Salvation
Obedient	Self-respect
Polite	Social recognition
Responsible	True friendship
Self-controlled	Wisdom

Try This

Rank Rokeach's instrumental and terminal lists of values according to how *you* value them. Rank each list of eighteen items separately. Give the lists to friends and have them rank the values. Compare your results. If there are differences, *why* did these differences occur?

may have a favorable attitude toward animals because our parents allowed us to have pets as children, or toward reading because our parents read to us often. Peers, teachers, parents, and even television personalities shape our attitudes. The more experiences we have, the more varied our attitudes are likely to be. Each attitude has four characteristics: *direction, intensity, salience* (importance), and *differentiation.*

Direction. An attitude's direction may be favorable, unfavorable, or neutral (no direction). In talking with others, it is often important to know the direction of their attitudes. If we are interested in persuading them, direction becomes vitally important. How we might begin, what words or arguments we choose, or how we structure our approach depends on whether the other person's attitude is favorable, unfavorable, or neutral.

When was the last time you wanted to convince someone of something? If, for example, you wanted to persuade a classmate to take a computer course with you, wouldn't it be helpful to know how the student felt about computers and their contribution to his or her career? To know how this classmate feels about computers would be to know the direction of his or her attitude.

Intensity. The intensity of an attitude refers to its strength. If a person we wish to persuade holds a particular attitude with great intensity, there is little likelihood that we will change it. Intensity can vary from zero (absolutely none) to infinity (a person willing to die for an attitude). Various people may hold attitudes in the same direction yet differ radically with respect to their intensity.

How might intensity be reflected in the example regarding computers? If you realized the student passionately hated computers, statistics, and mathematics, you might refrain from approaching him or her about taking a computer course, thinking, of course, that your efforts would have little result. The more intense an attitude, the more likely it is to produce consistent behavior.

Salience.   Salience refers to the perceived importance of attitudes. If you were an art student and hated computers, statistics, and mathematics, this attitude might not be as important—salient—for you as, perhaps, for a student in business administration. The more that things affect you directly—have a strong influence on your life—the more likely it is that attitudes regarding those things will be salient, even highly salient, for you. An attitude that is salient is less likely to change or be changed.

Differentiation.   Our discussion of direction, intensity, and salience may have suggested that attitudes are solitary or isolated elements. Yet attitudes seldom exist alone. That is, they are part of an interrelated mix. Attitudes with a large number of supporting beliefs are high in differentiation; those that are based on few beliefs are low in differentiation.

You may believe that a teacher is good because he or she is knowledgeable, organized, concerned about students, prompt, efficient, prepared, and humorous. Your attitude toward this teacher would be high in differentiation because it is relatively complex. On the other hand, suppose you voted against a candidate in the last election simply because he or she

Try This

List all the clubs, groups, organizations, and associations to which you currently belong—either formally or informally. Now, place a large check beside those that have the same—or nearly the same—values as you do. Can you articulate one or two of the specific values that each club, group, organization, or association actually espouses?

If one of these organizations were to change its values, would you leave it? How much of a change would it take? How easily could you change to conform to this group? If you wanted to initiate a change in the group's values, could you do it? How would you go about it?

Consider This

An attitude can be likened to a miniature theory in science, having similar functions and similar virtues and vices. An attitude, like a theory, is a frame of reference; saves time; because it provides us a basis for induction and deduction, organizes knowledge; has implications for the real world; and changes in the face of new evidence.

—Milton Rokeach, *Beliefs, Attitudes, and Values: A Theory of Organization and Change* (San Francisco: Jossey-Bass, 1968), p. 131.

supported the current administration. Your attitude toward that person, based on this one belief, would be relatively low in differentiation.

When attempting to change an attitude, it is helpful to know the degree of differentiation of that attitude. The more complex it is, the more difficult it is to change. It should be pointed out, however, that some attitudes which appear simple—low in differentiation—may be very complex once they are explored in depth. In the example regarding the candidate who supported the current administration, your attitude could be very high in differentiation if you were really voting against the administration's stand on the economy, foreign affairs, education, concern for the poor, and exploration of outer space.

Balance Theory: A Model of Attitude Change

When out attitudes are so deeply ingrained that we are hardly aware of them, they are very difficult to change. And, similarly, it is difficult for us to bring about attitude change in others. But attitude change can and does take place, especially if we are trying to be less rigid and more open and self-aware. The process of attitude change can promote growth (when we rid ourselves of an unhealthy bias) or it can be manipulative when we try to persuade someone to adopt an attitude we hold. Let's look at how this process takes place.

As a communication source or receiver, we should be aware of what happens when we state an attitude to another person (or vice versa) and when we try to effect successful attitude change. The model of attitude change we will use is one originally formulated by Fritz Heider, and it will help you understand the fundamentals of the process.

The theory rests on three assumptions: (1) that psychological imbalance is unpleasant or uncomfortable; (2) that we seek to maintain balance and to reduce imbalance; and (3) that one way we can achieve balance, or at least reduce imbalance, is to modify our attitudes.[9] **Balance** is mental and emotional steadiness.

It is not difficult to think of examples that demonstrate the concepts of balance and imbalance. If you like a particular professor you not only speak favorably of him or her, but you also look specifically for nice things to say. If you are a registered Democrat, you will generally vote for Democratic candidates. Conservatives support positions that reflect their philosophy.

It is easy to generate examples of imbalance. You return from a movie with a friend and discover she loved it; you hated it. You like freedom and lack of restriction, and yet you are enrolled in a class that is tightly structured and restrictive. A professor you admire recommends a book that you find distasteful. Awareness of similar imbalances may reveal the unpleasantness or discomfort of such situations.

The model of attitude change that follows is called **Heider's Balance Theory.**[10] Fritz Heider developed a model in which P refers to one person, O represents another person, and X stands for the topic being talked about. This is a useful way to picture the attitude change process.

Think of yourself as person one, or P. The relationships between you and O and X will be represented by plus and minus signs. A plus sign indicates a positive attitude; a minus sign, a negative attitude.

Heider proposed that in interpersonal relations, you are in a state of balance if the people you like have the same attitudes you do. You are in a state of balance, too, if people you dislike hold different attitudes from yours on the same topics. According to Heider, whenever you have three +'s or two −'s, the relationship will be balanced.

Try This

Here is a brief way to examine some of your *attitudes* on education. Complete the following statements:

1. I like classes that:
2. A teacher is a person who:
3. Students who pay for their own education:
4. I like textbooks that:
5. People who can use their education best are:
6. A student who cheats on exams, seldom does his or her own work, and tends to avoid classes:
7. Attendance in classes:
8. Compared with most other students, my education has been:
9. If I were to make one suggestion likely to improve higher education, it would be to:
10. Mandatory education should end with:

In Figure 7.2, let *X* be a certain movie. In A, you like the other person and both of you like the movie *(X)*. In B, you like the other person but neither of you likes the movie. In C, you like the movie and the other person does not, but you really do not care for him or her anyway. In D, you do not care for the other person or for the movie, even though the other person likes the movie. These are all what Heider calls states of balance. We feel comfortable in such situations because everything is in equilibrium.

If, on the other hand, you have three −'s or two +'s, the relationship will be unbalanced. In E of Figure 7.2, you don't like the other person and neither of you likes the movie. In F, both of you like the movie but you don't like the other person. In G, you like the movie and the other person, but the other person dislikes the movie. In H, you dislike the movie but you like the other person and he or she likes the movie. These are all what Heider would call states of imbalance. It's pretty obvious that you are more comfortable when people you like think the way you do.

When we are talking with a person we like very much and we realize that the two of us have different attitudes, we may try to bring our attitudes together; that is, we may **strain for balance.**[11] How hard we try depends on how strong and how salient or important our own attitude is. It also depends on how much we like the other person and how important the relationship is to us.

Any strain for attitude balance will affect our interpersonal relationship with this other person. The more we want to make our attitudes like those of someone else, the more likely we are to increase our communication with that person. And greater quantity of interaction—the sheer number of transactions—increases the probability that attitude change will occur.

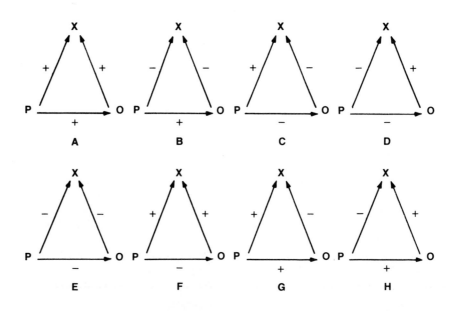

Figure 7.2
Heider's balance theory. (P) = first person, (O) = second person, (X) = topic under discussion, (+) = positive attitude, (−) = negative attitude.

Resolving Imbalances

Because we prefer a state of balance, we try to perceive things in a way that does not disturb our balance. Suppose the *X* in E and F of Figure 7.2 is the classic Marx Brothers movie *Duck Soup*. We see the movie with Arthur, whom we don't like. In E, we hate the movie, and so does Arthur. In F, we love it and Arthur does too. In both cases we are uncomfortable because we don't like Arthur and we would prefer that our tastes were different from his. In G and H of Figure 7.2, we see *Duck Soup* with Barb, a good friend, but in both of these cases one of us likes the movie and the other doesn't. Again we are uncomfortable because we would like to agree with Barb. How do we resolve these states of imbalance?[12]

1. We could criticize the source of the disturbing message. We could decide that Arthur and Barb don't mean what they say or simply don't know their own tastes.
2. We could say it doesn't matter. We may decide that disagreeing with Arthur or agreeing with Barb about this movie really isn't important.
3. We might go out and find additional information or other people to support us. This doesn't resolve the imbalance, but it may make us more secure about our position. We could probably find movie

reviews that reinforce our opinions of the movie whether they are positive or negative.

4. We might misperceive the other person's position. In the case of Arthur, this would mean thinking something like, "He said he didn't like it, but really he just doesn't like black-and-white movies," or "He said he liked it, but he laughed at all the stupid parts. He missed the really subtle humor." In the case of Barb our misperceptions might be more on the order of "She said she didn't like it, but really she was just too tired to enjoy it. She wasn't in the mood," or "She said she liked it, but she probably just thought I wanted her to say that."

5. We might tell ourselves that the conflicting attitudes are not relevant to each other. For both Arthur and Barb, this might mean *we* were looking at the movie from the point of view of a film connoisseur, while *they* were casual moviegoers. Our perspectives are just too different from theirs.

6. We could try to convince Arthur or Barb that our attitude is the right one. This, of course, means convincing the others that they are wrong. We might try to do this by citing movie reviews or what we perceive as "popular opinion." Or we might simply describe in detail what we thought was good (or bad) about the film.

7. We could change our own attitude. We could say we'd reconsidered and really did think *Duck Soup* was great (or terrible).

8. We could consider the imbalance a virtue. We might convince ourselves that it is healthy to admit we might agree with Arthur or disagree with Barb some of the time.

These methods of resolving imbalances show what we are up against when we set out to change someone's attitudes. We use some of these

Try This

What are some attitudes that you hold very dear? Are these attitudes likely to change by tomorrow? Next week? How about by next year? List some of these attitudes. Do they have anything to do with:

parents?	drugs?	dating?
school?	grades?	free time?
earning money?	how you use your money?	sex?
homework?	vacation time?	independence?
teachers?	cheating?	religion?
politics?	the opposite sex?	drinking?
selfishness?	music?	art?

methods to protect ourselves when we hear disturbing communications just as much as others do. But even if a change in attitude does occur, there is no guarantee that behavior will change correspondingly. Behavior changes will occur only if the direction, strength, and salience of the attitude are significant and if the context is appropriate. If Barb didn't like *Duck Soup* and we want to change her attitude and also get her to go to more Marx Brothers movies, we'll have to convince her of the direction, strength, and salience of our own attitude.

The relationship between attitudes and behavior can be very loose. There is no reason to assume that because an attitude changes, a behavioral change will follow. People can be enthusiastic about something one minute and bored with it the next.

Limitations of Heider's Model

There are a number of problems with looking at attitude change from Heider's perspective alone. The model does not, for example, take into account degrees of liking or disliking. Using Heider's model we are restricted to using plus and minus signs to indicate our attitudes. Another limitation is that Heider's model allows just one or two options to resolve an imbalance: change this plus or that minus. In reality, however, a number of options are open to people who feel tensions created by imbalance. For example, if you like Peggy much better than you like Carole and then find out that Peggy cares for Carole a great deal, you might be inclined to change your attitudes toward either one or both. The possibilities in this situation include: (1) changing your attitude toward Carole (she comes up in your estimation because of Peggy's interest in her); (2) changing your attitude toward Peggy (she comes down in your estimation because of her interest in Carole); or (3) changing your attitude toward both (they both come up or they both go down).

Heider's model suggests that attitude change is an all-or-nothing situation. It suggests that we change pluses to minuses—positive to negative—or vice versa, to restore balance. In many situations, however, we may change our attitude toward both attitude objects to establish a suitable midpoint at which balance is restored.

Another limitation of Heider's model is that there are situations to which it does not apply. For example, just because you love your dog and your dog loves to gnaw rawhide does not mean you, too, have to love to gnaw rawhide. Or that you have to start disliking your dog.

A final limitation of the model is that it does not take into account situations involving one object of judgment and more than two people. This further limits its applicability.

Despite these limitations, however, balance theory remains important. Its offshoots have spawned and will continue to spawn much valuable

Consider This

Yet we must deal with the world and its inhabitants, and therefore some understanding of it is necessary. In order to integrate the fragments of knowledge we do have and to bring some comprehensible order into the chaos of ignorance and some understanding into the complexity, we often do a peculiar thing—we create a world in our minds and pretend it is the real world. When as scientists we create a substitute world, we term it a theoretical model.

—E. E. Ghiselli, *Theory of Psychological Measurement* (New York: McGraw-Hill Book Co., 1964), p. 4.

research. Also, the model provides a useful beginning perspective. It offers the cornerstone of what one day may be an adequate theory of attitude change.

Attitude Change: For Better or Worse

It is important when studying attitudes to realize that what we are studying may *not* be observable. In addition, what we are studying may be outside the grasp of scientific analysis. To make matters more difficult, our assumptions about human behavior—in whatever context—may be subject to error. The point is not to discourage study, but to underscore the need to maintain an open mind. In this section I will discuss the likely duration of attitude change, the factors that affect the process of selecting influence strategies, and the ethics of interpersonal influence.

The Duration of Attitude Change

The point of discussing attitudes is to provide a base for understanding attitude change in ourselves and in others. What causes us to change our attitudes? Do we wake up one morning and say, "My attitude toward my family is poor. I think I'll replace it"? Not likely. We need time to realize the need for change and to make the change permanent.

We change our attitudes for a variety of reasons. Another person may give us a reward for changing our behavior or punish us for not changing it. Making a change under these circumstances is called **compliance.** We may comply for the moment but really not change our attitudes. This kind of change is frequently only temporary. For example, we know we will be punished if we get caught exceeding the speed limit. We may comply with the law, even if we object to it, when the threat of punishment is near—we see a police car—but the compliance is temporary if we speed up when the threat disappears.

We may change our attitudes because of **identification.** If someone we admire holds a particular opinion, we may try to be like that person by adopting similar attitudes. But when we are away from that person, our attitudes may change back to their original position. If we wanted to change another person's attitude through persuasion, one way to do it might be by using identification. We would try to present an honest, trustworthy, and credible image that the other person could identify with.

Internalization occurs when we adopt an attitude because we are truly convinced by it. If someone persuades us to quit smoking because it is harmful to our health, we may change our attitude toward smoking because we are truly convinced we will suffer if we do not. We may be inclined to change our attitude toward a pass-fail grading system if someone convinces us that prospective employers prefer job candidates who have taken courses for a letter grade. Changes such as these are likely to be long-lasting since they are based on intellectual and emotional agreement and do not depend on the presence of arbitrary reward or punishment or on another person.[13]

Up to this point, I've been talking about the ways we deal with challenges to our existing attitudes and how we adjust our thinking to maintain and protect those attitudes. However, we actually do change attitudes at times. There are reasons. For example, we might be **coerced** to change. If we do something illegal, law enforcement authorities may force us to change. Our attitude toward freedom may result in continual excessive speeding. The authorities may coerce us by (1) giving us a warning, (2) taking away our driver's license, or (3) putting us in jail. Whether the result is a change in behavior only or a change in attitude, too, could be a product of how effectively the authorities convinced us that speeding is inappropriate and whether we internalized their arguments. We might change our behavior to change our attitudes. We might change our attitudes, too, because of more subtle coercion, or **propaganda.** An organization may get us to accept its doctrines through "mass hypnosis, constant repetition, loaded language, the subtle use of social pressures, or the appeal to irrelevant loves, hates, and fears."[14]

We might also change our attitudes because of **manipulation.** A manipulator may exploit us, use us, or control us.[15] This may be blatant control, as when a friend says, "If you have that attitude, you will no longer be my friend." Or it may be more subtle, as when advertisers try to change our attitude toward their product by suggesting it will make us happier and more popular.

Try This

All advertising is meant to be persuasive. Advertisers assume they have to change our attitude toward their product to get us to buy it. On a P-O-X model, we are P, the advertisers are O, and the product being advertised is X. We can assume O will always be favorable to X.

Look at diagrams A, D, F, and H in Figure 7.2, where the O-X relationship is positive. Can you think of some television commercials which each of these diagrams describes? For example, diagram A describes a situation where we like both the product and the commercial. In D, we dislike both the product and the commercial. These are states of balance.

Obviously, advertisers hope the A situation exists much of the time, but we know that it doesn't. How do you resolve the attitudinal imbalance with advertisers represented by diagrams F and H? What would a P-O-X model look like when you are favorably disposed toward the company but dislike one of its commercials? Think of the methods discussed in the text.

Try This

When was the last time you changed one of your attitudes? Can you remember the reason why you changed it? Was the change caused by:

compliance?
identification?
internalization?
coercion?
manipulation?

Were you aware when the change occurred? Did you put up any resistance? What might have been the consequences had you not decided to change? Do you secretly wish that you had not changed?

The point is, there are many reasons for changing attitudes—some positive and some negative. We need to be aware of the forces at work on us. We also must try to avoid using coercion, propaganda, and manipulation in our interpersonal relations with other people. We should never use our knowledge of others for socially destructive behavior.

It may sound as if attitude change occurs rapidly or as the result of a single conversation. With compliance, this may well be the case. But it takes considerable time and usually a number of interpersonal transactions for important changes to occur. Ongoing interpersonal communication is vitally important in changing another person's attitude.

The Process of Selecting Strategies

Writers on strategies realize that there is a difference between what we plan to do and what we actually do. The same is true when it comes to the variables that affect strategy choice. Charles Berger points out that there are a number of variables that can affect which strategies persuaders (agents) select when they try to influence the behavior of others (targets).[16] Berger admits these variables are relevant *only* to reasoned behavior, and our assumption here will be that those who are engaging in influencing others are engaging in reasoned behavior. We will look briefly at seven variables.

Time available for goal achievement is important because with sufficient time, agents can examine potential consequences, situational elements, relationship effects, the personality of the target, and other elements of the interaction. Without the luxury of time, there is greater possibility of error, ineffectiveness, and lack of success. For example, if a decision on a purchase must be made immediately, judgments about quality, other possible alternatives, or even time to discuss the merits of the purchase are less likely to be made.

Affecting another person significantly is often a slow process. If we want to be successful in changing attitudes or behavior, we usually must commit ourselves to a long-term effort. Sometimes it may depend on how many different contacts with the target we are likely to have—the sheer number of times we meet increases the likelihood of change.

Degree of success has to do with how successful the strategy has proven in the past. If it worked before, why not try it again? We all know people who lack behavioral flexibility and depend on the same strategic plan despite its high rate of failure. Failure, of course, should not preclude further use of a strategy. The key is flexibility and adaptability in the use of strategies.

Legitimacy refers to an agent's right to use a particular strategy. Is it an employee's right to demand a raise from an employer? Should a student stand up in class and tell a teacher that class members should not be expected to complete an assignment just made? Does a person have a right to tell a casual friend that his or her choice of a spouse is inappropriate?

Relational consequences refers to the potential impact a strategy might have on the relationship of the agent and target. If a persuader wants to maintain the relationship or improve it, potential consequences need to be considered. A newly married man was watching television and wanted the channel changed. He asked his wife, who was in another room, to change the channel. The wife replied, "Change it yourself." The husband never again asked his wife to change the television channel. His request was an attempt to establish a precedent for future behavior; she made it clear that she had the same intent. Their behavior had a long-range effect on the relationship—a relational consequence. She later confirmed that her response worked.

Intimacy is closely related to relational consequences. Sometimes we are less considerate of the people close to us than we are of others. It may be that their love is "guaranteed," even if we hurt them. Often, just because they are so close all of the time, we do not think of them as being separate from ourselves. Whatever the situation, intimacy needs to be a concern. If you are involved in an intimate relationship, you are likely to find that many (perhaps most) of the persuasive or influence situations that you find yourself in will in some way bear on your intimate relationship, if not now, perhaps sometime in the future.

Personality of the agent will affect strategy selection. Assertive persuaders tend to use more direct strategies. Also, those agents who are cognitively complex—able to assess people and situations from a number of different perspectives—tend to select other-oriented strategies rather than self-oriented strategies. A cognitively complex person has a large number of attitudes that are high in differentiation. People like this tend to adjust their strategy to accommodate the other person such as "You know, if you go to the library with me, you'll do better on tomorrow's test," rather than the self-oriented strategy, "Go to the library with me. I need company when I study."

Relative power refers to the status of the agent compared with the status of the target. *Power* is the ability to affect the behavior of another person or group.[17] Berger suggests that those agents with high power have a wider range of strategy choices whereas those with low power tend to use less direct strategies. Let's look at the different kinds of power.

Think about whether or not you would change your behavior in these situations:

1. Your employer says you will get a raise if you would be willing to put in five more hours per week on weekends. (You currently do not work weekends and previously said you would not.)
2. Your girlfriend's (or boyfriend's) ex-relationship partner has come to you secretly and said, "You stop seeing *(name of your relationship partner)* or something dreadful is going to happen to one of you."
3. Your physician has told you that you must change your eating habits significantly or risk a life-threatening health problem in the next several years.

4. A celebrity whom you admire dresses in a distinctive and highly unusual manner and you have an opportunity to purchase similar clothing for yourself.

5. You have been stopped by a state police officer for speeding and she has chosen to give you a warning along with the comment, "If I ever catch you speeding in my jurisdiction again, I'll throw the book at you."

The question again is, "In which situations would you make a change in your behavior?" Why? Why not? Power and influence go hand in hand. Powerful people control situations, but, as illustrated in these situations, power comes in many forms.[18]

In the first situation, power occurs because the employer controls rewards. This is called *reward power*. In the second instance, you may respond to the ex-relationship partner out of fear. This is called *coercive power*. This could be similar to your response to a mugger demanding your wallet or to a bully pushing in line in front of you saying, "You're *after* me, jerk!"

In the third situation, you might change your diet in response to your physician's suggestion. This is *expert power*. You are unlikely to question your physician's judgment, just as you would probably not question a lawyer, scientist, or engineer who was making a specific suggestion within his or her field of competence.

The fourth situation involves a response to a celebrity, but it could be a response toward anyone who embodies moral or physical attributes that you admire. This is known as *referent power*. Have you ever chosen to wear something just because you saw someone you admire wearing it? This kind of imitation is a form of interpersonal influence.

The final situation involves a response to a police officer. This is called *legitimate power*. You comply *not* because the officer has a nice personality, or fulfills her duty appropriately, but because she represents the powers of the state. You might question her fairness if she chose to give you the speeding ticket, just as you might question the fairness of an assignment made by a teacher, but you cannot question the officer's right to give you a ticket or your teacher's right to make assignments.

Power is just one variable in strategy selection, but the use of power requires communication, and that is why it is of concern to us. But in order for an agent to influence behavior through power, targets must associate the behavior requested with the power held by the agent (the same holds true for the variable labeled legitimacy). All power is based on targets' perceptions. For example, if I don't believe my boss is in a position to give me a raise or if I don't believe the ex-relationship partner is in a position to carry out the threat, appeals to those powers are unlikely to result in influence. Also, unless the agent associates the influence attempt with the power, the attempt may be unsuccessful. Why, for example, does a plainclothes police officer immediately flash a badge to back up a request? To associate the influence attempt with the power.

The Ethics of Interpersonal Influence

The process of influencing others is an ongoing, natural, and important part of our daily lives. But, as mentioned in the Prologue, because persuasion may have an impact on others, because it involves choices about communicative means and specific ends (things we want or desire from others), and because it can be judged by standards of right and wrong, it involves ethical issues.[19] Throughout this book I have stressed the transactional nature of communication; it involves people in relationships with one another. With this in mind, ethics in influencing others should emphasize "shared responsibility for the outcome of the transaction."[20] The point of this approach is to try "to achieve the best possible outcome for all the participants in [the] transaction."[21] How do persuaders do this? There are ten items mentioned in the Prologue that will help achieve this goal. Two of the most essential items, according to Littlejohn and Jabusch, are openness and caring.[22]

Openness involves the honest and complete sharing of information. The point here is that only when information is honest and complete can a target make the proper choices. An example of lack of honesty and completeness would be someone trying to sell a used car that had significant problems without informing the target of these problems.

Caring involves concern for the well-being of self and others. As Littlejohn and Jabusch explain it, "It involves a feeling that what happens to others is as important as what happens to self. It is the spirit of good will."[23] Take, for example, the situation of trying to get a friend to go to a campus event when it is not in his or her best interests to do so. Consideration for the spirit of good will might cause the agent to back off when the target resisted. In fact, if all the situational variables were known to begin with, a caring agent might decide not to engage in influencing the target in the first place.

The point is that influencing others involves a transactional relationship. Any change in attitude or behavior that occurs in that relationship results from joint decisions and actions. Since both parties are participating in the process, both should take responsibility for outcomes—shared responsibility. For this reason, both agent and target need as much information as possible, and they need to reveal a caring attitude about each other as well. In any influence situation, then, agents need to keep openness and caring in mind as guiding principles for their behavior, approaches, and strategies.

Compliance Gaining

Compliance gaining is the process of getting others to do what we want. Whether we are requesting another person to help with our homework, buy an encyclopedia, study more, or give us a promotion, compliance-gaining strategies play an important role in our interpersonal behavior. It is unlikely that a single day goes by that you do not use one or more such strategies

and, in most cases, you use numerous ones over and over again. To learn how to use them will increase your chances for effectiveness and success in most interpersonal situations.

Most research in this area has been conducted within the last thirty years.[24] It is based on the principle that human experience involves interdependence: your goal outcomes (instrumental or terminal values) are dependent on others just as others' goal outcomes are likely to be affected by your behavior. Thus, it is useful to develop a repertoire of strategies by which to solicit others' cooperation (compliance) in achieving goals.[25]

There are some considerations that need to be observed before compliance-gaining strategies are chosen. The way receivers or targets of messages perceive the situation plays an important part. Some factors of situation perception include potential personal benefits to be gained, potential apprehension, potential resistance, justification for making the request, degree of intimacy between interactants, dominance, authority, control of one person over the other, and the potential consequences of the behavior. The extent to which sources of messages can diminish any negative aspects of these perceptions—or reduce their effect—will enhance chances that compliance will be attained.

What these factors suggest is that receivers are not empty, inanimate, vessels just waiting to be filled with your "choice" influence strategies! They may want to know what's in it for them. They may be apprehensive or nervous. They may be resistant to your persuasion. They may feel their rights are being threatened. They may think you have jeopardized your relationship with them. They may feel you have no authority to ask for a

Consider This

Read the following paragraph from both the agent's and the target's perspective. How might locus of control affect the kinds of strategies chosen by agents or the degree of resistance exhibited by targets?

> *Another personality variable of interest is internal-external locus of control.* People who are internal in their locus of control believe that their achievements will be rewarded, that they can have an impact on the world and help shape their own destinies, that the future is bright, and that they can prevent war, crime, and poverty. Internals believe that control of their behavior stems from their own internal motivations, abilities, and achievements. Externals, however, have little hope in controlling outcomes, feel that effort is not necessarily rewarded (one has to be in the right place at the right time to get rewards); they believe that their behavior is not motivated internally, but that they are responding to external pressures. Because of their strong achievement needs, internals are more likely to resist pressures to conform or to be influenced by experimenters. They are also more likely to be persistent in influencing others, that is, to try more strategies over time.***

* For a review of literature concerning internal and external locus of control, consult Michael J. Cody and Margaret L. McLaughlin, "The Situation As a Construct in Communication Research," in Mark L. Knapp and Gerald R. Miller, eds., *Handbook of Interpersonal Communication* (Beverly Hills: Sage, 1985); Herbert M. Lefcourt, *Locus of Control: Current Trends in Theory and Research,* 2nd ed. (Hillsdale, N.J.: Erlbaum, 1982).

** For example, see William J. Doherty and Robert G. Ryder, "Locus of Control, Interpersonal Trust, and Assertive Behavior among Newlyweds," *Journal of Personality and Social Psychology,* 37 (1979), pp. 2212–39.

—Erwin P. Bettinghaus and Michael J. Cody, *Persuasive Communication,* 4th ed. (New York: Holt, Rinehart and Winston, 1987), p. 189.

change, or they may sense that future consequences do not merit the request. The point is, once again, there is some interdependence operating that must be considered.

Once the receiver's perceptual base has been considered, other factors that affect the way an individual attempts to gain the compliance of another depends on how well the two people know each other—or their level of intimacy—and the power/status relationship between them.[26] Intimacy and power will be discussed later. Finally, the size of the request will influence the response. That is, how much targets feel they are being asked to do—the degree of imposition—will be a factor.

When dealing with such complex situations there are no guarantees. Because individuals, situations, and messages vary so much, it is better for those desiring compliance to have a variety of strategies at their command.

Consider This

There is a complex system operating in compliance-gaining strategies used by the actor on a target. The intentions of the actor must be recognized, and the inducements containing conditions for influence examined by the target.

—From "A Formal Account of Interpersonal Compliance-Gaining" by William J. Schenck-Hamlin, G. N. Georgacarakos, and Richard L. Wiseman in *Communication Quarterly,* 30 (Summer 1982), p. 173. Reprinted by permission of ECA.

Strategies

A number of lists of compliance-gaining strategies exist.[27] Henry Dan O'Hair and Michael J. Cody provide one of the most succinct lists. Their seven global strategies are the essential ones that overtly ask for compliance to requests. A brief explanation of each strategy follows.

1. *Direct requests* contain no information in addition to the request. "Will you take me to the airport?" is a direct request.
2. *Exchange* strategies are those that compromise or negotiate for compliance. "I'll take out the garbage if you'll wash the dishes" is an exchange strategy.
3. *Distributive* tactics occur when one person attaches some negative consequences or lays "a guilt trip" on another person for noncompliance. "If you don't go with me, I'll never help you again," or "If you don't talk to him for me, you're *never* going to hear the end of this," are examples of distributive tactics.
4. *Face-maintenance* strategies use emotional appeals that cast the other person in a positive light—as having good qualities. "Since you get along with her so well, will you talk to her for me?" would be a face-maintenance strategy.
5. *Supporting evidence* involves the use of reasoning and appeals to logic to gain compliance. "You can see from all these cancelled checks that you are going to have to be more careful this month," uses the cancelled checks as supporting evidence to gain compliance.
6. *Other-benefit* tactics are those that give receivers the impression that compliance will be in their best interests or will benefit them in some way. "I told her why this choice of a major would be the best one for her," is an other-benefit tactic.
7. *Referent influence* and *empathic understanding* are the final strategies grouped as a single item because of their similarity. In *referent influence,* sources appeal to the receiver's identification with them. "I know you'll like this movie because you like action and adventure just as much as I do," is an example of referent influence. In *empathic understanding,* sources appeal to the receiver's love and affection for them. "If you really loved me, you'd go to this movie with me," is an example of empathic understanding. Notice that both include the dependence on the relationship between the agent and the target.

Most individuals have their own ideas and perceptions about what strategies are most effective with which people. Many of these ideas and perceptions are based on either personal experience or the observations of others. Many, too, simply result from habit. It is probably best to use a variety of strategies, but whatever strategies are selected, careful analysis of the receiver and situation should occur first.

Limitations of Compliance-Gaining Research

Just as balance theory has its limitations (is anything perfect?), so does compliance-gaining research.[28] "Generally speaking, a request is a communicative act in which the speaker attempts to get the listener to perform an action at some time in the future, which the listener would not have performed otherwise".[29] Given the enormous variety in types of requests and the enormous number of goals speakers may have for making requests, one can begin to see some of the limitations of this type of research. First, most of the studies deal with a single message and a single situation as their examples. The same results are not obtained when multiple messages are used. And, it is reasonable to conclude that the same results will not necessarily hold in different situations. Along these same lines, if behavior is a function of both the person and the situation, then researchers need to look at both person and situation functioning together. You begin to realize the complexity of this issue when you consider the large number of individual difference variables versus the large number of situational variables. How would it ever be possible to catalog all the various interactions with all the possible results?

The second limitation involves the selection of strategies. Communicators act differently when asked to generate a spontaneous message than when asked to select a preformulated strategy. Individuals report that they tend to use more positive types of compliance-gaining strategies when selecting preformulated strategies than when spontaneously generating messages. Commenting on her research on the selection of communicative strategies, Ruth Anne Clark notes that:

> . . . *message composition is a form of behavior in which individuals engage regularly. By contrast, asking an individual to select among strategies requires the person to reflect on his or her behavior in a way which might never occur naturally.*[30]

The third limitation has to do with the abstract level at which strategies are formulated by researchers. They need to pay attention to how strategies are actually implemented at the level of discourse. What kinds of things do people *actually* say in compliance-gaining situations? Can strategies be identified in actual use?

The final limitation of compliance-gaining research is the lack of attention to the fact that communicators have multiple goals. Think about it. When you are attempting to gain compliance, is this your *only* concern at that moment? Often, you are also concerned about self-presentation (how you are presenting yourself to others), relational impact (how you are affecting the relationship you have with others), and responding to reservations (how the receiver is reacting to your message thus far). The job of making a request involves deciding when and how to be persuasive, when and how to be empathically sensitive, and when and how to push for

Consider This

It should be clear from this discussion of compliance gaining that interpersonal persuasion is complex and involves many factors. Compliance-gaining communication is a fact of social life. Our relationships are built on a base of consensus and compliance, give and take, offering and asking. Much of the time compliance is not a problem; it is accepted and negotiated as part of daily life.

—Stephen W. Littlejohn and David M. Jabusch, *Persuasive Transactions* (Glenview, Ill: Scott, Foresman and Company, 1987), p. 136.

Consider This

Do males and females *actually* differ in the strategies they use? Several studies have in fact documented gender differences, generally indicating that males are more blunt and direct and use more tactics of coercion than do females, who are less direct and, when employing pressure, are more likely to use some form of emotion-based tactic.* However, there is no *consistent* evidence that females select different tactics than males."

* For a review of these studies, consult David R. Seibold, James G. Cantrill, and Renee A. Meyers, "Communication and Interpersonal Influence," in Mark L. Knapp and Gerald R. Miller, eds., *Handbook of Interpersonal Communication* (Beverly Hills: Sage, 1985).
—Erwin P. Bettinghaus and Michael J. Cody, *Persuasive Communication,* 4th ed. (New York: Holt, Rinehart and Winston, 1987), p. 190.

compliance. In standard compliance-gaining experiments, subjects work with a restricted set of strategies that focuses on the persuasive aspect of situations with minimal attention to possible interpersonal goals.[31]

The point here is not to try to frustrate your attempts at compliance-gaining, nor is it to try to dissuade you from making such attempts. The point is simply to indicate the tremendous number of factors involved in the process. When you discover you haven't been successful, it is helpful to know that there are many potential explanations. These limitations should not *discourage* your attempts to influence others, but rather should *encourage* you to try again using a different approach, or the same approach at a different time, or a different combination of approaches.

Compliance Resistance

The purpose of using compliance-gaining strategies is to achieve effective control, maintain relationships, and create change. Much of the research in compliance gaining has focused on the potential persuader—the influence agent—as the active element in interpersonal persuasion. Yet, the target of a compliance-gaining message has the option of resisting compliance. And, as researchers on compliance resistance point out, "the type of strategy selected by the target to resist the compliance-gaining attempt is just as important as the agent's strategy."[32]

It should be noted that the target's unwillingness to comply may frustrate the agent's need. Not only that, it is likely to imply (1) that the agent lacks power to effect certain changes, or (2) that the agent has incorrectly assessed the situation. Such resistance, then, can result in rather serious relational consequences. For example, what if a person from whom you borrowed ten dollars said to you, "If you don't return that money, I am going to destroy your credit rating." Really? Could *this* person really affect your credit rating? With whom? However, not returning the ten dollars is likely to have a serious affect on *this* relationship for some time!

Unwillingness to comply also could indicate the agent has incorrectly assessed the situation. A friend tries to get you to defend your choice of a political candidate in front of a group of people you happen to be talking to. It isn't that you can't defend your choice, but you would rather not do it in front of *this* group of people. A friend trying to get you to steal something from the company you work for might not realize how highly you value honesty or your commitment to *this* company. An intimate friend trying to get you to be more romantic might have underestimated the impact on you of news of a relative's death. Depending on the persistance of the compliance-gaining strategy, your resistance in any of these situations could affect the relationship you have with the agent(s). As you read the three situations described in this paragraph, did you think of ways you would resist these influence attempts? Researcher Margaret McLaughlin and her colleagues have identified four basic compliance-resistance strategies: (1) identity management, (2) negotiation, (3) nonnegotiation, and (4) justifying.

Identity-management strategies involve indirect resistance in which the image of the agent, the target, or both is manipulated. For example, if someone wanted to borrow a sweater from you, you might say, "I can't believe anybody would ask to borrow my brand new sweater that I've only worn once," or you might say, "I've never asked to borrow any of *your* clothes."

Identity managing is primarily a manipulative strategy. It should be used with greater discretion in intimate situations than in nonintimate situations. Caution would be advised especially in intimate situations with long-term consequences. With nonintimates, identity managing would be effective only if both parties were committed to some sort of future interaction.

Negotiation strategies are, essentially, exchange strategies. In these cases, targets propose alternative behaviors to those suggested by the agent. Related to negotiation strategies are empathic-understanding strategies in which targets solicit discussion that will promote mutual accommodation. For example, a negotiation strategy would be used if you said, "I think ten dollars is too much to give; I'd be willing to give five, however." To show empathic understanding, you might say, "I'll tell you what, let's not decide that right now. Let's plan to talk more about it later today so we can come to some mutual agreement."

Negotiation strategies have high social desirability in all situations. In high-intimacy situations, negotiation is much more likely to be used— especially when the risk level is high and there could be long-term conse- quences. For example, relationship partners who had been dating for some

Consider This

What is the relationship between strategy use success and the influence situation? The following is the answer provided by the authors of a popular textbook on persuasion, one of whom is a researcher in the area of compliance gaining.

For years our students have asked us, "Don't the results of these studies [studies on compliance-gaining and compliance-resisting] depend on the situation?" Yes, many of our experiences are specific to certain types of situations or events. After being in similar types of situations over the years we learn which types of tactics failed and which succeeded, and we learn which type of tactic is effective and appropriate for particular kinds of events.

—Erwin P. Bettinghaus and Michael J. Cody, *Persuasive Communication,* 4th ed. (New York: Holt, Rinehart and Winston, 1987), p. 191.

time could decide to go somewhere with friends of one partner *if,* the next time they go somewhere with friends of the other partner.

Nonnegotiation strategies are straightforward, unapologetic tactics in which the target overtly declines to comply with the agent's request. For example, "I'm sorry, no," or "That topic is not open to discussion," would be nonnegotiation strategies. Nonnegotiation is less likely to be used in situations with long-term relational consequences, provided the relationship is highly intimate. In low-intimate situations there is greater likelihood that nonnegotiation strategies will be used.

Justifying strategies are used when targets feel the need to justify or defend their unwillingness to comply because of the potential outcomes, whether positive or negative, to self or others. "I told her that if I didn't go with her, I would get to use my father's car," would be one example, or, on the negative side, "I explained that I didn't want to participate simply because everyone already knew me and would make fun of me."

Justifying strategies might be used in high-intimacy situations only when the consequences are short term. That is, one would not want to appear argumentative or self-serving to an intimate if the situation were of great consequence. With nonintimates, one would be less concerned about identity management and more likely to use justifying strategies.[33]

Improving Skills in Influencing Others

There are many situations in which we would like to make people think or act differently, would like to have an effect, would like to persuade another person. There are situations, too, where we have carefully selected a compliance-gaining strategy, used it, only to be met by a compliance-resisting strategy that defeated us. What now?

To have an effect on others, we must first consider antecedent factors: What prior values and attitudes do they hold? Remember, too, that we are not the only influential factor. The strength of our message, the medium we use to convey our message, or the context in which the communication takes place can also have an effect. It is sometimes better to wait until circumstances are right before attempting persuasion. Internal processes such as perception, attention, and comprehension may also be important. Sometimes these elements are beyond our control. Looking at the situation in Heider's terms, are we attempting to unbalance the target and then provide a method for rebalancing—that is, attempting to destroy or weaken an attitude the target already possesses and then offering a replacement attitude that we think is better or stronger?

Let's look at a couple of brief examples concerning unbalancing. Suppose we tell a friend that the professor of a class she is planning to take gives very hard examinations. If we see that this has placed her in an unbalanced position we may try to rebalance it by adding that the professor gives excellent lectures and provides superior course material that is interesting and worthwhile. We might deliberately unbalance a source to determine the

salience of an attitude. Or is our goal simply to provide information that will rebalance an already unbalanced system? For example, we might find that a friend has negative feelings about a movie we want to see with him or her. The system is unbalanced. So we talk about people our friend knows who saw the movie and liked it. We mention reviewers who responded favorably to the movie, and we focus on the movie's strengths—or at least the features that would appeal to our friend. Is our final goal to change attitudes or to change values? How extensive is this goal? Obviously, when it comes to attitude change, there are a number of variables to consider.

In interpersonal situations, our personal credibility—the effect our character (competence, trustworthiness, and dynamism) has on the other person—will be highly important. But our effect on others depends on many other variables as well. If we are really interested in changing an attitude or behavior, being aware of these elements can help us improve the odds. The following are some additional specific suggestions for improving skills in influencing others.

Show that your proposal is approved by someone important to them.

This is the concept I earlier labeled as "referent influence."[34] Others have labeled it "bandwagon ethics." If others realize that people *they* consider important accept your ideas, your success will be more likely. Talking about friends, experts, or associates who already believe in what you are suggesting helps others put their present beliefs or actions in perspective.

Show that your proposal is consistent with their needs.

What are the personal needs of the people you hope to persuade? Abraham Maslow categorized seven types of human needs: needs related to physiology, safety, love, esteem, self-actualization, knowledge and understanding, and aesthetics. Think of these as a hierarchy: each level, beginning with basic physiological needs, must be taken care of before going on to the next one. (See Figure 7.3.)

Actually, the hierarchy is not as rigid as it sounds. Most people have these needs in about the order Maslow suggests, but there are exceptions. For example, there are people who seek esteem above all else, and there are people whose need to create takes precedence over any other need. Some people who have experienced long deprivation may be content for the rest of their lives with just having their most elemental needs satisfied. There are also some people who were so deprived of love in the earliest months of their lives that their need to give and receive love as adults is distorted.

Physiological needs. These are the most basic needs having to do with our survival. We need food, water, and sleep to survive. Unless these needs are satisfied, we cannot pay attention to anything else.

Safety needs. Once our physiological needs are satisfied, our next concern is safety. Our concern for safety in our environment is reflected in our need

---

Consider This

It's important to talk to people in their own language. If you do it well, they'll say, "God, he said exactly what I was thinking." And when they begin to respect you, they'll follow you to the death. The <u>reason</u> they're following you is not because you're providing some mysterious leadership. It's because you're following them.

—Lee Iacocca (with William Novak), *Iacocca: An Autobiography* (New York: Bantam Books, 1984), p. 55.

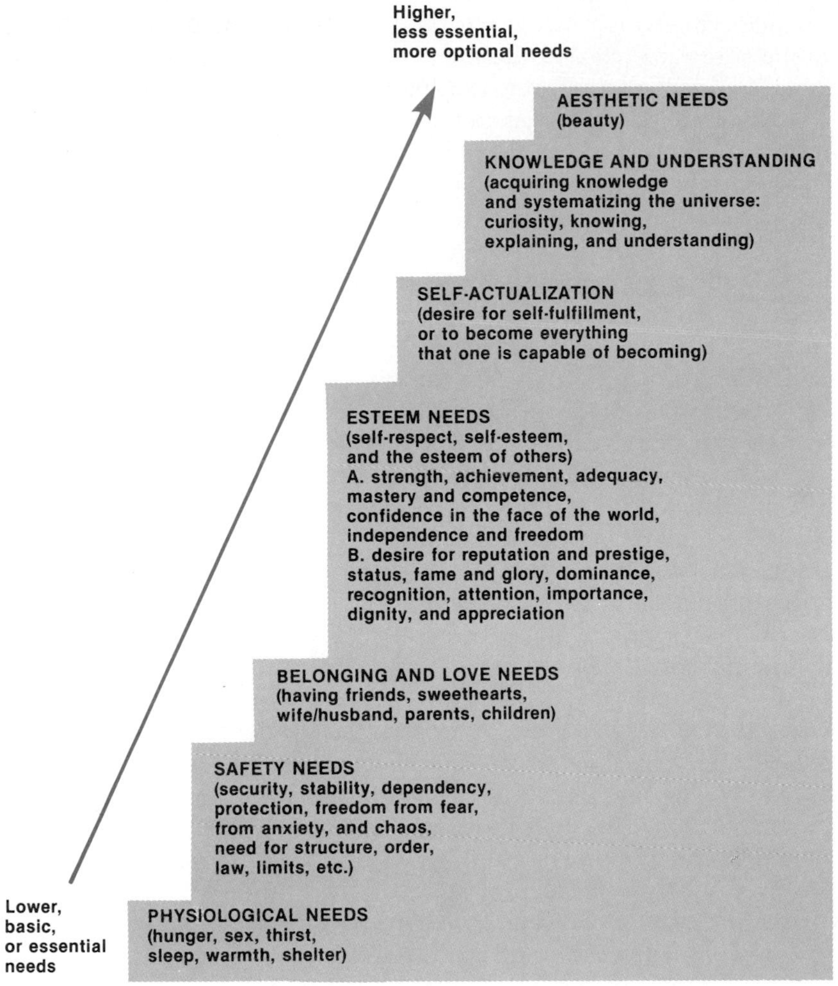

Higher,
less essential,
more optional needs

Figure 7.3
Maslow's hierarchy of
needs.[35]

AESTHETIC NEEDS
(beauty)

KNOWLEDGE AND UNDERSTANDING
(acquiring knowledge
and systematizing the universe:
curiosity, knowing,
explaining, and understanding)

SELF-ACTUALIZATION
(desire for self-fulfillment,
or to become everything
that one is capable of becoming)

ESTEEM NEEDS
(self-respect, self-esteem,
and the esteem of others)
A. strength, achievement, adequacy,
mastery and competence,
confidence in the face of the world,
independence and freedom
B. desire for reputation and prestige,
status, fame and glory, dominance,
recognition, attention, importance,
dignity, and appreciation

BELONGING AND LOVE NEEDS
(having friends, sweethearts,
wife/husband, parents, children)

SAFETY NEEDS
(security, stability, dependency,
protection, freedom from fear,
from anxiety, and chaos,
need for structure, order,
law, limits, etc.)

Lower,
basic,
or essential
needs

PHYSIOLOGICAL NEEDS
(hunger, sex, thirst,
sleep, warmth, shelter)

for shelter, clothing, and protection from heat and cold. We want to prevent any kind of threat; we resist changes that jeopardize our safety.

Belonging and love needs. Family and friends help us satisfy our need to love and to be loved. Our membership in groups fulfills a need to belong, to be accepted, and to have friends. Marriage and professional associations also satisfy this social need.

Esteem needs. We need to be respected by others. This need is related to our desire for status and a good reputation. If we seek recognition, aspire to leadership positions, desire awards, compliments, or acknowledgment for our work, our esteem need is operating. Our need for self-esteem is an important part of this need.

Self-actualization needs. When our more basic needs are satisfied, we can move toward self-actualization. This is our need to be everything we can be, to develop ourselves to our highest abilities.

The need for knowledge and understanding. We need to know and to understand in order to get along in society. For many people, knowledge and understanding are an important part of self-actualization. We need to inquire, to learn, to philosophize, to experiment, and to explain.

Aesthetic needs. Do you feel comfortable in a room where a picture on the wall is crooked? Many people find such a situation aesthetically displeasing, and they feel a need to remedy it. We have a wide range of aesthetic needs, but we all need to have things around us that we consider beautiful and orderly.

Exactly where our listeners are in their development along this hierarchy, and what they perceive to be the most pressing needs, will make a difference in how we approach them. If we want to persuade someone of something, we would do well to tie this to those needs most salient to our listener. If a person is hungry and desperately trying to feed a family, it is absurd to try to persuade that person to get a job on the grounds that it would be self-actualizing; the immediate need is for food. If we really want to change this individual's attitude toward working, we had better relate working to the most pressing needs.

Show that your proposal is consistent with alternative needs as well.
If appealing to one need does not work, perhaps another one will. Do not assume that satisfying one need is necessarily enough. New times mean new needs; people are always changing. We may have misperceived the other person's needs to begin with.

Know the power of fear in attitude change.
Our subconcious fears are constantly played upon by people who want us to change our attitudes. Advertisers, for example, try to convince us that social or professional success hinges on our buying their product. A teacher may say that our grade depends on the successful completion of a project; we complete the project because we fear failure. We may be persuaded to carry a credit card out of fear of what would happen if we lost a large amount of cash.

Fear influences our attitudes and our behavior. There is nothing new or wrong with that—a certain amount of fear is necessary and healthy in many situations. But if we arouse fear to get another person to accept our ideas, we should provide a means for removing the cause of the fear. Parents who persuade their children to wear boots in cold weather by saying they will get sick if they don't should make sure their children understand what they mean. That is, they need not suggest that pestilence and death will necessarily follow a few minutes with wet feet. And parents could say that the main point is not the boots themselves, but that the children are likely to stay healthier if they keep warm and dry.

Try This

Try to persuade someone of something you are not convinced of. Spend some time—even several days if necessary—continuing your effort.
Notice the effects you have on your listener. Were you successful? Why or why not? What kind of listener needs did you appeal to in trying to persuade? Did you find some needs easier to work with than others? What happened to your attitudes?

There is an element of manipulation in using the fear approach. Be aware when someone is trying to use it with you. It is a fairly low-level appeal and generally suggests a low evaluation of the person's intellectual powers. Still, a parent will use fear if necessary to keep a child from crossing a busy highway. You must decide for yourself if arousing fear as a means of persuasion has any place in mature communication.

Be persistent.   Just because one strategy did not work does not mean persuasive attempts must end. The strategy might work in a different context or situation, for example. Also, a different strategy might be more effective. For example, Mark deTurck, in his research on the effects of noncompliance, found that when agents "were confronted with noncompliance from persuasive targets . . . they increased their preference for reward-oriented message strategies more than punishment-based appeals on subsequent persuasive requests."[36] More rewards in future messages maximized the chances of obtaining their goals while minimizing the chance of relational damage.

DeTurck also discovered that after targets' noncompliance with two compliance-gaining requests, agents turned to *threat* as their most-preferred message strategy. Yet, previous compliance-gaining research indicates that threat is typically the least-preferred strategy in any relational context.

Offer a reward or incentive.   How much of an incentive we need to offer to get a person to change an attitude depends upon the attitude, the listener, ourselves, and the situation. There is no way this can be determined without knowing the variables that operate in a given case. Sometimes another person will go along with an idea if our reward is as simple as saying, "If you do it, I'll go with you." Sometimes it is not so simple. But generally our society operates on a system of rewards and incentives; people want something in return for something. That "something" may be as small as a word of praise at the right time, or it may be as elaborate as a large and expensive gift. The reward that works best depends wholly on the circumstances.

Think small.   Perhaps the most important suggestion for changing attitudes is to first try to change others in some small way that is consistent with their long-range goals.[37] Small changes are often more acceptable and create less conflict and defensiveness than big changes and may show results more quickly, making bigger changes easier to come by later on.

There is nothing simple about the process of influencing others. But knowing the importance of attitudes and values, the ways in which attitudes can be changed and the process of resolving imbalances, the criteria for selecting various compliance strategies, and various ways to improve your skills in influencing others should help improve effectiveness and success. The next chapter discusses emotion, a subject that is closely related to influencing others.

Notes

[1] Edwin A. Weinstein, "The Development of Interpersonal Competence." In *Handbook of Socialization Theory and Research*, eds. David A. Goslin and David C. Glass (New York: Rand McNally, 1969).

[2] Karen Tracy, Robert T. Craig, Martin Smith, and Frances Spisak, "The Discourse of Requests: Assessment of a Compliance-Gaining Approach," *Human Communication Research*, 10 (Summer 1984): p. 513.

[3] William Labov and David Fanshel, *Therapeutic Discourse: Psychotherapy as Conversation* (New York: Academic Press, 1977), p. 94.

[4] Robert F. Mager, *Developing Attitudes Toward Learning* (Palo Alto, Calif.: Fearon, 1968), p. 14.

[5] Irving Sarnoff, "Psychoanalytic Theory and Social Attitudes," *Public Opinion Quarterly*, 24 (1960): p. 261.

[6] Gordon W. Allport, "Values and Our Youth," *Teachers College Record*, 63 (1961): pp. 211–19.

[7] Milton Rokeach, *Beliefs, Attitudes and Values: A Theory of Organization and Change* (San Francisco: Jossey-Bass, 1968), p. 160.

[8] See Milton Rokeach, *Value Survey* (Sunnyvale, Calif.: Halgren Tests, 1967).

[9] William J. McGuire, "The Current Status of Cognitive Consistency Theories," in *Cognitive Consistency: Motivation Antecedents and Behavioral Consequences*, ed. Shel Feldman (New York: Academic Press, 1966), p. 1; Chester A. Insko, *Theories of Attitude Change* (New York: Appleton-Century-Crofts, 1967), esp. pp. 161–76.

[10] Fritz Heider, "Attitudes and Cognitive Organization," *The Journal of Psychology* 21 (1946): pp. 107–12. Reprinted by permission of the Helen Dwight Reid Educational Foundation © 1946. The theory is developed more extensively in his *Psychology of Interpersonal Relations* (New York: John Wiley & Sons, 1958).

[11] This is called "symmetry theory," and is developed in Theodore M. Newcomb, "An Approach to the Study of Communicative Acts," *Psychological Review*, 60 (1953): pp. 393–404. Robert B. Zajonc, "The Concepts of Balance, Congruity, and Dissonance," in *Foundations of Communication Theory*, ed. Kenneth K. Sereno and C. David Mortensen (New York: Harper & Row, 1970), p. 185, suggests that Newcomb's notion of "strain toward symmetry" will lead to a similarity of attitudes between P and O and X if P is attracted to O.

[12] Herbert W. Simons, "Persuasion and Attitude Change," in *Speech Communication Behavior: Perspectives and Principles*, ed. Larry L. Barker and Robert J. Kibler (Englewood Cliffs, N.J.: Prentice-Hall, 1971), p. 239.

[13] Herbert C. Kelman, "Process of Opinion Change," *Public Opinion Quarterly*, 25 (1961): pp. 57–78.

[14] Franklyn S. Haiman, "Democratic Ethics and the Hidden Persuaders," in *Readings in Speech*, ed. Haig A. Bosmajian (New York: Harper & Row, 1965), p. 196.

[15] Everett L. Shostrom, *Man, the Manipulator* (New York: Abingdon Press, 1967), p. 15. Used by permission of Everett Shostrom.

[16] Charles R. Berger, "Social Power and Communication," p. 486, in *Handbook of Communication*, eds. Mark L. Knapp and Gerald R. Miller (Beverly Hills, Calif.: Sage, 1985). Reprinted by permission.

[17] James C. McCroskey, Virginia P. Richmond, and Robert A. Stewart, *One On One: The Foundations of Interpersonal Communication* (Englewood Cliffs, N.J.: Prentice-Hall, 1986), p. 186.

[18] John R. French and Bertram Raven, "The Bases of Social Power," in *Studies in Social Power* (Ann Arbor: University of Michigan Press, 1959).

[19] Richard L. Johannesen, *Ethics in Human Communication*, 2d ed. (Prospect Heights, Ill.: Waveland Press, Inc., 1983).

[20] Stephen W. Littlejohn and David M. Jabusch, *Persuasive Transactions* (Glenview, Ill.: Scott, Foresman, 1987), p. 16.

[21] Littlejohn and Jabusch, *Persuasive Transactions*, p. 16.

[22] I credit Littlejohn and Jabusch with the selection of the factors of openness and caring as essential to responsible interpersonal communication.

[23] Littlejohn and Jabusch, *Persuasive Transactions*, p. 16.

[24] I am using as a beginning date the work by Gerald Marwell and David R. Schmitt, "Dimensions of Compliance-Gaining Behavior: An Empirical Analysis," *Sociometry*, 30 (1967): pp. 350–64. In their article, Marwell and Schmitt mention many of the preceding authors who provide lists or sets of strategies. Most date from about 1960. They mention B.F. Skinner, *Science and Human Behavior* (New York: Macmillan, 1953), who, they say, has "the most inclusive list of types of techniques" (Marwell and Schmitt, p. 354).

[25] See Leslie A. Baxter, "An Investigation of Compliance-Gaining As Politeness," *Human Communication Research*, 10 (Spring 1984): pp. 427–56.

[26] Karen Tracy, Robert T. Craig, Martin Smith, and Frances Spisak, "The Discourse of Requests: Assessment of a Compliance-Gaining Approach," *Human Communication Research*, 10 (Summer 1984): pp. 513–38.

[27] The most-often cited is the list of 16 strategies of Marwell and Schmitt, previously cited. Also see Gerald Miller, Frank Boster, Michael Roloff, and David Seibold, "Compliance-Gaining Message Strategies: A Typology and Some Findings Concerning Effects of Situational Differences," *Communication Monographs*, 44 (March 1977): pp. 37–51; William J. Schenck-Hamlin, Richard L. Wiseman, and G. N. Georgacarakos, "A Model of Properties of Compliance-Gaining Strategies," *Communication Quarterly*, 30 (Spring 1982), pp. 92–100. There are many other sources. See Erwin P. Bettinghaus and Michael J. Cody, *Persuasive Communication*, 4th ed. (New York: Holt, Rinehart and Winston, 1987), pp. 185–87.

[28] Tracy, Craig, Smith, and Spisak, "The Discourse of Requests," pp. 516–17.

[29] Tracy, Craig, Smith, and Spisak, "The Discourse of Requests," p. 514.

[30] Ruth Anne Clark, "The Impact of Self Interest and Desire for Liking on the Selection of Communicative Strategies," *Communication Monographs*, 46 (November 1979): pp. 257–73.

[31] Tracy, Craig, Smith, and Spisak, "The Discourse of Requests," pp. 516–18.

[32] See Margaret L. McLaughlin, Michael J. Cody, and Carl S. Robey, "Situational Influences on the Selection of Strategies to Resist Compliance-Gaining Attempts," *Human Communication Research*, 7 (Fall 1980): pp. 14–36.

[33] For more information on resisting compliance-gaining strategies, see McLaughlin, Cody, and Robey, as cited above.

[34] Herbert C. Kelman, "Compliance, Identification, and Internalization: Three Processes of Attitude Change," *Journal of Conflict Resolution*, 2 (1958): pp. 51–60.

[35] Data (for diagram) based on Hierarchy of Needs in "A Theory of Human Motivation" in *Motivation and Personality*, 2d ed., by Abraham H. Maslow. Copyright © 1970 by Abraham H. Maslow. By permission of Harper & Row, Publishers, Inc.

[36] Mark A. deTurck, "A Transactional Analysis of Compliance-Gaining Behavior: Effects of Noncompliance, Relational Contexts, and Actor's Gender," *Human Communication Research*, 12 (Fall 1985): pp. 54–78.

[37] A summary of the findings that support this generalization can be found in C. A. Kiesler, *The Psychology of Commitment* (New York: Academic Press, 1971), pp. 14–17.

Further Reading

Erwin P. Bettinghaus and Michael J. Cody, *Persuasive Communication*, 4th ed. (New York: Holt, Rinehart and Winston, 1987). This textbook covers the major topics relevant to the study of persuasive communication today. The authors examine the use of persuasion in contemporary situations. They offer a thorough, research-based approach designed for advanced students.

Daniel Cohen, *Re: Thinking: How to Succeed by Learning How to Think* (New York: M. Evans & Co., 1982). Cohen offers ways to change old thinking habits and to develop new ones. He vividly illustrates how you must first comprehend how your mind works and then find the right techniques for strengthening it. This book offers a very direct, practical approach for improving your thinking skills.

Fritz Heider, *The Psychology of Interpersonal Relations* (New York: John Wiley & Sons, 1958). This book contains a complete description of Heider's theory of attitudes.

Chester A. Insko, *Theories of Attitude Change* (Englewood Cliffs, N.J.: Prentice-Hall, 1967). Insko provides a thorough and detailed summary and evaluation of research studies which bear on the major theories of attitude change. A valuable resource for the study of attitude change.

Daniel Katz, "The Functional Approach to the Study of Attitudes," *Public Opinion Quarterly* 24 (1960):163–204. Katz offers a fairly complete description of the functions that attitudes can serve. He also examines the implications of each of these functions for attitude arousal and change.

Stephen W. Littlejohn and David M. Jabusch, *Persuasive Transactions* (Glenview, Ill.: Scott, Foresman, 1987). The authors base this undergraduate textbook on four premises: (1) persuasion is a transactional, rule-based process, (2) it occurs in all communication contexts, (3) it is best understood through an eclectic approach, and (4) persuasive competence involves a blend of theoretical understanding, sensitivity, and skill. An excellent, well-written book.

William J. McGuire, "The Nature of Attitudes and Attitude Change," in *The Handbook of Social Psychology*, 2d ed., Vol. 3, ed. G. Lindzey and E. Aronson (Reading, Mass.: Addison-Wesley Publishing Co., 1969), pp. 136–314. Pages 172–265 of this impressive chapter contain a scholarly and often-cited review of research. McGuire outlines the major variables involved in persuasive communication and attitude change.

Milton Rokeach, *Beliefs, Attitudes, and Values* (San Francisco, Calif.: Jossey-Bass, 1972). In this textbook, Rokeach provides a philosophical and scientific approach to attitude and value formation. This book is highly recommended to the student interested in an in-depth exploration of the development of attitudes, beliefs, and values.

Harry C. Triandis, *Attitude and Attitude Change* (New York: John Wiley & Sons, 1971). This is a scholarly, worthwhile, and thorough presentation of attitudes and beliefs.

Philip G. Zimbardo, Ebbe B. Ebbesen, and Christina Maslach, *Influencing Attitudes and Changing Behavior*, 2d ed. (Reading, Mass.: Addison-Wesley Publishing Co., 1977). This is a book of both theory and practice. The authors pose the problems of personal influence and social change, examine the theories of attitude and behavior change, and then discuss the tactics and strategies involved in attitude change.

8

Experiencing Emotion: Sharing Our Feelings

Learning Objectives

When you have finished this chapter you should be able to:

- Explain the nature of emotions.
- Explain why it is important to understand emotions.
- Describe and briefly explain the three phases of recognizing emotions.
- Make specific suggestions for controlling emotions.
- Explain how to read another's emotions.
- Develop an approach for dealing with others' emotions.
- Explain several guidelines that can help you determine when it is appropriate to share your feelings with others.
- Make suggestions for clearly and vividly expressing your emotions.
- Explain how you can change your emotions.
- Describe and briefly explain the principles that serve as guidelines for improving skills in expressing feelings and emotions.

Imagine, for a moment, waking up one morning surprised to find heavy rain outside rather than the clear, sunny day you had anticipated. You turn to look at the clock and panic because you have overslept your first class. Impatient with yourself, you dress quickly and with only fifteen minutes to spare, you decide to grab coffee and a doughnut on the way to your second class. You become irritated at the fellow for his slowness in serving the coffee, but you express your gratitude anyway with a hasty "Thanks a lot." In class, you quickly become anxious when you realize you left today's assignment at home on your desk. The class leaves you bored, and your mind wanders just as you are asked by the instructor for

Consider This

Not to be aware of
one's feelings, not to
understand them or
know how to use or
express them is worse
than being blind, deaf
or paralyzed. Not to
feel is not to be alive.
More than anything
else feelings make us
human. Feelings make
us all kindred.

—David Viscott, *The Lan-
guage of Feelings* (New
York: Arbor House, 1976),
p. 11. Copyright © 1977
by David Viscott. Re-
printed by permission of
Arbor House Publishing
Company.

a response. You are embarrassed; you didn't hear the question. Slightly disgusted with yourself, you ask the instructor to repeat the question. She does. Relieved (you know the answer) and happy, you answer correctly. You leave the class cheerful and more alert. Just outside, you become excited by seeing your best friend and call out in a friendly manner. The frustration of missing your first class passes quickly as you enjoy chatting with your friend.

Notice how many emotions have been experienced in this short sequence: surprise, panic, impatience, irritation, gratitude, anxiety, boredom, embarrassment, disgust, relief, happiness, cheerfulness, excitement, and friendliness. Think of the range of emotions that we can experience in a short span of time. Emotion is so basic to human existence that Darwin suggested that some patterns of emotional expression are innate in both animals and humans—although the meaning of such expressions may vary from culture to culture. In this chapter I will begin by looking at the derivation of emotions. What are they and where do they come from? Then I will explain why it is important to understand them. What difference does understanding emotions make? In the third section, I discuss how we recognize our emotions. What is required for recognition? A fourth area covered in this chapter is the control of emotions. Since they are powerful forces in influencing behavior, and since they can be triggered in an instant, we need to know how to control them. Finally, I discuss whether or not emotions should be shared with others. Just because we experience them, does this mean we should share them? This final section ends with some practical ideas on how to share our emotions successfully with others.

What Are Emotions?

Often we describe people as too emotional or not emotional enough. We know some people who can hide their emotions very well, whereas others are like an open book, wearing their emotions on their sleeves for all to see. *Emotions are felt tendencies toward stimuli.* Because emotions are feelings and feelings are emotions, I will use these terms interchangeably. You might wonder what a "felt tendency" is. It is an internal physiological reaction to your experiences.[1] Physiological cues probably contribute to the intensity of felt emotions. Emotions have the power to motivate us to action.

When we experience emotions, especially strong emotions, many bodily changes are likely to occur. Our heart rate increases, our blood pressure rises, our adrenaline secretions increase, our blood sugar level may increase, our digestive process may slow down, and our pupils may dilate. We may tremble or sweat. Tears may come. These are just a few of the physiological reactions that may occur. They provide some evidence that our physiological reactions probably contribute to the intensity of felt emotions. Notice how many physiological reactions can come into play at the same time. Here, for example, a woman describes what she felt in the presence of her father, who, she said, always seemed to get her angry: "I'm easily irritated and ready to snap. My face and mouth are tight, tense, and hard. My whole body is tense. My teeth are clenched and my muscles are rigid. I get a tight, knotted feeling in my stomach."

Feelings are always internal states, but we use overt behaviors as we communicate our feelings to others. For example, we often use nonverbal behaviors. Our posture, gestures, and facial expressions are major clues. A young man who often felt depressed explained his nonverbal behaviors this way: "I feel heavy and sluggish. I am physically less responsive. My body seems to slow down." Body positioning and distance are additional nonverbal clues that indicate our emotional state. The young man describing his depression added, "I feel a certain distance from others; everyone seems far away. There is a sense of unrelatedness to others; I am out of contact, can't reach others. I feel as if I'm in a vacuum. I don't want to communicate with anyone. There is a sense of being deserted; my body wants to contract, draw closer to myself." In this case the internal states are profoundly felt.

In addition to nonverbal behaviors, we use verbal behaviors to communicate our feelings to others. We use several ways of expressing our feelings verbally.[2] Sometimes we do it very briefly, saying just "I feel guilty," "I'm furious," or "I'm afraid/sad/happy/confident/hopeful/confused/eager." Some people are limited to these single-word descriptions. The language they use to describe their feelings is impoverished, and they have difficulty

going beyond a few basic feelings such as "good" or "bad," "happy" or "sad," "terrible" or "great."

Another way of expressing feelings verbally is by using more descriptive phrases, like "I'm all mixed up inside." A student emerging from an examination was overheard saying, "I'm on top of the world." Another said, "That was the pits. I'm in the doghouse now!" After a lively class discussion, one student said, "I'm totally in the dark." About a perplexity in a relationship, a woman said, "That leaves me between a rock and a hard place." As long as the phrases are not too obscure, they can serve to effectively describe emotional states.

A third way of expressing emotions verbally is by describing what is happening to you, like "I feel as though he's always watching me." One student in a group said, "I feel like nobody here gives a damn." One in a relationship said, "I still feel that he cares about me." A third, also in a relationship, said, "I still feel she loves me." These are effective expressions because they are clear, specific, and vivid.

A fourth and final way of expressing emotions verbally is by describing what you'd like to do, like "I just feel like crying my head off." After getting a flower from her roommate, the other roommate said, "Oh, I just feel like hugging her." A young woman getting ready for an exciting date said, "I just feel like singing at the top of my lungs!" A student frustrated by his grades said, "I feel like giving up." Although most if the time these expressions are clear, sometimes they can be confusing. For example, we cry from anger and fright as well as from great joy. We laugh nervously in fear; we laugh

Try This

Awareness is the first step in beginning to understand emotions. How do you feel inside when you experience the following emotions?

affection	disgust	love
anxiety	elation	pity
apathy	grief	pride
confidence	hate	reverence
contentment	inspiration	serenity
depression	jealousy	shame

Can you state how you feel in each case clearly and specifically? Can you recall specific situations in which you have felt any of these emotions? Does recalling specific situations help you state how you feel when you experience the emotion

Try This

Being able to state your emotions concretely is important to effective communication. Concreteness means being clear and specific instead of vague and general. Notice the difference between the following statements:

"Life isn't going too well."
"I'm really frustrated. I want to go to a movie with John, but I have one of my sinus headaches."

The first one is so general that it could mean almost anything. The second one is clear, specific, and concrete.

The following are general statements. Based on your own experiences, behaviors, and emotions, provide a concrete, clear, and specific statement to substitute for each of the following:

"I have a bad headache.
"People are bothering me."
"School is OK right now."
"I think I messed everything up with my mom yesterday."
"What you say stirs up a lot of feelings in me."

—From *You and Me* by Gerard Egan. Copyright © 1977 by Wadsworth Publishing Company, Inc. Reprinted by permission of Brooks/Cole Publishing Company.

in uncomfortable situations to reduce tension; and we laugh, too, in happiness and pleasure. I remember once at an awards banquet noticing one mother with tears streaming down her face. I thought she was feeling bad and asked her if she would like someone to take her home. She said, "Oh no, I'm enjoying this so much! These are tears of joy!" The clear, specific, and vivid expression of emotions is essential to effective communication.

Why Is It Important to Understand Emotions?

Emotion is important in daily life and in interpersonal communication. It has been suggested that feelings of competence and mastery over the environment are basic to survival. Understanding our emotions and emotional responses adds to our competence—how suitable or fit we feel. Emotions are of fundamental importance to all living creatures. If we learn to understand them properly, it is likely that we can better control and share the emotions we experience.

Try This

It is helpful to have different ways for expressing emotions. Try to express each of the following emotions (1) in a descriptive sentence, (2) by describing what's happening to you, and (3) by describing what you'd like to do. Be creative.

ashamed, embarrassed	capable, competent
feeling defeated	feeling bad about yourself
confused	satisfied
guilty	misused, abused
rejected	without energy
depressed	distressed
peaceful	loving
frustrated	bored
pressured	hopeful

—From *You and Me* by Gerard Egan. Copyright © 1977 by Wadsworth Publishing Company, Inc. Reprinted by permission of Brooks/Cole Publishing Company.

Emotion Is Part of the Human Condition

Emotion and the expression of emotions are an essential part of the human condition. Because it underlies every communication exchange, emotion needs to be understood as an ingredient in understanding others and their messages.

Emotion Is an Element in Empathy

Empathy, discussed in Chapter 4, can be considered a process or encounter between individuals that aids in solving problems and mediating tensions between people.[3] Since emotion is a prime factor in achieving empathy, a clearer understanding of emotion is likely to add to the potential usefulness of empathy—when we project our own personality into that of another in order to understand and "feel" the other better.

Emotion helps us in each of the four phases of empathy discussed in Chapter 4. Identification is essentially a "feeling" phase—where we let another's feelings act on us. To incorporate their feelings into ourselves, the second phase, we must try to feel as they do. Reverberation, the third phase of empathy, has us actually interact with the feelings experienced by the other. We achieve the fourth phase, detachment, if we have engaged successfully in the previous phases. We are likely to gain a more accurate picture if we have participated fully in what the other person is feeling.

Emotion Is an Aspect of Individual Uniqueness

However similar human beings are, there is something distinctive and unique about each one. One aspect of that uniqueness is the way each of us has of experiencing and expressing emotions. If our goal is to understand what is individual and distinctive in people, then an understanding of emotion and the expression of emotions is essential.

Emotion Is a Supplement to Reason

In our culture, the traditional way to study a situation is to use our reason. But if we want to understand another person in depth, we cannot rely on reason alone. A combination of the rational and emotional is needed to gain a better understanding of human behavior and motivation.

Emotion Is a Means to Self-Understanding, Self-Control, and Security

An understanding of emotions offers an opportunity for appreciating, explaining, and analyzing ourselves and our own inner experiences. Who are we? How do we experience ourselves? With greater self-understanding comes

the greater likelihood of control—the control of our emotional responses. With self-understanding and control, too, comes security. Once we are more proficient in our use of emotions, we know we have a reliable communication channel at our command. We can then direct our emotions better, and we are likely to become more spontaneous as well. Spontaneity results from our knowledge that we are in control. When we are more secure in our responses, we are then able to trust our own feelings and instincts. Thus, *anything* we can learn about the emotions, and emotional expression, will contribute to self-growth.

How to Recognize Your Emotions

Recognition involves three phases: (1) awareness, (2) responsibility, and (3) investigation. They normally occur in this order. We cannot take responsibility for something of which we are unaware. Unless we take responsibility, we are unlikely to do any investigation—why bother? Once we become aware of, take responsibility for, and investigate our emotions, there is a stronger likelihood that we will begin to experience more, express more, and understand more. There will be greater personal and emotional involvement as well as control.

A belief that we have no control over our environment can lead to giving up and eventually to death, even in previously healthy individuals.[4] Emotionally caused deaths sometimes occur in prison camps and in response to voodoo curses. Many cultures make no distinction between physical and mental diseases or between natural and supernatural causes. This is not to suggest that you will die without some understanding of the emotions! It is simply to point out the importance of the emotions to self-control and the relationship of self-control to good health.

Be Aware of Your Emotions

Before we share our emotions with others, we must be aware of them ourselves. There are numerous ways to get in touch with your feelings:

- Notice the changes in your body. Because emotional reactions cause physiological changes, physiological changes can signal the presence of emotions.
- Monitor your nonverbal clues. Examine your facial expressions. Keep track of your vocal tone. As you talk, be responsive to your paralanguage. Notice your posture and gestures. Are the clues you notice fluid and natural or are they rigid and tense?
- Recognize emotional expressions in your self-talk. How are you communicating with yourself? What messages are you receiving?

Consider This

Intellect is to emotion as our clothes are to our bodies; we could not very well have civilized life without clothes, but we would be in a poor way if we had only clothes without bodies.

—Alfred North Whitehead, *Dialogues of Alfred North Whitehead* (Boston: Little, Brown & Co., 1954), p. 232.

Try This

It takes practice to know what you are feeling. It involves getting to know your body and the signals it gives to tell you what you are feeling. It also involves becoming familiar with the typical pattern of thoughts that go along with specific feelings for you.

To help you start this process, use the sample feeling chart below. When you want to know what you're feeling, look at the chart and select the word that best approximates how you feel at the moment.

FEELING CHART

Positive

relaxed	secure	peaceful
calm	strong	confident
glowing	happy	interested
warm	busy	turned on
sexy	content	ambitious
excited	loving	imaginative
willing	bubbly	close to you

a little
/
I feel . . . somewhat
\
very

Negative

grouchy	alone	frustrated
sad	dumb	sorry
anxious	trapped	incompetent
tired	put down	rebellious
ashamed	silly	confused
bored	shy	listless
hurt	guilty	depressed
restless		

After you make your selection, make a note of the signals that that emotion has for you. Are you feeling anxious? Well, where does your body show it? Are there specific muscle groups that are tense—neck? hands? jaw? chest? gut? Is it hard to talk? Is your mouth dry? Are you sweating? Keep a diary of your own personal signs of emotions. Let your body teach you about yourself.

What were you thinking? Make a record of what you were thinking when you experienced each emotion. Then study your notes about your body and your thoughts. Eventually your signs of emotion should alert you to how you are feeling.

—Reprinted with permission from Gottman, J., Notarius, C., Gonso, J., and Markham, H., *A Couple's Guide to Communication* (pp. 32–33). Champaign, Ill.: Research Press, 1976.

Consider This

As people become more open with their feelings there's less need to guard against things in the world that are threatening; for instead of hiding from feelings, the open person uses them as a guide that interprets the world he is experiencing. People who rely solely on their intellect to find their way through the world are not as likely to be as in harmony as people who also use their feelings. The highest accomplishments of man are not in the precision of his science, but in the perfection of his art. Man's art is the celebration of his feelings at their most coherent point.

—David Viscott, *The Language of Feelings* (New York: Arbor House, 1976), p. 14. Copyright © 1977 by David Viscott. Reprinted by permission of Arbor House Publishing Company.

- Look at the verbal messages you send to others. "I hate you" is an obvious expression of anger just as "I feel *so* bad" can signal unhappiness, boredom, fear, embarrassment, or even guilt.

Take Responsibility for Your Emotions

Awareness of emotions is important, but if we make excuses for our emotions, blame others for them, or otherwise escape responsibility for them, we are unlikely to increase our understanding of ourselves or move closer to maturity. Maturity assumes responsibility. It means recognizing that others don't make us angry or happy, embarrassed or disgusted. Rather than saying, "You really make me mad," it means saying, "I feel angry when you say you'll stop by and then don't show up or call." *We* are responsible for the way we react. *We* are responsible for the emotions we feel. If we do not take responsibility for them, we will feel no need to change them if they are damaging or negative.

For example, Jeffrey found himself unable to smile or laugh easily. He was becoming less able to cope with his daily activities. It was almost as if he had lost the power to act or move. Finally, Jeffrey determined that he was "feeling fear" and that this fear concerned an upcoming, major examination. The moment he realized the cause of his jumpiness and jitteriness, he was able to try to change. He created a schedule for daily study that would assure that he covered all the required material and allowed for final, concentrated study just before the exam. Although Jeffrey's new study procedures did not eliminate all his concerns, he reduced his fear to a manageable and normal level of anxiety about the exam. He might have blamed his teacher; instead, Jeffrey took responsibility for his fear.

Investigate Your Emotions

When you trace emotions to their roots, you may get surprising results. One thing you may find is that the emotions you express or reveal have their roots in personal problems or situations. I have a friend, for example, who appears hostile and spiteful. She seems to condemn almost everything. But if you listen long enough, you realize that much of her bitterness stems from the fact that she feels life has been unfair to her. She has an inferiority complex that manifests itself in excessive aggressiveness and a domineering attitude.

Another thing you may find is that the emotion being experienced is just one of a couple or several. Diane and Dave, for example, had had a great evening. Just after dinner, two friends of Diane, Vern and Donna, came over to their table. Diane and Dave had been involved in some self-disclosing and Diane repeated a "juicy" anecdote to Vern and Donna. After Vern and Donna left, Dave became silent. Soon they left the restaurant. Dave was angry. His mouth was tight, his body was tense, he had a knotted feeling in his stomach. Dave's anger may have been justified, but had he expressed the *real* cause of his anger—the fact that he was embarrassed by the information Diane had revealed—it might have been easier for Diane to understand his reaction.

Anger often arises from other emotions. Ramon became angry at Maria because he was jealous of her relationship with José, her former boyfriend. Jealousy, not anger, was the root emotion. Deona became angry at her roommate, Athena, because she resented the time Athena spent with girlfriends down the hall and not with her. Resentment was the true cause of Deona's anger. Allen carried anger toward Sean. Once he investigated the cause, he realized he was envious of Sean's advantages and possessions. Envy caused his anger.

Try This

The following is suggested as a relaxation technique:

1. Sit quietly in a comfortable position.
2. Close your eyes.
3. Beginning at your feet and progressing up to your face, deeply relax all your muscles. Keep them relaxed.
4. Breathe through your nose. Become aware of your breathing. As you breathe out, say the word <u>one</u> silently to yourself. Continue the pattern: breathe in . . . out, "one"; in . . . out, "one"; and so on. Breathe easily and naturally.
5. Continue for 10 to 20 minutes. You may open your eyes to check the time, but do not use an alarm. When you finish, sit quietly for several minutes, first with your eyes closed and later with your eyes opened. Do not stand up for a few minutes.
6. Do not worry about whether you are successful in achieving a deep level of relaxation. Maintain a passive attitude and permit relaxation to occur at its own pace. When distracting thoughts occur, try to ignore them and return to repeating <u>one</u>. With practice, the response should come with little effort. Practice the technique once or twice daily but not within two hours after any meal, since the digestive processes seem to interfere with eliciting the relaxation response.

—Reprinted by permission of the Harvard Business Review. An exhibit from "Time Out for Tension" by Ruanne K. Peters and Herbert Benson (January/February 1978). Copyright © 1978 by the President and Fellows of Harvard College; all rights reserved.

- Ask yourself, "Where did my anger come from?"
- Trace the origin of your emotion(s).
- Is your emotion rooted in personal problems, related situations, or other reactions?

How Can We Control Emotions?

Think about the last time you became emotional. What did you do? Probably, for most of us, the negative situations are easier to remember than the positive ones simply because we are likely to be more demonstrative in negative situations. For the most part, research on emotion has concentrated on the negative emotions (primarily anxiety and fear), while neglecting the positive emotions such as love, happiness, and contentment.[5]

What did you do the last time *you* became emotional? Sherrie yelled. Todd cursed. Rebecca felt like hitting. Gus threw something. Amanda broke something. Jonathan struck someone. Chances are that just before each of these people did what they did, they felt tense, wound up, maybe even nervous. Some people describe these feelings by saying, "I feel tied up in knots." Our physical response often is a way of releasing the body tension that strong emotions cause. One of the first ways of reducing this tension is to relax in some way. I don't want to assume that all emotional expression is negative; however, for the purposes of this section, let's assume we are dealing with the expression of strong negative emotions. Often, the negative expression is what causes problems. How can we control it? Here are a few suggestions.

Try This

Think about a recent situation in which you became emotional. Imagine yourself experiencing the situation and the feelings again. Now, write down the emotion-producing statements (the negative labels) that you made. Look for all such labels. Were there statements or feelings that you made that:

1. made you look bad?
2. provided proof that you were no good?
3. proved that things had to be <u>entirely</u> the way you wanted them to be?

Write down the negative statements you made. Now, write an alternative positive statement that disputes the negative one.

Negative Label
1. "She knows I hate going to parties with her friends. She did this purposely to spite me."
2. "She has no respect for my wishes."

Positive Alternative
1. "She knows I hate these parties, so she must have a reason for saying we'd go. Maybe this is something special."
2. "I'm the only one she likes to go out with, and I have asked her to go to parties with *my* friends."

Notice how we tend to jump to conclusions? Notice how inclined we are to place negative labels on situations? If the choice is fifty-fifty, why is it we generally choose the negative viewpoint or perspective rather than the positive?

Learning to Relax

Stress is the body's response to environmental demands, positive or negative. It is an inevitable part of life, and one we must learn to cope with rather than try to avoid. In Chapter 10, stress management is discussed in relation to conflict. Here, relaxation is discussed in relation to emotional buildups. Taken together, these sections will help us cope with situations of high emotional intensity.

There are many ways to reduce tension, and these ways can be learned. Once we have learned relaxation skills, we can control emotional buildup in all areas of our life. Lisa learned one method in her public-speaking class. Just before rising to give a speech, she would close her eyes, take a deep breath, exhale slowly and forcefully, and give herself a pep talk: "Okay, stay calm and relaxed now. This isn't a life-or-death situation. You can do it, and you can do it well."

There are other methods, too. Monica uses yoga; Daniel uses meditation along with deep muscular relaxation. All these methods include breathing exercises, reduction of muscular tension, and a focus on internal bodily sensations.

Many situations escalate to an emotional outburst because of the buildup of tension. Relaxation along the way can help defuse the situation. The earlier a building-emotional situation can be detected, the sooner relaxation skills can be instituted.

Learning Self-Control

The most commonly heard excuse for becoming excessively emotional is that people are "out of control." In some cases, loss of control becomes an excuse for any actions that occur. Once "out of control," people claim they are no longer responsible for what they do. "Loss of control," for some, makes their behavior acceptable. I find it difficult to accept the fact that people *can't* control their behavior, easier to accept the fact they *don't* control their behavior. Perhaps it is just that it is easier to place blame for our behaviors than to accept responsibility for them. Self-control takes practice, but it can be learned if we accept responsibility for our own behavior.

Reading Others' Emotions

Because of the transactional nature of communication—the relationship that occurs between interacting partners—dyadic partners have an important and ongoing influence on each other. They do not operate independently. Thus, if you have learned to relax and have gained some self-control, this is likely to influence your relationship partner. Let's assume, for a moment, that you are calm and relaxed, but your partner has a potential emotional problem. How do you read his or her emotions?

According to the research, our most immediate source of information about a relationship partner's feelings is our own feelings.[6] Our own feelings can be easily observed and felt, they are important (since they *are* our own), and they are directly experienced. The second most immediate source of information about feelings is the partner's nonverbal emotional expression.[7] We judge emotion in others to a large extent on the basis of their nonverbal behavior; much of the overt behavior in emotion is learned in accordance with cultural norms and expectations. Facial expressions, gestures, posture, and tone of voice are important clues. Paralanguage, too, is an important clue. Nonverbal behavior is assumed to be a more direct and less-censored reflection of our underlying emotional feelings.[8] Verbal explanations are a third way to determine others' feelings. Although verbal behavior is often preempted by more immediate information about feelings, this is not always the case. Some people are especially sensitive to verbal disclosure and emotions. Often, this occurs when people are frank in their communication and engage in verbal sharing.[9]

In the following example, "A Case Study in Dealing With Others' Emotions," Penny, a student who is upset and angry with a grade she received, approached Dr. Williams, her teacher. Dr. Williams determined that the appropriate response was to calm Penny. Notice the number of different things Dr. Williams does in dealing with Penny.

A CASE STUDY IN DEALING WITH OTHERS' EMOTIONS

Penny was furious. She had just gotten her paper back and her grade was a "C." Penny had never received less than a "B" on her papers, so she followed her instructor to her office. On the way, she became more and more incensed. When she entered Dr. Williams's office, she exploded. But while she yelled, Dr. Williams remained calm. She responded to Penny's aggression with calmness. Dr. Williams's facial expression, her posture and gestures, and her tone of voice modeled calmness. Penny calmed down.

There were other things that Dr. Williams did to help calm Penny. She encouraged her to talk. She allowed her to explain why she was upset. She even asked open-ended questions such as "What exactly upset you?" "Why did this bother you so much?" and "How do you suppose this happened?" In addition, Dr. Williams listened openly. She was paying close attention to what Penny was saying— and she showed it. She looked directly at Penny, nodded her head when appropriate, avoided interrupting, and even leaned toward Penny to show her concern and seriousness.

As Penny continued talking, Dr. Williams demonstrated that she understood what Penny was telling her. She used statements such as "I see what you mean," "I can understand that," and "I know how that must make you feel." She used the paraphrasing response discussed in Chapter 4 by restating the content of Penny's ideas. Dr. Williams would say back to Penny, in her own words, the essence of what Penny had said. In this way, she let Penny know that she was trying hard to stay with her and with what she was saying.

Dr. Williams also revealed empathy—the most effective way she had to communicate understanding to Penny. She concentrated more on what Penny was feeling than on what she was saying, and Dr. Williams let her understanding of Penny's feelings be known. To reveal empathy, Dr. Williams did several things. She:

1. tried to put herself in Penny's place.
2. asked herself what Penny was feeling and how strongly she was feeling it.
3. tried to understand Penny's feelings.
4. noticed what Penny said but also how she said it (tone, speed, loudness of words, breathing rate, stammering, sighing, gestures, posture, facial expressions).

Dr. Williams also helped calm Penny through reassurance. She tried several ways to reassure her. She told her, for example, "It's going to be okay," and "Let's work through this one step at a time." She also said, "I'm really interested in helping you solve this problem." The purpose of reassurance is to reduce threat, arouse hope and optimism, clear up ambiguities, and make clear your willingness to help solve the problem. In addition to the words, Dr. Williams was warm and sincere when appropriate. Although she did not touch Penny, sometimes a touch, such as a hand on the other's shoulder, also provides reassurance.

The final thing Dr. Williams did to help calm Penny was to help her save face. She did not corner or humiliate Penny. She said that she would be willing to reread the paper, which was a concession on her part. In addition, she said she would be willing to change the grade *if* she found sufficient justification for it; this could be a compromise. In this way, Dr. Williams offered Penny at least part of what was being emotionally demanded. In doing this, Dr. Williams remained calm and self-controlled. She avoided comments that would be perceived as provoking, belittling, critical, threatening, or overly impatient.

Consider This

Man is an extremely complex emotional organism, and the way in which he copes with his emotions is probably what separates him most widely from the rest of the animal kingdom. His greatest pleasures in life come from the realistic fulfillment of his emotional drives. If his emotions are mishandled, however, this not only can lead to unhappiness but also may actually interfere with the normal healthy functioning of his body.

—Leo Madow, *Anger: How to Recognize and Cope with It* (New York: Charles Scribner's Sons, 1972), p. 71.

Sharing Emotions

Just because we experience an emotion does *not* mean we should or need to share it with others. Fortunately, there are some guidelines that we can use to determine when it is appropriate to share our feelings. In this section, how to decide whether to share our emotions will be discussed first, when to share them will be discussed next, and, finally, some specific methods for sharing emotions successfully will be offered.

Deciding Whether to Share Your Emotions

Maybe you have gotten to this point in this chapter still wondering *why* you should share your feelings, let alone when and how. Sharing is risky, even scary sometimes. But, in interpersonal communication, sharing emotions with others can help solve problems, resolve conflict, benefit our physical health, and increase intimacy with others. The questions raised in this section may help you decide whether or not to share your emotions with others.

Do you have problems that need to be solved? Interpersonal problems such as hurtful patterns of communication or unpleasant job conditions can often be alleviated when people share their feelings about them. If one or both partners in a relationship have problems that they are not talking about with each other, then their relationship is not a very full one. When problems are solved together, there is mutual investment in the relationship and the relationship will grow stronger.

Do you have conflicts that need to be resolved? Conflicts such as disagreements over money, politics, religion, and the raising of children are easier to deal with when feelings are shared. The sharing of feelings does not provide the answers but sets up an atmosphere in which effective negotiation and compromise can occur. A common response is "I didn't know you felt that way! Now that I know, we can do something about it."

Are you impairing your physical health by holding in emotions? Expressing emotions can help us physically. Just as emotions are accompanied

Consider This

BILL T.: At first I was wary about bringing up some of the things that were bothering me about our relationship. I guess I figured they will work out in time. But this Bible-study group we belong to emphasizes honesty and openness in relationships. So we agreed to give it a try by telling each other some of the things we were unhappy with. I told Laurie I don't like the way she plans every move on our weekends and expects me to go along with it, and I don't like it when she mothers me. There was some tension for a while and some hurt feelings, but you wouldn't believe what a productive discussion we wound up having. It turned out that Laurie was really bothered by some things I do too, and I had no idea they irritated her so much. Now that we both know how the other feels, we can work the problems out. We couldn't before because we didn't talk about them.

DR. SPENCER, MARRIAGE COUNSELOR: Be careful about communicating. Just because you talk about a "problem" doesn't mean you've solved it. It's not enough to bring something up. You have to decide to do something about it. The popular myths say just talk about it. But once the issue is on the table, it must be resolved.

—Gerald M. Phillips and Julia T. Wood, *Communication and Human Relationships: The Study of Interpersonal Communication* (New York: Macmillan Co., Inc., 1983), p. 140.

by physiological changes, the tension that occurs when we hold in emotions—especially strong emotions—also can have physiological results. One physician suggests that when there is no discharge of the energy buildup that results from getting emotional, some of the results include headaches, gastrointestinal disorders, respiratory disorders, skin disorders, genito-urinary disorders, arthritis, disabilities of the nervous system, and circulatory disorders.[10]

Are you involved in an intimate relationship that has the potential for greater closeness if you could express how you *really* feel on some issues? Expressing how we feel appropriately and on an ongoing basis with a relationship partner can bring us closer together. Notice in the "Consider This" on page 284 Henrietta's explanation of how her fights with Jack are resolved. Henrietta and Jack are very affectionate and demonstrative with each other; thus, the warmth and support they provide each other following emotional flareups is likely to be rich and rewarding—as well as anticipated by both partners.

Suppose that we have answered some (or all) of these four questions affirmatively. Suppose we do have problems to be solved, conflicts to be resolved, physical needs for emotional release, and needs for greater intimacy. Should we share our feelings? Since we cannot always open up to others indiscriminately, or easily, or without taking some responsibility for our actions, there are a number of factors that may need to be taken into consideration. When is it appropriate to share our feelings? Questions like the following may help in deciding:

- What do you want to achieve in this situation? Will expressing the emotion help achieve it? I remember a snowy evening when our teenage daughter was driving a group of her friends to a concert. Fifteen minutes after the group had left, the mother of one of the other girls called our house to express her worries about driving in such weather. Of course we told her that we understood her worries and assured her that we would not have let our daughter drive on such a night if we hadn't felt sure she could handle it. But what purpose did the call serve? It was too late to cancel the outing—and I suspect that the mother hung up the phone just as worried as before, despite our reassurance. Had she thought her response through first, it would have been better for her *not* to share her feelings in this case.
- Is this the appropriate person to share this with? Could you be misdirecting your emotion? A student became enraged at what appeared to be a new policy imposed by his instructor and went immediately to the director of the course. After listening to the student, the director suggested that the student talk directly to the instructor. When the matter was finally clarified, it was simply a misunderstanding. Had the student gone to the instructor at once, there would have been no reason for getting upset.
- Can you express your emotion honestly and responsibly, describing exactly what the emotion is and what you really want? Bruce was having difficulty understanding Trina's behavior. One day she would talk about ending their relationship, the next day she seemed to really want to be with him. Finally, they had a long talk. Trina expressed her feelings honestly and responsibly when she said, "I'm confused by my feelings about you. Sometimes I feel that we are just too different and ought to call it off. But I also want you to know that I love you very much." Although expressing her confusion did not solve the problem, at least it helped Bruce understand her on-again, off-again behavior and laid the groundwork for open discussion of their differences.
- Can you make certain that you express your feelings clearly? Can you provide brief reasons for feeling the way you do? Can you express the feeling directly rather than indirectly? Jim had reached the point of not wanting to go home—he felt that his father was always "on his case." If it wasn't his messy room, it was the way he left the bathroom, or the chores he forgot to do. One evening at the family dinner table, Jim decided to speak up. He told his father that he felt he was coming down too hard on him for every little

Consider This

HENRIETTA: Well, if something does happen, it starts out with one or the other saying something the other does not like, and getting a little defensive, and you can feel tension and we get angry. There's never anything said about <u>you rotten person</u> or something like that. It's always: "I don't like it when you do this," or, "You make me feel bad because of this." We get pretty emotional sometimes—sometimes I cry, sometimes he cries, sometimes we both cry, but usually when we see how bad the other is dealing with it, we tend to try and comfort each other through it too. So it's conflicting and comforting that ends up with us realizing how much we care for each other.

—Excerpt taken from pp. 392–393 of *American Couples* by Philip Blumstein and Pepper Schwartz. Copyright © 1983 Philip Blumstein and Pepper Schwartz. By permission of William Morrow and Company, Inc.

thing. Instead of stopping there, Jim got specific: "Dad, just in the five minutes before dinner you got-after me for not returning a screwdriver to the workbench, not standing up straight, and not starting my homework the minute I got home from school." To his astonishment, his father admitted that he'd been too hard on him, wanting him to be "too perfect," and agreed to try to back off a little. The direct expression of feelings worked well for Jim.

- Can you keep the feeling centered on specific circumstances rather than on things in general? We all have ups and downs. Can you focus on the "down" of the present moment only? Joan was increasingly annoyed at finding hair in the bathroom sink after her husband, Zach, shaved in the morning. She had let him know before they were married that she would never be his household slave. When she told him how she felt about having to clean up after him every morning, she was careful *not* to mention the socks he dropped on the floor, the newspaper he forgot to put away, or the milk carton he left out on the counter. Joan focused on one specific circumstance only—and she chose the one that bothered her the most.

Sometimes it can help to talk your emotions over with someone else— a friend or a neutral party. This can help you understand what you are really emotional about and how to communicate it. It might be helpful to tell yourself first. Use intrapersonal communication. Sometimes, too, if the emotional reaction is very strong, it is a good idea to use some delaying tactics to give yourself time to understand your feelings. Count to ten. Put yourself in the other person's shoes. Walk around the block. Time provides perspective and, perhaps, a sense of humor.

In every discussion of sharing emotions with others, there is one question that always seems to be brought up: Why is it that whenever your relationship partner becomes emotional, he or she always seems to take it out on you—first! If you think about this, however, you are the person your immediate relationship partner is around the most. Not only that, you are the person with whom he or she is probably most comfortable. In addition, you are the one from whom he or she is likely to get the most support and comfort. An advantage, too, is that two heads are often better than one. One relationship partner can calm the other; suggest possible alternatives for the other; and, perhaps, provide the only outlet that the relationship partner needs! Sometimes all we need is a listener—or a shoulder to cry on. Relationship partners, often, are excellent channels for emotional outlet. Think of it as a compliment; your relationship partner thought enough of you to come to you first!

Our emotions and their expression give us an opportunity to learn more about ourselves. By looking honestly at how we feel and how we can best share our feelings with others, we can grow beyond immature reactions. Emotions are energy. Learning to channel them can provide great satisfaction and can turn problems into solutions.

Deciding When to Share Your Emotions

Because emotions are powerful, they have the potential for stirring people up. Thus, the time and place where they are shared is important. In general, the sooner we share our emotions the better. Research indicates that information that is more immediate has greater influence on understanding.[11] When sharing is immediate, the feelings are fresh, specific, and easier to identify;[12] thus, the results of immediate sharing are likely to be favorable. There will be less confusion, less difficulty trying to reconstruct the circumstances, and less misinformation.

On the other hand, it is probably best *not* to share emotions right away if you are:

- rushed. Sometimes the emotion is so strong that you need time to think it over and get a little perspective on it.
- very disturbed. You may overstate your anger, saying or doing things that you'll regret later.
- too tired to exert the effort necessary to solve the problem.
- not ready to listen to what the other person has to say.

If we know that immediacy is best, but recognize that we can sometimes be too rushed, too disturbed, or too tired, this will help us determine when to share our emotions. Sharing is important, and we need to seek the best

Consider This

Most divorces occur because of incompatibilities of values, ethics and emotional needs.

—From "Letter to the Editor" by SaraKay Cohen Smullens, "Trauma of Divorce," *TIME,* February 27, 1989, p. 7. Reprinted by permission of the author.

possible opportunity—soon—if we are to make the sharing pay rich dividends in increased understanding. The problem is that the issue of when to share your emotions is not a clear one. Sometimes it is better to do it at once, sometimes it is better to wait. You are the only person who can make that judgment.

Sharing Your Emotions Successfully

Earlier in this chapter it was stated that the clear and vivid expression of emotions is essential to effective communication. Knowing *how* to be clear and vivid, however, is not all that simple. More than anything else, it requires practice. For example, look at the following pairs of sentences:

- You don't let me know how you feel about our relationship.
- When you don't let me know how you feel about our relationship, I get frustrated and insecure.

- Since we had our fight, I haven't been able to say anything to you.
- Since we had our fight, I've said nothing to you because I've been hurt and confused.

Notice that the second statement in each of the pairs above includes a clear and specific emotional expression. The first is emotionally void. Sometimes people think they are expressing themselves emotionally, but they are not providing emotional content. I am not discussing paralanguage here, simply the words that we choose to use. For example, "I feel like going to the party," or "I feel we've been seeing too much of each other," are emotionally void statements. In the first of these sentences, the word "feel" is being used as a synonym for "want to": "I want to go to the party." In the second example, "feel" is being used as a synonym for "think": "I think we've been seeing too much of each other." Add an emotive word to each sentence and notice the changes:

"I feel

alone	friendly
anxious	happy
curious	jealous
depressed	lonely
desperate	needy
disappointed	optimistic
eager	proud
excited	weary

and I want to go to the party."

or "I think we've been seeing too much of each other and I feel:

afraid	glad	out of control
closed	hopeful	overcontrolled
confined	hopeless	pessimistic
concerned	hostile	pleased
contented	hurt	pressured
cut off from others	immobilized	proud
dependent	impatient	restrained
deprived	inhibited	secure
despondent	insecure	terrified
exhilarated	misunderstood	threatened

The point of listing all these words is to demonstrate in how many directions the statement can go once the emotional term is added. Complete the statement using each word and sense the differences. Notice how clear and specific the statement becomes and how the emotional term adds to the communication.

A final point needs to be made in discussing the nature and expression of emotions. We have discussed their physiological nature as well as their nonverbal and verbal expression. Much of our reaction to an emotion, however, depends on how we label it. Think, for example, what a difference it makes when we label a person as a "friend" or as an "enemy." How we respond to that person depends on the label we have chosen. The same is true when we face emotional situations: we must remember that we control our emotional response, and we can label the situation in any way we choose. Labeling, then, can change our emotional viewpoint toward a situation, just

Consider This

Notice how Philip G. Zimbardo labeled his own behavior as a lecturer, then changed his responses through relabeling:

I notice I'm perspiring while lecturing. From that I infer, I am feeling nervous. If it occurs often, I might even label myself a "nervous person." Once I have the label, the next question I must answer is, "Why am I nervous?" Then I start to search for an appropriate explanation. I might notice some students leaving the room, or being inattentive. I am nervous because I'm not giving a good lecture. That makes me more nervous. How do I know it's not good? Because I'm boring my audience. I am nervous because I am a boring lecturer and I want to be a good lecturer. I feel inadequate. Maybe I should open a delicatessen instead. Just then a student says, "It's hot in here, I'm perspiring and it makes it tough to concentrate on your lecture." Instantly, I'm no longer "nervous" or "boring."

—*Philip Zimbardo, Shyness.* Reading, Massachusetts: Addison-Wesley Publishing Company, Inc., 1977, pp. 76–77.

as the way we think about ourselves has profound effects on all aspects of our lives. Many people are too ready to pin labels on themselves. The label becomes a self-fulfilling prophecy. If we perceive ourselves as depressed, we will act depressed, others will respond to our depressing actions, and their responses will confirm the fact that we are, indeed, depressed. All of this *can* begin with the way we choose to label a situation. Saying "I am angry" will probably make you feel the physiological clues for anger. We may be able to change the situation by selecting a new label: "I am disappointed." The new word is likely to make you feel the physiological clues for disappointment—which are unlikely to be as strong as those of anger. The point is, *we* control the words we choose. With more care in our language choices, we exert more control over ourselves *and* our environment.

The way we label situations becomes a powerful persuader. In an important experiment on shyness, subjects were asked how they would react in certain kinds of situations or with certain kinds of people. The researcher found that those who labeled themselves shy did not differ significantly in their reactions from those who said they were not shy. The difference was that those who labeled themselves shy blamed *themselves:* "I am reacting negatively because I am too shy, it's something I am, something I carry around wherever I go."[13] If these people could relabel these experiences and focus on external causes, they could work to change the situation.

An important element in emotional control and emotional sharing that has been discussed in this chapter needs further emphasis. Stressed throughout has been the fact that emotions occur within us, they are ours, and *we* control them. We not only cause them to occur, we sometimes increase their intensity and prolong them. Then, having fanned the emotions ourselves, we may even blame ourselves because we have them. It's a curious process: we become emotional because we became emotional! The point is, the emotions are ours to control. And if we realize that we are in control, we can just as easily change our emotions—reduce their intensity—or create positive ones to replace those that are negative as we can create them in the first place.

Nobody can *make* you disappointed or irritated. *You* do this to yourself. And if you do it, you can undo it. In their book *A New Guide to Rational Living*, Albert Ellis and Robert Harper say it best: "*You* create and control your feelings. You *can* change them."[14] To bring on this kind of change requires that we *push* ourselves. When we feel afraid, angry, anxious, bored, defensive, disappointed, frustrated, guilty, hurt, inferior, jealous, lonely, rejected, repulsed, sad, shy, or suspicious—some of the most commonly experienced negative emotions—we should use these as cues that we need a shove! Change won't happen by itself. Tell yourself, "I can change this emotion from negative to positive or from negative to *less* negative." Think about it, then do it!

Improving Skills for Expressing Feelings and Emotions

Although expressions of feelings and emotions are important to the success of interpersonal transactions, they should not be an end in themselves. That is, you do not need to express *every* feeling and emotion. Yet many people fear their emotions and live emotionally sterile interpersonal lives as a result. This is the other side of the same coin. Notice how these positions are opposite ends of a continuum. (See Figure 8.1)

Notice in the figure that responsible expression of feelings and emotions occupies the middle area of the continuum. It does *not* involve expressing all feelings and emotions, nor does it involve suppressing them totally. How often and how much to express are part of responsible assertiveness. Gerard Egan has suggested that the following principles can serve as guidelines: legitimacy, genuineness, constructiveness, immediacy, and control.[15]

Recognize the Legitimacy of Your Feelings and Emotions

A basic, underlying principle that governs the expression of all feelings and emotions is their humanness. That is, because you are a human being, you have feelings and emotions, and it is legitimate to have and to express them.

If you hesitate to express them because you feel they are barriers to interpersonal effectiveness, you undoubtedly question their legitimacy. It may be that you have not experienced the breadth, depth, or flavor they can add to relationships.

Let Your Feelings and Emotions Be Genuine

Feelings and emotions should be honest reflections of your mental state. Sometimes people hide behind manufactured emotional reactions or repress emotions that should be expressed. Sometimes this results from trying to do what is "right" or what is "expected." Some people have little problem demonstrating negative emotions: anger, annoyance, exasperation, sorrow, misery, outrage, or hate. But these same people cannot (or do not) show joy, pleasure, delight, ecstasy, affection, or elation. Others reveal the positive emotions but not the negative ones. This may be culturally induced behavior. Feelings and emotions, whether positive or negative, are not good or bad. It is the way they are expressed that can be constructive or destructive.

Express Your Feelings and Emotions Constructively

Because of the power of emotions and feelings and the effect they can have, they can be used destructively in many ways. Some people, for example, save feelings up and then dump them all at once on another person in an emotional barrage. Others release them slowly (and sometimes painfully) over time in cynical or sarcastic ways to undermine another person's credibility or strength. Still another destructive use of emotions is for manipulation; for example: "If I act as if I'm hurt, they'll leave me alone," or "If I get angry and upset, I'll get my own way."

Constructive expression means taking the responsibility for your feelings and emotions. You need to be aware of them, admit them, investigate them, report them in a factual, objective manner, and integrate them with your other thoughts and feelings.[16] An example of the constructive expression of feelings would go something like this: "I'm feeling very defensive. I don't like to talk about my previous relationships. It just gets me upset and angry. Perhaps we could find something else to talk about."

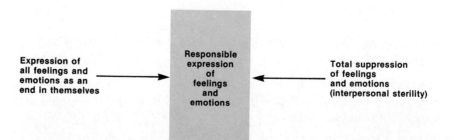

Expression of all feelings and emotions as an end in themselves → **Responsible expression of feelings and emotions** ← **Total suppression of feelings and emotions (interpersonal sterility)**

Figure 8.1

Give Immediacy to Your Expression of Feelings and Emotions

The timely expression of feelings and emotions allows you and others to deal with them while they are still manageable. To deal with them when they come up or soon afterward keeps them in the context in which they arose rather than having to reconstruct the context through explanation and description, like "Remember two days ago when we were talking about such and such, and you said. . . ." Reconstruction of past events is often vague and general, and sometimes the feelings and emotions being pinpointed get lost in the ambiguity of the description.

Another function of immediacy is **ventilation.** Expressing feelings and emotions immediately offers a channel for release and avoids saving them up and cashing them in all at once in a gigantic emotional avalanche. Most people are unprepared for such emotional outbursts. Immediacy supplies the readiness to explore various reactions and experiences as they occur—while they are clear and meaningful.

Exercise Control Over Your Feelings and Emotion

Though you may be willing—even eager—to share your feelings and emotions, discipline is still required. Working through periods of intense feelings and emotions is not easy. An overall desire to explore the issues that give rise to the intensity is important.

Control has both positive and negative sides. Positively, control allows communication to continue in a supportive, open environment. Negatively, control can be used to punish, controlling the expression of feelings and emotions by repressing them, holding back cooperation, lapsing into silence, showing coldness, or offering cynicism. Control, here, means guiding and managing the expression of feelings. Even strong emotions, or the strong expression of emotions, can be controlled.[16] People who are in control do not give in to the strength of their feelings and emotions. Such people might respond to an intense situation in this way: "I really hate what you are saying. You are attacking some values that I care about very deeply. I want to blow up right now, but that isn't going to do either of us any good. I want to strike out at you for what you are saying—and yet I want to know why you are saying these things and why I am reacting so strongly."

There is nothing simple about the subject of emotions. But it is important to try to understand them because they are an essential part of daily life, an essential part of interpersonal communication. Communicating feelings is one of the most frequent sources of difficulty in relationships. We are likely to encounter opposition, conflict, and defensiveness as we deal with both emotions and attitudes. Some disagreement is always likely. And yet we should be able to stand up for our rights, defend our emotions and feelings, and effectively express our attitudes—in other words, to be assertive. Assertiveness will be discussed further in the next chapter.

Notes

[1] David W. Johnson, *Reaching Out: Interpersonal Effectiveness and Self-Actualization*, 2d ed. (Englewood Cliffs, N.J.: Prentice-Hall, 1981), p. 110.

[2] These ways are described by Gerard Egan in *You & Me: The Skills of Communicating and Relating to Others* (Monterey, Calif.: Brooks/Cole, 1977), pp. 87–88.

[3] This definition comes from Robert L. Katz, *Empathy: Its Nature and Its Uses* (London: The Free Press of Glencoe, 1963), p. viii.

[4] Philip G. Zimbardo and Floyd L. Ruch, *Psychology and Life*, 9th ed. (Glenview, Ill.: Scott, Foresman & Co., 1975), p. 405.

[5] Zimbardo and Ruch, *Psychology and Life*, p. 368.

[6] Alan L. Sillars, Gary R. Pike, Tricia S. Jones, and Mary A. Murphy, "Communication and Understanding in Marriage," *Human Communication Research* 10:3 (Spring 1984): p. 342.

[7] Sillars, Pike, Jones, and Murphy, "Communication and Understanding in Marriage," p. 342.

[8] See Mark L. Knapp, *Nonverbal Communication in Human Interaction*, 2d ed. (New York: Holt, Rinehart & Winston, 1978).

[9] Sillars, Pike, Jones, and Murphy, "Communication and Understanding in Marriage," p. 342.

[10] Leo Madow, *Anger: How to Recognize and Cope with It* (New York: Charles Scribner's Sons, 1972), pp. 71–85.

[11] Sillars, Pike, Jones, and Murphy, "Communication and Understanding in Marriage," p. 341.

[12] Sillars, Pike, Jones, and Murphy, "Communication and Understanding in Marriage," p. 341.

[13] Philip G. Zimbardo, *Shyness: What It Is. What to Do About It* (New York: Harcourt Brace Jovanovich, 1977), p. 78.

[14] Albert Ellis and Robert A. Harper, *A New Guide to Rational Living* (North Hollywood, Calif.: Wilshire Book Co., 1975), p. 211.

[15] Gerard Egan, *Interpersonal Living: A Skills/Contract Approach to Human-Relations Training in Groups* (Monterey, Calif.: Brooks/Cole Publishing Co., 1976), pp. 36–37.

[16] John Powell, *Why Am I Afraid to Tell You Who I Am?* (Allen, Texas: Argus Communications, 1969), pp. 87–93.

Further Reading

Joel R. Davitz, *The Communication of Emotional Meaning* (New York: McGraw-Hill Book Co., 1964). The primary purpose of this book is to present a series of researches by different writers on emotional communication. Although it represents only a beginning of research in the area, it shows some of the ways that the studies of emotion have been conducted.

Joel R. Davitz, *The Language of Emotion* (New York: Academic Press, 1969). In this research-based book, Davitz introduces a line of inquiry into the language of emotion. Important inclusions are a dictionary of emotional meaning and clusters of clues that help to identify each emotion.

Gerard Egan, *You & Me: The Skills of Communicating and Relating to Others* (Monterey, Calif.: Brooks/Cole, 1977). This book is intended for people who wish to improve their interpersonal self-awareness, communication skills, and assertiveness. Egan offers a systematic skills-oriented approach for the lay reader. An excellent collection of activities and exercises is included with each chapter.

Albert Ellis, *How to Stubbornly Refuse to Make Yourself Miserable About Anything—Yes, Anything!* (Secaucus, N.J.: Lyle Stuart Inc., 1988). Ellis claims that emotional turmoil is unnecessary and that we create our own feelings. We are the ones who choose to think and feel in self-harming ways. This is Ellis's most recent book on rational-emotive-therapy. It is an easy-to-read, enthusiastic, and interesting book that could help readers deal with anger, anxiety, and depression.

Albert Ellis and Robert A. Harper, *A New Guide to Rational Living* (North Hollywood, Calif.: Wilshire Book Co., 1975). Quoting from the foreword: "All the emotional problems to which human beings are prone are dissected by Drs. Ellis and Harper in a brilliant and all-encompassing manner" (p. vii). Excellent chapters on "You Feel As You Think," "Feeling Well by Thinking Straight," and "What Your Feelings Really Are." An easy-to-read book full of practical advice and suggestions for moving in a positive direction.

William Glasser, *Control Theory: A New Explanation of How We Control Our Lives* (New York: Harper & Row, 1984). Glasser believes that all behavior is made up of three components: what we do, what we think, and what we feel. He claims we are motivated completely by forces inside ourselves and with better control of our emotions and actions can live healthier and more productive lives.

Robert Plutchik and Henry Kellerman, eds., *Emotion: Theory, Research, and Experience*, Vol. 1: *Theories of Emotion* (New York: Academic Press, 1980). To indicate the sophisticated research basis for this book, the editors draw on the disciplines of psychology, sociobiology, ethology, psychosomatics, psychiatry, linguistics, and neurology. In all cases they treat theoretical issues, methodological problems, research findings, and practical and clinical applications. Many excellent research sources are included.

K. T. Strongman, *The Psychology of Emotion*, 2d ed. (New York: John Wiley & Sons, 1978). The author provides a broad coverage of emotion and suggests guidelines for its study and research. Strongman shows a leaning towards the behavioral in his suggestion of research strategies. A book for the serious student.

David Viscott, *The Language of Feelings* (New York: Arbor House, 1976). Viscott shows how such feelings as hurt, anger, guilt, anxiety, and depression can be converted from crippling to freeing influences, leaving one free and clear of emotional debt. Viscott's approach is simple and direct as he relates his personal understanding of feelings, what they mean, where they come from, and what they can do for you.

R. Reid Wilson, *Don't Panic: Taking Control of Anxiety Attacks* (New York: Harper & Row, 1986). This is a self-help book for overcoming panic and coping with anxious fears. In the first part, six chapters, he identifies and describes the problem. In the second part, fourteen chapters, he shows readers how to take control of anxiety attacks. This is an information-packed, practical book full of "how to" advice.

9

Getting There from Here: Assertiveness

Learning Objectives

When you have finished this chapter you should be able to:

- Define assertiveness and explain the problems that result from *not* being assertive.
- Explain what it is that keeps people from being assertive.
- Distinguish between assertiveness, nonassertiveness, and aggression.
- Illustrate a negative cycle of self-doubt.
- Provide specific assertive, nonassertive, and aggressive responses to situations with which you are familiar.
- Define a script and the various levels of scripts.
- Explain, illustrate, and construct a DESC script.
- Describe the ingredients of a personal development program designed for changing interpersonal behavior.
- Briefly explain each of your assertive rights.
- Explain the purpose, identify the three elements, and provide an example of an "I message."

Have you ever found yourself suffering in class because you had something to say but just couldn't bring yourself to ask a question or volunteer an idea? Have you ever accepted an invitation to a party that sounded boring because you just could not bring yourself to say "no"? Have you ever felt close to another person and yet found it impossible to tell him or her how much you cared? These are typical of situations in which assertive behavior could have lessened the discomfort and improved the quality of the communication involved.

We've all had the experience of needing to assert ourselves with loved ones, teachers, doctors, salesclerks, and public employees. With friends and with strangers. With children and with people much older than we are. How do we handle it? In this chapter I'm going to consider different ways of coping with situations that too often end up awkward and leave us with bad feelings about ourselves and other people. I'm going to look at how our attitudes, ideas, and values affect our choices. The information here will help you pinpoint your real feelings and improve your skills in direct, honest, and appropriate communication.

What Is Assertiveness?

Assertiveness is the ability to share the full range of your thoughts and emotions with confidence and skill.[1] It means speaking and acting in a way that communicates who you *are* and what you *want*. You can be assertive without infringing on the rights of others and feel comfortable about your behavior.[2]

According to psychologists Alberti and Emmons, people express their emotions situationally. That is, they have difficulty expressing themselves only in particular circumstances.[3] Most of the time they are fairly effective, but in certain circumstances or with specific people they lack either the skill or the confidence necessary. Do you find it easy to express hate or anger but difficult to express affection? Do you reveal confidence and strength with friends as you explain how you plan to confront your boss but fail to stand up for your rights in his or her presence? Effective interpersonal behavior involves identifying the times when assertive behavior would be useful and valuable and then being assertive at those times to the best of your ability.

The cycle in Figure 9.1 shows how assertive action and reaction contribute to and affirm your personal assertive power. Say, for example, that you no longer want to lend course material to a classmate who is depending on you entirely to pass a course he or she is not attending. You are attending class and working hard while this person is playing the role of a leech. You take action by refusing to lend your notes to this classmate.

Figure 9.1[4]
Cycle of assertive behavior.

Then you assert yourself and express it in this way: "I don't feel right about giving you my notes. I don't mean to hurt you, but if you don't plan to attend class or do any of the other work yourself, you're going to have to find someone else to depend on in this class." If the classmate protests that you are not being fair, a responsible reaction might be: "Perhaps not in your eyes. However, I feel this action is right, and it will make me feel better about myself. I have never felt good about just giving you all this material."

If this solves the problem, you can be assured that your own personal, assertive power will be reinforced. You have extricated yourself from a difficult, emotion-draining situation.

We have the right to be ourselves and express ourselves and to feel good about doing so as long as we do not hurt others in the process.[5] No matter how confident or successful we feel, there are still times in our lives when we may hesitate to claim our rights, where we are anxious about our feelings, where we are unable to respond to anger, or where we feel powerless in our relations with people. But each of us has the right to be treated with respect. Each of us has the right to have and to express feelings, opinions, and wants; to be listened to and taken seriously by others; to set our own priorities; to be able to say "no" without feeling guilty; and to get what we pay for. These are some of our fundamental rights.[6]

You may wonder what's ineffective about *not* being assertive. Here are some of the problems that arise from not asserting ourselves:

1. We may end up with shoddy merchandise and service.
2. We bottle up our real feelings.
3. We are not doing anything to improve a bad situation.
4. We are cheating another person out of a chance to air the real issues.
5. We get involved in situations we would rather not be in.
6. We end up being a "yes" person—having to do all the work while others sit by and watch.
7. We run into communication barriers because nobody is willing to say what he or she *really* wants.

What, in any given situation, might make us hold back from asserting ourselves? A few possibilities include:

1. Laziness,
2. Apathy,
3. Feelings of inadequacy,
4. Fear of being considered unworthy, unloved, or unacceptable,
5. Fear of hurting the other person or making him or her angry,
6. Fear of getting no reinforcement,
7. Not knowing how to accomplish our desired goal, and
8. Feeling that if we don't do it, someone else will.

Acting in our own best interests is a matter of personal choice. Who knows better than we do what is best for us? The key to assertiveness *is* choice. Along with choice, of course, comes taking responsibility for the choice. There is rarely any one way that we *must* act in a particular situation. True, some situations have prescribed or "proper" ways of acting, but even within such guidelines, there is often great latitude for individuality and variety. For example, we know that we would act with a certain amount of deference if we were introduced to the President of the United States—that is a generally prescribed guideline—but within the realm of deference, we can still be ourselves. The main point is that we need not be manipulated by circumstances or by people. We must choose for ourselves how to act.

Assertiveness, Nonassertiveness, and Aggression

You have come to meet with an instructor to discuss a research paper you wrote and that she recently returned with a lower grade than you feel you deserved. She is a strict teacher who scares you a little by her manner and approach. You put a great deal of time and effort into your paper and feel the grade is not justified. A girl you know wrote her paper the night before it was due and got an A; you spent the better part of a week on yours and received a low C. Your instructor begins the conversation with "Well, I'm glad we are going to have a chance to discuss your paper . . ."

You have many different options as far as your response to this instructor is concerned. You might reply: (1) "I'm sorry the paper didn't live up to your expectations. I really tried, but . . . you know . . . I guess I just didn't give the paper enough time . . ." or (2) "You have no right to give me a C on my paper! I worked harder than the girl down the hall and she got an A. Teachers are really unfair; they never give you credit for the work you do. If you don't change my grade, I'm going to see the dean" or

(3) "I think you should know how hard I worked on this paper. I spent most of last week researching and writing. I really thought the paper deserved more than a C. Will you tell me your reasons for the grade? Then at least I would know how to approach the next assignment."

These three alternatives are oversimplified for the purposes of explanation. You would, of course, have other options as well. You could discuss the grade and the reasons for it without becoming apologetic or defensive at the outset. Discussion that is free from apology or defensiveness is likely to create a positive climate and yield satisfying results as well. Discussion should be conducted in an atmosphere of strength and conviction. That is, you should not sacrifice your values or compromise your standards; you should be able to defend your work and support your overall effort. Discussion is a process of give-and-take that involves *mutual* compromise—not self-sacrifice, apology, or defensiveness. Effective discussion can and should take place in a climate of assertiveness.

Clearly, the (1) and (2) responses in this example are inadequate. In (1) you apologized and used the "excuse" technique. This nonassertive behavior is both dishonest and unfair. You did not really express your feelings, and you denied your teacher honest feedback to her evaluation of the paper. In (2) you showed little sensitivity to the instructor's feelings and used aggressive language that would probably put her off. Only in (3) could you save yourself and the instructor embarrassment, hurt, or awkwardness by a straightforward, assertive response.[7] Your initial response sets the tone for all the communication to follow.

Consider This

Interpersonal relationships appear to be superior for assertive people. In the area of marital relationships, for example, assertiveness is related to satisfying marriages. Marital problems are frequently caused by one of the partners being dominant and exhibiting aggressive behavior or by both of the partners behaving in a nonassertive manner. When one person is aggressive, the other experiences fear and anger. If the second person is nonassertive, she or he may remain in the marriage, but be highly dissatisfied; if the second person is assertive, she or he may leave the marriage; if she or he is aggressive, open conflict may ensue. When both partners are nonassertive, a lack of understanding often occurs, with neither partner communicating openly and honestly with the other. Marriages with two nonassertive people may withstand the test of time, but they are frequently reported to be unsatisfying.

—Judy Cornelia Pearson, *Gender and Communication* (Dubuque, Iowa: Wm. C. Brown Publishers, 1985), p. 137. Reprinted by permission.

Consider This

Shyness is not necessarily a barrier to success. While some shy people choose to work in low-level, invisible jobs, others may become famous in their fields. According to Kagan,* both T. S. Eliot and Franz Kafka were shy from a very early age. Some shy people even become performers. Zimbardo** counts among the "shy extroverts" such celebrities as Johnny Carson, Carol Burnett, Barbara Walters, and Michael Jackson. Clearly, some shy people, even those with the genetic dice loaded against them, can come up winners.

* See J. Kagan, J. S. Reznick, and N. Snidman, "The Physiology and Psychology of Behavioral Inhibition in Children," *Child Development,* in press.
** Philip Zimbardo is a psychologist at Stanford University. His bestselling book is called *Shyness: What It Is, What To Do About It* (Reading, Mass.: Addison-Wesley, 1977). Also available from Jove Publications, Inc. (Harcourt Brace Jovanovich), 1977.

—From "Triumphing Over Timidity" by Jules Asher in "Born to be Shy?" from *Psychology Today,* 21 (April 1987), p. 64. Copyright © 1987 (PT Partners, L. P.). Reprinted with permission.

A person who is too politely restrained, tactful, diplomatic, modest, and self-denying—whose behavior falls at the extreme **nonassertive** end of the continuum—may be unable to make the choice to act. A nonassertive person says, in effect, that he or she will let someone else decide what will happen to him or her. We reveal a nonassertive style when we do the following things:

1. Never speak up in groups;
2. Always stick to the middle-of-the-road position or refrain from taking a stand;
3. Allow others to make decisions for us;
4. Pass by potential friendships because they seem like too much effort;
5. Always keep our voice low or avoid eye contact to keep from calling attention to ourselves;
6. Verbally agree with others despite our real feelings;
7. Bring harm or inconvenience to ourselves to avoid harming or inconveniencing others;
8. Procrastinate to avoid problems and to keep from making decisions;
9. Always consider ourselves weaker and less capable than others;
10. Always escape responsibility with excuses and "good" reasons.

Nonassertiveness can cause the beginning of a **negative cycle.** In the example given above, if we go along with the teacher's evaluation without question or discussion, we may acquire a whole new set of doubts: "What is wrong with me? I am not cut out for college. I cannot compete. I'll never succeed." These doubts can lead to further and sometimes intensified inadequate behaviors (see Figure 9.2). We may come to think of ourselves as wholly inadequate when, in fact, we may simply have misunderstood the assignment.

If we are nonassertive we deny ourselves and fail to express our actual feelings. We leave it to someone else to decide what will happen to us and we may *never* reach our desired goals. This places an unnatural and uncomfortable burden on our interpersonal communications. How do we know how others feel unless they are willing to tell us? Interpersonal communication should not be a game where people must cleverly try to find out what the other person *really* thinks. Assertive behavior can help reduce game-playing and makes interpersonal communication more effective.

The **aggressive** style of response is essentially the complete opposite of the nonassertive style. If we are aggressive, we might:

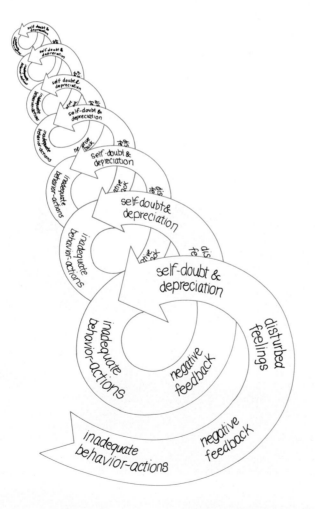

Figure 9.2
Self-doubt may lead to further inadequate behavior.

1. Interrupt others when they are speaking;
2. Try to impose our position on others;
3. Make decisions for others;
4. Use and abuse friendships;
5. Speak loudly and otherwise call attention to ourselves;
6. Accuse, blame, and find fault with others without regard to their feelings;
7. Bring harm or cause inconvenience to others rather than bring harm or cause inconvenience to ourselves;
8. Speak beside the issue, distort the facts, or misrepresent the truth to get our solutions accepted quickly;
9. Consider ourselves stronger and more capable than others;
10. Accept responsibility and positions of authority for the purposes of manipulation or to give us a means of vehemently expressing ourselves.

If we use aggressive behavior we try to accomplish our life goals at the expense of others. Although we may find this behavior expresses our feelings, we may also hurt others in the process by making choices for them and by implying they are worth less than we are as people.

The **assertive** style, in contrast, is self-enhancing because it shows a positive firmness. The assertive style is revealed when we:

Consider This

Several reasons for verbal aggression in interpersonal communication have been suggested:* *frustration* (having a goal blocked by someone, having to deal with a disdained other); *social learning* (individuals are conditioned to behave aggressively and this can include modeling, where the person learns the consequences of a behavior vicariously by observing a model such as a character in a television program); *psychopathology* (involves transference, where the person attacks with verbally aggressive messages those people who symbolize unresolved conflict); and *argumentative skill deficiency* (individuals resort to verbal aggression because they lack the verbal skills for dealing with social conflict constructively).

* See Dominic A. Infante, J. David Trebing, Patricia E. Shepherd, and Dale E. Seeds, "The Relationship of Argumentativeness to Verbal Aggression," *Southern Speech Communication Journal, 50* (Fall 1984):pp. 67–77.

—From "Verbal Aggressiveness: An Interpersonal Model and Measure," by Dominic A. Infante and Charles J. Wigley III in *Communication Monographs, 53*, March 1986, p. 62. Reprinted by permission of the Speech Communication Association and the authors.

1. Allow others to complete their thoughts before we speak;
2. Stand up for the position that matches our feelings or the evidence;
3. Make our own decisions based on what we think is right;
4. Look to friendships as opportunities to learn more about ourselves and others and to share ideas;
5. Spontaneously and naturally enter into conversations using a moderate tone and volume of voice;
6. Try to understand the feelings of others before describing our own;
7. Try to avoid harm and inconvenience by talking out problems before they occur or finding rational means for coping with unavoidable harm or inconvenience;
8. Face problems and decisions squarely;
9. Consider ourselves strong and capable, but generally equal to most other people;
10. Face responsibility with respect to our situation, needs, and rights.

As truly assertive people, we feel free to reveal ourselves. We communicate in an open, direct, honest, and appropriate manner. We go after what we want and make things happen. Finally, we act in a way that we, ourselves, can respect. We know that we cannot always win. We accept our limitations, but no matter what the situation, we always make a good try so that we will maintain our self-respect.[8]

Try This

Make up an aggressive, an assertive, and a nonassertive response to each of the following questions and statements. This will help you become familiar with the differences between these response styles.

1. May I nominate you for president of our organization?
2. Would you carry in the things from the car?
3. Prepare a speech for us on why we should abolish grades.
4. Help me with my homework.
5. Could you take me downtown?

6. Would you babysit Saturday night while we go to the movie?
7. Go to the lecture and take notes for all of us.
8. Would you tell him for me?
9. We're all going. Aren't you going to join us?
10. Tell him he expects too much.

With which of the response styles do you feel most comfortable? Most uncomfortable? What additional information about these situations would help you determine a response style?

At different times we may be nonassertive or aggressive or assertive. The problems occur when we are nonassertive or aggressive too often— when it is a habit for us to be one way or the other. The idea is to be assertive when we need to be—not controlled by the habits of others or by situations. When we can no longer choose for ourselves how we will act, the trouble begins.

Changing Negative Scripts

The word **script** is used in this context to mean a rule governed, habitual pattern of behavior. Thomas Harris defines scripts as decisions about how life should be lived.[9] Muriel James and Dorothy Jongeward suggest that there are various levels of scripts: (1) **cultural,** which are dictated by society; (2) **subcultural,** defined by geographical location, ethnic background, religious beliefs, sex, education, age, and other common bonds; (3) **family,** the identifiable traditions and expectations for family members; and (4) **psychological,** people's compulsion to perform in a certain way, to live up to a specific identity, or to fulfill a destiny.[10] In this section I will discuss psychological scripts: our ongoing program for our life drama which dictates where we are going with our life and how we are going to get there.[11]

Scripts are shaped by past experiences. You are not always responsible for the scripts that govern your behavior. Your inability to swim, for example, may be a result of limited experience around the water. Your fear of dogs may result from an attack by a neighbor's dog when you were young. Past experiences—or the lack of past experiences—may be responsible for negative reactions in certain situations or unpleasant associations connected with specific circumstances. Behavior is shaped, in part, by experience. James and Jongeward label these "scripts with a curse."[12]

You may behave nonassertively because of inadequate or incomplete learning. But assertive behavior—or increased assertiveness—can be learned. You are not helpless. A history of nonassertive behavior does not sentence you to a similar future. But because of the time that the negative scripts have had to become well established, serious, concentrated work to reverse trends and establish new behaviors is necessary. You will need to set new goals and learn new styles of expression and responding if you seriously want your style of communicating—your current scripts—to change.

Positive expectations can aid your communication effectiveness. Have confidence in yourself. Be willing to experiment by striking up conversations with interesting people, getting help when you are confused, defending your rights, expressing your feelings and emotions when appropriate, and asking others to clarify or explain their feelings and emotions. Do not begin all at once, but realize that you *can* increase your assertive repertoire; you *can* become more confident; you *can* increase your skills as an interpersonal communicator.

Sharon and Gordon Bower have devised what they call a **DESC script** for use in planning your response in specific situations or for maintaining your rights.[13] DESC is short for Describe, Express, Specify, and Consequences. A DESC script forces you to state clearly what you want, and yet it permits freedom of response for the other person. A convenient way to think about it is in terms of "This is who I am, this is what I think and feel, and this is what I want." In completing a DESC script, you should include the characters (you and the other person in the relationship), a plot (something that occurred that left you dissatisfied), a setting (the specific place and time of the occurrence), and a message (both the verbal and the nonverbal cues of the characters).

Describe.   Describe the situation or idea as clearly and specifically as you can: "I want Anita to date only me," "I want Daryl to stop ignoring me," or "I want Mom and Dad to give me more freedom." Specific and objective description allows you to explain the character, plot, setting, and message and to define your needs and goals as well.

Express.   How do you feel about this situation? What feelings does this situation evoke in you? "I feel tense because I'm afraid I'm going to have to compete for Anita with some other guy," "I am irritated because Daryl doesn't notice me," or "I am upset because Mom and Dad treat me like a kid." The use of *I, me,* or *my* makes these personal, emotional statements. Notice that these statements refer to how you are feeling and what you are thinking.

Try This

Plot some DESC scripts for several situations that you are involved in now. Notice how a DESC script clarifies situations and specifies exact behaviors for approaching those situations. The more general the situation or the behavior specified, the less useful the DESC script.

Specify. What is it you want? This should include a specific deadline as well. In this way, there is a goal for action: "I would like Anita to let me know this weekend if she will date only me." "I want Daryl to talk to me after class this afternoon." "I would like to have Mom and Dad let me know before the next vacation whether I will have curfews when I'm home." Specifying is a two-way process. This is where freedom of response for the other person is permitted. Others may find aspects of your behavior annoying. Compromise may be necessary. Assertive behavior often requires give-and-take.

Consequences. What are the results of meeting and/or not meeting your desires? "If I don't get a commitment from Anita this weekend, I am going to find someone from whom I *can* get such a commitment." "If Daryl doesn't talk to me after class this afternoon, I'm going to ask *him* some questions about class to encourage conversation." "If Mom and Dad do not drop my curfews, I will have to negotiate with them during my next vacation period to get the curfews relaxed." Try to emphasize positive outcomes.

Bringing About Personal Change

We need more than just an attitude and a DESC script to bring about change. We need specific ideas to aid us. Presented next is a brief program for personal development. If changing your interpersonal behavior is an important goal for you, then this program will help.

Here and now. Live in the present. Try to forget your past, because most history will not be helpful. It is what is going on now that is important.

Focus on what is and what could be. Avoid dwelling on harmful behaviors of the past. Use the past only if you can use some past success as a model for future behavior.

Look at behavior and not feelings. If you start changing behavior, feelings will start changing too. Begin to build a personal reserve of effective, positive behaviors on which you can depend—behaviors such as being concrete, being open and straightforward, being convincing, maintaining a firm position, expressing your wants and goals, and setting clear, reachable targets. Practice using them over and over so that they can become definite, clearly expressed, explicit scripts.

Responsibility.   Stop looking outside yourself for excuses for your behavior. When you find yourself saying, "If only he would . . . " or "Why does this always happen to me?" you are limiting the likelihood that "Maybe *I* can . . . " will occur. Even knock out the "Maybe" so that possible behavior becomes probable. "I can" is more definite and assertive than "Maybe I can."

What is required at this stage is an acceptance of what you need to do. What you do not need are excuses, self-pity, rationalization, and blaming: "This is a cruel world," "Such an undertaking is too much for me," "I'm not ready for this yet," or "It's my parents' fault." All this denial dams up your sense of responsibility for your behavior.

When you begin to take responsibility for your life, life becomes more meaningful. You will begin to fulfill your needs. Responsible behavior also involves awareness of the needs of others. Thus, as you begin to fulfill your own needs, this fulfillment embodies concern, consideration, and respect for the needs and feelings of others. Assertiveness is *not* a selfish one-way process.

Alternatives.   If change is to occur, you need alternatives. Often it is self-doubt that limits you. Sometimes, however, it is simply your lack of imagination; you close out possibilities of change.

If you give your imagination free rein often enough on a variety of different problems, you will quickly discover that you are developing a facility for creative problem-solving. Alternatives make assertiveness more likely because assertive people are flexible and flexibility requires choices. Action is more likely when you have many different possibilities for action.

Plan of action.   Taking responsibility and having alternatives are not final points in an agenda of growth and development. You must be willing to take action, which may require compromise, readjustments of values, or a new life-style. To become more social, for example, may mean giving up some of the time you have had alone—some of the solitude you value. When friendships develop, commitments of time and energy are required to maintain those friendships. Are you willing to give up some of your independence to nurture a friendship?

After you have considered various alternatives and the consequences of each, you must choose which plan of action to pursue. The more

Consider This

Nothing keeps you
  bound
except your Me—
until you break
its chains, its hand-
cuffs,
and are free.

—From *The Book of An-
gelus Silesius,* translated
by Frederick Franck. Copyright © 1976 by Frederick
Franck. Reprinted by per-
mission of Alfred A.
Knopf, Inc.

alternatives you have, the easier this job will be because many plans are a combination of various alternatives. Evaluation of plans involves judging to see how well each one meets your needs. Seek a plan, or a combination of plans, with the most pluses and fewest minuses.

Commitment.   However carefully mapped out, a plan of action will remain a dream unless there is some commitment to change. Is the change important to you? Do you want to put in the time, effort, and pain necessary to bring it about? How badly? Are there obstacles? Can you surmount them? Do you have sufficient involvement to overcome any barriers that confront you as well as any negative or hesitant attitudes that occur? Commitment to a plan of action must be more than "I'll *try* to do it" or "I *might* do it." What is needed is "I *will* do it," "I *am* going to win," "I *want* to do this more than anything else." These are the attitudes of a person of commitment. Commitment must be 100 percent; why waste time and effort with a plan doomed to failure because of lack of commitment or self-doubt?

Success.   Too often we think of success in absolute terms—complete success or complete failure. Instead, we need to think of it in terms of constant effort, evaluation, and progress. Thus, we must design short-range

Consider This

Human interaction is a two-sided coin. On the opposite side of assertiveness is responsiveness. You are responsive when you tune into, show understanding for, and respect the rights and resources of other people. It is not enough to be aware of your own rights and resources, to feel positive about yourself; it is essential, also, to be aware of and responsive to "the other." As is the case with assertive behavior, responsive behavior requires action. People do not know that you are interested, concerned, understanding, empathic, available unless you show it. People do not know that you want or need their knowledge, their affection, their energy, their influence, unless in some fashion you demonstrate that desire. Responsive behavior is an overt demonstration of your interest and concern for the resources and rights of the other. At times it may be as simple as an expression of curiosity or interest. At other times it may be reflected in a change in your own behavior. For example, if you become aware that your approach to conducting meetings is distracting other people from participating, perhaps frightening them or causing them to withdraw, you then have to reassess your own behavior based on your sensitivity and awareness of what is going on in the group.

—Malcolm E. Shaw, Emmett Wallace, and Frances N. Labella, *Making It, Assertively* (Englewood Cliffs, N.J.: Prentice-Hall, 1980), pp. 28–29.

goals—small steps—that can be accomplished. Each small success is a step toward a new success.

With respect to success, too, being assertive does *not* guarantee getting the results you seek. There are simply too many variables involved. Assertiveness is a positive, success-oriented, clear expression that is more likely to lead toward success than a nonassertive or aggressive response in most situations.

Improving Skills in Assertiveness

Where do we begin? If we are serious about learning to assert ourselves we must understand our rights. Our rights as human beings are the framework upon which we build positive interpersonal relationships. If we often allow our rights to be violated, we will begin to find it difficult to express our individual selves to others. Trust may give way to suspicion, compassion may evolve into cynicism, warmth and closeness may disappear, and love (if it exists at all) may acquire an acid bite. In his book *When I Say No, I Feel Guilty*, Manuel J. Smith talks about our humanness, about our responsibilities for ourselves and our own well-being, and about what other people should be able to expect from us.[14] The advice that follows is drawn from Smith's discussion.

Take responsibility for yourself.   If we take responsibility for ourselves, then we are in control of our own thinking, feeling, and behavior. When someone, for whatever reason, reduces our ability to be the judge of what we do, we are being manipulated and our most basic right is in jeopardy.

When we can put this primary assertive right into practice, we will learn how to work out ways to judge our own behavior. Through trial and error we will discover standards of behavior that fit our own personality and life-style. These standards need not be logical, consistent, or permanent; in fact, they may make no sense to others. But our own judgment is *our* guide. This means we take full responsibility for our own happiness and well-being. Our other rights are everyday applications of this prime right. They provide the foundation for assertive behavior.

Don't overapologize.   When we return merchandise, we are accustomed to explaining what went wrong with it. When we cannot go somewhere with a friend, we usually explain why we cannot go. But we often tend to overexplain. We offer lengthy apologies when a brief one would do. While some word of explanation is both polite and helpful, people are hardly ever interested in long, involved excuses. When others demand our explanation to convince us that we are wrong, they are manipulating our behavior and feelings. No friendship should be based upon the requirement that we explain our behavior at every turn. In asserting this right, we should, of course, observe common courtesy. Not to give a reason when one would be helpful may be seen as a negative reaction, especially if we are accustomed to giving reasons and if others expect them from us. But it's best to be brief.

Don't try to rearrange someone else's life.   A friend may come to us wanting us to help him or her become healthy and happy. We may be compassionate and we may give advice and counsel, but the person with the problems has the responsibility of solving them. Our best course in such situations is to assert who we are and the limits of what we're able to do. We should help the other person do the same. As much as we might wish good things for our friends, we really do not have the ability to create mental stability, well-being, or happiness for anyone else. We might temporarily be of some help, but real change requires hard work from the person who wants to change. The reality of the human condition is that everyone must learn to cope on his or her own.

Feel free to change your mind.   A common view in our society is that people who change their minds are irresponsible, two-faced, scatter-brained, or unreliable. If we do change our minds, we are expected to justify our new choice or say that we were in error before. We're often afraid to vacillate because this can affect our credibility: "Don't trust him, he'll just turn around and change his mind!"

Human beings do, however, change their minds. We may make a decision about how to do something and no sooner get started than we find

Consider This

Regarding specific traits she [Dr. Patricia Bull, a consultant to women professionals in the criminal justice system] said, "Women have special qualities to offer. We may have knocked them in the past, but now we realize they are pretty neat. I mean, the tender things like love, caring and nurturing. Women were confused about that for a while. They thought maybe they ought to be aggressive instead." Bull does not perceive women and men as fitting just one role or being limited by society's expectations. She advocates a wide range of behaviors for both sexes: "What is best is to be able to choose from the whole spectrum of emotions and attitudes, to be aggressive at times, tender at others. I should be free to be the person I am, not present a half-person because of my womanness."

—From *Sex Differences in Human Communication*, p. 79, by B. W. Eakins and R. G. Eakins, Copyright © 1978 by Houghton Mifflin Company. Reprinted by permission of Harper & Row Publishers, Inc.

a better way. Our goals and interests are constantly changing. Our choices may work for us in one situation, but there is no reason to believe they will work for us in another. To keep in touch with reality, to promote our own well-being and happiness, we must believe that changing our minds is both healthy and normal.

Feel free to make mistakes. If we have a horror of making mistakes, we leave ourselves open to manipulation every time we make one. We may feel compelled to retreat and not call attention to ourselves for awhile. In that submissive posture, we are fair game for people who want to make us pay for our error or who want to put us down for it.

If you make an error of judgment, admit the mistake as soon as you realize it. Apologize to anybody who may have been hurt, do what you can to repair the damage, and then forget it. "It seemed like a good idea at the time" is often the most honest, simple explanation. You may well be genuinely sorry if others were hurt by your mistake; the important thing is not to feel subhuman for having made it. When you realize you've erred, simply show that you are responsible. In this way, you admit that you made the mistake, that it made trouble for the other person, and that, like everyone else, you make mistakes.

Learn to recognize unanswerable questions. Some questions are unaswerable. Some you may have heard are: "Didn't you know that would happen?" "Why didn't you remember to . . . ?" "What would this world be like if everyone . . . ?" What can we say to such questions? We do not need to have immediate answers for questions people ask us.

News reporters depend on the fact that most people are very uncomfortable leaving questions dangling, unanswered. Almost everyone will give *some* kind of answer, no matter how preposterous the question, but we should learn to see that questions in themselves do not demand answers. We need not be intimidated by inquiries.

We can recognize other people's attempts to manipulate us by phrases that begin with "What kind of a friend (or son or daughter) would . . . ?" To deal with questions like this, we simply need to say, "I don't know." No one can know all the possible consequences of his or her own behavior. If someone else wants to know, let him or her speculate! This is not a defense of irresponsibility, but there *are* limits to how much we can know.

Feel free to say "I don't know." There are legitimate, answerable questions that we just do not have the answer to. Either we don't have the facts, we have not had time to think about them, or we do not have enough evidence to make a judgment. Whatever, the best response to questions like these is, "I don't know." Sometimes others will try to commit us to a premature response or to force a quick answer to a question that is complex or confusing. It is better to say "I don't know" than to make the commitment. We should feel free to say we want more time to think about it.

Don't be overly dependent on the goodwill of others. Everyone likes to be liked. Everyone needs to be liked. But although we all need other people, they don't all need to be our brothers and sisters. No matter what we do, someone is not going to like it or is going to get his or her feelings hurt. If we feel that we must have other people's goodwill before dealing with them, we become open to manipulation.

Why do you suppose we have the stereotype of the smiling, friendly used-car dealer? Because the assumption is that we will feel liked and will want to keep the dealer's goodwill by buying a car. There are many examples of the "I like you" smile used for manipulative purposes. Parents control children by withholding smiles, politicians win supporters with a broad grin, and advertisers generate sales by showing happy, smiling faces.

We are mistaken if we believe we must have the goodwill of anyone we relate with in order to deal with them. The next time you catch yourself thinking like this, think again. Do you really care if this salesclerk (or whoever) likes you and the way you live your life? Would you accept this person's judgment on what you should or shouldn't have for lunch? Of course you wouldn't! So why let him or her judge *you?* We may have great difficulty saying "no" to someone if we assume that a relationship is impossible to maintain without 100 percent mutual agreement. We cannot always live in fear of hurting other people's feelings. Sometimes we may offend others. Such is life.

Feel free to be illogical. Logic is not always the answer in dealing with wants, motivations, and feelings. Our emotions occur in different degrees at different times. Logical reasoning may not help in understanding why we want what we want or in solving problems created by conflicting motivations.

Logic has its place, of course. We turn a paper in on time because we know if we don't we will lose a grade. We fill up the gas tank when it's nearly empty because we know that if we don't, we could get stranded. But being logical works best when we are dealing with things we completely understand, and often solutions to problems lie outside these limits. In some cases we just have to guess, no matter how crude or inelegant the results. We must calculate the risks of the guesses. It is our right to be illogical at times. Human behavior often is illogical.

Feel free to say "I don't understand." We understand as a result of experience. But experience teaches us that we do not always understand what another person means or wants. People may try to manipulate us by implying we are expected to know something or to do something for them. We may not understand a teacher's explanation of a concept or a gas station attendant's directions. Rather than blame ourselves automatically for not "getting" something, we should ask for clarification or restatement. How do we know the other person is being as clear as possible?

We can hardly be expected to always understand what other people's needs are. Sometimes when we don't guess correctly, people think we are irresponsible or ignorant. Often, this manipulation occurs after a conflict. People who believe they have been wronged may expect us to understand that they are displeased with our behavior, that we should know what behavior has displeased them, and that we should change so that they will no longer be hurt or angry. If we allow this manipulation, we end up blocked from what we want to do and often do something else to make up for wanting to do it in the first place. We have difficulty enough trying to read our own minds, without trying to perform this service for others.

Feel free to say "I don't care." If we set ourselves up to be perfectly informed and concerned about all matters, we will be disappointed and frustrated. It can't be done. Some things will matter more to us, others less. We have the right to say that we do not care about certain things. We do not need perfect knowledge of what someone else has determined to be *the* important category. Some people may try to manipulate us into thinking we need to improve until we are perfect in all things.

The teacher who says, "How can you call yourself a history major when you know nothing about medieval England?" and the athletic coach who says, "How do you expect to run the 440 when you eat sugar instead of honey?" are trying to impose their standards on us. If we submit, we fall into the trap of being affected by someone else's arbitrary choice of what constitutes perfection. We end up apologizing for failing in our obligation to become perfect in all things. The only certain way to stop this manipulation is by asking ourselves, "Am I satisfied with my own performance and with myself?" We should be free to make our own judgment about whether or not we wish to make a change.

Another writer in this field, Ronald B. Adler, has expanded Smith's list, giving specific tips on how to express one's needs and wants effectively.[15] His suggestions are discussed below.

Learn to make "I messages." When you are the one who is dissatisfied with a situation, you are the one with the problem. If your roommate is irritating you by leaving the room messy, *you* are the one dissatisfied, and it is your problem because your roommate will be content to go on as before. If your neighbors play loud music, *you* are the dissatisfied party if the loud music annoys you. If you are losing sleep because of unsatisfactory working conditions, it is *your* problem. When the circumstances prompting the dissatisfaction are troublesome primarily to you, leading you to want to speak up about them, then it is a problem *you* need to own—to take responsibility for.

Once you have identified a problem and declared ownership, then your statement of concern should contain three elements that can be discovered by answering three questions:

Try This

Create "I messages" for the following relationship situations. In each case you are <u>trying to get a relationship partner to</u>:

open up and communicate more.

take things (life) more seriously.

spend his or her money more wisely.

stop bringing up past (other) relationships.

show more love and respect for you.

be less possessive.

give you more freedom.

stop his or her drinking (or taking drugs).

spend more time with you.

understand <u>your</u> feelings about premarital sex.

1. *Behavior:* What is the behavior that presents the problem?
2. *Consequences:* What are the concrete, observable consequences of the problem?
3. *Feelings:* What feelings do you experience as a result of the problem?

Once these three questions are answered, the three parts can be framed as an "I message." An "I message" simply starts with "I" and claims ownership: "I have a problem. When you (behavior), (consequences) happen, and I feel (feelings)." For example, with the messy roommate: "I have a problem. When you leave your clothes all over the room (behavior), I have to look at them, step over them, and even move them (consequences). I feel angry and I get upset (feelings)." This formula works in all situations where *you* own the problem, where there are direct consequences, and where your feelings are involved. The order of the parts is not as important as their presence—they should all be present, but they can be offered in whatever order feels most comfortable.

Learn to repeat assertions. In most cases, the "I have a problem" approach proves successful. But not always. There are times when it may not be clearly or accurately received. Or it may be clearly and accurately received and nothing may happen. Or what happens is not what you want to happen. All of these are less than satisfying responses. Since there is little likelihood that the problem will be resolved under these circumstances, the original assertion needs to be repeated. This should be done in a calm, genuine manner. Notice, for example, how Shirley gets Greg to set a time to talk about their relationship—which Greg has been avoiding:

SHIRLEY: You know, Greg, we need to set a time when we can talk about our relationship. When can we get together? [Assertion]

GREG: Tomorrow I have that big calculus exam, and I just can't stop thinking about it right now.

S: I know—you really have to study for it. When can we get together? [Repeated assertion]

G: Next week that history project is due, and I have plans to go home for the weekend.

S: It doesn't have to be this weekend, but we need to find a time when we can get together. [Repeated assertion]

G: Hmmm, I don't know . . .

S: Since we won't be able to get together this weekend or next, how about the next weekend? [Repeated assertion]

G: Well, I know Jim and Bill are going to want to do something . . .

S: Okay, but let's plan Saturday night just for us—no one else—and we are going to discuss our relationship. [Repeated assertion]

G: All right. That sounds good.

Sometimes we fail to make an assertive request a second or third time for fear of being seen as pushy and obnoxious. Although this is possible, it may be the only way to get our message across or to let the other person know how important it is to us. Even if the other person thinks less of us because of our persistence, sometimes this is necessary for self-respect.

Feel free to make requests. Requests are made to satisfy needs. For example, you ask your date to please arrive on time because you *need* to be at the concert promptly at eight or you won't be seated. You ask friends to go to the party with you because you *need* companionship. You ask an instructor for more information because you *need* to clear up some confusion. Requests and needs are not the same; requests are based on needs.

Sometimes it is best to state the need clearly before the request. Doing this helps others understand the importance of the request. Also, because the need is clarified, there is more chance that the request will be satisfied. For example, if a friend comes up to you at a party and says, "I am really feeling ill. Could you take me home?" you will be much more inclined to help out than if the request was, "Could you take me home right now?"— especially if you were having fun!

Another reason for stating the need before the request is that there may be better ways to solve the problem. If you can't suggest other alternatives, maybe someone else can. For example, if the friend is feeling ill, maybe an aspirin or some stomach remedy could take care of the problem. Maybe he or she simply needs to lie down for a bit. When my family and I were

traveling around the world, we found that when we accompanied our requests for directions—which occurred often!—with the fact that we were new there (a need for help), we would get a totally different reaction than when we simply asked for directions. Sometimes the natives responded by taking us on informal, informative sightseeing tours.

Feel free to say "no."   Sometimes we get unreasonable, undesired, or unworkable requests. In such cases, we must bring ourselves to say "no"—firmly and unequivocally. Of course it is easier to do this when the person doing the requesting has no personal importance to us. A waitress urges us to order a dessert we don't have room for. A door-to-door solicitor is seeking contributions to a cause we don't support. A co-worker who does not repay his debts asks for five dollars for the weekend.

But it is not always easy to say "no" when your dignity or an important personal principle is threatened. Embarrassing others or breaking personal commitments could threaten your dignity. A group of friends invites you to join in on some gossip about an absent friend, or a party hostess asks you to take a drink when you abstain. Nonnegotiable principles might include breaking the law. A friend asks you to bring home some supplies free from the office, or you are asked to forge an instructor's signature so that a friend can drop a class without failing. What if a close friend asks you for a copy of a paper you've written—and you know he or she is planning to use it as his or her own? It is difficult for us to stand by our guns when friends are urging us to compromise our principles. Peer pressure rears its ugly head!

It is not easy to say "no" either when the issues are unimportant but the people matter to you. Friends want you to join them for a study session at the library, and you don't feel like going. A neighbor asks you to help move some furniture, and you are just ready to leave the house to run some errands you've been postponing. An employer asks you to stay late to work on a noncritical project when you have already made other plans.

People often find it difficult to say "no." One reason for this difficulty is that they want to be accepted and approved of. Sometimes when we strive for this acceptance and approval we cause inconvenience to ourselves, and we lose self-respect. Sometimes the problem is that we are trying to please more than one person at the same time, and they have conflicting needs. You may have seen this happening—for example, when you are out with a person, run into friends of his or hers, and notice a sudden behavior change. The person has been sincere, appreciative, and serious with you and suddenly becomes playful, callous, and obnoxious—trying to please the friends, not you. Trying to win acceptance and approval from everyone can be exhausting and discouraging.

Another reason some people find it difficult to say "no" is that they are trying to meet everyone's needs. This is their way of appearing perfect. To be perfect, they must do favors, lend money, run errands, and solve others' problems. Sometimes these people are viewed as selfless martyrs, but more often as suckers or doormats. People who constantly let others take advantage of them often begin to feel resentment and frustration, seldom expressed because it would detract from their "perfect" image. But the emotions often find an outlet in indirect aggression such as criticism and gossip about those who make the demands of them.

The best way to say "no," especially to strangers or people who don't mean anything to you personally, is directly and with no adornment. You are under no obligation to explain yourself, although you may choose to do so to keep from appearing curt or brutal. With friends, you may want to provide an explanation to let the other people know the reason behind your choice: "No, I really can't go—I have two tests tomorrow I have to study for." Explanations like this, framed in the first person, show that *you* accept responsibility for your refusal and are not blaming the refusal on someone else.

One other alternative to saying "no"—especially when you are faced with an undesirable request—is to withhold your decision until you have

Try This

Practice assertive responses for each of the following situations:

1. Someone pushed in front of you in line.
2. You must tell someone you no longer wish to date him or her.
3. You are trying to study and someone is making too much noise.
4. You are angry with your parents.
5. You must insist that your roommate does his or her fair share of the cleaning.
6. You must ask a friend to do a favor for you.
7. You have been served unsatisfactory food in a restaurant.
8. You want to express your love and affection to a special person.
9. A professor has made a statement that you consider untrue.
10. Someone you respect has expressed an opinion with which you strongly disagree.
11. A friend of yours is wearing a new outfit that you like.
12. A friend has made an unreasonable request of you.
13. A person is being blatantly unfair.
14. A friend has betrayed your confidence.
15. You want to ask a friend to lend you a few dollars.
16. Someone keeps kicking the back of your chair in a movie.
17. Someone interrupts you in the middle of an important conversation.
18. A friend has criticized you unjustly.

thought about the request. Who says you must respond at once? Of course, if this is simply a delaying tactic, a way to avoid assertiveness, then it would be better to say "no" and have the decision completed. But you are under no obligation to answer most requests immediately. Assertiveness does not require a quick reply. "Hmmm, I'd really like to think about it" is an acceptable response. You have the right to think it over. Just because you can think of no logical reason for saying "no" does not mean you must say "yes"—especially when you are caught off guard. Withhold your decision until you've had time to make sure that your eventual "no"—or "yes"—is a true expression of your thoughts and feelings.

Two final notes on assertiveness. If you plan to be assertive, you must plan and expect assertiveness—even conflict—in return. Life is a two-way street. If you are confronted, make sure you know what the other person is saying. Use paraphrasing to gain clarification if you are confused. Explore the confrontation nondefensively with the goal of mutual sharing, mutual discovery, and mutual growth. If a change in attitudes or values is being requested, try experimenting with the new behavior. Just as you do not expect others to change suddenly, neither can you. Do not try to take care of the change all at once. Second, being assertive does not guarantee getting what you think is due you. It can be especially frustrating and discouraging when you summon up your courage and become assertive, only to be met with an equally assertive response. Assertiveness alone does not guarantee success.

Being assertive will help us communicate directly, honestly, and appropriately in dyadic communication situations. Assertiveness encourages goodwill and self-confidence and aids in pinpointing our real feelings. It is a means of self-expression and has the added advantage of making us feel good about ourselves. Asserting ourselves is how we get from here to there, from being an object or a pawn to being a human being with rights that should be recognized.

This freedom of positive expression will result in greater openness in the communication of genuine, positive feelings toward other people. Such open communication, combined with increased assertiveness, may make us more likely to encounter opposition, conflict, and defensiveness. Some disagreement is always likely. How to overcome the opposition, conflict, and defensiveness that stand in the way of successful interpersonal communication is the subject of the next chapter.

Notes

[1] Ronald B. Adler, *Confidence in Communication: A Guide to Assertive and Social Skills* (New York: Holt, Rinehart & Winston, 1977), p. 6.

[2] Lynn Z. Bloom, Karen Coburn, and Joan Pearlman, *The New Assertive Woman* (New York: Dell Publishing Co., 1975), p. 15.

[3] Robert E. Alberti and Michael L. Emmons, *Stand Up, Speak Out, Talk Back! The Key to Self-Assertive Behavior* (New York: Pocket Books, 1975), p. 53.

[4] Adapted from *It Depends: Appropriate Interpersonal Communication*, 1981, p. 200, by Beverly Byrum-Gaw by permission of Mayfield Publishing Company.

[5] Robert E. Alberti and Michael L. Emmons, *Your Perfect Right: A Guide to Assertive Behavior* (San Luis Obispo, Calif.: Impact, 1974), p. 6.

[6] Bloom, Coburn, and Pearlman, *The New Assertive Woman*, pp. 11–12.

[7] Gerard Egan, *Interpersonal Living: A Skills/Contract Approach to Human-Relations Training in Groups* (Monterey, Calif.: Brooks/Cole Publishing Co., 1976), pp. 36–37.

[8] Herbert Fensterheim and Jean Baer, *Don't Say Yes When You Want to Say No* (New York: Dell Publishing Co., 1975), p. 20.

[9] Thomas A. Harris, *I'm OK—You're OK: A Practical Guide to Transactional Analysis* (New York: Harper & Row, 1969), p. 45.

[10] Muriel James and Dorothy Jongeward, *Born to Win: Transactional Analysis with Gestalt Experiments* (Reading, Mass.: Addison-Wesley Publishing Co., 1971), pp. 69–79.

¹¹ James and Jongeward, *Born to Win*, p. 69.

¹² James and Jongeward, *Born to Win*, p. 81.

¹³ Sharon Anthony Bower and Gordon H. Bower, *Asserting Yourself* (Reading, Mass.: Addison-Wesley Publishing Co., 1976), pp. 87–102.

¹⁴ Manuel J. Smith, *When I Say No, I Feel Guilty*, pp. 27–71. Copyright © 1975 by Manuel J. Smith. Used by permission of the Dial Press.

¹⁵ Ronald B. Adler, *Confidence in Communication: A Guide to Assertive and Social Skills* (New York: Holt, Rinehart, & Winston, 1977), pp. 219–45.

Further Reading

Robert E. Alberti and Michael L. Emmons, *Your Perfect Right: A Guide to Assertive Living* (San Luis Obispo, Calif.: Impact Publishers, 1986). In this fifth edition of the book that popularized assertiveness training in 1970, the authors have totally revised and expanded the original material. In addition to basic information on assertiveness, chapters on assertive sexuality, goal setting, and on-the-job assertiveness are included. A classic book well worth reading.

Wayne Dyer, *The Sky's the Limit* (New York: Pocket Books, 1980). Here, Dyer presents a program designed to help readers to transcend their average or normal selves and evolve into people they might never have dreamed of becoming. Readable and enjoyable.

Jeffrey Eisen with Pat Farley, *Powertalk! How to Speak It, Think It, and Use It* (New York: Simon & Schuster, 1984). Advice on how to speak confidently, positively, and forcefully, how to be polite but not obsequious, and how to be precise and concise. Practical and useful.

Nancy Foreman, *Bound for Success* (New York: Simon & Schuster, 1985). Foreman provides tough-minded, practical lessons for making the most of yourself and your career. Included is the captivating Horatio Alger story of how Foreman rebuilt her own life. Her strategies for unleashing our constructive energies are clear, practical, and workable.

Barbara Forisha-Kovach, *Power & Love: How to Work for Success and Still Care for Others* (Englewood Cliffs, N.J.: Prentice-Hall, 1982). An interesting book about how we can balance our need for personal achievement and our need for caring relationships. Numerous personal illustrations and practical examples.

Meryle Gellman and Diane Gage, *The Confidence Quotient: 10 Steps to Conquer Self-Doubt* (New York: World Almanac Publications, 1985). If you are plagued by self-doubt, this book is for you. Gellman and Gage provide a clear, practical look at the foundations of effective assertive behavior.

Irene C. Kassorla, *Go for It! How to Win at Love, Work and Play* (New York: Dell Publishing Co., 1984). What is it that separates winners from losers? Kassorla claims that we all have within us the power to become winners. Essentially, this is a book of practical exercises designed to develop self-confidence and a greater sense of self-worth. An exciting book full of enthusiasm and support.

Richard J. Leider, *The Power of Purpose* (New York: Ballantine Books, 1985). A hands-on workbook, complete with self-assessment questionnaires, checklists, and exercises designed to help us acquire meaning and purpose in our lives. This is an excellent, challenging book full of interesting material not found in other sources.

Harvey L. Ruben, *Competing* (New York: Pinnacle Books, 1980). What does successful competition require? Ruben tells us how to compete rather than how to win, with advice on how to understand the nature and effects of competition in your life, how to weigh your limitations and assets, and how to use this knowledge to your advantage.

Malcolm E. Shaw, Emmett Wallace, and Frances N. LaBella, *Making It, Assertively* (Englewood Cliffs, N.J.: Prentice-Hall, 1980). The authors take a holistic (total) approach, emphasizing that assertiveness is a two-way interactive process. An overall strength is the rational, problem-solving approach they offer as well as the tools for self-improvement they provide.

10 Overcoming Barriers: Coping with Conflict

Learning Objectives

When you have finished this chapter you should be able to:

- Compare and contrast how society views conflict and how you view conflict, and explain what happens when people disagree.
- List and briefly identify the five elements that can cloud or destroy an atmosphere of acceptance.
- Describe Blake and Mouton's two-dimensional scheme for categorizing the ways in which people handle conflict.
- Compare and contrast the five styles of handling conflict.
- Understand the requirements of effective interpersonal communication when it comes to choosing appropriate conflict-management strategies.
- Explain several possible stress-management techniques and how you can personally adjust to stress.
- List and briefly explain the four main elements for managing stressful conflict situations.
- Explain why manipulation occurs.
- Briefly explain the four types of misunderstanding that are likely to escalate conflict.
- Construct, label, and explain a model of conflict management.

I have discussed attitudes and the nature of attitude change; feelings and emotions and how to recognize, accept, and constructively express them. I have also discussed assertive behavior and how to improve our skills in assertiveness. As we attempt to deal with attitudes, feelings, and assertiveness, we often run into conflict. We'll begin this chapter by considering how our society views conflict and how each of us reacts to it personally.

Try This

Can you think of specific people who fit the following phrases?

1. She really is kind.
2. Aren't they friendly?
3. They would do anything in the world for you.
4. He'd give you the shirt off his back.
5. She always has a smile on her face.
6. Isn't he sweet?
7. It wouldn't be a party without him.
8. She really is all heart.

Can you think of other phrases that emphasize nonaggressiveness?

Then I'll discuss ways of coping with conflict with suggestions for some skills to practice. Understanding the nature of conflict will help us facilitate cooperative behavior, resolve problems, and enhance our interpersonal relationships and contacts. We can't eliminate conflict, but we can start to look at it as something we can handle or lessen.

How Society Views Conflict

Conflict is often considered undesirable in our society. You may believe that conflicts cause marriages to dissolve, employees to be fired, and demotions, demerits, demoralization, and divisiveness to occur. Certainly arguments, disagreements, and fights do force people apart and damage relationships. But more than likely it is not the conflict itself that causes the break in these relationships, but the poor handling of the conflict.

Anger is one of the underlying causes of conflict. And yet anger may be viewed as not "gentlemanly," "ladylike," "nice," or "mature." The mere mention of fighting is enough to make some people uncomfortable. They may talk of their "differences" or of their "silly arguments" but never of "fights," because they feel fighting implies a lack of maturity and self-control. (Fighting here means verbal and nonverbal quarreling, not physical battle.) Actually, not to admit to conflict or fighting implies a *lack* of maturity. When we are on intimate terms with another person, our closeness may be characterized by quarreling and making up. We may try to live in harmony and agreement with another person, but this desire alone creates a need for conflict—just to establish and maintain *our* notion of harmony and agreement.[1] We also fight to resolve conflicts and to release frustration.

Our society has conditioned us to dislike personal aggressiveness. Well-liked people are described with such phrases as, "She is very kind; she'll do anything for anyone" or "He doesn't have a nasty bone in his body" or "She wouldn't raise her voice to anyone." Think of people you know who are admired and the phrases people use to describe them. Nonaggressiveness is praised and admired.[2]

Our society's attitude toward nonaggressiveness may be responsible for the vicarious pleasure many people get from watching the violent acts of other people. Sports such as hockey, football, and boxing include elements of violence; violence also is prominent in the news, in movies, and on television. Although anger and aggressiveness are officially taboo, as a society we apparently admire and are fascinated by aggressive people. Our heroes and heroines are powerful, robust, forceful characters. There seems to be a difference between what we give lip service to and what we actually like. There is no doubt that conflict *can be* destructive. Whether it is harmful or helpful depends on how it is used.

How You View Conflict

Healthy interpersonal communication is *not* conflict-free. Conflict is a part of all the relationships we have with other people. It can be constructive or destructive, depending on how we manage it.[3] Conflict is often the constructive means we use to challenge established norms and practices, and at times it is the means through which we are our most creative and innovative. Conflict often motivates us to summon up our untapped abilities. Some of our most eloquent moments result spontaneously from situations that occur when we have been stopped from doing something or need to get our way. We should concentrate on managing interpersonal conflict to gain the maximum benefit for the relationship, discovering our own best style of handling it in the process.

Any time we get together with another person for more than a short while, conflicts may arise that are serious enough to destroy the relationship if we do not know how to handle them. There are no magic formulas for overcoming barriers and resolving breakdowns. But we can look at those breakdowns in a fresh way. The fact that we are unique and that we experience the world in a unique way is enough to generate conflict because conflict occurs when human differences or uniquenesses meet. Remember, too, that we selectively perceive; thus, what is a conflict to one person may not be a

Consider This

Suppose a friend lit up a cigarette in an enclosed space and you found this fact irritating. You might consider any one of the following actions or responses:

Grab the cigarette from the person's mouth and crush it.
"Put out that cigarette before I get upset."
"If you'll quit smoking right now, I'll buy you a drink."
"How can you keep on smoking, knowing that it causes cancer? You should put it out."
"Do me a favor by putting out the cigarette; I have an allergic reaction to them."
In each case a form of control is being exercised between you and the other person.

—William J. Schenck-Hamlin, G. N. Georgacarakos, and Richard L. Wiseman, "A Formal Account of Interpersonal Compliance-Gaining," *Communication Quarterly* 30 (1982): 173. Reprinted by permission of Communication Quarterly, Eastern Communication Association.

conflict to another person. In addition to being unique, each of us is also able to make choices. We can decide how to handle the disagreements we encounter.

It may seem discouraging to think that even in the very best of relationships there is going to be conflict and that, on top of that, there is no guarantee that the conflict can be resolved. *But we can change the way we deal with it.* First we need to confront our own feelings. To know what happens when we disagree is a useful starting point.

What Happens When People Disagree

Conflict is simply a situation in which we, our desires, or our intentions are in opposition to those of another person. Opposition means incompatibility: if our desires predominate, the other person's will not.[4] If we want to go to one movie and our friend wants to go to another, a state of conflict results. If we feel we deserve an A and our instructor thinks a B is all we deserve, we are in conflict. If we believe that one interpretation of a poem is correct and our classmates think another one is more appropriate, we have another conflict situation. These are, of course, honest and unavoidable differences of opinion that lead to conflict. But there are also barriers and breakdowns in communication that create conflict and can be avoided.

Communication Barriers and Breakdowns

An atmosphere of acceptance is essential to preventing breakdowns in communication. Technically, communication cannot break down. If we cannot *not* communicate, breakdowns cannot occur. We will use the term breakdown to refer to distortions and misinterpretations. Without acceptance, messages may not be received at all or may be distorted if they are received. Not receiving a message or distorting it causes conflicts. John Keltner identifies five elements that can cloud or destroy an atmosphere of acceptance: contrary attitudes, newly acquired contrary opinions, jumping to conclusions, low credibility, and hostility.[5]

Contrary attitudes.

Our prejudices, biases, and predispositions affect the way we interact with and perceive others. This will become a barrier to communication unless we make a concerted attempt to be open-minded. One student's father saw a picture of her bearded professor and immediately decided that the professor was a left-wing, radical ex-hippie. Nothing the student could say would make him change his mind. She explained to the professor that her father's contrary attitude resulted from his service as a Marine gunnery sergeant.

Newly acquired contrary opinions.

Converts to a religious belief are generally thought to be stronger believers than those who have been brought up with the belief. The closer we are to the time we acquired a new opinion, attitude, or belief, the more rigid we may be in defending it. And the more rigid we are, the less amenable we are to change. Conflict is most frustrating when neither person is willing to be flexible. As time passes, we may begin to be more receptive to contrary ideas, even though we may still firmly hold our original belief. If we are conscious of the effects of the passage of time on creating an atmosphere of acceptance, we will be more careful about our timing when we need to present a new and potentially controversial idea to someone.

For example, Darrell was in desperate search of a college major and a lifetime goal. But each semester, as a result of taking different classes, he had become a quick convert to another new course of study. Nobody could persuade him to step back, be objective, and weigh the alternatives. Darrell began as a music major, switched to education, then to business, and now was changing to his fourth major, speech communication. His best friend, Alicia, was trying to persuade him to remain a business major until he was more sure of his specific goals, but she was getting nowhere. Darrell had taken one speech-communication course—a requirement—and was convinced he wanted to make that his major. No matter how much Alicia argued, Darrell was convinced *he* had the answer—and no one, including Alicia, was about to change his mind!

Try This

Every day we encounter many conflict situations. Of the following situations, which do you consider critically important? Which seem irrelevant to you?

1. Conflict with another person for control of your life;
2. Conflict over what you should eat;
3. Conflict about how you spend your money;
4. Conflict about how you relate to other people;
5. Conflict over how clean you keep your living area;
6. Conflict about how you spend your time;
7. Conflict over your lifetime goals;
8. Conflict over what you want to believe in;
9. Conflict over your use of tobacco, marijuana, alcohol, or drugs;
10. Conflict about how you think of your self (your self-respect, self-esteem, or ego).

Jumping to conclusions. The problem with jumping to conclusions is that it destroys the climate of acceptance. We make a decision before we have enough facts on which to base the judgment. When we do not really listen, review the facts, or try to examine all the messages we are receiving, we create an atmosphere that works against effective communication. Janet was absolutely convinced Robert was seeing someone else. She had called him twice and got no answer; he hadn't called her at the regular time; and Janet's best friend said she had seen him at the library with Ellen. What else could he be doing? When Janet and Robert met, Janet immediately became angry, upset, and nearly out of control. Robert tried to calm her down. Once he was able to speak, he explained that he *had* called but got no answer. He said, "I was very concerned about that big chemistry test; Ellen is in the same class and was helping me study. Al was there, too. Now that it's over, we can celebrate!"

Low credibility. Acceptance is affected if one of us perceives the other to be a person of low credibility. If we suspect someone of being unfair, biased, unreliable, hostile, or contradictory, we are not likely to hear what he or she says. This basic lack of acceptance creates a serious handicap to communication. Focusing on the content of the message and not on the person will help, but a climate of low credibility is difficult to overcome. Don told both Maurice and Virginia that Geography 253 was a lousy course and that they shouldn't take it. Both Maurice and Virginia argued with him, but he seemed to have the facts: incompetent teaching, terrible exams, and too much work. After Don left, Maurice and Virginia had a chance to talk.

They reminded themselves that Don was a poor student who hated attending lectures, taking exams, or doing any work. He seldom went to class. Since Don had low credibility in this situation, they decided to enroll in the class anyway.

Hostility.   In the presence of outright hostility, it is very hard to achieve an atmosphere of acceptance. Hostility begets hostility. When we become aware of hostility directed toward us, we are likely to respond with a potentially hostile posture—prepared, alert, and equipped for a self-defensive action. Hostility then intensifies and communication is blocked. Joe and Sara were in a speech-communication class together. As the term progressed, Joe began to like Sara less and less because, it seemed to Joe, every time he wanted to say something, Sara would interrupt. At the end of the term Sara gave a persuasive speech promoting a petition to get a crosswalk at an important student crossing on campus. Asked why he wouldn't sign the petition, Joe said, "Why can't you just keep quiet for a while? You've interrupted me constantly all term." His response had nothing to do with her speech, but the presence of hostility made it hard for Sara to achieve an atmosphere of acceptance.

Styles of Handling Conflict

Robert R. Blake and Jane S. Mouton have developed a two-dimensional scheme for categorizing the ways in which people handle conflict.[6] This scheme represents a significant improvement over the simpler view that people either cooperate or compete. One dimension, labeled "cooperativeness," is concerned with the extent to which individuals attempt to satisfy the concerns of others. The second dimension, "assertiveness," deals with the extent to which individuals attempt to satisfy their own concerns. Five specific conflict-handling modes can be identified in terms of their location along these dimensions (see Figure 10.1). These five modes are competing

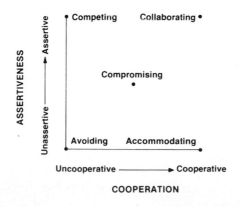

Figure 10.1
Styles of handling conflict.

(assertive, uncooperative), collaborating (assertive, cooperative), avoiding (unassertive, uncooperative), accommodating (unassertive, cooperative), and compromising (intermediate in both cooperativeness and assertiveness).[7] Much of the following discussion is based on the work of Kenneth W. Thomas and Ralph H. Kilmann.[8]

Competing takes place when individuals desire to meet their own needs and concerns at the expense of others. As Figure 10.1 indicates, it is the most assertive and least cooperative people who use this style, wielding whatever power is available to get the outcome they want. There is nothing wrong with power; it is how it is used that becomes important. One writer on negotiation suggests that power is a crucial variable in any negotiation situation.[9]

Collaborating involves maximum use of both cooperation and assertiveness. A collaborative style aims to satisfy the needs of both parties. Those using this style move through a series of important steps: (1) acknowledging that there is a conflict; (2) identifying and acknowledging each other's needs; (3) identifying alternative resolutions and consequences for each person; (4) selecting the alternative that meets the needs and concerns and accomplishes the goals of each party; and (5) implementing the alternatives selected and evaluating results.

Since collaborating requires more time, energy, and commitment than the other styles, an accurate assessment of the conflict situation is important. Do the needs and concerns of the parties involved warrant the use of this method? Are both parties committed to the resolution? If the answer to either question is "no," another method should probably be used.

Avoiding results from uncooperative and unassertive behavior by either or both parties. There is no attempt to address the conflict or to discover or confront each other's needs and concerns. One or the other member evades the other, withdraws from the other, or leaves before a resolution is agreed upon.

Avoidance is not always negative—unless it becomes a permanent method for resolving conflicts. It can give people enough time to cool down if the conflict has become heated. It can provide time for more information to be accumulated. If an issue is relatively unimportant, avoidance may be a way to avoid conflict, but of course the problem here is "*Who* says it is unimportant?" Avoidance may also be helpful if there is not enough time to come to a solution or if the problem is a symptom of a more extensive problem that must be dealt with later. A final reason for choosing to avoid confronting the situation may be that others can resolve the conflict more effectively, efficiently, or easily.

Accommodating involves cooperative, unassertive behavior. When you accommodate others, you place their needs and concerns above your own. Accommodating is an appropriate method if one party is not as concerned as the other. For example, you are trying to decide with a friend where to go first. If you *really* don't care, it is easy to accommodate your friend's needs and concerns. Accommodating tends to build goodwill, and it leads to cooperative relationships; however, it should not become one's only style of managing conflict. Although the method can promote harmony, avoid disruption, and reduce the power factor in a relationship, it can also mean that you are always suppressing your own needs and concerns, always deferring to the other person, which is not a healthy situation.

Compromising is, as Figure 10.1 shows, a middle position. It requires moderate amounts of cooperativeness and assertiveness. Through compromise, both parties search for a mutually acceptable solution. Although the solution reached is mutually acceptable, it only partially satisfies each person's wants and needs. So, with respect to gaining a satisfying result, compromising is second to collaborating.

Compromise has an advantage if short-range solutions are sought for complex issues. Compromise works, too, when time is short. If the goals of both parties are moderately important but not worth the effort and time collaborating requires, compromise may be appropriate. It is also an effective backup strategy when collaboration breaks down.

You may have noticed from the discussion of each conflict-management style that there is nothing inherently right or wrong with any of them. Any one of them may be appropriate or effective depending on the situation or the people involved. You will need to assess situations and people carefully to determine which method is best. Consistently using the wrong approach can cause serious damage to a relationship. On the other hand, interpersonal communication can be enhanced if conflict is handled effectively. Effective interpersonal communication, then, requires flexibility—the ability to use whichever strategy is appropriate in the particular situation.

Stress Management: Personally Adjusting to Stress

Stress is a state of imbalance between demands made on us from outside sources and our capabilities to meet those demands.[10] Often, it precedes and occurs concurrently with conflict. Stress, as you have seen, can be brought on by physical events, other people's behavior, social situations, our own behavior, feelings, thoughts, or anything that results in heightened bodily awareness. In many cases, when you experience pain, anger, fear, or depression, these emotions are a response to a stressful situation like conflict.

Sometimes, in highly stressful conflict situations, we must cope with the stress before we cope with the conflict. Relieving some of the intensity of the immediate emotional response will allow us to become more logical and tolerant in resolving the conflict. In this brief section, some of the ways in which we can control our physical reactions and our thoughts will be explained.

People respond differently to conflict just as they respond differently to stress. Some people handle both better than others do. Individual differences are not as important as learning how to manage the stress we feel. The goal in stress management is self-control, particularly in the face of stressful events.

Stress reactions involve two major elements: (1) heightened physical arousal as revealed in an increased heart rate, sweaty palms, rapid breathing, and muscular tension, and (2) anxious thoughts, such as thinking you are helpless or wanting to run away. Since your behavior and your emotions are controlled by the way you think, you must acquire skills to change those thoughts.

Controlling physical symptoms of stress requires relaxation. Sit in a comfortable position in a quiet place where there are no distractions. Close your eyes and pay no attention to the outside world. Concentrate only on your breathing. Slowly inhale and exhale. Now, with each exhaled breath say "relax" gently and passively. Make it a relaxing experience. If you use this method to help you in conflict situations over a period of time, the word "relax" will become associated with a sense of physical calm; saying it in a stressful situation will help induce a sense of peace. Refer also to the "Try This" on page 276 of Chapter 8, which provides a specific six-step sequence for relaxation.

Another way to induce relaxation is through tension release. The theory here is that if you tense a set of muscles and then relax them, they will be more relaxed than before you tensed them. Practice each muscle group separately. The ultimate goal, however, is to relax all muscle groups simultaneously to achieve total body relaxation. For each muscle group, in turn, tense the muscles and hold them tense for five seconds, then relax them. Repeat this tension-release sequence three times for each group of muscles. Next, tense all muscles together for five seconds, then release them. Now, take a low, deep breath and say "relax" softly and gently to yourself as you breathe out. Repeat this whole sequence three times.

You do not need to wait for special times to practice relaxing. If, during the course of your daily activities, you notice a tense muscle group, you can help relax this group by saying "relax" inwardly. Monitor your bodily tension. In some cases you can prepare yourself for stressful situations through relaxation *before* they occur. Practice will help you call up the relaxation response whenever needed.

For other ways to relax, do not overlook regular exercise. Aerobic or yoga-type exercise can be helpful. Personal fitness programs can be tied to these inner messages to "relax" for a complete relaxation response.

Controlling your thoughts is the second major element in stress management. Managing stress successfully requires flexibility in thinking. That is, you must consider alternative views. Your current view is causing the stress! You must also keep from attaching exaggerated importance to events. Everything seems life-threatening in an moment of panic; things dim in importance when viewed in retrospect.

Try to view conflict from a problem-solving approach: "Now, here is a new problem. How am I going to solve this one?" (A specific problem-solving approach will be discussed in the next section.) Too often, we become stressed because we take things personally. When an adverse event occurs we see it as a personal affront or as a threat to our ego. For example, when Christy told Paul she could not go to the concert with him, he felt she was letting him know she disliked him. This was a blow to Paul because he had never been turned down—rejected—before. Rather than dwell on that, however, he called Heather, she accepted his invitation, and he achieved his desired outcome—a date for the concert.

One effective strategy for stress management consists of talking to ourselves. We become our own manager, and we guide our thoughts, feelings, and behavior in order to cope with *stressors*—that is, the events that result in behavioral outcomes called *stress reactions*. Phillip Le Gras suggests that we view the stress experience as a series of phases. Here, he presents the phases and some examples of coping statements:

1. *Preparing for a stressor.* What do I have to do? I can develop a plan to handle it. I have to think about this and not panic. Don't

be negative. Think logically. Be rational. Don't worry. Maybe the tension I'm feeling is just eagerness to confront the situation.

2. *Confronting and handling a stressor.* I can do it. Stay relevant. I can psych myself up to handle this, I can meet the challenge. This tension is a cue to use my stress-management skills. Relax. I'm in control. Take a low breath.

3. *Coping with the feeling of being overwhelmed.* I must concentrate on what I have to do right now. I can't eliminate my fear completely, but I can try to keep it under control. When the fear is overwhelming, I'll just pause for a minute.

4. *Reinforcing self-statements.* Well done. I did it! It worked. I wasn't successful this time, but I'm getting better. It almost worked, Next time I can do it. When I control my thoughts I control my fear.[11]

The purpose of such coping behavior is to become aware of and monitor our anxiety. In this way, we can help eliminate such self-defeating, negative statements as "I'm going to fail," or "I can't do this." Statements such as these are cues that we need to substitute positive, coping self-statements.

If the self-statements do not work, or if the stress reaction is exceptionally intense, then we may need to employ other techniques. Sometimes we can distract ourselves by focusing on something outside the stressful experience—a pleasant memory, a sexual fantasy—or by doing mental arithmetic. Another technique is imaging. By manipulating mental images we can reinterpret, ignore, or change the context of the experience. For example, we can put the experience of unrequited love into a soap-opera fantasy or the experience of pain into a medieval torture by the rack. The point here is that love and pain are strongly subjective and personal, and when they cause us severe stress we can reconstruct the situation mentally to ease the stress. In both these cases the technique of imaging helps to make our response more objective—to take it *outside* ourselves. The more alternatives we have to aid us in stress reduction, the more likely we are to deal with it effectively. The following suggestion offers suggestions for approaching the conflict itself—successfully.

Coping with Conflict: A Successful Approach

An approach has been designed for managing all stressful conflict situations that puts a high priority on creative coping and on maintaining self-esteem. How successfully we use these coping behaviors depends on our recognition of a conflict situation and on our ability to keep our wits about us as we put this approach into action. The four main elements of this approach are (1) gaining information, (2) organizing ourselves, (3) striving for independence, and (4) anticipating conflict situations.[12]

Information: Get Enough of the Right Kind

In any communication setting, whether conflict-laden or not, we act best when we are well informed. In a conflict situation, we need to find out all we can about the problem to assure ourselves that we have more than one way to deal with it. The information we pick up may involve the nature of the communication itself or it may involve the other person. Problems with information may develop in three major ways: through overload, through manipulation, and through ambiguity.

Communication overload.
If one person provides another person with more information than he or she can handle, a problem will arise.[13] We call this "overload." The information I am referring to here has to do with the content of a communicator's message to a listener, not with information of a general nature about a conflict situation, as discussed above.

A human being can handle only so much information at one time. This has to do not only with the capability of the human brain to decipher material, but also with the various ways that emotions get bound to certain experiences. Often the root causes for conflict are closely tied to our emotional response pattern. In such cases, as sure as conflicts are bound to come up, so are the emotions that go along with them. If we are having an emotionally involving experience, it is difficult to take on and fully comprehend a new "load" of information at the same time. Our senses are preoccupied. If someone else tries to share some vital news with us while our feelings are thus tied up, interpersonal conflicts may result. We may experience this when we try to listen to a classroom lecture just after we've heard some upsetting news. The intensity of the emotional experience overshadows any material the teacher could offer. We simply don't have room for any more information.

Manipulative communication.
Barriers to communication are likely to occur when a listener feels information is being offered with manipulative intent. You may have experienced manipulation at one time or another when you felt someone was using you or trying to control you. People manipulate other people for various reasons. In some cases, a person looks to others *for support*. Not trusting them to give it, he or she manipulates them to steer them in the right direction. Manipulation may also result *from love*. The problem is described by Everett Shostrom:

> We seem to assume that the more perfect we appear—the more flawless—the more we will be loved. Actually, the reverse is more apt to be true. The more willing we are to admit our weaknesses as human beings, the more lovable we are. Nevertheless, love is an achievement not easy to attain, and thus the alternative that the manipulator has is a desperate one—that of complete power over the other person, the power that makes him do what we want, feel what we want, think what we want, and which transforms him into a thing, our thing.[14]

Erich Fromm has said that the ultimate relationship between human beings is that of love—knowing a human being as he or she is and loving that person's ultimate essence.[15] Loving someone's "ultimate essence" is just the opposite of manipulation.

A third reason that manipulation occurs is *out of frustration with life*. People who feel overwhelmed may decide that since they cannot control everything, they will control nothing. They become passive manipulators. It should be clear, however, that passive manipulation can be a form of control. Passive manipulators may use various devices and tricks to accentuate their helplessness. They will try to get other people to make decisions for them and carry part of their burden, manipulating through their own feeling of powerlessness.

There are two other reasons why manipulation occurs that appear to be near opposites. People may deal with others ritualistically in an effort *to avoid intimacy or involvement*. An example of ritualistic communication is the teacher who cannot deal with students in other than strictly teacher-student terms. The same type of ritualistic behavior might be seen in employer-employee and doctor-patient relationships.

Another reason people manipulate is *to gain the approval of others*. There are people who think they need to be approved of by everyone. They may be untruthful, trying to please everyone in their quest for acceptance. An example of this behavior is the friend who tells us everything we do is "great" just to keep us as a friend.

Ambiguous communication.   Ambiguous information may contribute to a conflict situation because ambiguity almost always leads to misunderstanding.[16] Ambiguity can result when not enough information is provided or when it is too general. If one of your friends tells you that everyone is going to the show tonight and that you should meet them downtown, you

Consider This

It would appear, therefore, that "healthy" marriages, in the large, are those in which the husband is secure enough in his own identity that he can be supportive of his wife's effort to find herself in her new role. In such marriages, conflicts are settled more easily precisely because the husband is able and willing to be supportive, conciliatory, and trusting. Such behavior is, of course, reinforcing because the wife responds positively since her need for sympathy and support is satisfied. Thus, mutual growth is fostered.

—William A. Barry, "Marriage Research and Conflict: An Integrative Review," *Psychological Bulletin,* Vol. 3, No. 1 (Arlington, Va.: American Psychological Association, 1970), p. 52. Reprinted by permission of the author.

might easily misunderstand. Who is "everyone"? Where exactly should you meet them? What time? Also, the more abstract our language is, the more likely it is to be ambiguous and conflict-promoting.

Whenever we find ourselves in a conflict situation, we should pay special attention to the kind of information we are exchanging: Is there enough? Is there too much? Is it manipulative? Is it ambiguous? It will be helpful to remember that every receiver of messages creates his or her own meaning for that communication based upon what he or she perceives. We can never know exactly which stimulus aroused meaning in someone else's head. The kinds of phenomena that can provoke meaning are limitless—there is no way anyone can control with certainty all the variables that will eliminate potential conflict situations.

Finally, remember that the message a receiver gets is the only one that counts in a conflict situation. The message that he or she acts upon may be quite different from the information that was sent. To discover precisely what message was received is useful in coping with conflict. We may need to ask the other person, "Now, what did you hear?" or "What is it that you understand?" or "What are you going to do?" As far as possible, we need to know how the other person understands the situation if we are to deal successfully with conflict.[17]

Organization: Sort Things Out

Think of a situation to which you had a powerful emotional response: fear, anger, grief, or passion. If you needed to cope with conflict at that time, you may have found your judgment was affected. To reestablish stability and a sense of right and wrong we need to organize ourselves within ourselves—we need to get ourselves together.[18]

This is not to say we should avoid emotional experiences. Feelings of fear, anger, grief, and passion are healthy and normal and should not be repressed. But when in the throes of strong emotional experiences, we must remember that our senses are affected, that we cannot depend on our perceptions. This is why, for example, people are wise to make funeral arrangements *before* a person dies. In the emotional aftermath of the death of a loved one, decision making is difficult and judgments are not as rational as they are at other times.

When our perceptions are distorted, conflict is likely to escalate because of the misunderstandings exchanged. One such misunderstanding has been labeled by David W. Johnson as **"mirror image."** In conflict, "mirror image" occurs when both people think they are right, both think they were the one maligned, both think the other person is wrong, and both think they are the only one who wants a just solution.[19]

Johnson labels a second perceptual distortion the **"mote-beam mechanism."** This occurs when we are blind to the insensitive and mean things we do to others but clearly see all the vicious and underhanded things they do to us. Johnson derives this label from Jesus' question in the Sermon on the Mount: "Why beholdest thou the mote [speck of sawdust] that is in thy brother's eye, but considerest not the beam [thick timber] that is in thine own eye?"

Another kind of misunderstanding occurs, according to Johnson, when one person sees identical acts committed by both sides but considers those of the other person illegitimate, unfair, unjust, and unreasonable while viewing his or her own as legitimate, fair, just, and reasonable considering the circumstances. For example, why should one person in a relationship be allowed to "play around" while the other must remain faithful? Why are rules "bent" for one person and not for another? How can a father or mother make one set of rules for the oldest child and another for the others? This is known as the **"double standard."**

In conflict situations, too, according to Johnson, thinking becomes **polarized.** Both individuals might come to have an oversimplified view of the conflict. In this uncomplicated view, anything the other person does is bad and everything we do is good. It is the oversimplification that distinguishes polarized thinking from mirror image and double standard. Obviously, when such misunderstandings are at work, it is difficult to organize our thinking.

When we are aware that we are not coping rationally, we would do well to seek help from others. It's a good idea to go to trusted friends for help in making decisions and carrying out plans. To recognize that we cannot make competent decisions until we have reorganized our thinking is not a weakness; it is realistic and mature.

To be organized within ourselves is an awareness function. People who "have it together" are responsive, alive, and interested; they listen to

Try This

It is human nature to blame others for conflict in which we find ourselves. More often than not, however, a combination of factors, and our own personality, thoughts, or feelings, are part of the problem. Conduct a self inventory by answering the following questions:

1. Do you consider your thoughts to be more important than those of others?
2. Are your feelings more positive than those of others?
3. Do you speak with authority?
4. Do you like to give orders to people?
5. Do you believe that your principles are superior to those of our society?
6. Do you believe in saying what you feel in dealing with other people?
7. Is your chief concern for your own individuality?
8. Do you admire forceful people more than cooperative ones?
9. Are you able to listen to others when you are annoyed by them?
10. Are you highly tolerant of other people's negative feelings?
11. Do you care for the people with whom you talk?

If you answered these questions honestly, and if your answers to the first eight questions were predominantly "yes," then it may be that your concern for yourself and for control engenders or aggravates much of the conflict in your life.

—Paraphrased from a survey reprinted in Charles T. Brown and Paul W. Keller, *Monologue to Dialogue: An Exploration of Interpersonal Communication* (Englewood Cliffs, N.J.: Prentice-Hall, 1979), pp. 260–63. Used by permission of Charles T. Brown, Western Michigan University.

themselves. The attitudes they express are based on firmly rooted values. An organized person takes time to think, to monitor, and to reevaluate before responding.

Independence: Be Your Own Person

Most conflict situations we deal with on a daily basis are not the extremely taxing kind. The better we know ourselves, the better we will be able to cope with daily conflict. The better organized we are, too, the more likely we are to be our own person—autonomous. We need to be free to act and to deal with conflict and we must avoid being pushed into action before we are ready.[20]

The people best prepared to cope with conflict are spontaneous. They have the freedom to express their full range of potentials, to be the masters of their own lives and not to be easily manipulated. Successful copers are open and responsive. They can assert their own independence without trying to stifle another person's. They show their independence by expressing their wants and needs instead of demanding them, by expressing their preferences instead of ordering, by expressing acceptance of each other rather than mere tolerance, and by being willing to surrender genuinely to another person's wishes when it is appropriate to do so rather than simply pretending to submit.[21]

Anticipation: Be Prepared for Conflict

Conflicts are more likely to become crises when they catch us totally unaware. Try to anticipate conflict situations. Try to control your emotional reactions before they escalate. If we are ready for conflict and confident in our ability to deal with it, we'll be much less anxious if and when conflict develops.

By anticipating a conflict situation, we will be more likely to have some control over the context in which it occurs. Instead of focusing, for example, on whose fault the conflict is, we can try to get in touch with where we and the other person are and attempt to work from there.

In addition, with some anticipation, we can take responsibility for our feelings and actions. We can plan, in advance, to say such things as "I am angry" instead of "You make me angry," or "I feel rejected" instead of "You are excluding me again," or "I am confused" instead of "You don't make sense." In this way, we own our feelings—we take full responsibility for them. We claim, "*I*" feel this way or "*I* am this way." To do this rids us of the scapegoating we learn so well when we are young: "Billy made me do it." It is not only a move toward assertive behavior; it is a move toward maturity. And we convey our feelings to others, thereby creating trust in the process.

Consider This

People find themselves in a dilemma. They see two ways to negotiate: soft or hard. The soft negotiator wants to avoid personal conflict and so makes concessions readily in order to reach agreement. He wants an amicable resolution; yet he often ends up exploited and feeling bitter. The hard negotiator sees any situation as a contest of wills in which the side that takes the more extreme position and holds out longer fares better. He wants to win; yet he often ends up producing an equally hard response which exhausts him and his resources and harms his relationship with the other side. Other standard negotiating strategies fall between hard and soft, but each involves an attempted trade-off between getting what you want and getting along with people.

—From *Getting to Yes* by Roger Fisher and William Ury. Copyright © 1981 by Roger Fisher and William Ury. Reprinted by permission of Houghton Mifflin Company.

Finally, anticipation can cause us to be more aware. Resolving interpersonal conflict is easiest when we listen to the other person and respond to him or her with feedback. Conflict is likely to be reduced when we try to support and understand the other person.

Improving Skills in Conflict Management

The following ideas will aid in developing a constructive approach to dealing with conflict situations. Remember that there are no guaranteed solutions or sure-fire approaches. Remember, too, that not all conflicts can be resolved but that we can always choose how to handle them. This is an expansion of the collaborating style of conflict management.

Define the conflict. [22]   How we view the cause, size, and type of conflict affects how we manage it. Thus, it is important to be as specific as possible when defining the conflict. If it is multi-faceted (as many are), each part should be defined individually. If we know what events led up to the conflict and especially the specific event that triggered it, we may be able to anticipate and avoid future conflicts. We should learn to see the true size of a conflict: the smaller and more specific it is, the easier it will be to resolve. When a large, vague issue or principle is involved, the conflict is often escalated and enlarged. We can get very upset over how the system of higher education stifles individual initiative and growth, but that is a large, vague issue. To narrow the cause of the conflict, we might focus directly on a particular professor with whom we are having problems. Also, it is important to remove as much emotion as possible. We should strive for objectivity—a true representation of the conflict—rather than subjectivity—the conflict as it is attached to our feelings and emotions. Honesty is important as well. If the problem is not honestly defined from the beginning, no solution will resolve it.

View the conflict as a joint problem.   There are two general ways of looking at a conflict—as a win-or-lose situation or as a joint problem: **win-win.** If we look at a conflict as a joint problem, there is a greater possibility for a creative solution that results in both of us being satisfied. If we are having trouble with our English professor, we could easily turn the situation into a win-lose confrontation. We might say, "She thinks she's so great, I'm going to show her. I'll go to the department head . . . . " If we perceive the conflict as a joint problem, we might say, "Perhaps she has a point; maybe if I go in to see her, we could talk about this." The way we label a conflict partly determines the way we resolve it. A win-win attitude in conflicts suggests that there are creative alternatives and an infinite number of solutions for every problem. A win-win attitude also suggests that each party in the conflict assumes responsibility for his or her own behavior.

Defining conflict as a joint win-win problem means trying to discover the differences and similarities between ourselves and the other person. There is always the question of not just how *we* define the problem but also of how the *other person* defines the problem and how our definitions differ.

State the problem.   We'll have a better chance of resolving a potential conflict quickly if we have a clear idea of what behavior is acceptable or unacceptable to us and if we express our position to the other person. When we say, "When you interrupt me when we are talking to other people, I feel put down and unimportant" or "Every time you publicly criticize the way I dress, I get angry with you," we explain specific behaviors that are unacceptable to us. And we can then discuss or change those behaviors.

When we focus on a specific bothersome behavior, we reveal what is going on inside us. We take responsibility for our feelings by using "I" language instead of "you" language. This lessens the likelihood of defensiveness by not placing the blame on the other person as we would if we said, "You insult me" or "You make me angry."

Check your perceptions.   Under any circumstances, it is easy to be misunderstood, misquoted, or misinterpreted. Especially in a conflict situation, we should always check to make certain our message has been received accurately. We should also make sure we understand the other person's responses by paraphrasing them before we answer. Because our emotions intensify in times of conflict, further hurt or resentment can occur quickly through distortions caused by expectations or predispositions. Empathic listening is critical. We can determine where we are in our conversation with another person through paraphrases and summaries.

Generate possible decisions.   It is important, once we have shared what is bothering us, to consider how change can occur. We need not come up with all the decisions ourselves. A joint, cooperative decision is more likely to work. Flexibility is important in this process. Julius Fast views

flexibility as extremely valuable, calling it "an awareness of alternative solutions as well as the ability to discard one solution if it doesn't work and select another."[23] What is needed? What can the other person do? What can we do? What can be done together? These are realistic questions that should be raised. As we get possible answers to these questions, we should paraphrase and summarize them so that we are certain that both of us know what has been suggested and what alternatives exist.

Reach a mutually acceptable decision.

When we have considered all the possible alternatives we and the other person could generate, we should decide which of them would be mutually acceptable. It is important that we find an answer somewhat agreeable to everyone involved. But we cannot stop there. We all should understand the possible outcomes of implementing the decision. What is likely to happen? We should also understand what needs exist for cooperative interaction. In what ways, for example, will a particular decision require us to work together? When we have come to a final agreement on how to settle our conflict, we should make certain everyone fully understands what we agreed on by paraphrasing and summarizing the results. If we cannot reach an agreement we should stop. Plan another meeting. Try again later. Getting away from the problem for awhile may generate new insights.

Implement and evaluate the decision.

Before we put the proposed solution into effect, we should try to agree on how we will check it later to see if it solved the problem. Plan a meeting to evaluate progress. After we implement the decision, we'll want to find out if the results are mutually satisfying. If they aren't, we might have to go back to the beginning, possibly to our original definition of the conflict. We should have some way of knowing how to tell if the implemented decision worked well or did not work at all. If we have moved through the conflict successfully or are at least making progress, some gesture of appreciation might be appropriate from one (either!) party to the other.

It should be clear that these suggestions for coping with conflict are designed to provide a general framework (see Figure 10.2). No two conflict situations are identical; thus, no two ways of dealing with conflict will be exactly the same. Many of the decisions we face must be made instantaneously; how we cope is often a function of how quickly and accurately we are able to respond. However, successful coping may also result from slow, deliberate action. The discussion of ways to improve our skills in conflict management is not designed to make the situation more complex than necessary nor to prolong solutions unnecessarily. The point has been to set the tone or the appropriate frame of reference for decisions, whether quick or slow.

Conflict in interpersonal communication is an inevitable human experience. We are unique, the next person is unique; when these uniquenesses meet, conflict can occur. Conflict does not need to fracture friendships, dissolve marriages, or break up other interpersonal relationships. There is nothing inherently destructive, threatening, or mysterious about conflict.

Figure 10.2
Conflict management model.

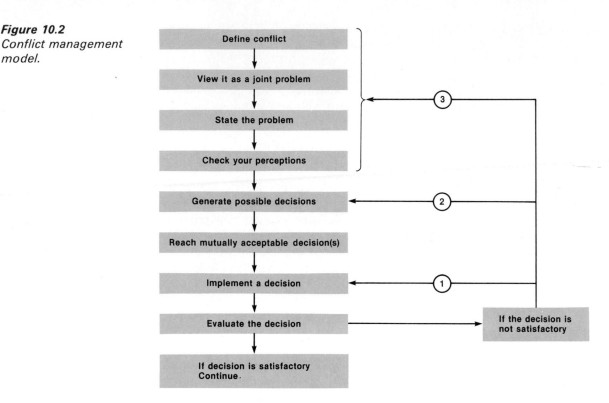

1. Other decisions may be implemented, if more than one mutually acceptable decision was agreed upon.

2. If no alternative decisions are available, a new set of decisions may have to be generated at this point.

3. When all else fails, it may be necessary to redefine the conflict. This may be especially necessary if the conflict was not honestly defined from the beginning, if it was not viewed as a joint problem, or if the problem was incorrectly or improperly stated.

How well we handle it while maintaining our values and our self-esteem and, at the same time, protecting the values and self-esteem of other people, will help determine our effectiveness in interpersonal relationships.

Notes

[1] George R. Bach and Peter Wyden, *The Intimate Enemy: How to Fight Fair in Love and Marriage* (New York: Avon Books, 1968), pp. 25–26.

[2] George R. Bach and Herb Goldberg, *Creative Aggression: The Art of Assertive Living* (New York: Avon Books, 1974), p. 82.

[3] Robert J. Doolittle, "Conflicting Views of Conflict: An Analysis of the Basic Communication Textbooks," *Communication Education* 26 (March 1977): 121.

[4] Kenneth E. Boulding, *Conflict and Defense* (New York: Harper & Row, 1962), p. 5.

[5] Based on pp. 172–76 from *Elements of Interpersonal Communication* by John W. Keltner. Copyright © 1973 by Wadsworth Publishing Company, Inc., Belmont, California 94002. Used by permission of John W. Keltner.

[6] Robert R. Blake and Jane S. Mouton, *The Managerial Grid* (Houston: Gulf Publishing Co., 1964). See also Robert R. Blake and Jane S. Mouton, *The New Managerial Grid* (Houston: Gulf Publishing Co., 1978), p. 11.

[7] Kenneth W. Thomas, "Conflict and Conflict Management," in *Handbook of Industrial and Organizational Psychology*, Vol. II (Chicago: Rand McNally, 1976).

[8] Kenneth W. Thomas and Ralph H. Kilmann, *Thomas-Kilmann Conflict Mode Instrument* (Sterling Forest, Tuxedo, N.Y.: Xicom, 1974). For an excellent interpretation of their work, see Martin B. Ross, "Coping with Conflict," in *The 1982 Annual Handbook* for Facilitators, Trainers, and Consultants, ed. J. William Pfeiffer and Leonard D. Goodstein (San Diego, Calif.: University Associates, 1982), pp. 135–39. Table 10.1 is adapted by permission from this source.

[9] See Herb Cohen, *You Can Negotiate Anything* (New York: Bantam Books, 1980), pp. 49–113.

[10] I am indebted to L. Phillip K. Le Gras, "Stress-Management Skills: Self-Modification for Personal Adjustment to Stress," in *The 1981 Annual Handbook for Group Facilitators*, ed. John E. Jones and J. William Pfeiffer (San Diego, Calif.: University Associates, 1981), pp. 138–40, for his development of these ideas.

[11] Le Gras, "Stress-Management Skills," p. 139.

[12] Julius Fast, *Creative Coping: A Guide to Positive Living* (New York: William Morrow and Co., 1976), pp. 187–88.

[13] W. Charles Redding, *Communication Within the Organization* (New York: Industrial Communication Council, 1972), p. 87.

[14] From *Man, the Manipulator* by Everett Shostrom. Copyright © 1967 by Abingdon Press. Used by permission.

[15] Erich Fromm, "Man Is Not a Thing," *Saturday Review*, March 16, 1957, pp. 9–11.

[16] Richard C. Huseman, James M. Lahiff, and John D. Hatfield, *Interpersonal Communications in Organizations: A Perceptual Approach* (Boston: Holbrook Press, 1976), p. 99.

[17] Redding, *Communication Within the Organization*, pp. 28, 30, and 37.

[18] Fast, *Creative Coping*, p. 187.

[19] David W. Johnson, *Reaching Out: Interpersonal Effectiveness and Self-Actualization*, 3rd ed. (Englewood Cliffs, N.J.: Prentice-Hall, 1986), p. 212.

[20] Shostrom, *Man, the Manipulator*, p. 50.

[21] Shostrom, *Man, the Manipulator*, p. 53.

[22] This approach is a variation of Dewey's problem-solving method. See John Dewey, *How We Think* (Chicago, D.C. Heath, 1910).

[23] Fast, *Creative Coping*, p. 53.

Further Reading

Deborah Borisoff and David A. Victor, *Conflict Management: A Communication Skills Approach* (Englewood Cliffs, N.J.: Prentice Hall, 1989). In this 201-page paperback, Borisoff and Victor provide a communication skills approach to managing interpersonal conflict. Their first three chapters focus on defining conflict and the necessary communication skills for dealing with conflict. Their second three chapters explore conflict in specific contexts—gender differences, intercultural situations, and writing. They incorporate realistic case studies and examples in each chapter. Also, they list 245 references for further reading. Their numerous exercises target the intervention strategies and skills essential for effective conflict management.

Robert M. Bramson, *Coping with Difficult People* (New York: Ballantine Books, 1981). Bramson discusses how to deal with hostile-aggressors, complainers, unresponsive people, wonderfully nice people, negativists, know-it-alls, and indecisive stallers. More than anything else, Bramson instills the attitude that coping with difficult people is possible!

Leon Chaitow, *Your Complete Stress-Proofing Programme: How to Protect Yourself Against the Ill-Effects of Stress* (New York: Thorsons Publishers Ltd., 1985). Chaitow traces the causes and nature of stress, the physical effects of stress, how to assess your stress, the ways we have for stress-proofing ourselves, relaxation exercises, meditation, and the use of the power of the mind for healing. A useful feature is the checklists provided for assessing your own levels of stress.

Edward A. Charlesworth and Ronald G. Nathan, *Stress Management: A Comprehensive Guide to Wellness* (New York: Atheneum, 1984). This is a 327-page book full of complete descriptions and explanations of management techniques based on many years of clinical psychological work. Included are techniques such as progressive relaxation; time-planning; life-change management; imagery training; controlling Type A behavior; managing anger, self-doubt, and irrational beliefs; assertiveness; exercise and weight control; and many more. The authors offer innovative strategies for coping with the hazards of time-urgent living. An excellent resource.

Herb Cohen, *You Can Negotiate Anything* (New York: Bantam Books, 1980). Cohen discusses everything from mergers to marriages and from loans to lovemaking. He views the world as a giant negotiating table. This is a very practical guide in how to use the win-win approach. An enjoyable book full of useful advice.

Roger Fisher and William Ury, *Getting to Yes: Negotiating Agreement Without Giving In* (Boston, Mass.: Houghton Mifflin Co., 1981). What is the best way for people to deal with their differences? This is a practical presentation of the method of principled negotiation developed at the Harvard Negotiation Project which decides issues on their merits rather than through a haggling process focused on what each side says it will and won't do. A useful book.

Joseph P. Folger and Marshall Scott Poole, *Working Through Conflict: A Communication Perspective* (Glenview, Ill.: Scott, Foresman & Co., 1984). The authors of this book support two themes: (1) that people can successfully work through conflicts, and (2) that productive work can be accomplished through conflict. This textbook is written for undergraduates with little or no background in this area. The authors provide a balance between theory and practical advice. Numerous case studies are provided for explanation and discussion. Well-researched and thorough.

Joyce L. Hocker and William W. Wilmot, *Interpersonal Conflict*, 2d. ed. (Dubuque, Iowa: Wm. C. Brown Publishers, 1985). A thorough, well-researched textbook that covers the nature of, power in, and structure of conflict as well as conflict styles, analyzing issues and setting goals, strategies and tactics, and intervention principles and practices. A useful bibliography is included.

Fred E. Jandt, with Paul Gillette, *Win-Win Negotiating: Turning Conflict into Agreement* (New York: John Wiley & Sons, 1985). Jandt shows how to turn conflict into a positive force that paves the way for communication, teamwork, and healthy change. The techniques are practical and applicable to almost all situations; the writing style is comfortable; and the examples are useful and interesting.

Alfie Kohn, *No Contest: The Case Against Competition-Why We Lose In Our Race to Win* (Boston: Houghton Mifflin, 1986). In this 257-page paperback, Kohn argues that competition is inherently destructive. In this well-researched, carefully reasoned study, Kohn demonstrates that gaining success by making others fail is an unproductive way to work and learn. Any win/lose structure, he argues, is psychologically destructive and poisonous to relationships. An impressive, challenging, and thoughtful work.

11

Experiencing Growth and Change: Communicating with Family and Friends

Learning Objectives

When you have finished this chapter you should be able to:

- Justify a section on family communication in a textbook on interpersonal communication.
- Relate assumed or assigned roles to family communication.
- Identify some communication barriers likely to occur in families.
- Explain the problems associated with restricted freedom, emotional buildups, possessiveness, and double standards.
- Briefly describe a six-stage system for maintaining family relationships and for acquiring good arguing skills.
- Clarify the general characteristics of the art of friendship. Why can it be called an art?
- Explain why people pursue friendships. Distinguish between the needs for security, affection, self-esteem, freedom, and equality.
- Briefly characterize some of the major factors that influence communication among friends.
- Illustrate the differences in breadth and depth of self-disclosure between strangers, acquaintances, and close friends.
- Explain cultural identity, how it evolves, and its value.

We exist only through our relationship to the world around us. Our relationships with family, friends, work associates, and others provide context and meaning for our lives. Growth without these relationships is not likely; it is through them that life takes on meaning.

Obviously such concepts as perception, self-disclosure, listening, and verbal and nonverbal communication, discussed in earlier chapters, are meaningful only in the context of interaction with others. In this chapter we put it all together and discuss the special needs and demands of communicating interpersonally in two vital areas of our lives: family and friends. We all have certain conceptions and expectations for our family and friends. What are they based on? What are our values in these areas?

We need some additional skills in order to gain the most from these important relationships. These skills are really extensions of ideas already mentioned; they are discussed here again because of their particular relevance to communication with family and friends.

Family

"The greatest happiness and the deepest satisfaction in life, the most intense enthusiasm and the most profound inner peace," says Sven Wahlroos in *Family Communication*, "all come from being a member of a loving family."[1] The reverse is also true: some of the greatest pain can come from family relationships. We choose our friends, but we do not choose our family. We can move in and out of relationships with most people, but it is often more difficult with family members. Our choices and our freedom are more limited within family relationships. Family relationships present unique problems and unique satisfactions in interpersonal communication.

The Familiar Question: Who Am I?

A useful way to begin to think about communicating with our families is to think about the various family roles we all may have assumed or been assigned. "Sister" or "daughter" are some obvious roles, but for most of us things are more complicated than that. There are other influences that decide

Try This

Which adjectives best describe how you were perceived by other family members when you were growing up?

active	disorderly	kind	self-centered
affectionate	dumb	lazy	self-confident
agreeable	emotional	mischievous	selfish
aggressive	friendly	naughty	shy
alert	generous	noisy	slow
antisocial	gentle	odd	smart
apathetic	gloomy	outgoing	sociable
awkward	happy	peculiar	stable
cautious	high-strung	persistent	stingy
cheerful	hostile	pleasant	strong
complaining	impatient	quarrelsome	stubborn
confident	impulsive	quiet	talkative
cooperative	independent	rebellious	timid
cruel	irresponsible	reliable	tolerant
demanding	irritable	responsible	unattractive

How have these perceptions affected you? Have you seen their influence on your relationships with others? Are there other adjectives that better describe how you were perceived by other family members when you were growing up?

—This list of adjectives was borrowed, in part, from David W. Johnson, *Reaching Out: Interpersonal Effectiveness and Self-Actualization*, © 1972, pp. 29–30. Reprinted by permission of Prentice-Hall, Inc., Englewood Cliffs, New Jersey.

our roles for us. Whether we are male or female may have determined whether we mowed the lawn or did the dishes, carried out the garbage or cleaned the house, were given freedom in dating or were more controlled— just to cite some obvious examples. Our sex may have affected how we were perceived: forthright, aggressive, athletic, awkward, friendly, or mischievous. Larry Feldman has summarized the numerous research studies on sex roles. His findings are given in Table 11.1. Birth order also strongly influences family roles. First-born children are often more restricted than those born afterward. Older children, too, are often treated as more mature and responsible; younger children may be spoiled or treated as irresponsible, delicate, or dependent.

Physical and mental attributes also affect the role we may have assumed or been assigned. The physically biggest child in a family may be perceived as the clumsiest or may be given the most responsibility. The smartest may

Table 11.1
Psychological dimensions of the female and male roles.

The female role. Women are expected to be (or allowed to be) the following:
1. Home-oriented, child(ren)-oriented.
2. Warm, affectionate, gentle, tender.
3. Aware of feelings of others, considerate, tactful, compassionate.
4. Moody, high-strung, temperamental, excitable, emotional, subjective, illogical.
5. Complaining, nagging.
6. Weak, helpless, fragile, easily emotionally hurt.
7. Submissive, yielding, dependent.

The male role. Men are expected to be (or allowed to be) the following:
1. Ambitious, competitive, enterprising, worldly.
2. Calm, stable, unemotional, realistic, logical.
3. Strong, tough, powerful.
4. Aggressive, forceful, decisive, dominant.
5. Independent, self-reliant.
6. Harsh, severe, stern, cruel.
7. Autocratic, rigid, arrogant.

—Larry B. Feldman, "Sex Roles and Family Dynamics," Table 14-1, in *Normal Family Process*, ed. Froma Walsh (New York: Guilford Press, 1982), p. 355. Used with permission.

have had "success" in school drilled into him or her since kindergarten. Family members may peg a highly emotional child as the family troublemaker, the one who starts arguments. These qualities (and many more) do determine our roles to a great extent. Because they tend to be constantly reinforced, they come to be the roles with which we feel most comfortable. Being perceived as a clown or a peacemaker, moody or jolly, gentle or cruel in family relationships will strongly affect how we relate to people outside the family. It is important to understand where we fit and what our role may be. It is important, too, not to be locked into these roles.

Communication Barriers in the Family

Although the emphasis here is on the family in which you grew up, because of its importance in establishing many of your patterns of communication, some of these things will operate in the family you may form for yourself later on. You will be establishing another pattern of roles in that family. These roles will be based, in part, on what your growing-up experience was.

Family roles provide a subtle but continuing influence on our lives. One of the first communication barriers that may develop out of family roles is the tendency within the family to see a family member *only* in one role. This does not allow for growth or change. Despite the fact that we may have become outgoing or more independent, family members may still treat us as if we are shy or dependent. We may become a corporation president, but family members may still perceive us as a helpless kid sister. This not only may limit our own possibilities for change but may cause breakdowns in communication resulting from misperceptions and false assumptions.

There is a related communication problem, the assumption that no matter *what* we actually say, the other members of our family will understand us. Though family members often communicate with each other very efficiently by means of a kind of communication shorthand, sometimes we come to depend too much on this system of signals and implied meanings. An example of this is the son who agreed with his father that whenever he wanted to use the family car, he would make arrangements with him in advance. The son used the car and the father accused him of violating the agreement. The son insisted he had told him: "You saw me washing and waxing the car, and you know I never do that unless I'm planning to use it." Our meaning is not always as clear as we might think, even within our own family.

In the family relationship, much mutual "picture taking" goes on. That is, members are often involved in forming mental pictures of how others are feeling, reacting, or thinking. As Virginia Satir, a leader in the field of family therapy, states in *Peoplemaking:* "The people involved may not share their pictures, the meanings they give the pictures, nor the feelings the pictures arouse."[2] Those involved guess at meaning and then assume those guesses are facts. This guessing procedure results in a great many unnecessary family communication barriers.

We simply cannot assume that another person always knows what we mean, even if we have grown up with that person. The reason this assumption causes special problems in the family is that people who share such a close relationship feel they *should* be able to read each other's minds. Everyone is supposed to know how everyone else feels—no one needs to say or show

MISS PEACH, Courtesy of Mell Lazarus. © 1990, Mell Lazarus.

what he or she feels. Serious misunderstandings can result when this doesn't work. Think of a time when you felt *very strongly* that the family should take a specific vacation, make a certain purchase, or eat at a certain restaurant. Did you reveal this strong feeling to other family members? Just because you felt it does not mean you showed it to others. We are not as transparent to others as we are to ourselves.

This extends to our policy of criticizing and complimenting other family members, too. Whether we're aware of it or not, we look to our families for reinforcement and rewards. We may not voice praise or gratitude because we expect family members to know our feelings without spelling them out. But our message doesn't always get through, and it should. A pat on the back is not only welcomed but needed from time to time. Not surprisingly, family members are often less inclined to hold back criticisms of each other. When the free and heavy flow of criticism gets to be too much, family relationships may turn into nothing more than opportunities for negative exchanges, with estrangement and resentment resulting. Wahl-roos even goes so far as to say that "the main reason for . . . discord [in families] is simply that the consciously felt love and the good intentions harbored by the family members are not *communicated* in such a way that they are recognized."[3]

It should be acknowledged, too, that not all family relationships are conducted by healthy people in healthy situations. What is offered in this chapter is an ideal scenario. It may be that some families have to work very hard just to create a climate for communication. "Making contact," as Satir calls it, can be a major accomplishment in family situations involving child abuse, alcoholism, or other serious problems. In some such situations, professional counseling is needed to facilitate communication among family members.

Other Behaviors That May Cause Problems

Such behaviors as restricting the freedoms of others, allowing emotional buildups, possessiveness, and double standards can cause problems in family relationships as well.

Restricted freedom simply means less opportunity to behave at any moment just as you please. Living with others may affect the time you may study, eat, sleep, dress, or even use the bathroom. When freedoms are restricted, interpersonal stress results. For example, one parent may have just come home after a harried day of decision making at work. It may be later than usual. As he or she comes in the door, a new set of decisions may have to be faced: homework that is not finished, television-related requests, civic or community events, invitations from friends, requests for use of the car, and on and on. Such demands and responsibilities are part of family membership, but they can also cause stress. Often they carry with them unstated assumptions and understandings, such as: to be a "good father" you should help Tim with his homework, or to be "good neighbors" you should go over to the Joneses' open house tonight, or to be "good parents" or "good citizens" you should go to the school board meeting tonight. As well as assumptions and understandings sometimes such decisions also carry emotional freight. This can occur when one spouse makes an informal commitment to something, and the other spouse makes a decision that does not correspond with or counters the other. One spouse, for example, may decide to go golfing or bowling when the other believes that that time should be spent with the children.

It may take a while for someone who has been used to living alone to become "we" oriented. It takes a while to learn how to share one's space, time, and physical objects with another person, to be able to say, in response to an invitation, "I can't tell you whether or not we can come; I'll have to check with _____" or "I'll have to check our calendar." With the relinquishment of certain freedoms, tension and stress must be accommodated.

Emotional buildups result when we store up our thoughts and feelings. To the words, phrases, and situations that we are involved in, we add emotional associations. Sometimes the emotional link is already so strong that all another person has to do is refer to it, like saying, "I saw Fred today," to activate the emotional avalanche, "I thought we agreed that you were never going to see him again!" The more intimate the relationship, the more likely emotional buildups are to occur. Questions such as "Have you studied?" "Have you practiced?" "Can I use the car?" or "Can I borrow your tools?" are likely to have powerful linkages because of many shared past experiences. Think of all the shared recollections that are likely in such situations: times when studying or practicing was not given a first or even a high priority, or times when the car was left dirty or out of gas, or still other times when tools were lost or misplaced. When these shared experiences have occurred, a question that looks like a simple request for information is no longer perceived that way. Emotional linkages will affect the way the question is asked, the way it is perceived, and the behavior that is likely to follow.

Possessiveness in family relationships occurs when members feel they have a right to control or influence the behaviors of one another. This is a normal feeling that grows out of the interpretation of family situations by members belonging to the family. You hear it said, "That's my girl . . ." or "As long as you live in this house, you aren't going to do that." Or people may make statements like "He's my husband," or "He's my son." There are expectations that accompany these statements and feelings—expectations that imply control.

Parents are known to say such things as, "If you really cared about us you would . . . ," or "If you loved us, you wouldn't act that way." Although

Consider This

It is often little habits, more than important things, that wear upon people who are engaged in mutual activities or who live together. A toothpaste tube that is habitually left uncapped, or a coffeepot that is imperfectly rinsed, can grate upon the nerves more insistently than a serious flaw of temperament or character.

—From "Strictly Personal" by Sydney J. Harris, *Toledo Blade,* June 19, 1985. By permission of NAL, Inc.

it is natural to want to please those we love, it is when others' expectations include changes in behavior that control and possessiveness are demonstrated.

Control and possessiveness tend to make other people defensive. Jack Gibb has examined defensive communication in detail, pointing out that defensive behavior occurs when individuals perceive or anticipate threat.[4] Defensiveness then leads to distortions in communication. People who feel defensive spend unnecessary time thinking about how they appear to others, how they may be seen more favorably, how they may win, dominate, impress, or escape punishment, or how they may avoid or mitigate a perceived or an anticipated attack. Such defensiveness creates defensiveness in others and provokes defensive listening.[5]

If listeners listen defensively, they become less able to perceive accurately. The attitudes and values of the other person are distorted, and the efficiency of communication is lessened. Gibb says that you must expect defensiveness if you reveal the following behaviors:[6]

1. **Judgmental behavior:** "You should not talk like that," or "Talking like that is bad."
2. **Controlling behavior:** "When you are in this house, you do it our way."

Try This

On what issues do members of your family have strong emotional linkages? Are they attached to such issues as:

religion?	your friends?
politics?	how late you stay up?
sex?	how much television you watch?
studying?	what you read?
your use of time?	where you go?
how seriously you take school?	what you eat?
what you wear?	your appearance?

How do you face these issues—when you know strong emotional linkages are present? Can you avoid emotional explosions over them? Is avoidance one of the techniques you use? Is it easier to talk to some family members about them than others? Do you think complete avoidance contributes to a healthy interpersonal relationship? Is it likely that emotional linkages will change on some of the issues above? If so, what may contribute to the change?

Try This

You have undoubtedly found yourself engaged in defense-producing behavior. Can you remember the last time? Which type of behavior was it?

judgmental	neutral
controlling	superior
strategic	certain

Can you remember what you said or did that reflected this climate? Which of the following types of behavior would have helped reduce the defensiveness?

descriptive	empathic
problem-oriented	equal
spontaneous	provisional

Is it possible to identify specific behaviors—things you might say or do—that would result in these supportive climates?

---

3. **Strategic behavior:** "A thoughtful person would have done it without being asked."
4. **Neutral behavior:** "Let's not get emotional, just give me the facts. Be objective, and you can solve this problem . . ."
5. **Superior behavior:** "As your father, I can tell you what *I* would do in such a situation . . ."
6. **Certain behavior:** "There is only one way to look at it; only one point of view that is acceptable . . ."

Gibb has provided parallel, correlated supportive climates for each of the six defense-producing climates given above.[7] This means that descriptive behavior helps reduce defensiveness caused by judgmental behavior; problem-oriented behavior reduces defensiveness caused by controlling behavior, and so on. Practicing each of the following behaviors will help reduce the possibility of defensiveness:

1. **Descriptive behavior:** "How do *you* feel about the situation?"
2. **Problem-oriented behavior:** "Let's look at this idea together with no predetermined attitudes or solutions."
3. **Spontaneous behavior:** "It is important to be straightforward and honest. The best way to deal with situations is by being direct."
4. **Empathic behavior:** "I think I know how you feel. Perhaps we could talk about the problem a bit more. Sharing feelings like this seems to help."

5. **Equal behavior** (showing mutual trust and respect): "Isn't it neat that we can discuss problems from the same viewpoint? We can push aside our differences and really have a meeting of the minds."
6. **Provisional behavior:** "There are no sure ways to approach this situation; let's just try something and if it doesn't work, we'll try something else."

The purpose of these supportive behaviors, though perhaps slightly exaggerated above, is to increase trust between family members. They allow identification to occur: they enable one family member to get a sense of what the other is feeling. In this way, accuracy of communication is likely to increase.

Double standards can also cause problems among family members. Double standards emerge when parents expect their children to follow rules or perform rituals from which they, as parents, are exempt. Parents often follow a "Do as I say, not as I do" philosophy. The rules may have to do with lying, stealing, or, on a smaller scale, interrupting others, or talking with one's mouth full. Rituals may prescribe proper eating habits, going to church, or other daily or weekly occurrences. Often there is a distinct gap between what the parents do and what they expect of their children.

A double standard may also be operative between other segments of the family. For example, there may be a stiff requirement that one child must keep a bedroom neat because it is visible to everyone, including guests, whereas the other children, whose bedrooms are in another part of the house, do not have the same requirement. It may occur, too, over the way chores are assigned or over who must fill in when someone is not present. The cry of "It's not fair" is a common one in some households. Some parents stress to their children that things are *not* equal: life is not equal for all. Different privileges may be considered appropriate for male and female children. A teenage boy, for example, may be allowed to travel alone some distance from home whereas a teenage girl may be more restricted. The point here is not whether double standards operate, or whether they are good or bad, but simply that they can become points of conflict within a family.

Maintaining Family Relationships

Most people want to maintain or improve their family relationships. Aware, open people, or those who want to become more aware and open, can utilize the following system. This system provides the knowledge, understanding, and equipment that will enable people to make conscious, deliberate use of the process of interaction in family situations. It is from such interaction in meaningful situations that change and growth can occur. If a family already has established a foundation of mutual affection and shared interests, then acquiring good arguing skills will give them a much better chance of having healthy, satisfying interactions that are likely to continue into the future.[8]

Stage 1: Seek information.   Although this stage appears obvious, it is not. If we have been offended by someone's else's actions, we may charge into the situation without investigating how the other person feels, trying to get even without sufficient knowledge or a solid foundation on which to base our response. We tend to "shoot from the hip" because it is easier, because we let our emotions take over, or because that is our problem-solving style.

Seeking information is a continual, rational process that requires time and commitment. It requires that we step back from the immediate situation occasionally and answer some crucial questions. Although these questions should be answered with respect to the immediate situation, answers will not be as difficult to discover if the process has, indeed, been ongoing:

1. Who am I in this family?
2. How do I relate to others?
3. How do they relate to me?
4. How do we communicate?
5. How do we normally resolve problems?

Seeking information means being aware of and sensitive to what is occurring around you. Keep your eyes and ears open all the time. Then, when problems arise, they occur in an already established matrix of information and knowledge.

You may be asking, "But how do I keep my emotions in check?" First, if emotions are intense, it might be wise to put off any discussion of the immediate problem until after a brief cooling-off period (twenty to thirty minutes). Second, it is important to understand that emotional involvement is a natural, normal part of family problem solving. Emotions lie at the heart of everything we think and do. Third, they are an intetgral part of the information-seeking stage, and another set of questions needs to be asked:

1. What are my feelings on this issue?
2. How intense are they?
3. What are the other's feelings on the issue?
4. How intense are they?
5. How will our feelings interact?
6. How are feelings likely to affect those involved? To affect others—even those not directly involved with the problem now?

The final aspect of Stage 1 has been labeled by psychologist John Gottman as **"mind-reading strategies."**[9] This is when we strive to put the pieces of the puzzle together. This may entail methodical, consistent detective work. It may mean taking the position of an outsider—someone outside the immediate situation—and trying to respond as an objective bystander would. Or we may gain such a picture as the result of the "Aha!" experience—the meaning suddenly occurs to us. Whatever process we use, we must try to lay the foundation for later stages by trying to understand as much about the feelings, opinions, and motives of the other person as possible—guessing, anticipating, perceiving, and observing—and combining these with all other interacting ingredients.

Stage 2: Share meanings.

No situation has exactly the same meaning for each of the people involved. If two or more people do not sit down and organize the data and identify (together) the various thoughts and feelings that bear on the problem, they are likely to continue to act unilaterally.

Sharing meanings is a give-and-take process. It involves open, trusting, honest interaction between people. It allows underlying wishes, guilts, and jealousies to be brought to the surface. It helps clarify options and evaluate their appropriateness and workability.

In his article on "Avoiding Couple Karate," Anthony Brandt provides an example of the benefits of sharing meaning:

The happily married couples come to all agreements fairly readily, either through one partner giving in to the other without resentment or through compromise:

>*"We spent all of Christmas at your mother's last year. This time let's spend it at my mother's."*
>
>*"Yeah, you're right, that's not fair. How about 50-50 this year?"*[10]

Perhaps the biggest barrier to sharing meaning is our tendency to blame. Hating to be found wrong, we may blame another for our difficulty and simply not listen to the other's side of the discussion. Or we may place all the blame on ourselves, no matter what the situation, and begin the sharing in a one-down position. The best sharing is equal, allows give-and-take, deals with the facts, has both parties taking responsibility, and strives for mutual growth and understanding.

One warning regarding open communication within the family is necessary. There are sometimes collusions (secret agreements) that are years old that when revealed, can create more problems and emotional responses rather than helping. The best advice here is a gradual opening of communication channels with lower levels of self-disclosure before any "heavy" revelations of emotional "stashes."

Stage 3: State alternatives. In 1910, in his book *How We Think*, and as part of the plan he labeled "reflective thinking," John Dewey called for the "cultivation of a variety of alternative suggestions."[11] Once again, the need to state alternatives may seem too obvious a stage of problem solving to deserve mention. But think about how open and receptive you are to various other ways of proceeding when you think *you* have the answer, the right method, or the only way. We tend to see the world through self-prescribed lenses.

In this stage, the partners make conscious and deliberate efforts to discover and evaluate all possible alternatives. This can be an opportunity to be speculative and adventuresome. "Alternatives" do not need to be polished proposals. They can be merely suppositions and guesses.

Stage 4: Select solutions. From the mixture developed in Stage 3, partners need to weigh the advantages of the alternatives suggested as well as the strengths and weaknesses of possible combinations of those alternatives. Often, it is a combination that best satisfies both parties.

Looking back to our discussion of "Styles of Handling Conflict" in Chapter 10, it is clear that there are really five basic ways that decisions are made in families, and that these can be identified in terms of the dimensions of assertiveness and cooperation. A family member who is highly assertive and uncooperative uses a competing style of problem solving characterized by power, persuasion, and coercion. If another family member wants to prevent conflict or avert a potential blowup, he or she may assume an avoiding style—despite its weaknesses. Sometimes a problem is just not

Consider This

Family communication patterns can encourage or discourage satisfying relationships . . . three needs should be met in our interactions with the members of our families: (1) establishment of the individual's need for autonomy, (2) maintenance of the family's need for interdependence, and (3) development of awareness of the recurring interactional patterns and the changes within the family system.

We allow members to be autonomous, or separate, functioning people when we permit open and honest self-disclosure for all family members. People of both genders and all ages need the opportunity to share their feelings, thoughts, and ideas, even when they are discrepant from the rest of the family . . . .

The family is an interdependent unit, which means that each member of the family has needs that are satisfied by the others in the group, and each in turn satisfies the needs of the others. Interdependence is maintained as family members engage in active listening and empathic understanding . . . .

We need to develop an awareness of the recurring interaction patterns and the changes that occur within our family systems . . . .individual families go through major alterations. Family members are born, others die, some move away, and others move back home. Some family members work while others lose their jobs, some begin to attend college while others graduate or drop out. As they mature, family members agree to take on new tasks within the home and are able to perform them; others relinquish particular duties because they feel the tasks are no longer appropriate for them to do. These changes strongly impact on the communication patterns in the family and on the resulting satisfaction that people feel.

—Judy Cornelia Pearson, *Gender and Communication* (Dubuque, Iowa: Wm. C. Brown Publishers, 1985), pp. 309–11. Reprinted by permission.

worth getting upset over or spending time on. But when avoiding becomes *the* way to achieve peace, the family members lose mutuality, and the avoiding person loses a voice in problem solving.

The highly cooperative and nonassertive person seeks to satisfy the other person(s) at all costs. This accommodating style may be appropriate for short-range, unimportant, unemotional issues. Some people can build relationships based on accommodation because, as we saw in Chapter 10, it can build goodwill, promote harmony, avoid disruption, and reduce the power factor in a relationship. Its major weakness is that it depends on a high degree of nonassertiveness in one of the members. Mutuality—the coming together of people on a near or equal footing—requires some degree of assertiveness by all parties.

The middle position on both dimensions is compromising. Here people give in or agree even though they may not be pleased or satisfied with the decision.

Collaborating is the method that involves the highest degree of both assertiveness and cooperation. In collaboration, respect is shown for everyone, and the solution will be based on what is appropriate and constructive for the family as a whole. In solving problems, it is not necessary for all parties to agree. They could agree to disagree. They could agree to allow all those involved to do as they wish. Collaboration is based on every family member's appreciation of and respect for one another's uniqueness and for the preservation of the family relationship as a whole.

Stage 5: Start implementation.

Selecting the solution is of little value if no effort is made to put it into practice. Sharing meaning is important at this stage, too, to make certain both sides perceive the same solution and the same methods of implementation. How often have you found yourself saying, "Yes, I remember what we agreed upon, but I thought we were going to do it this way." Feelings and reactions need to be controlled. Judgment of final outcomes needs to be suspended until the solution is tried.

The most important ingredient we can contribute to starting the implementation process is personal responsibility. We should feel responsible for helping the agreed-upon solution work. We should feel responsible because we care about others. We should feel responsible, too, because of a commitment to the relationship. We also should feel responsible because of our human need to learn and grow. But we can only feel responsible for implementing the decision if we have had input into it and agree with it. Indeed, that is what collaboration is all about.

Stage 6: Survey results.

There are no guarantees that solutions will work when they are implemented. Surveying the results of Stage 5 may be a continuation of Stage 1: seeking information. We need to monitor the process, asking such questions as:

1. Is the solution working?
2. Is everyone pleased with the results?
3. Are there changes that need to, or can be, made to improve effectiveness or pleasure?

Surveying also is a continual process of sharing meaning. In many cases, a number of different solutions will be going on at the same time. To make certain that the relationship is continuing as expected, communication between participants must be a regular feature. One family member may think things are all right while the other is playing the silent role. Many people have well-entrenched habits of assuming they know what the other person means, thinks, feels, or intends. Surveying should involve adapting to each other under the new conditions, altering circumstances as needed, and gaining renewed balance or stability in the relationship. Although surveying results is a final stage in the problem-solving system, it is also an integral part of the ongoing process of interaction. It really never ends.

This six-stage program can be useful for problem solving if your commitment to maintaining and improving family relationships is strong, and if you want to grow closer to the other members. Putting it into effect takes work and practice. Do not let occasional failures deter you. Gradually, sometimes laboriously, you will find yourself altering old ways and shifting from former habits. Eventually, perhaps even unknowingly, the process will become second nature.

Friends

As we saw in the earlier chapters of this book, a great deal of personal growth is possible within our friendships. As we become wiser in the ways of human beings, more sensitive to ourselves and more perceptive about others, we become more careful about the kinds of friendships we begin. The more we know about the types of personalities with whom we should or should not become involved, the more likely we are to choose friends with whom a relationship will last a long time. Many of the skills for communicating effectively within the family are applicable in this section as well.

Often people view the art of acquiring and holding friends as a passive process. They feel fortunate when they find a friend and are happy when that friendship lasts, but they do not realize that friendship involves commitment, giving, and energy. Often people are too lazy to make friendships work. These people never discover what friendships can be and do, and the mutual needs that can be fulfilled. Andrew Greeley, in *The Friendship Game*, calls friendship "the most pleasurable and most difficult of specifically human activities."[12]

In forming and maintaining relationships, all our interpersonal skills come into play. Friendship involves making choices that are not always based on logic. There is a chemistry that occurs between good friends. Sometimes an instant rapport is deceptive and dangerous; we learn to distinguish this from what is authentic. The skills described here for forming and maintaining relationships assume that you know someone with whom friendship seems likely and you wish to proceed. The purpose of this section is to help you think more clearly about the problems and challenges of friendship, especially close friendships.

Why We Form Friendships[13]

A **friendship relationship** is one marked by very close association, contact, or familiarity. Usually a warm friendship has developed as a result of a long association, but this is not always the case. Sometimes friendship develops suddenly. Friendship relationshps are very personal or private in nature and are often characterized by different types of communication.

There is no doubt that many factors govern the nature, development, maintenance, and dissolution of friendship relationships. As bases for friendship relationships, Mark Knapp lists personality and background factors, situational and developmental factors, cultural guidelines, emotional considerations, self-fulfillment, self-surrender, and commitment.[14] Many of these factors have been discussed elsewhere in this book.

We seek friendship relationships for many reasons. These reasons may operate singly or in conjunction with each other. Many overlap. In some situations, with some people, one of these reasons may sustain a relationship while in others several are likely to operate. The more needs that are fulfilled in a relationship, the more solid the foundation upon which the relationship rests. We seek friendship relationships to fulfill five basic needs: the need for security, affection, self-esteem, freedom, and equality.[15] They are not necessarily ranked here in order of importance.

Security is one need that friendship can fulfill. The primary concern here is the psychological security to be gained from the absence of threat.

Consider This

In our . . . society, no clear lines mark the beginnings of a friendship; often none mark the ending either. Relations of blood generally end in death—clear and unequivocal. But friendships usually just fade away. Beginnings are equally unambiguous in the family: A baby is born and instantly there are mother, father, sister, brother, aunts, uncles, cousins. With marriage also, beginnings and endings are strikingly clear: Marriages start with a wedding and end with death or divorce. But for us, friendship is a *non-event*—a relationship that just *becomes*, that grows, develops, waxes, wanes and, too often perhaps, ends, all without ceremony or ritual to give evidence of its existence.

—From *Just Friends: The Role of Friendship in Our Lives* by Lillian B. Rubin. Copyright © 1985 by Lillian B. Rubin. Reprinted by permission of Harper & Row, Publishers, Inc.

The nature of the threat differs. It may be being single in a society that prizes relationships. It may be the threat of no commitment, since making a commitment to another person is one of the most important events in most people's lives. Security is gained from situations in which there is much ego-supportive communication and a healthy amount of predictiveness. Maslow lists it as the second most basic need humans have—second only to satisfying such needs as hunger, sex, thirst, sleep, warmth, and shelter.

Affection relates to a sense of belonging. This could encompass sexual gratification, but does not need to. Affection suggests a moderate feeling toward or emotional attachment to another person. When you feel tender attachment for others or pleasure in being with them, you are experiencing affection. As discussed in Chapter 7, Abraham Maslow labels this "belonging and love needs," placing this need among the basic or essential needs after "physiological" and "safety" needs.

Self-esteem is felt when you are recognized or appreciated by others. Sometimes being with someone enhances your status. Also, if other people attribute a joint identity to your relationship with another person, this may also increase your self-esteem. Self-esteem is affected because such a high premium is often placed on dating and "going steady." Maslow places self-esteem needs only one step higher than affection—as slightly less essential and more optional.

Freedom is another reason for friendship. You may think of friendship situations as just the reverse: restrictive, confining, and limiting. This is one area that needs to be negotiated in most friendships. In some areas, for example, you may want self-reliance and independence; in other areas you may want dependency and reliance. You may want independence when it comes to going around with whomever you want but reliance on a set of friends when it comes to going out and doing things together. You then negotiate, sometimes subtly, for freedom of movement for yourself and for control of your social calendar.

Another area of freedom often negotiated is how much the friends will be together. Suppose one person in a friendship enjoys what you might label a "smothering" relationship, whereas you want more openness, less togetherness. Can openness be negotiated? Is flexibility possible? You may end up weighing your reasons for maintaining this friendship against your need for freedom. People need *self*-fulfillment, and this is best realized when they are not too limited or restrained by their relationships with others. David Viscott, a psychiatrist, expresses it this way:

> *No relationship can provide everything needed for the complete experience of being yourself. Many important answers must come from ourselves, not from another person. The role of another person in our search for ourselves will at times be little more than that of a friendly, accepting bystander. The greatest burdens in our lives will clearly fall upon our own shoulders, not on our relationship with another person.*[16]

Consider This

The following information is based on the nearly 300 interviews that Lillian B. Rubin conducted in connection with writing her book on friendship.*

'What is a friend?'—a question I asked everyone I talked with. The answers I heard varied somewhat depending on class, gender, and generational perspectives. But regardless of the experienced reality of their lives and relationships, most people presented some idealized definition of friendship. Trust, honesty, respect, commitment, safety, support, generosity, loyalty, mutuality, constancy, understanding, acceptance. These are the most widely heralded qualities of friendship, the minimum requirements, if you will, to be counted as a friend.

* These were in-depth interviews, each lasting several hours, with men and women aged 25 to 55, both single and married, from working class to upper-middle class backgrounds.
—From *Just Friends: The Role of Friendship in Our Lives* by Lillian B. Rubin. Copyright © 1985 by Lillian B. Rubin. Reprinted by permission of Harper & Row, Publishers, Inc.

Try This

To find whether you have the base for a fruitful and productive friendship, ask yourself the following questions. If you can answer yes to most of the questions, it is likely that the friendship will grow and develop; if not, it is likely to become troublesome.

1. Are you willing to risk—to overcome fear of the unknown?
2. Are you attracted to the other person?
3. Do you share values and goals with the other person?
4. Do you have some of the same interests, commitments, and expectations?
5. Are you willing to be open and honest? To acknowledge your part in the relationship? To respond to the other person authentically?
6. Can you count on each other to be responsible and reliable?
7. Can you play together—let yourselves go and have fun without feeling embarrassed or ill at ease?
8. Does the relationship enable you to see yourself more clearly?
9. Does the relationship allow you to remain open to other kinds of relationships with other people?
10. Does the relationship feel good?

If you answered no to many of these questions, then you should probably either get out of the relationship or begin at once looking for ways to improve it. Neither solution will be painless, but the longer you wait, the harder it will get.

Equality is difficult to define. Also, the need for equality is linked with all of the other needs. I have discussed this in Chapter 1, where I labeled equality between people as a symmetrical relationship and inequality as a complementary one. There may be times when you need to be superior, times when you need to be subordinate, and times when you need to be equal. These needs may even change so that in a situation when you were previously superior or dominant, you now want to be equal or subordinate. The point is that there are needs in relationships for equality; sometimes these are negotiated. Relationships tend to be stronger when people's needs for equality and inequality are met.

Communication in Friendship Relationships

The communication that occurs in friendship situations can be affected by all of the preceding factors. It is often personal and unique—highly idiosyncratic (peculiar to the constitution and temperament of the individuals involved). Much of the earlier discussion of communication within families (barriers, defensiveness, defensive-reducing strategies, steps for maintaining relationships) also applies to communication between friends. In this section I'd like to focus on the special qualities that characterize communication between friends.

The communication that goes on between friends represents a special case of exchanged discourse that has had little attention from researchers.[17] Among the kinds of communication that characterize friendship relationships, Mark Knapp lists self-disclosure, constructive discourse, forms of expressions, commitment, nonverbal messages, private jargon and meanings, and shared experiences as being the most important.[18] Each of these will be discussed in the following sections.

Self-disclosure.   Self-disclosure by friends contributes to the growth of relationships. Personal self-disclosures increase as relationships progress. Most disclosures prompt disclosures by others. Sometimes this does not occur immediately; however, it usually balances out over the duration of relationships. (See Figure 11.1.) It should be noted, too, that *perceived disclosure and perceived reciprocity of disclosure may be more important than what actually takes place.*

In one study of close relationships, Gerald Phillips found that disclosure was *not* an essential feature. What was essential was **regularity**—that is, our frequency of contact with another person is likely to be more important than the amount or kind of disclosure that occurs.[20] Phillips lists several kinds of contact; essentially, anything that brings us together regularly becomes important.

Constructive discourse.   Not only does disclosure occur more regularly in positive relationships, but there will be more positive disclosures than negative ones. For example, just the fact that Mike and Yvonne share ideas about anything and everything means that there are likely to be more positive disclosures than negative ones. When subjects come up, they discuss

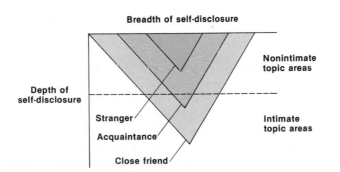

Breadth of self-disclosure

Depth of self-disclosure

Nonintimate topic areas

Stranger

Acquaintance

Intimate topic areas

Close friend

Figure 11.1[19]
Notice how the level of intimacy of a relationship affects both the breadth and depth of self-disclosure in that relationship. This figure also shows how breadth and depth of self-disclosure differ between you and a stranger, an acquaintance, and a close friend.

them. Sometimes their discussions lead to "heavy" topics, but more often "light" topics are the substance of their sharing.

Mike and Yvonne recognize the value and purpose of constructive discourse. Their attitudes toward it are positive. They know, for example, that conflict is a natural part of all human relationships, that not all conflicts can be resolved, that the feelings of the other person must be taken into account because the relationship is more important than the conflict, and that the good of all concerned is of more value than a personal victory.[21]

Forms of expressions. In strong friendship relationships, participants often use supportive forms of expressions—especially when relationships begin. **Absolute** statements such as "You are the most energetic person I've ever seen" often appear early but are not as prominent as relationships develop and more rationality takes over. Also, as relationships begin, forms of expression like "You're the greatest" or "I think you're fantastic" tend to be *repeated* over and over. Participants also use the *present tense* in friendship relationships: "We can see more of each other," or "I want to be your friend forever." There is a tendency toward hyperbole at the outset of most new relationships; this tendency is, perhaps, what helps relationships get off the ground.

Forms of address also change as relationships become closer. The more intimate we feel toward someone else, the less formal will be the form of address we use with them. You are introduced to a Mr. Richardson at a party. As you talk with him, you say, "I'm sorry, I didn't catch your name." He replies, "Howard." In talking to others you discover that his friends call him "Rich." Later, after much self-disclosure and considerable intimacy, you hear that his grandmother used to call him "Butch," and because this is a family (intimate) name, you adopt it for "Mr. Richardson." If you become his relationship partner or spouse, you may sometimes switch and call him "Honey" or "Sweetheart" for variety, and as the mood dictates.

Notice the stages through which the changes in forms of address occurred. "Mr. Richardson" is a formal form of address. "Howard" is ambiguous formal—ambiguous because it is capable of being understood in two possible senses: first, as informal if you do not know other alternative names and, second, as formal since this is Mr. Richardson's formal first name. "Rich" is informal. And "Butch," "Honey," or "Sweetheart" are used to show affection.[22]

Commitment. No satisfying relationship can exist for long without commitment. This is just as important in friendships as in family relationships. In his study, Phillips found there was a possessive element in most relationships.[23] This is revealed in a relationship when a third party intervenes. A third party often functions as an irritant, altering the relationship to accommodate the real or possible displacement of affection.[24]

A commitment is an obligation or pledge. In a relationship, this commitment is not revealed through possessiveness alone. Loyalty is another

Consider This

To be without friends is a cause for shame, a stigma, a symptom of personal deficiency that none of us takes lightly. Indeed, in notable ways, our very sense of ourselves is connected to our ability to negotiate the world of friendship.

—From *Just Friends: The Role of Friendship in Our Lives* by Lillian B. Rubin. Copyright © 1985 by Lillian B. Rubin. Reprinted by permission of Harper & Row, Publishers, Inc.

Consider This

While most of us want a close friendship, we also fear that in the process of meeting someone and becoming known to this person we may be found undesirable. For some people, this fear of rejection results in the formation of a false front, a mask to avoid being known. Hidden behind this mask is usually the belief, conscious or implicit, that to be one's real self is dangerous, that exposure of real feeling will lead to being un-wanted: "If people found out what I was really like, they wouldn't want any part of me."

—Joel D. Block, *Friendship* (New York: Collier Books, 1980), p. 180.

aspect of commitment. Loyalty involves faithfulness to the other person—steadfast affection, firm in adherence to promises that are (or have been) made or firm in observance of duty. Loyalty between partners means dependability—each partner can depend on the other.

A related aspect of commitment is constancy, or the word we have used for constancy, regularity. Phillips found that "in order to keep relationships going, constant talk and contact was imperative."[25] I prefer the word *regular* to *constant*, but the idea is the same. Behaviors tend to lose their value over time. That is, behavior that is immediate (now!) is vibrant and meaningful. Thus, to keep a relationship going, readjustments and continued negotiation are necessary. Relationships come apart when communication patterns become stereotypical. New behaviors need to be developed or old behaviors need to be examined with new eyes.[26] This requires commitment—a commitment to the friendship.

Commitment boils down to one essential question: How much do you care? People who want a friendship realize that friendships require time and energy. They require reciprocation. Whatever you expect to receive, you must be willing to give. In a relationship as in the marketplace, you get what you pay for.

Nonverbal messages.   Nonverbal messages become more important as relationships continue. For a moment look back at Figure 11.1. If the figure is relabeled on the left side "Areas of touch" and at the top "Amount of touch," the figure would reveal that we touch strangers nonintimately and occasionally touch acquaintances intimately, such as the goodbye kiss or the friendly pat on the shoulder. Only with close friends is touch intimate—especially with respect to areas and amounts. With strangers and acquaintances, we rely on widely understood and stereotyped touching. Intimacy brings about the use of a broad spectrum of nonverbal communication—including touch.[27]

Try This

Think of a friendship that has been worthwhile and meaningful for you. How has it required discipline, concentration, and patience? Have you noticed times during the development and maintenance of the friendship where you or the other person showed supreme concern? Think of some specific examples. Would you say that you have shown deep love for each other in this friendship? In what ways?

The nonverbal messages exchanged among friends are likely to vary dramatically from pair to pair. Some people tend to be "touchers"; others do not touch as much. The nonverbal messages exchanged among intimates will be associated with greater liking, warmth, and affection than those used with strangers or close acquaintances. Also, they are likely to occur more frequently.[28] Touches, for example, are likely to be greater in number, in length, and in number of places.

Eye contact among friends occurs more frequently than with strangers or acquaintances. Eye contact is likely to be held longer as well. Mutual eye gazing signals that communication channels are open, psychologically reduces physical distance, and is a useful method for gaining visual feedback.

Many other nonverbal behaviors increase as well. Friends are likely to nod more, lean toward each other more, maintain open arms and body, and direct the body orientation toward the other. Positive facial expressions of happiness, interest, joy, and amusement are likely to predominate over negative facial expressions.[29] Vocal characteristics may also reveal friendship. Friends may use a lower vocal pitch, softer voice, slower rate of speech, and somewhat slurred enunciation.[30]

Private jargon and meanings.   Friends often develop interpersonal jargon (terminology characteristic of only that pair) that reflects private symbols and private meanings. Certain common words and phrases come to have special meanings for them. Have you ever winked, smiled, or glanced at a close friend when one of "your" words or phrases was used publicly? These words and phrases come to be considered private possessions.

This can occur nonverbally as well. Have you ever shared a "special look" with a friend? The mutual eye gazing referred to in the previous section may provide opportunities for such exchanges—private worlds being shared in public situations through private means.

Shared experiences.   Over a period of time friends establish a relationship that is a unique enterprise with its own characteristic talk. In a sense, friends develop a unique cultural identity. A **cultural identity** is the distinguishing pattern of shared behaviors that includes thoughts, emotions, speech, and actions by which a relationship can be identified.

A cultural identity evolves; it cannot be forced. However, the more friends communicate, establish understandings, or share experiences, the sooner a cultural identity can be identified. The greater the shared expectations, experiences, and assumptions—and the more easily these can be pinpointed by both parties—the clearer, or more precise, the cultural identity.

So what? What is the value of a cultural identity? There are numerous values. Here are some: First, if necessary, a cultural identity makes it clear to the participants that a distinct relationship exists. Second, it helps define the relationship. The kind of relationship, depth of commitment, or level of intimacy can be determined once a definition of the relationship is discovered. Third, if the relationship is good, a cultural identity provides a positive history on which the participants can build. If the relationship is weak, it may offer ideas for change, growth, or progress. Also, the cultural identity may offer the suggestion that the relationship should be terminated. Fourth, it lets outsiders know that some mutual commitment has been made. Others may begin to treat the two of you as one—as members of the same relationship. This can be especially important where intervening third parties are involved.

I have included this chapter on family and friends because it is within such relationships that so much of our interpersonal communication occurs. Our success in these relationships depends largely on how much we care about succeeding. It is based on our attitude. No growth or change can occur if we do not care—if we do not commit ourselves to these relationships.

As friendships continue they sometimes develop into intimacy. At other times, intimate relationships develop separately from friendships. This chapter serves as a useful foundation for the next one on intimacy.

Notes

[1] Sven Wahlroos, *Family Communication: A Guide to Emotional Health* (New York: New American Library, 1974), p. xi.

[2] Virginia Satir, *Peoplemaking* (Palo Alto, Calif.: Science and Behavior Books, 1972), pp. 51–56.

[3] Wahlroos, *Family Communication*, p. xii.

[4] Jack R. Gibb, "Defensive Communication," *Journal of Communication* 11:3 (1961): 141–48.

[5] Gibb, "Defensive Communicatin," p. 141.

[6] From "Defensive Communication" by Jack R. Gibb, *Journal of Communication* 11:3 (1961): 147. Reprinted by permission.

[7] Gibb, "Defensive Communication," p. 147.

[8] Anthony Brandt, "Avoiding Couple Karate: Lessons in the Martial Arts," *Psychology Today* 16 (October 1982): 38. Brandt's conclusion is based on the work of John M. Gottman, *Marital Interaction: Experimental Investigations* (Orlando, Fla.: Academic Press, 1979).

[9] Brandt, "Avoiding Couple Karate," p. 41.

[10] Brandt, "Avoiding Couple Karate," pp. 41–42. Reprinted by permission of the author.

[11] John Dewey, *How We Think* (Boston: D. C. Heath & Co., 1910), p. 36.

[12] Andrew M. Greeley, *The Friendship Game* (Garden City, N.Y.: Doubleday & Co., 1971), p. 15. See also pp. 25–32, 46–56, 74–83, and 135.

[13] For more information on intimate communication see Gerald M. Phillips and Nancy J. Metzger, *Intimate Communication* (Boston: Allyn & Bacon, 1975), and Murray Davis, *Intimate Relations* (New York: The Free Press, 1973).

[14] Mark Knapp, *Interpersonal Communication and Human Relationships* (Boston: Allyn & Bacon, 1984), pp. 189–202.

[15] Knapp, *Interpersonal Communication*, pp. 197–99. Also see Robert E. Eubanks, "Relationships: The Manifestations of Humanness," in *Human Communication: The Process of Relating*, ed. George A. Borden and John D. Stone (Menlo Park, Calif.: Cummings Publishing Co., 1976), pp. 185–90.

[16] David Viscott, *How to Live with Another Person* (New York: Arbor House, 1974), p. 155.

[17] Gerald M. Phillips, "Rhetoric and Its Alternatives as Bases for Examination of Intimate Communication," *Communication Quarterly* 24 (1976): p. 11.

[18] Mark Knapp, *Social Intercourse: From Greeting to Goodbye* (Boston: Allyn & Bacon, 1978), pp. 174–75.

[19] Adapted with permission from Irwin Altman and W.W. Haythorn, "Interpersonal Exchange in Isolation," Figure 3, *Sociometry* 28 (1965): p. 422.

[20] Phillips, "Rhetoric and Its Alternatives," p. 21.

[21] Knapp, *Interpersonal Communication*, p. 216.

[22] Knapp, *Interpersonal Communication*, pp. 228–31.

[23] Phillips, "Rhetoric and Its Alternatives," p. 21.

[24] Phillips, "Rhetoric and Its Alternatives," p. 21.

[25] Phillips, "Rhetoric and Its Alternatives," p. 21.

[26] Phillips, "Rhetoric and Its Alternatives," p. 21.

[27] Knapp, *Interpersonal Communication*, p. 234.

[28] Knapp, *Interpersonal Communication*, p. 234.

[29] Albert Mehrabian, *Nonverbal Communication* (Chicago: Aldine Publishing Co., 1972).

[30] Joel R. Davitz, *The Communication of Emotional Meaning* (New York: McGraw-Hill Book Co., 1964), p. 63.

Further Reading

Steven A. Beebe and John T. Masterson, *Family Talk: Interpersonal Communication in the Family* (New York: Random House, 1986). The authors wrote this book to help readers better understand and improve communication in families. They divide the book into three parts: (1) Understanding Family Communication, (2) Improving Family Communication Skills, and (3) Managing Family Decisions, Conflict, and Change. This textbook includes chapter objectives, summary and application sections, discussion questions, activities, and suggested readings—a complete educational tool.

Joel D. Block, *Friendship* (New York: Collier Books, 1980). This book is the end product of a study based on 500 interviews, social science literature, and a national questionnaire survey completed by 2063 people. The author examines women, men, same-sex friendships, marriage, and divorce. In a final chapter he discusses the key ingredients in making friendship work: authenticity, acceptance, and direct expression.

Harold H. Bloomfield with Leonard Felder, *Making Peace with Your Parents: The Key to Enriching Your Life and All Your Relationships* (New York: Ballantine Books, 1983). Bloomfield and Felder offer a practical book full of examples and suggestions to help readers deal with family relationships. How do you express anger and love with your family? How do you deal with difficult parents? How do you deal with aging, dying, and death? Their final chapter is on becoming your own best parent. A useful book.

Kathleen M. Galvin and Bernard J. Brommel, *Family Communication: Cohesion and Change*, 2d ed. (Glenview, Ill.: Scott, Foresman & Co., 1986). This is an outstanding textbook that examines the family from a communication perspective. Depending heavily on the available research, the authors support the premise that communication undergirds family functioning. The focus is descriptive rather than prescriptive.

Eugene Kennedy, *On Being a Friend* (New York: Ballantine Books, 1982). From his perspective as a professor of psychology and former priest, Kennedy offers comforting insights into the joys and sorrows, laughter and tears, and rewards and difficulties of friendship.

Mark L. Knapp, *Interpersonal Communication and Human Relationships* (Boston: Allyn & Bacon, 1984). This fine textbook is about the way people communicate in relationships that are either developing or deteriorating. Full of examples based on research, the book offers very clear descriptions of the importance of communication in all relationships—with a strong emphasis on male-female dyads. The final chapter, "Developing Communication Skills," is an important resource for students.

Gerald M. Phillips and H. Lloyd Goodall, Jr., *Loving & Living: Improve Your Friendships and Marriage* (Englewood Cliffs, N.J.: Prentice-Hall, 1983). The authors offer readers an inside look at how ordinary, untroubled people communicate to make their marriages and friendships work. The book is based on ten years of extensive interviewing, and it is sprinkled with valuable advice from counseling professionals.

Gerald M. Phillips and Julia T. Wood, *Communication and Human Relationships: The Study of Interpersonal Communication* (New York: Macmillan Co., 1983). This is an interesting textbook, enriched by case histories of ordinary people, and focusing on sex roles as primary issues in contemporary relationships. The authors contend that people choose how to define themselves as well as how to deal with one another.

Lillian B. Rubin, *Just Friends: The Role of Friendship in Our Lives* (New York: Harper and Row, 1985). This is one of the best books on friendship I have discovered. Rubin includes a comprehensive bibliography, numerous footnotes, and depends on close to 300 interviews for her observations and suggestions. She is a noted social scientist, writer, and psychotherapist. In this book, she helps us understand ourselves and our relationships more fully.

Virginia Satir, *Peoplemaking* (Palo Alto, Calif.: Science and Behavior Books, 1972). Provides basic ideas for helping families discover the causes of some of their problems and offers creative ways of working through them. This is a clear and comprehensive treatment of family living—a workbook designed to enhance self-awareness, to stimulate partner conversation, and to induce new levels of family communication.

12 Seeking Closeness: The Course of Intimate Relationships

Learning Objectives

When you have finished this chapter you should be able to:

- Define intimate relationships and briefly explain each element of the definition.
- List and briefly describe some of the factors in others that affect how we feel about them.
- Identify the six stages of relationship development.
- Define small talk and explain its functions.
- Explain the verbal and nonverbal cues that reveal that integrating has occurred.
- Explain how intimate relationships can be maintained and nurtured.
- List and briefly explain the four characteristics of relational change.
- Explain the causes of relationship disintegration.
- List and briefly describe each of the five stages of relational disintegration.
- Describe four specific ways to improve intimacy skills.

Intimate relationships provide much of the structure of our society. Marriage is the best example—an institution in which intimacy is maintained over a period of time. Intimacy contributes to our personal needs by offering protection from loneliness. Intimate relationships also offer warmth, confidence, self-esteem, and love.

Obviously, not all dyadic relationships develop into intimacy. But intimacy is central to everyone's growth and fulfillment. One does not need marriage to achieve intimacy. It can occur in friendships as well as in romantic relationships, and, also in male-to-male or female-to-female relationships. No matter the type of relationship involved, the same factors in others have the same effects on how we feel about them, the same stages of relationship development and disintegration occur, the relationships are maintained and nurtured in much the same way, the same characteristics of relational change occur, and the same ways to improve intimacy skills apply.

And what are we likely to gain from intimacy? Most intimate relationships are deeply personal. Only with an intimate partner can we be and experience ourselves. They are emotionally gratifying. Only with an intimate partner can we express and share the range of emotions. They are mutually rewarding. Healthy relationships offer each partner gratification, affection, joy, and understanding. In intimate relationships both partners can candidly express themselves and not be rejected, share their tremendous joys and horrendous sorrows, and be spontaneous without concern for how they talk or how they will be received. How wonderful to be accepted despite weaknesses!

In this chapter, I will first discuss the nature of intimacy and some of the reasons we form intimate relationships. We will then look at the course of relationship development, at relational maintenance, and the promotion of relational growth. After examining relational change and the causes of disintegration, I will describe the stages of relationship disintegration and what happens when a relationship has been terminated. Finally, there is a brief section on how to improve intimacy skills.

What Is Intimacy?

When Stan began picking up Pete each day on his way to work, he had no idea how close they would soon become. During their half-hour ride together every morning, they first found themselves talking about their work, since that was what they seemed to have most in common. The discussion quickly moved to their backgrounds and families and then to their goals and aspirations. Although they were of different religions and political parties, they minimized these differences because they enjoyed each other's company. Besides, their differences seemed to add a unique dimension to their discussions: each approached life and its problems from a somewhat different perspective. They began calling each other in the evenings, and soon their families got together for barbecues and croquet. Stan and Pete shared an intimacy from which both gained benefits.

Alan Sillars and Michael Scott have defined intimate relationships as those "*in which there is repeated interaction, high self-disclosure, high interdependence (i.e., mutual influence), and high emotional involvement.*"[1] This definition assumes some important connection between the two indi-

viduals, and it emphasizes those elements distinctive to intimate and ongoing relationships. In this section I will briefly examine each element of the Sillars and Scott definition.

Repeated Interaction and High Self-Disclosure

The first two elements that help define intimate relationships suggest that intimates share a great deal of common experience. This is likely to increase their mutual understanding. Because of increased mutual understanding, those in intimate relationships are more likely to predict their partner's attitudes accurately, possess greater attitude similarity, predict the other's word choice in hypothetical conversations, possess specialized codes for communicating, and reveal greater efficiency in communication than non-intimates.

Repeated interactions and self-disclosure will cause communication between intimates to become more individualized. As couples become more intimate, this helps reduce any erroneous perceptions that may have resulted from reliance on cultural and social stereotypes earlier in the relationship. For example, one may have assumed that a partner was highly reliant on a close, tight-knit family (a cultural stereotype) but closer acquaintance shows that he or she is really quite independent. Or the assumption that a partner prefers quiet evenings at home rather than partying (a social stereotype) may be negated as one finds that he or she enjoys an active social life.

One interesting negative aspect of these first two elements is that having a great deal of information about someone *can* be misleading! For example, familiarity increases our confidence in our understanding of others. This confidence may lead us to take too much for granted. Individuals tend to overestimate how much they and their relationship partners know about each other, and therefore tend to seek less information. For example, if I think I *knew* that you would want to be with your family on *all* holidays or that you would *never* want to go to loud parties, I may never ask you about these matters.

Many examples of such overestimations exist. One partner, for example, knows the other supports causes that promote minorities and the underprivileged and assumes (without gaining further information) that this partner also supports a political candidate who espouses these causes. In another example, one partner knows the other likes to hike and explore the outdoors and assumes he or she also likes camping.

Another negative aspect, according to Sillars and Scott, is that repeated interactions and high self-disclosure may lead to the entrenchment of existing impressions. Familiarity leads individuals to believe their partners are constants—never changing. When new behavior occurs, they tend to view it as a continuation of previous behavior. This means that when individuals undergo personal changes, misperceptions may occur between intimate partners. The point is that the more we know, the more difficult it may be to accept new information. Relational change, as we will see in a later section in this chapter, is always difficult.

Interdependence

Each person's behavior in a relationship is partly a response to the other relationship partner. Interdependence is high in most intimate relationships because of the negotiation that occurs. Intimate partners, for example, negotiate unique modes of conduct, specialized communication codes, and even a joint identity.

The negative aspect of interdependence is that as it grows, we may reach a point where we feel we know *why* the partner behaves the way he or she does. We think we know the underlying traits, attitudes, intentions, or perceptions that cause the behavior. In fact, however, the partner could be exhibiting a new behavior that has no roots in the traits, attitudes, intentions, or perceptions with which we are familiar! For example, suddenly at a party, one partner becomes animated, engaging in friendly put-downs of others and telling jokes, whereas she has previously tended to be a wallflower. It may be that, unbeknownst to her partner, she is suddenly trying to be more outgoing, assertive, and fun-loving. And this is her debut!

This negative aspect is reinforced in conflict situations. When the reason for a behavior appears ambiguous, it is all too easy to blame the

Consider This

What does interdependence look like in relationships today? Francesca Cancian's position, from her book *Love in America* (Cambridge University Press, 1988), as interpreted by Pamela Black for *Psychology Today*, is this:

> . . . the new relationship models born mostly of the social upheavals of the 1960s and '70s are more equal but not necessarily less committed. They are based on self-fulfillment rather than sacrifice of one partner to the other, flexible gender roles and intimate, open communication.
>
> Interdependent partners both contribute to the economic and emotional well-being of the relationship. They are separate but not independent. Cancian points out that the values of the larger society tend to encourage independent over interdependent relationships.

—From "Alone Together" By Pamela Black in *Psychology Today,* 22 (April 1988): p. 72. Copyright © 1988 (PT Partners, L. P.). Reprinted with permission.

other person for the conflict. Also, when relationship patterns are involved in interdependent situations, partners may overlook many of the effects of their own behavior on others. For example, Sharon and Robb had agreed not to discuss politics because Sharon had been brought up in a rock-solid Democratic household whereas Robb's background was die-hard Republican. After a news broadcast, Sharon made a negative comment about what one news analyst said about the local Democratic candidate. Robb made no comment but discussed the news analyst's comment with coworkers the next day, and he told Sharon about the discussion at dinner that night. Sharon became upset since she thought they had agreed *not* to discuss politics. Robb thought Sharon was taking it all too seriously—getting upset because of a conversation he reported—but he blamed her for starting the conflict. Sharon thought it was Robb who was taking it too seriously by talking to his coworkers. At this point, their mutual distress was having an effect on each other, and the political issue had receded into the background. The actual reason for the conflict was a bit ambiguous; thus it was easy for each to blame the other!

Emotional Involvement

Sillars and Scott state that "emotions are felt most strongly and expressed most spontaneously between intimates."[2] These researchers cite evidence to support the claims that conflicts among intimates have greater potential to become physically emotional, that even milder forms of negative behavior occur more often, that relationship partners are less polite and interrupt each other more, show more disapproval of one another, communicate less positively, and use more emotional and abrasive conflict-resolution strategies.

There are three concerns with respect to emotionality among intimates. First, it tends to bias the interpretation of messages. Intimates presume greater agreement than actually exists and greater disagreement than actually exists. Sillars and Scott say, in addition, "We suspect that there may be an equal though less well-documented tendency for intimates to distort, by contrast, the meaning and affective intent of messages exchanged during emotionally involving conflicts."[3] In other words, when you get into a conflict with an intimate, the chances of misinterpretation are high.

The second concern suggests that intimates focus heavily on the negative and more dramatic actions of their partner and give less consideration to a partner's less noticeable behavior or to their own behavior. In other words, emotional expressions capture our attention just like a blinking neon light

Consider This

Notice how, in the following description, Katharine and David Viscott had to adapt to the ebb and flow of their relationship. There are two sides to intimacy—one is emotional and euphoric, the other is rational and challenging.

It was not always smooth. The arguments and the negativity Katharine and I sifted through often overwhelmed us. We sometimes lost our belief that we loved each other and became disillusioned and discouraged. We both considered calling it quits, but we realized that only people who are as close as we are could have such power to hurt each other. We came to accept that we were both still growing and that we needed to build self-confidence and trust and to hold our arsenals in check so we didn't retaliate, even when deliberately provoked. We believed in each other, and our love prevailed.

Being loved, feeling loved, and working out the difficulties between us proved to be the most important part of my own emotional growth. I was challenged at my weakest points and encouraged to become my best. I was supported in taking risks that previously I had barely dared to think about. If a goal made me happy, it was important to Katharine that I reach it. I learned that being loved was like having another self that loved the best *in me and insisted on seeing and communicating with it even when I had lost sight of it. I discovered that love was about being your best selves together.*

—David Viscott, *I Love You, Let's Work It Out* (New York: Simon and Schuster, 1987), p. 12.

in a neighborhood of lights of many colors and sizes. Thus, when a partner becomes highly emotional, we pay greater attention to the emotional presentation.

The third concern is that emotionality tends to short circuit any cognitive response. For example, in situations of high stress "individuals experience a drop-off in their ability to engage in complex integrated thought."[4] This drop-off results in less desire to pursue further information, failure to discriminate between items of information and points of view, and inability to see the difference between stereotypic and retaliatory responses and the perception of only one side of issues. Emotionality simply clouds issues and makes rational thinking and analysis difficult. Essentially, this supports the cliche, "My mind is made up, don't confuse me with the facts."

The point of the foregoing is not only to define intimacy, but it is also to point out some of the concerns and problems with intimacy. The four elements that clearly define intimate relationships are the same elements that can lead to relationship myopia (shortsightedness). Those who are entering an intimate relationship for the first time are especially prone to looking at the relationship through rose-colored glasses—in a way that makes everything look terrific. That is not necessarily bad; it is just unrealistic. This discussion of potential problems is not meant to appear pessimistic, but rather to serve as a challenge to potential relationship partners. The point is that we need to seek a balance; the same elements that define intimacy can lead to the destruction of intimacy.

Formation of Intimate Relationships

Why do we form intimate relationships with others? What is it about others that attracts us to them? In this section, we will focus on some of the factors in others that affect how we feel about them. These include competence, attractiveness, similarity, liking, and self-disclosure.

We Are Attracted to Competent but "Human" People

There is no doubt that we like people who are qualified, fit, and able. Surrounding ourselves with such people makes *us* feel qualified, fit, and able, and sometimes we think that, by association, their skills may rub off on us. But all the associations are not necessarily positive. Their competency may well make us look poor by comparison! Also, they may make us feel uncomfortable because they appear too unapproachable, perfect, and unlike us. Thus, when we think others are too competent, we are more attracted to them when they also appear human—capable of failing, of revealing some imperfections, of blundering now and then. We are attracted by competence, but we don't especially like perfection!

Try This

Before you begin this section, do your own survey of the top five characteristics others look for in a mate. While you are asking, find out the five least desirable characteristics as well. Tell others that you are involved in a psychological study. What you are likely to discover is that the most-preferred characteristics are those that anyone with a sense of caring, commitment, and self-esteem could easily fulfill!

We Are Attracted to Physically Attractive People

I think most of us would like to believe that people's personality, character, integrity, sincerity, and honesty are the qualities that attract us to them. And, indeed, if relationships continue, these traits are often responsible for that continuance, and the physical attraction that first may have brought us together recedes in importance. Initially, however, physical attractiveness is likely to be the *most* important factor that draws people together. No matter how old, no matter how committed to a current relationship partner, no matter how convinced we are that personality features are important, we can still be affected by a pretty face, a nice body, or a handsome profile. "Physical appearance is one of the most powerful determinants of attraction," says Don E. Hamachek, summarizing the research on this subject in his book on interpersonal relationships.[5]

One reason we are attracted to attractive people is probably that an attractive person seems to enhance our own credibility—it makes *us* look and feel good to be able to attract people with good looks, and others may think more highly of us because of it! Second, research suggests that we associate positive traits with good looks. Karen Dion and her colleagues found that good-looking people are generally thought to be more sensitive, kind, interesting, strong, poised, modest, sociable, outgoing, and exciting.[6] But Hamachek cautions that "attractive physical features may open doors but apparently, it takes more than physical beauty to keep them open."[7]

We Are Attracted to People Who Are Similar to Us

The essential element here is that the similarity occurs on core issues. Core issues are mutually important issues as opposed to trivial ones. For example, agreement on a favorite movie or brand of toothpaste would probably not be as important as agreement about vegetarianism, religion, politics, money, the family, and so on.

Why is similarity so important? First, when someone who is important to us agrees with us, it provides reinforcement for our own feelings. Second, when there is agreement on major issues, it helps avoid many of the needless, daily little hassles. For example, if both partners agree that being on time is important, the little annoyances of lateness are likely to be avoided. Third, similarity reduces the chances that we will have to change in any way. Change is difficult, especially on core issues.

It is useful to note that we do not like *all* people who are similar to us. When those with similar backgrounds and attitudes behave in strange or socially offensive ways, we tend to dislike them. Our dislike of them keeps them at arm's length and preserves and protects our self-image. Dislike of them also reduces the disturbing anxiety that we may have more in common with them than we may want to admit!

We Are Sometimes Attracted to Opposites

We often hear that opposites attract and, indeed, if they complement each other, they *do* attract because one partner's needs and characteristics help the other become more complete and well-rounded. But if the two are opposite on core issues or core personality traits, then their opposition may keep them at a distance. A dynamic, assertive individual may not get along with a low-energy, nonassertive individual. An orderly, neat person may find it difficult living with an unkempt, sloppy person. A deeply religious person may have trouble with an individual who is not at all religious.

The other side of this opposites coin is positive, however. One individual might be a person who makes quick, snap decisions and drives himself or herself very hard. The other may take his or her time making decisions and, thus, have a tempering, rational, calming effect on the partner. One person draws out the other while the other is slowed and relaxed. This could occur as well when one partner is dependent and emotionally needy and the other is highly nurturing and giving, or when one is dominant and the other is submissive.

We Are Attracted to People Who Like Us

Don't you experience a warm feeling when you hear that someone likes you? Hamachek considers this to be one of the most powerful influences in attraction. "Knowing that a person likes us, or even loves us, may be enough to start a relationship, but it is seldom enough, it seems, to keep a relationship going."[8]

We may not be attracted to someone who likes us, though, if we think they may have ulterior motives for doing so. Think of the anonymous telephone caller who begins by inquiring how you are. It sounds like a friend

Consider This

Some people have a deep fear of dressing attractively or looking sexy. There can be two reasons behind this. The first reason is a lack of self-esteem. If you see yourself as a loser, it may feel more natural to dress in plain, unappealing clothes. This also helps you keep your anxieties low, because if you don't come on too strong, people won't notice you and it won't seem as if you really have to compete for a mate. By maintaining a low profile, you won't have to confront your fears of rejection.

—David D. Burns, *Intimate Connections* [New York: New American Library (A Signet Book), 1985], p. 74.

calling, which immediately makes you want to respond. When you begin to suspect that the other person is after a sale, a donation, or some other favor, you may be less inclined to respond. Also, if the praise or feedback we are getting differs radically from our own estimation of what is appropriate, we may dislike those who like us. If somebody thinks we are beautiful, and we know we have only average looks, or if someone says we are brilliant and we know we are of average intelligence, we may feel an urge to pull away—to doubt the other's motives, to be suspicious, to remain skeptical and alert for hidden causes.

We Are Attracted to People Who Disclose Themselves to Us

For you to tell me something personal about yourself involves risk. But that risk indicates the presence of trust and an atmosphere of goodwill. That trust and goodwill are likely to cause me to trust you and to self-disclose in return. A cycle of mutual trust and reciprocity has begun which tends to increase attractiveness. Reciprocity and mutuality are necessary for a strong, enduring attraction to occur. Those unwilling to say much about themselves are likely to find few people attracted to them.

As we saw in Chapter 3, there are some guidelines for appropriate self-disclosure. To jump in with deep self-revelations too early in a relationship can reflect immaturity, insecurity, and phoniness. Timing is important. Also, people who disclose too much may be perceived as boring.

Stages of Relationship Development

Mark Knapp has identified five stages of relationship development.[9] I have included one additional stage suggested by writer Julia T. Wood.[10] These six stages of relationship development are initiating, experimenting, intensifying, integrating, revising, and bonding. These stages are not always discrete or clearly separated. These stages and the five stages of relationship disintegration (which will be discussed later) are presented in Table 12.1 along with some representative dialogue.

Initiating

The initiating stage may take as little as fifteen seconds and includes all those processes that occur as people first come together. We are at a party and see a stranger for the first time. We assess the person's attractiveness. We decide whether or not we want to initiate communication. We try to determine if the person is likely to be accepting: Is the person alone? In a group? Is he or she occupied? In a hurry? Next, we likely search for an appropriate

	Stage	Representative Dialogue
Relationship Development	Initiating	"Hi, how's it going?" "Fine, how about you?"
	Experimenting	"You like movies?" "Yes, very much."
	Intensifying	"I really love you." "I love you, too."
	Integrating	"What is mine is yours." "And what is mine is yours too."
	Revising	"We need to spend more time together." "You're right . . . let's try."
	Bonding	"Would you marry me?" "Oh, yes, yes, yes!"
Relationship Disintegration	Differentiating	"I do not like your friends." "I don't like yours either."
	Circumscribing	"How did work go today?" "Did you get the mail?"
	Stagnating	"I have nothing to say to you." "And I have nothing to say to you either."
	Avoiding	"I have too many things to do. I have no time to talk." "I'm not around when you are free anyway."
	Terminating	"As far as I'm concerned, our relationship is history." "That goes for me, too."

Table 12.1
Stages of relationship development and disintegration.

Adapted from *Interpersonal Communication and Human Relationships* by Mark L. Knapp. Copyright © 1984 by Allyn & Bacon, Inc. Used with permission. The stage of "Revising" is excerpted from *Human Communication: A Symbolic Interactionist Perspective* by Julia T. Wood, copyright © 1982 by Holt, Rinehart and Winston, Inc., reprinted by permission of the publisher.

opening line: "What brings you here?" "Do you know the host?" "Would you like a drink?" "Did you happen to hear on the evening news about . . .?"

In the initiating stage, often our goal is simply to present others with an attractive package—ourselves. We try to come across as pleasant, warm, friendly, empathic, and socially adept. In a sense, all we are doing is trying to present an attractive first impression that will open channels of communication for more contact and talk.

Experimenting

The goal of experimenting is to explore the unknown. Once initiation has occurred, you want to find out who this stranger is and what you have in common. This is the stage of "small talk," in which some rather standard information is collected in an informal, unstructured, and relaxed manner. We are not conducting an interview but engaging in comfortable give-and-take. Answers that are given are often expanded upon as mutual self-disclosure takes place. Examples and illustrations are used to fill in details and to make the experimentation stage interesting and enjoyable.

Small talk, Knapp suggests, often fulfills important and sufficient functions in relationships:

> *(1)It is a useful process for uncovering integrating topics and openings for more penetrating conversation. (2) It can be an audition for a future friendship or a way of increasing the scope of a current relationship. (3) It provides a safe procedure for indicating who we are and how another can come to know us better (reduction of uncertainty). (4) It allows us to maintain a sense of community with our fellow human beings.*[11]

Thus small talk is *not* necessarily a waste of time, as most people believe. Experimenting is a rewarding stage because communication at this point is usually pleasant, relaxed, casual, and uncritical. There are few commitments, and acquisition of information is usually interesting and unthreatening. Small talk, then, is the beginning of the disclosure process. If the small talk goes well, the relationship may proceed to the intensifying stage.

Many of my students want guidance at this stage—that is, they want some suggestions about what kind of information to discover. Of course, it would be inappropriate to begin grilling a person after just meeting him or her. Such behavior would be likely to end any potential relationship right there! But a variety of questions can be naturally and comfortably worked into conversations during the experimenting stage. You might want to try one or more of the following:

- What is your name?
- What do you do (like to do)?
- Where are you from (do you live)?
- What are your hobbies?
- What do you do for fun?
- What do you do for relaxation?
- Do you enjoy traveling?
- Are you a sports fan?
- Who is your favorite author?
- What kind of movies do you like to go to?
- Do you enjoy classical music (jazz, rock)?
- Who are your heros (heroines)?
- Are you active in politics?
- What is your religion? Do you attend services regularly?
- What would you like to be doing five years from now?

The point of all this may be to gain breadth, to pass the time, or even to prevent the relationship from developing further. We can maintain relationships at this level, and we often do. In fact, most relationships do not go beyond this stage.

It should be noted that some people consistently connect with others on a rather shallow level. They enjoy pleasant experiences and light conversation for a while and may be very impressed with each other's physical appearance. But they never bond more deeply. Their relationships are very different from those who choose to deepen their commitment, trust more, and bond more strongly. Many intelligent, educated people prefer the lighter style. A particular relationship may be only one of many valuable things in their personal life. Some people find relationships expendable. This may be especially true of those who have been previously wounded by intimacy—especially if they have been wounded deeply. Such a wound may create a lasting preference for lighter, less risky involvement.

Intensifying

When the intensifying stage is reached, an acquaintance has become a close friend. This includes greater commitment to the relationship, an increase in self-disclosure, and a willingness to make yourself vulnerable. You may wonder what signs indicate that the intensifying stage has been reached. Knapp offers six verbal cues:

> *(1) Forms of address become more informal—first name, nickname, or some term of endearment. (2) Use of the first personal plural becomes more common—"We should do this" or "Let's do this." (3) Private symbols begin to develop, sometimes in the form of a special slang or jargon, sometimes using conventional language forms that have understood, private meanings. (4) Verbal shortcuts built on a backlog of accumulated and shared assumptions, expectations, interests, knowledge, interactions, and experiences appear more often; one may request that a newspaper be passed by simply saying, "paper." (5) More direct expressions of commitment may appear—"We really have a good thing going" or "I don't know who I'd talk to if you weren't around." Sometimes such expressions receive an echo—"I really like you a lot." "I*

really like you, too." (6) Increasingly, one's partner will act as a helper in the daily process of understanding what you're all about —"In other words, you mean you're . . ." or "But yesterday, you said you were . . ."[12]

More reliance on nonverbal communication also occurs. Sometimes couples will replace talk with a touch or a gesture. To emphasize their commitment, individuals may allow their possessions and space to become more accessible to the other, and they may coordinate the clothes they wear to emphasize their growing relationship. In a sense, they are beginning to declare, publicly, a partnership.

Integrating

This stage represents greater commitment. The two individuals begin to blend, fuse, and coalesce. An important aspect of this stage (important because we will see a reversal of this when relationships disintegrate) is that the "I," "me," and "mine," that frequent the communication of individuals, becomes "we," "us," and "ours"—signifying sharing and mutuality. The relationship takes on a uniqueness that distinguishes itself from other relationships and from partners acting alone. Partners now share in perceptions, outlooks, and decisions. Rules, roles, definitions, and strategies are secured and tested at this stage.

Because individuals are so enthusiastic about each other in this stage, some distortion occurs. Optimism and euphoria sometimes cause partners to see what they want to see. Much as Sandy hates fishing, for example, she loves Paul so much that she takes fishing trips with him in order to be together and to get to know each other better. Raymond dislikes Christa's smoking, but he overlooks it because he knows how difficult it would be for her to give it up.

Once again, Knapp provides the verbal and nonverbal cues that reveal that integrating has occurred:

(1) Attitudes, opinions, interests, and tastes that clearly distinguish the pair from others are vigorously cultivated—"We have something special; we are unique." (2) Social circles merge and others begin to treat the two individuals as a common package—one present, one letter, one invitation. (3) Intimacy "trophies" are exchanged so each can "wear" the other's identity—pictures, pins, rings. (4) Similarities in manner, dress, and verbal behavior may also accentuate the oneness. (5) Actual physical penetration of various body parts contributes to the perceived unification. (6) Sometimes common property is designated—"our song," a joint bank account, or authoring a book together. (7) Empathic processes seem to peak so that explanation and prediction of

behavior are much easier. (8) Body rhythms and routines achieve heightened synchrony. (9) Sometimes the love of a third person or object will serve as glue for the relationship—"Love me, love my rhinos."[13]

Revising

Julia T. Wood adds a stage at this point. She suggests that after the intensity and infatuation of the integration stage, "individuals need time to think over what has happened, to get back in touch with themselves, and to consider the desirability of continuing the relationship."[14]

It is at this stage, after a rather emotional integrating stage, that rationality takes over. This is a highly intrapersonal stage because much of the assessment takes place as self-talk. "Can I learn to like fishing?" "Can I tolerate her smoking?" "Is he too dependent on me?" We may compare this relationship with others or this relationship partner with others. We may also consider other alternatives available to us. Are there other (better?) prospects?

Another set of considerations involves the kinds of changes likely to take place. Will I have to change to accommodate Bill's assertiveness, Lisa's intelligence, Steve's athletic ability, Tanya's attractiveness, Vince's generosity, or Cherie's orderliness and efficiency? Often, we compare ourselves with our partners. Am I willing to modify my values, attitudes, or behaviors? Who am I becoming because of this relationship, and do I like it? The revising stage allows us time to take stock. If we are unhappy, we may end the relationship at this stage. If not, we may pursue it.

Try This

What kinds of questions would you ask if you were to do a fairly complete assessment of your relationship at the revising stage? Here are some questions, perhaps you can think of others.

1. Do you listen to and empathize with each other?
2. Do you give each other encouragement and support?
3. Do you play together?
4. Do you express your feelings openly and freely?
5. Do you ask each other for things you are not getting?
6. Do you accept and work through your differences?
7. Do you identify, define, and solve problems together?
8. Do you work together well as a team?
9. Do you share opinions, thoughts, and ideas without becoming defensive?
10. Overall, are you satisfied with the relationship?

If we have decided to pursue a relationship, we may conclude that revisions or modifications are necessary. These revisions are usually negotiated in this stage as a result of requests from the partner. "I wish you would spend more time with me." "Maybe you could just try golf." "Your swearing is really obnoxious." "I wish you wouldn't watch so much TV." Such requests require some modification of behavior to make continuance of the relationship attractive and possible.

There is no doubt that this stage can breed anxiety, tension, and defensiveness. Accepting constructive criticism—even from a loved one—is difficult. Trying to change may be even more challenging. Changing is tough. How would *you* like to be asked to change your manner of dress, drinking habits, friends, language, or the way you deal with others? Such requests are normal at this stage, and such negotiation is often necessary to lay the proper foundation for the next stage. Establishing the proper atmosphere in the revising stage requires listening skills and maintaining a supportive climate. Anxiety, tension, and defensiveness can be reduced by sensitive, empathic, supportive communication between partners. Success at this stage is likely to lead to bonding.

Bonding

The main difference between this stage and all the others is that the others are processes; bonding is both an event *and* a process. Bonding is a commitment to the revised relationship. A bonding ceremony may be public or private. If it's public, such as marriage or going steady, the relationship gains social or institutional support because the couple can rely on laws, policies, or precedents for guidance. If private, the couple must rely on each other to keep the relationship intact. Bonding is simply the contract for the union of the two individuals.

Features of the bonding event are that it is voluntary, for an indefinite period (who knows how long it will last?), and under special rules. The voluntary commitment can be a powerful new force in the relationship. Individuals have new freedom to interact and discuss without worrying that trivial concerns will break up the relationship. They can be themselves more.

The indefinite period of commitment causes a hardening of the relationship to occur. Partners cannot leave each other as easily. There is likely to be a change in the language used between partners as they become more relaxed and informal. The contract itself may be a frequent topic of conversation.

Special rules refer to the social and institutional, formal and informal guidelines that assist partners who are going steady, engaged, or married. No longer are partners as free to see former boyfriends and girlfriends. There may be some restrictions on partners' freedom to see their former group of friends, perhaps even other family members. More time is spent together. Generally, individuals in a relationship support each other when in the presence of others. Decisions are now made jointly. When a decision that

affects both partners or the relationship must be made, each individual must consult the other and not behave as though the other does not exist. And when and where individuals in relationships go—and their freedom to go—is usually negotiated. One partner usually knows where the other is. All of this because bonding has occurred! New rules causing new adjustments resulting in new behaviors!

Bonding is a process too. Once a commitment has been made, the relationship will continue to evolve. To think of bonding just as an event may lead people to believe that evolution stops. Those who have bonded recognize the need to view what happens next as relationship maintenance, negotiation, adjustment, and readjustment. To suggest that the development of a relationship ends here—with the possible exception of disintegration or dissolution—is to deny the rewards, excitement, challenges, and interest that relationship partners who have moved to this stage can and often do experience. Indeed, I believe that this stage, at most times, may be equated with peak communication—"complete emotional and personal commun-ion."[15] Some may believe this correlation with peak communication is too zealous or enthusiastic, but at least it should be viewed as a goal or as a realistic possibility.

Maintaining and Nurturing Intimate Relationships

The chances of two people sharing the same blueprint for a relationship are rather slim. But the chances decrease dramatically when there is no communication. Without communication frustration is likely to result and both partners may give up whatever ideals they brought to the relationship, either settling for a mediocre relationship or allowing whatever relationship existed to disintegrate.

But let's assume for the moment that intimacy is desired and achieved. How do people maintain it? What are the keys to sustaining interest? We will examine communication, sharing activities, constant effort, and protecting individuality.

Communication

Intimacy involves talking together. Without talk, relationships become stalemated, partners become walled off from each other, and any exchanges that do take place become superficial, unable to touch the deep, real concerns of the participants.

Why is communication essential? Often, relationships are thought to be stable, static, fixed entities. However, this is far from true. A relationship is a dynamic, fluid, constantly changing mixture that reflects the changes in

---

Try This

One of the problems with relationships is that we seldom discuss—within the relationship itself—matters that relate to the relationship. Allow some time in your current relationship to sit down and talk. The following questions are designed to give you something to talk about:

What is an intimate relationship? What does it ask of me? Of you?

What are our expectations of this relationship? Of each other?

Does our relationship mean exclusivity? What kinds of freedom will be provided? Is it us, only us, and no one else but us?

Does our relationship mean long evenings talking and laughing together?

Does our relationship mean sharing a closeness both physically and psychologically?

Does our relationship mean having sex? Living together? Having gourmet meals?

Where do the two of us want to be—with respect to this relationship—in six months? One year? Five years? Ten years?

---

the relationship partners and in their life situations. Without communication, these changes may not be understood, may cause surprise or even shock, and may lead to deterioration rather than growth of the relationship.

Changes in relationships cause inevitable and constant difficulties. Partners must adjust and face the obstacles together. How they do this is unique to each relationship and, often, cannot be predicted. But with open communication at a deep, meaningful level, the chances for adjustment improve and the chances for relational growth improve as well. Relationship partners who stubbornly resist change and growth may find growing dissatisfaction in their relationship with concurrent problems and crises and likely disintegration.

Sharing Activities

Intimacy involves both talking *and* doing together. Talking and doing enhance each other. Activities offer opportunities to see into each other. We not only get a better look at our relationship partner, but we can approve

---

Try This

Tensions develop from time to time in any relationship. Healthy relationship partners take the time to study the tensions that exist, explore some of their underlying dynamics, and take some steps toward resolving them constructively. This is accomplished together as the partners share ideas, insights, and suggestions. Take time out with your partner to air, clarify, and possibly resolve any discomforts, frustrations, hurts, or irritations (however slight). Find a comfortable, quiet place, and the two of you, *each* complete the following sentences:

One of the ways I sometimes hurt you is . . .
One of the ways I sometimes make you angry is . . .
One of the ways I sometimes frustrate you is . . .
One of the ways I sometimes make it difficult for you to love me is . . .
One of the ways I sometimes make it difficult for you to give me what I want is . . .

Listen as your partner completes the sentences. Feel free to discuss and expand on responses that are given. This is a time for sharing. Change the sentence stems, as necessary, to make them apply directly to your relationship and your relationship needs.

—Nathaniel Branden, *"If You Could Hear What I Cannot Say": Learning to Communicate with the Ones You Love* (New York: Bantam Books, 1983), p. 162. Copyright © 1983 by Nathaniel Branden. Published by Bantam Books.

of what we see as well. Earlier we labeled this benefit of relationships as ego building—contributing to the positive development of self. We want our partner to accept that part of the self we expose. The sharing of activities can bring people very close.

Some shared activities are *rituals*. A ritual is a patterned interaction that is predictable. Because ritual behavior is governed by rules (either given or negotiated), it is also recognizable by other members of the culture and repeatable at other times and places. Anniversaries, honeymoons, and birthdays are rituals as well as such holidays as Thanksgiving, Christmas, Valentine's Day, and Easter. But rituals also can include the once-a-week lunch dates, the Friday afternoon happy hour with partner and friends, the weekly dinner out, or the nightly walk around the block. Rituals affirm the value partners place on spending time together, and they serve to anchor the bond and promote relational growth. They are a great means for sharing activities.

Constant Effort

Andrew Greeley has said, "Intimacy . . . is always difficult, and when it stops being difficult it stops being intimacy."[16] Not only is intimacy difficult to achieve, it is difficult to sustain. It requires both work and patience. The ideal relationship is sometimes described as a 50-50 effort. But with this ratio, if either partner decides to let the relationship slide, intimacy will suffer. The best guideline, if you want intimacy badly enough, is for *each* partner to give the relationship 100 percent of their effort, and the relationship will absorb the extra energy. When Eric and Linda were in school, they found increasing tensions between them. When they talked about it, both realized they had let the pressures of school eclipse the importance of their relationship with each other. Although school was important to both of them, they decided to set aside a specific amount of time each week just for themselves. And they soon found their relationship once again growing pleasurable. Such decisions are not easy. They must take into account the age of the relationship partners, their goals, and the nature of their relationship.

Protecting Individuality

Talking about marriage in *The Prophet*, Kahlil Gibran says, "But let there be spaces in your togetherness, and let the winds of the heavens dance between you." Gibran continues in this way:

> Love one another, but make not a bond of love:
> Let it rather be a moving sea between the shores of your souls.
> Fill each other's cup but drink not from one cup.
> Give one another of your bread but eat not from the same loaf.

Sing and dance together and be joyous, but let each one of you be alone,
Even as the strings of a lute are alone though they quiver with the same music.[17]

Intimacy must not destroy individuality, but too much individuality can destroy intimacy. A useful way to view dependence, independence, and interdependence in a relationship is in terms of an A, H, and M frame, as illustrated in Figure 12.1.[18] The A frame represents dependence. Absorption in the other is so strong that if one partner lets go, the other falls. In the reverse situation, shown in the H frame, there is strong individual identity, a great deal of self-sufficiency, and no couple identity. If one partner lets go, the other hardly feels it. Finally, in the M frame, there is interdependence, a combination of dependence and independence. If one partner lets go, the other feels a loss but recovers balance. There is meaningful couple identity without sacrifice of individual identity.

Although partners must give themselves to the relationship and to each other, they must also exist as individuals. When people grow together as a couple, they must be free to grow as individuals as well—the M frame. Whose responsibility is this? Partners need to guard each other's personal need for individual freedom to grow and yet protect interdependence. This underscores the reasons why constant communication is essential, because with growth comes change. When intimacy becomes oppressive, partners need to back off before coming back together for more intense involvement or, perhaps, for a newly redefined level of involvement.

A FRAME

DEPENDENCE

If one lets go, the other falls.

No individual identity

Self absorbed in the other

Strong couple identity

H FRAME

INDEPENDENCE

If one lets go, the other hardly feels a thing.

Strong individual identity

Self-sufficient

No couple identity

M FRAME

INTERDEPENDENCE

If one lets go, the other feels a loss but recovers balance.

Healthy individual identity

Self relates meaningfully to the other

Meaningful couple identity

Figure 12.1
Levels of dependence in relationships.

Consider This

The husband was not willing to take the time to do with her [the wife] what she enjoyed. He was caught up in restoring old cars. When it became evident his endless hours in the garage were tearing their relationship apart, she made her decision. Donning a pair of coveralls, she entered the garage, crawled under a car beside her husband, pointed to what he was working on and said, "What's that?" He described the transmission to her and she permitted him to turn her into an automobile nut like himself. Now the endless hours together in the garage restoring old cars have revitalized their relationship.

—Charles M. Sell, *Achieving the Impossible: Intimate Marriage* (New York: Ballantine Books, 1982), pp. 40–41.

Relational Change

The development and maintenance of relationships always involves change. Richard Conville, a researcher of interpersonal communication, has speculated about change. He claims that change in any part of the relationship is likely to affect the whole relationship. Conville identifies four characteristics of relational change: (1) predictability, (2) uniqueness, (3) obliqueness, and (4) exchange.[19] These characteristics affect partners whether the relationship is developing, being maintained, or disintegrating.

Predictability

Predictability refers to the nature and order of change. Conville suggests that relational change that alters the relationship itself follows a predictable course. Once change begins, certain other stages of change must follow. After three years of living with John, Diane realized that her romanticized world was not what she really wanted. As a result, Diane lost a clear picture of the future. Her relationship with John became ambiguous. No clear definition of the relationship seemed possible because of her new perspective. Because normal humans cannot exist long without anchors in the future and anchors, as well, in significant others, Diane struggled for stability. She finally found it in her own values. This, according to Conville, is a predictable course of events.

Changes in relationships create new concerns not previously faced. Thus, the way partners evaluate and assess change, like Diane and John's need to evaluate and assess her changed view, need to change as well. Part of predictability is also the struggle necessary to obtain stability within the relationship. Diane and John faced a new situation. This potential change in their relationship may make it stronger or weaker, but whatever happens, it will be different because of the change, and Diane and John will evaluate the relationship differently both now and in the future.

Uniqueness

Because relational change is unique to each couple, there are no sure-fire, guaranteed methods for dealing appropriately with it. Whenever change occurs, partners are forced to fight for survival. Whether it involves a change in jobs or geographical location, the death of a parent, a divorce, a religious conversion, or a risk-laden journey, individuals seldom can rely on past experiences for guidelines on how to respond. People are severely jolted, forced to rely on their own resources, and faced with the need for an intense struggle. In many cases, it is just such a struggle—partners working together in a battle for the survival of the relationship—that brings individuals closer together and cements the bond. But *how* the partners deal with the change, and how that cementing occurs (if it does), is likely to be unique.

Obliqueness

One meaning of oblique is "indirect" or "not straightforward." Conville suggests that when partners are in the midst of relational change, they cannot see what is happening. "Their awareness of the change is indirect—not straightforward. Partners may be aware that some change is occurring, but it is only upon reflection—looking back—that the individuals may be able to understand the true nature of the change and its effect on them.

Moving closer to a partner's parents may be a good example of obliqueness. Such a move is likely to have profound effects on a relationship. These effects may occur so rapidly that it is impossible to digest them all: more meals with the relatives, more coordination of plans, more visits, more exchange of gifts, more interference with personal plans, less time together for the relationship couple, etc. Nothing can be done about it. However, after a move away from this situation, both partners are able to look back on the situation and understand its effect. They use the experience as a basis for sharing stories and advice with others. But at the actual time of the experience their only thoughts may have been how to change the situation.

Of course, a situation does not have to be *past* before partners can look at it objectively. Sometimes, when the emotional attachments are low, or when there is low differentiation in the attitudes toward the situation, partners might be able to adjust to situations to face them with equanimity. Sometimes, it takes both time and distance from a situation to achieve the objectivity and calm rationality required to deal appropriately with it.

Exchange

Change also involves exchange. Conville claims it is "the exchange of certain present securities for certain future securities."[20] Take the case of Don and Mary Ann. Their present securities include spending time together, having a "traditional" DINK (Double-income-no-kids) relationship with a "traditional" division of labor, and the security of experiencing no change. Mary Ann is considering accepting a promotion to supervisor. Possible future securities include increased income, one partner (the wife) having a higher-status position, and the likelihood of acquiring a new group of friends (her new colleagues). Would these individuals risk exchanging their present securities for these future securities?

Sometimes, individuals choose to maintain a relationship because present securities are better than what they see as *no* securities. For example, having a guaranteed date, transportation, companionship, and a group of friends may seem much better than having none of these securities at all, or trying to build a new relationship with someone else. "It's not the best relationship or the ideal person," one may say, "but it is better than none at all!" When change occurs, all of us must assess our relationship in terms of exchange. Is the exchange of securities worth the risk?

Why Relationships Disintegrate

Disintegration can be caused by either partner, both partners, or neither partner. Either partner may decide to go a separate way, to take on a new partner, or to go it alone while the other wants to continue the relationship. Both partners may come to an agreement that separation would be best. Or both partners may want to continue, but other situations may intervene that cause disintegration. The partners, for example, become unavoidably separated by distance, or one partner who had free time takes on a job, or the life-styles of the partners change. Although neither wants the change in intimacy, it happens nonetheless. Sometimes outside threats will strengthen relationships, at other times weaken them or tear them apart.

One way to view disintegration would be with respect to our total energy bucket. Think of each one of us having a bucket 100 percent full of energy. We can distribute that energy in any way we choose. (See Figure 12.2.) Now, what happens to the energy distribution when we become preoccupied with ourselves? When we have a massive inferiority complex? When we feel unloved or unworthy? Some of the energy shifts to ourselves, and we have less available to give to the relationship.

The same thing (a shift in energy) occurs when we become preoccupied with a task. Less energy remains for the relationship. Once we get our own personal problems solved, and once our work can be a balanced, normal,

Figure 12.2
How much energy do we have to give to a relationship? When we are preoccupied with ourselves, or preoccupied with a task (our work), the relationship is likely to suffer.

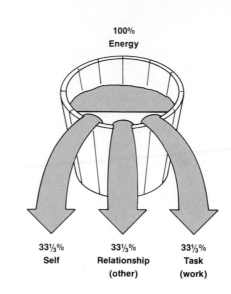

100%
Energy

33⅓%
Self

33⅓%
Relationship
(other)

33⅓%
Task
(work)

integrated part of our lives, then we are likely to have more energy to give to the relationship, and disintegration is less likely to occur.

Sometimes partners need to weigh the costs versus the rewards of continuing the relationship. It may be that disintegration is the best thing. Phil and Sam, partners in a small business, realized, for example, that they were doing everything together. Phil wanted his independence—partly to free himself to seek new business contacts. Alice and Paul realized that they were both being smothered by their relationship. They decided they both needed more distance to give them a chance to think about themselves, each other, and the relationship.

An important consideration for people embarking on an intimate relationship for the first time is the restriction that intimacy tends to impose. Chris wondered, for example, how willing she should be to give up other potential relationships. She quickly discovered that her new relationship was likely to prevent her from making other new friends. Keith recognized that his new relationship was preventing him from exploring different types of relationships with different people. He wanted freedom to experiment and explore.

Each relationship is different. What may be benefits for some may be burdens for others. It is impossible to offer specific guidelines for couples, but those who are experiencing some waning interest in a relationship might want to discuss the benefits of staying together or breaking up. In many cases, such discussions offer lessons that can be used later. Gene learned from one such discussion that every time a relationship reached intimacy, he lost interest in it. With that knowledge, he began to approach intimate situations differently. Table 12.2 is Michael Cody's list of the causes that can precipitate disintegration of a relationship—or what he calls "relational disengagements."

1. I realized that he/she had too many faults (personality and otherwise).
2. I felt his/her personality was incompatible with mine.
3. I felt that she/he was too demanding.
4. The partner behaved in ways that embarrassed me.
5. Generally, the partner's behaviors and/or personality was more to blame for the breakup than anything else.
6. I realized she/he was unwilling to make enough contributions to the relationship.
7. I felt that he/she no longer behaved towards me as romantically as she/he once did.
8. I felt that he/she took me for granted.
9. I felt that he/she wasn't willing to compromise for the good of the relationship.
10. I simply felt that the relationship was beginning to constrain me and I felt a lack of freedom.
11. Although I still cared for the partner, I wanted to start dating other people.
12. While this relationship was a good one, I started to get bored with it.
13. The partner made too many contributions, and I started to feel suffocated.
14. I felt that she/he was becoming too possessive of me.
15. Although I still liked the partner, I felt that the romance had gone out of the relationship.
16. I was primarily interested in having a good time and not with maintaining a relationship.
17. I felt that he/she was too dependent upon me.
18. The two of us simply developed different interests and had less in common.
19. I realized that I couldn't trust him/her.
20. One of us moved away and we couldn't see each other very much.
21. Most of my friends (or all of them) didn't like him/her (most of his/her friends didn't like me), causing problems that detracted from the relationship.
22. Generally, the relationship itself didn't seem right and the faults of the relationship could not be blamed on any one person in the relationship.
23. My parents didn't approve of him/her (or her/his parents didn't approve of me).
24. The partner showed too much physical affection (or was too aggressive).

From Michael J. Cody, "A Typology of Disengagement Strategies," *Communication Monographs* 49:3 (September 1982): 162. Reprinted by permission of the Speech Communication Association and the author.

Table 12.2
Causes precipitating relational disengagements.

Relationships disintegrate for many different reasons. John and Tracey had formed a relationship just when their previous intimate relationships had terminated. But both had formed new support groups, and they now felt their needs for each other had virtually ceased. Dan and Sandy had established an intimate relationship in high school. Dan went to work for his father in an independent insurance company, and Sandy went on to college. It was in Sandy's junior year that it became clear to her that her attitudes had become incompatible with Dan's, that her intellectual interests and abilities had outdistanced Dan's, and that her major goals had changed. Their relationship had begun to wobble and was now coming unglued.

Stages of Relational Disintegration

There is no inevitability in relational disintegration. That is, just because a relationship begins to disintegrate does not mean there is no turning back. Knowing the stages and what *can* happen helps couples become aware of a problem. Entering the first stage of disintegration may be enough to create the awareness of a need for renewal. In such cases couples may:

Consider This

Dissatisfied partners tend to keep their unhappiness secret at first as they contemplate, brood on, and quietly assess the situation. This allows them to continue participating in routine aspects of life with the other person. As unhappiness grows, they begin to reveal it but often in a vague and ill-defined manner.

These early attempts to communicate dissatisfaction usually take the form of complaints aimed at changing the other person or the relationship to better suit the needs of the initiator. He or she may complain, for example, about how the other person spends leisure time. "Why do you watch TV all the time? Why don't you turn it off and do something else?" But television isn't usually the issue. The initiator may be questioning the partner's level of commitment or the appropriateness of a relationship with a person who has nothing better to do than watch the tube.

Such complaints fail to communicate that the relationship is the real problem. At this stage, the initiator may not be able to articulate the deeper reasons for his or her unhappiness. The partner, trying to be cooperative, may even turn off the television, thus eliminating the symptom but not the problem.

Instead of complaining, initiators may use sullenness, anger and a decrease in intimacy to suggest unhappiness . . . .

—Diane Vaughan, "The Long Goodbye," *Psychology Today*, 21 (July 1987): p. 38. Adapted from *Uncoupling: Turning Points in Intimate Relationships* by Diane Vaughan, Oxford University Press, 1986.

- confront problems
- renegotiate roles
- get back in touch
- institute new rituals
- renegotiate rules

- explore changes
- revise their world
- redefine their relationship
- recommit themselves
- get outside help

We need not assume that when something interferes with an intimate relationship, disintegration will follow. What really determines the effect of the interference is *commitment: the obligation partners feel toward each other and the relationship.* Relationship strength is often directly related to commitment strength. How much do partners care? When the commitment is very strong, many obstacles can be overcome and the process of disintegration can be reversed. Partners need not allow themselves to be victims of disintegration, or victims of negative influences. They *can* fight back if they use the strategies suggested for maintaining intimacy and those at the end of this chapter on improving intimacy skills. Even if disintegration has begun, it should be clear that at *any* stage partners may decide to reverse the process by using the renewal strategies listed above.

Knapp suggests that there are five stages of disintegration. These are differentiating, circumscribing, stagnating, avoiding, and terminating.[21]

Differentiating

Since this is the first stage of disintegration, it is simply a signal that problems are occurring. Differentiating partners make clear the differences they see in each other. Instead of focusing on the other and on the relationship, individuals begin to focus on themselves. How are *they* different? Perhaps the best sign of this change in focus is the change in language. The "we," "us," and "our" that become a signal that integrating was occurring reverts to the "I," "me," and "mine" used before the relationship began. Shared possessions, shared friendships, and shared times become less important. Conversations focus on the awareness of differences.

Circumscribing

The point of circumscribing is to control areas of discussion and restrict communication to safe areas. This means fewer interactions, less depth in the subjects discussed, and shorter communications. Partners avoid risky topics, topics related to basic values or hidden secrets, or topics that require extended discussion. A whole new set of ground rules comes into play, prescribing what is acceptable and unacceptable as far as permissible interaction topics.

Couples avoid inappropriate discussion with comments like, "I'd rather not talk about that," "Let's call discussion of *that* off limits," "*That* is none of your business," or with silence. Sometimes, to avoid a discussion, one partner will simply change the topic.

Stagnating

Stagnation means no motion or activity. As the disintegration progresses, partners decide that total silence in each other's presence is better than oral communication. Most areas and topics are closed off from discussion, even the superficial. Participants just mark time now until the end. When they have to talk they treat each other as strangers. Any discussion of the relationship is off limits. Knapp characterizes communication at this stage, when it occurs, as "more stylized, difficult, rigid, hesitant, awkward, and narrow."[22] The main theme characterizing this stage, according to him, is "There is little sense bringing anything up because I know what will happen, and it won't be particularly pleasant."

You may wonder why anyone would delay at the stagnating stage. There may be a number of reasons. Individuals may be gaining rewards outside this relationship—at work, in their primary family, or with another relationship partner. Some may simply be avoiding the eventual pain of termination or even hoping to revive the relationship. Some, too, may enjoy giving the pain they think they have already suffered—an eye for an eye!

Consider This

Because couples have differences does not mean they need to terminate their relationship. Couples who are making it have developed their own private and unique ways to continue their commitment. Notice how Rick A. chooses to continue his relationship:

RICK A.: Like all people, me and Susan have topics we don't like to hear about. I can't stand it when she talks about her cousins. I hate her cousins. She doesn't like locker-room talk—you know, bad jokes and stories about what the guys do. So we agreed we'd get phone pals. She found a cousin willing to talk about cousins all night, and I got one of the guys who would swap yarns with me almost any time I wanted to, and when one of us brought up a forbidden topic, the other one would give a signal to get on the phone, and then that person would leave the room so he or she wouldn't have to listen to the phone call. Learning that little trick taught us how to be very honest with what we could tolerate. I think it saved us a lot of pain.

—From Gerald M. Phillips and H. Lloyd Goodall, Jr., *Loving & Living: Improve Your Friendships and Marriage* (Englewood Cliffs, N.J.: Prentice-Hall, 1983), p. 125.

Avoiding

This is a transition stage between stagnating and terminating the relationship. In avoidance, however, individuals attempt to remove themselves from the same physical environment. Participants seek to avoid face-to-face or voice-to-voice interaction of any kind. "I don't want to see you," or "I want to avoid communicating with you," are the messages being sent at this stage. Unfriendliness and antagonism may accompany these messages.

If partners are unable to avoid one another, they will act as if the other is not present. They remove themselves from any interactions. They may inject negative evaluations of the other when possible. They seldom offer any rewards to the other like a "Congratulations" for getting a raise, or a "Good luck," when facing a difficult situation. These tactics tend to lower the other's self-concept and, perhaps, lead him or her to question "Am *I* still all right?" "Am *I* still lovable?"

Terminating

Often the terminating stage is not a stage at all but just an end or an announcement of final separation. Individuals settle their final "joint" concerns such as property, custody of children and pets, or the last phone bill. Also, they construct necessary psychological barriers to create distance: "It was bound to happen sooner or later," "It will be better for both of us," or "We were never *really* meant for each other." These make any final grieving—if it occurs—easier.

Termination dialogue is characterized by messages that create distance and disassociation. But these messages are likely to vary with the kind of relationship being dissolved and how the final dissolution takes place. Was there a lengthy commitment? What was the relative status between the partners? What kind of relationship was it? What kind of future relationship was desired? How was the dialogue conducted? By telephone? By letter? Face-to-face?

When Terminating Is Over

As anyone who has been part of a serious relationship knows, sometimes terminating is *never* over. The relationship remains in our consciousness forever—sometimes with good and sometimes with bad residual effects. But relationships change people. We are different people because of them. They may alter our values, attitudes, and behaviors as well as our future plans, needs, and expectations. We may reassess ourselves, and we may alter the criteria we use to judge potential relationship partners or relationships. We may decide to wait until *we* are more mature, more secure, or more prepared. We may choose never to enter a relationship again. We may choose to avoid people who are neurotic, nervous, smothering, mothering, domineering, or

"You are about to experience something rare in your life, Stan—rejection."

Drawing by Koren; © 1988 The New Yorker Magazine, Inc.

untrustworthy. Whatever the case, terminated relationships provide an enduring point of comparison for all future relationships.

Improving Intimacy Skills

The concept of intimacy demands several things of relationship partners. Success in intimacy often results from a union of differences.[23] The following sections describe how couples can use these differences to enhance their relationships.

Accept each other's differences.   For a satisfying relationship, partners must learn to accept each other's differences. One of the joys of intimacy is learning to receive and know fully a person different from yourself. Too often these differences are allowed to drive people apart because one partner is unwilling to allow the other to be himself or herself.

Another problem is competition. Sometimes we reject our partner's differences and begin to compete with them. This happened in the beginning of my own relationship with my wife. Once we talked about it, we both realized that a strength for one of us—either one of us—was a strength for both of us. Although competition may be friendly at first, it can become critical and destructive.

See differences as a chance for intimacy.   Differences can provide a great opportunity for intimacy. One of the biggest contributions we can make to the development of trust and respect in a relationship is to understand the other as a unique human being. Frank had recently been overlooked for a promotion. He was feeling depressed, but he didn't feel he could talk to his good friend Jim about it. Frank and Jim were opposites. Jim was very assertive, outgoing, and buoyant. He seemed to sail through life without problems. Frank was unassuming and rather shy. How could he expect a person like Jim to understand how he was feeling? When he finally decided to talk to Jim, he found Jim not only supportive but helpful in suggesting some options. Sharing his feelings with someone very different from himself gave him a new perspective on his problems—and served to strengthen their friendship.

See differences as complementary.   A good relationship rests on the formula "One plus one equals three." This simply means that the whole is greater than the sum of the parts. Each person in an intimate relationship is a unique human being who brings this uniqueness to the relationship. When you add the strength of one partner to the strength of the other, the result is a sum that could not be achieved by either acting separately: hence three instead of two in the formula.

Sometimes it is the differences that keep the intimacy relationship strong. One partner is a socially quiet person and the other is an outgoing person. The socially quiet person helps contain the excesses of the other while the outgoing person helps draw out and encourage the other. Robin is easily depressed and Andy is lighthearted. He helps her with her down moods much as Jim helped Frank in the previous example:

> *Depressed again, she sits in her dormitory room wondering how she can make it through the evening. Then she hears his Suzuki coming down the street and her sadness begins to lift.*
>
> *When she meets him at the door, she says: "I'm really down tonight." Not letting it faze him, he invites her to hop on and off they go for an evening of mirth that has her laughing as she walks back into her dorm room. How she loves him; like no one else he has brought happiness into her life.*[24]

It is Robin's and Andy's differences that make their relationship strong because they add dimensions not present in their relationships with others.

See communication as essential.   Lack of communication in a relationship may indicate general withdrawal, unwillingness to engage in self-disclosure, and reduced supportiveness—all indicators that the relationship may be disintegrating. But communication in itself does not guarantee intimacy. If we are using communication to deceive our partner or simply evaluate him or her, the relationship may be faltering.

Consider This

I must be ready to accept you as you are. If either of us comes to the relationship without this determination of mutual honesty and openness, there can be no friendship, no growth; rather there can be only a subject-object kind of thing that is typified by adolescent bickering, pouting, jealousy, anger and accusations.

—John Powell, *Why Am I Afraid to Tell You Who I Am?* (Allen, Texas: Argus Communications, 1969), p. 63.

Good communication allows us to manage relationships to the mutual satisfaction of both partners. Whether the relationship is to be changed or dissolved, communication is essential to such negotiation.

Honesty is the most important element. Can partners express their needs, dissatisfactions, fears, and unfulfilled ambitions? Can partners look honestly at themselves, at each other, and at the relationship? Flexibility is also important. Can partners bend and change? Can they remain open to the other's feelings and to alternative points of view? Tentativeness is important too. Can partners phrase their ideas so they do not become absolutes? Can they look at decisions so they are not permanent, absolute, or final? Refraining from judgments is essential as well. Can partners keep from an "I'm right and you're wrong" frame of mind? Can they avoid name calling, labeling, and other biased approaches so that true discussion and sharing can take place?

Concluding Remarks

In this chapter I have discussed the nature and meaning of intimate relationships. I have also discussed some of the nourishing ways of relating that can lead to the development and maintenance of such relationships. This chapter brings us full circle. As the book began, I showed how our strength and our security are built on self-esteem and self-acceptance. But it is clear from this chapter that self-esteem and self-acceptance can best be nourished within our intimate relationships. The ultimate in human interaction is intimate one-to-one relating.

Notes

[1] Alan L. Sillars and Michael D. Scott, "Interpersonal Perception Between Intimates: An Integrative Review," *Human Communication Research*, 10 (Fall 1983): p. 154. See Sillars and Scott, pp. 153–176, for a summary of the research findings on intimate relationships.

[2] Sillars and Scott, "Interpersonal Perception Between Intimates," p. 162. They claim that a number of sources affirm this everyday observation.

[3] Sillars and Scott, "Interpersonal Perception Between Intimates," p. 163.

[4] Sillars and Scott, "Interpersonal Perception Between Intimates," p. 164.

[5] The factors described in this section have been selected and discussed by Don E. Hamachek in *Encounters with Others: Interpersonal Relationships and You* (New York: Holt, Rinehart and Winston, 1982), pp. 52–70.

[6] Karen Dion, Ellen Berscheid, and Elaine Walster, "What is Beautiful is Good," *Journal of Personality and Social Psychology*, 24 (1972): pp. 285–290.

[7] Hamachek, *Encounters with Others*, p. 59.

[8] Hamachek, *Encounters with Others*, p. 65.

[9] Mark L. Knapp, *Interpersonal Communication and Human Relationships* (Boston: Allyn and Bacon, 1984), pp. 35–39.

[10] Julia T. Wood, *Human Communication: A Symbolic Interactionist Perspective* (New York: Holt, Rinehart and Winston, 1982), pp. 178–180.

[11] Knapp, *Interpersonal Communication and Human Relationships*, p. 36.

[12] Knapp, *Interpersonal Communication and Human Relationships*, p. 37.

[13] Knapp, *Interpersonal Communication and Human Relationships*, p. 38.

[14] Wood, *Human Communication*, pp. 178–179.

[15] John Powell, *Why Am I Afraid to Tell You Who I Am?* (Allen, Texas: Tabor Publishing, 1969), p. 62.

[16] Andrew Greeley, *Sexual Intimacy* (Chicago: Thomas More Press, 1973), p. 26.

[17] Kahlil Gibran, *The Prophet* (New York: Alfred A. Knopf, 1975), pp. 15–16.

[18] From *Illusion and Disillusion*, 3d ed., p. 49, by John F. Crosby. © 1985 by Wadsworth, Inc.

[19] I am indebted to Richard L. Conville for the ideas in this section. See Richard L. Conville, "Second-Order Development in Interpersonal Communication," *Human Communication Research*, 9 (Spring 1983): pp. 195–207.

[20] Conville, "Second-Order Development," p. 205.

[21] Knapp, *Interpersonal Communication and Human Relationships*, pp. 40–44.

[22] Knapp, *Interpersonal Communication and Human Relationships*, p. 42.

[23] Charles M. Sell, *Achieving the Impossible: Intimate Marriage* (New York: Ballantine Books, 1982), p. 46.

[24] Sell, *Intimate Marriage*, pp. 49–50.

Further Reading

Michael J. Beatty, *Romantic Dialogue: Communication in Dating & Marriage* (Englewood, Colo.: Morton Publishing Co., 1986). This is a 156-page paperback textbook on communication in relationships. Beatty treats the nature of romantic love, acquaintance, conflict and power, the need for dialogue, listening, and problem-solving. The book is basic, well-written, practical, and useful.

Philip Blumstein and Pepper Schwartz, *American Couples: Money, Work, Sex* (New York: William Morrow, & Co., 1983). American couples are in a state of transition. What are the issues that confront all American couples today? This book reports the results of a study based on thousands of questionnaires and more than 300 interviews.

Nathaniel Branden, *"If You Could Hear What I Cannot Say": Learning to Communicate with the Ones You Love* (New York: Bantam Books, 1983). Branden presents a sentence-completion technique that enables relationship partners to explore such sensitive topics as sex, money, marriage, personal expectations, emotional security, and the past. Much of this book is designed for readers to fill in their own ideas, but the technique, itself, is exciting and valuable. It works.

David D. Burns, *Intimate Connections* (New York: New American Library, 1985). In this exciting and useful book, Burns applies the principles of cognitive therapy to show how to eliminate the negative thinking and low self-esteem that cause loneliness and shyness. With sensible and sensitive advice, case histories, and revealing exercises, Burns offers a step-by-step program that shows readers how to rid themselves of attitudes that keep them apart from others and, thus, develop fulfilling relationships.

John F. Crosby, *Illusion and Disillusion: The Self in Love and Marriage*, 3d ed. (Belmont, Calif.: Wadsworth Publishing Co., 1985). An inquiry into the psychodynamics of intimate relationships, this book guides the reader toward a meaningful and fulfilling relationship with a primary partner.

C. Edward Crowther and Gayle Stone, *Intimacy: Strategies for Successful Relationships* (New York: Dell Publishing, 1986). Based on his work as a therapist and teacher, Crowther, with Stone, offers a practical book on how to rate intimacy levels, cope with fears of intimacy, avoid emotional sabotage, spot symptoms of burnout, and know whether relationships are worth saving. A book full of examples, anecdotes, and practical advice.

Mark L. Knapp, *Interpersonal Communication and Human Relationships* (Boston: Allyn & Bacon, 1984). This book is about the way people communicate in developing and deteriorating relationships. One of the book's strengths is its discussion of interaction sequences for coming together and coming apart. Knapp includes two chapters related to intimacy: "The Foundations of Intimate Dialogue," and "The Language of Intimacy."

Alan Loy McGinnis, *The Romance Factor* (San Francisco: Harper & Row, 1982). Based on his counseling practice, McGinnis considers how to ignite romantic love, choose the right partner, build intimacy and still be yourself, weather marital storms, avoid affairs, and build a lasting relationship. A book full of examples, anecdotes, and practical advice.

Gerald M. Phillips and H. Lloyd Goodall, Jr., *Loving and Living: Improve Your Friendships and Marriage* (Englewood Cliffs, N.J.: Prentice-Hall, 1983). This book is a source of ideas you can apply to your own relationships. The authors discuss why we spend our lives with others, what people say about their mates, and how love ends, as well as how to handle problem relationships and relationship problems.

Charles M. Sell, *Achieving the Impossible: Intimate Marriage* (New York: Ballantine Books, 1982). Sell discusses three essentials to love: commitment, sacrifice, and love. His is a warm, sensible book that explores the dynamics of communication and companionship, the keys to intimate marriage. The book is designed to make relationships stronger and happier.

Appendix: Interpersonal Communication in the Workplace

Learning Objectives

When you have finished this Appendix you should be able to:

- Briefly explain the interpersonal skills found to promote success with coworkers.
- Explain the skills considered to be most important for successful job performance.
- Discuss the meaning and components of communicative competence on the job.
- Describe which influence styles tend to work best for *both* males and females trying to exert influence in the workplace.
- Provide a summary of the factors considered most important for getting a job.
- Identify the steps necessary for preparing for the job search.
- Clarify each of the three ways to conduct an initial inquiry: (1) by letter, (2) by telephone, and (3) in person.
- List the minimal requirements for a résumé.
- Briefly explain how interviewees can make a good impression in job interviews.
- Describe the decisions interviewees can make during job interviews.

One of the areas in which interpersonal communication skills are most essential is the world of employment. In this Appendix we will look at some of the communication skills identified by researchers as essential for success on the job. We will then review the job-seeking process and the all-important employment interview. This first section is divided into three parts. What communication skills are necessary for success on the job? What communication skills reflect on-the-job communicative competence? And what skills are necessary for influencing others in the workplace? We will look closely at a number of studies that have identified these specific skills and consider their applications.

Communication Skills for Your Career

A list of the interpersonal skills that have been found to promote success with coworkers—of any type of rank—would probably be familiar to you. It would include listening and feedback; verbal, nonverbal, and persuasive skills; controlling and sharing emotions; being appropriately assertive; and coping successfully with conflict (similar to the chapters of this book!). Indeed, many of these are among the skills identified as essential in a survey of business-college graduates.[1] The respondents mentioned the following six skill areas, listed in descending order of frequency, as being important:

1. *Listening*—both to those above them and to those below them. The respondents emphasized the feeling that listening was one of the most important communication skills.
2. *Public speaking and presentation of technical information*—the need for presentations to groups of twenty or less and the need for adequate training in the organization of material.
3. *Writing*—with an emphasis on clear, accurate and organized writing.
4. *Small group leadership and problem solving communication*—most of the respondents prefaced their remarks with a comment indicating frustration with the small groups they had been a part of.

Consider This

. . . It is evident that stronger emphasis must be given to interpersonal communication where the ability to work well with others on a one-to-one basis (handle human relations and conflict management), to perceive and interpret nonverbal cues, and work effectively in small groups [is important]. If students do not have the understanding and skills these courses provide undoubtedly they will lack the "outcomes" necessary for functioning effectively in the market place, much less the competencies and experiences important to function as a productive family member and citizen in our democratic society.

—From "National Preferences in Business and Communication" by Dan B. Curtis, Jerry L. Winsor, and Ronald D. Stephens, in *Communication Education,* 38 (January 1989). Copyright © 1989 by the Speech Communication Association. Reprinted by permission of the Speech Communication Association and the authors.

5. *Human relations*—whether stated explicitly, or implied. There was an emphasis on the ability to relate and be sensitive to the needs of those they came in contact with in the day-to-day work environment.
6. *Persuasion and attitude theory*—a concern was expressed about how to understand what makes others behave in certain ways and about how to motivate others.

Most of the interpersonal skills have been discussed elsewhere, and methods for improvement in each area have been outlined. In the next few pages I will delineate the skills identified in these studies because they can provide a focus for concentrating your future effort. Achieving proficiency in these skills will enhance not only your overall success on the job but also your ability to communicate with your coworkers and to influence others in the workplace.

Preparation for a Successful Career

Researcher V. Linquist asked 178 corporate employment officers what advice they would give a high-school senior planning to attend college the following fall.[2] He concluded that the best advice was to secure a well-rounded education *without* overspecialization. The respondents stressed the importance of a strong liberal arts or general education orientation supplemented by business, technical, and computer coursework and the development of both written and oral communication skills.

William Bennett, former Secretary of Education, cites two studies highlighting the value of a liberal arts education, the first a survey of 1300 recent liberal arts graduates of the University of Texas; the second a study of AT&T's management system.[3] The latter revealed that 43 percent of the employees who had achieved at least a fourth-level promotion had majored in liberal arts. Only 32 percent of the employees who achieved this distinction were business majors and 23 percent engineering majors. Bennett claims that the success of liberal arts graduates is based on their development of skills indispensable to all areas of work such as research, writing, speaking, and analyzing. The more specialized "salable" skills, he says, can be developed in on-the-job training, through internships, or in graduate school.

Ann Howard, another researcher working in this area, supported Bennett's conclusions. Using numerous assessment factors, she concluded that humanities and social science majors have the best overall performance in business. They surpass the other majors (business, engineers, science, math, education, inter-disciplinary, etc.), she claims, on intellectual ability, creativity, solving business problems, decision making, written communication skills, and interpersonal and verbal skills.[4]

Dan Curtis, Jerry Winsor, and Ronald Stephens surveyed 172 personnel managers in the greater Kansas City area to identify the factors or skills important for successful job performance.[5] It is interesting to note that the top four factors are communication related. (See table A.1.)

Table A.1
Factors/skills important for successful job performance.

Rank/Order	Factors/Skills Rated Important	Score
1	Interpersonal/human relations skills	4.364
2	Oral (speaking) communication skills	4.337
3	Written communication skills	4.159
4	Enthusiasm	4.116
5	Technical competence	4.076
6	Persistence/determination	4.000
7	Personality	3.811
8	Work experience	3.798
9	Poise	3.640
10	Dress/grooming	3.532
11	Interviewing skills	3.351
12	Specific degree held	2.976
13	Grade point average	2.952
14	Résumé	2.530
15	Physical attractiveness	2.514
16	Letters of recommendation	2.224

From "National Preferences in Business and Communication Education" by Dan B. Curtis, Jerry L. Winsor, and Ronald D. Stephens, in *Communication Education* 38 (January 1989). Copyright © 1989 by the Speech Communication Associations. Reprinted by permission of the Speech Communication Association and the authors.

The same researchers also present an ideal management profile based on the optimal balance of traits and skills that the personnel managers said young managers should possess to advance in an organization. The top five abilities are basically oral communication skills. If these studies are correct, it appears that oral communication, listening, enthusiasm, and written communication skills are considered to be most important for successful job performance. In the next section we'll look at some additional factors that relate to what others perceive to be on-the-job competence. (See table A.2.)

Communicative Competence on the Job

If you want to be perceived as likable and easy to work with, what should you do? Four factors have been identified as indicative of communicative effectiveness and social attractiveness in the workplace.[6] The first of these, *impression leaving*, means the tendency to be remembered because of what one says and/or how one says it. This involves using frequent, unique (memorable) nonverbal mannerisms and gestures and frequent unique verbal expressions.

Openness is another factor that reveals communicative effectiveness and social attractiveness. This means revealing personal things about yourself, easily expressing feelings and emotions, and being frank and sincere. "Open" people are characterized by frequent statements of personal opinion or experience, high-risk self-disclosure statements, and attempts to facilitate openness in conversations as a whole.

Animation is a third factor. It means providing frequent eye contact, using facial expressions, and gesturing often. Animated people vary the range, pitch, and loudness of their voice. They use frequent and varied body movements, facial expressions, eye movements, and "communicative" (purposeful) gestures.

Finally, a person reveals communicative effectiveness by being *relaxed*. David Brandt defines this as "a tendency to be calm and collected, not nervous under pressure, and to not show nervous mannerisms."[7] He says we detect a relaxed state when a person leans back in his or her chair, speaks in a "steady" voice, seldom mentions apprehension or nervousness concerning the interaction, and reveals little or no rigidity of posture.

Brandt also lists three traits characteristic of workers who are perceived as desirable working partners or associates.[8] Such people are attentive,

Rank	Trait/Skill	Score
1	Ability to work well with others one-on-one	4.494
2	Ability to work well in small groups	4.491
3	Ability to gather accurate information from others to make a decision	4.420
4	Ability to listen effectively and give counsel	4.374
5	Ability to give effective feedback (appraisal)	4.247
6	Ability to write effective business reports, etc.	4.205
7	Knowledge of job	4.105
8	Ability to present a good public image for the organization	3.994
9	Ability to use computers	3.535
10	Knowledge of management theory	3.488
11	Knowledge of marketing	3.467
12	Knowledge of finance	3.452
13	Knowledge of accounting	3.414
14	Ability to use business machines	2.871

From "National Preferences in Business and Communication Education" by Dan B. Curtis, Jerry L. Winsor, and Ronald D. Stephens, in *Communication Education*, 38 (January 1989). Copyright © 1989 by the Speech Communication Association. Reprinted by permission of the Speech Communication Association and the authors.

Table A.2
Ideal management profile.

friendly, and precise. *Attentive* people have a tendency to listen, to show interest in what others are saying, and to deliberately react in such a way that others know they are being listened to. Indicators of attentiveness include the amount and duration of eye contact, the frequency with which communicators repeat, rephrase, or paraphrase others' statements back to them, the frequency of requests for additional information pertaining to previous statements made by the others, and the communicator's postural orientation.

Friendly people have a tendency to encourage others, to acknowledge others' contributions to the interaction, and to openly express admiration. People who are perceived as friendly show frequent agreement with and/or acknowledgment of the worth of others' statements. They smile, lean forward, and use other gestures of warmth and friendliness. They make statements that reflect their interest in what others are saying and they frequently reinforce and use "stroking" statements—statements of support and encouragement.

Finally, those who are perceived to be desirable working partners are *precise.* They use very specific language and try to say exactly what they mean. They frequently use examples and illustrations to clarify their statements. They use definitions. They may elaborate on a previous statement, and they generally use correct grammar. These qualities promote productivity and efficiency through the choice of words.

Consider This

Research shows that the average executive spends 75 to 80 percent of most working days communicating—about 45 minutes of every hour.* One survey of almost a hundred companies showed that 80 percent of the respondents conducted interviews, 78 percent gave spoken instructions to subordinates, 76 percent gave oral reports, and 75 percent spoke with clients as part of their jobs.** Communication is just as important in other fields: lawyers interview clients and speak in court, medical practitioners work with patients and colleagues, teachers face students, ministers preach, and social workers counsel.

* C. S. Goetzinger and M. A. Valentine, "Problems in Executive Interpersonal Communication," *Personnel Administration,* 27 (1964): pp. 24–29.

** J. D. Wyllie, "Oral Communications: Survey and Suggestions," *American Business Communication Association Bulletin* (June 1980): pp. 14–15.

—From Ronald B. Adler, *Communicating at Work: Principles and Practices for Business and the Professions* (New York: Random House, Inc., 1986), p. 5.

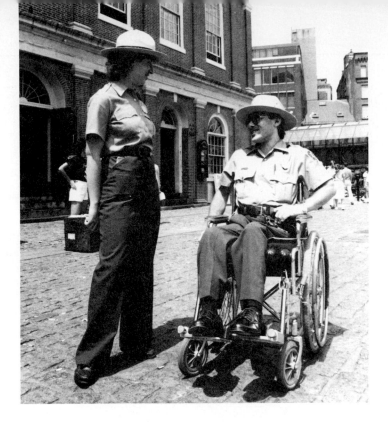

Influencing Others in the Workplace

Many people believe that pushing for what you want and refusing to take no for an answer are essential qualities for success on the job.[9] Ask several friends to name the characteristics of the fast-track, highly successful, movers and shakers of the business world, and you are likely to come up with words such as assertive (maybe even aggressive), self-confident, brash, persistent, risk-takers.

Stuart Schmidt, a professor of human resource administration, and David Kipnis, a professor of psychology, both at Temple University, examined the consequences of different influence styles in the workplace. Their "studies involved employees from hundreds of firms in industries ranging from manufacturing to financial services."[10]

Schmidt and Kipnis surveyed workers, supervisors, sales representatives, and chief executive officers to determine how frequently people influence their superiors using the six strategies described in Table A.3: reason, assertiveness, friendliness, coalition, higher authority, and bargaining. They then grouped people into four influence styles based on the way they used the strategies.

1. *Tacticians*—These people actively try to influence others, relying on reason and logic.

Table A.3
Different ways of getting your way.

Reason	Explain the reason for your request. Write a detailed plan.
Assertiveness	Repeatedly remind. Confront face to face.
Friendliness	Make person feel important. Act humble and polite.
Coalition	Obtain support of coworkers. Obtain support of subordinates.
Higher Authority	Make a formal appeal to higher levels. Obtain the informal support of higher-ups.
Bargaining	Propose an exchange. Offer to help in exchange for what you want.

From "The Perils of Persistence: Refusing to Take No for an Answer Can be Costly Both Personally and Professionally" by Stuart M. Schmidt and David Kipnis, in *Psychology Today*, 21 (November 1987): 34. Copyright © 1987 (PT Partners, L. P.). Reprinted with permission.

2. *Ingratiators*—These people are active in their persuasion, but they rely on ingratiation and flattery.
3. *Shotguns*—These people refuse to take no for an answer. Shotguns use all six strategies to get their way. When one strategy fails they shift to another.
4. *Bystanders*—These people seldom attempt to influence others; they stand by watching the action like wallflowers at a dance.

The results provide useful lessons for those interested in making their mark in the workplace. Schmidt and Kipnis found that shotguns received low performance evaluations, earned less than those using other strategies, experienced high levels of job tension and personal stress, and expressed less satisfaction with all aspects of their work. This discovery held true at different organizational levels and in numerous occupations and firms. This finding does not mean that the shotgun style is always inappropriate; in certain situations there may be no other choice when someone refuses to respond to reasoning.

Schmidt and Kipnis found traditional sex-stereotypical differences with respect to which influence style received the best performance evaluations. The highest performance ratings were given to male Tacticians—those who relied on reason and logic. Women who received the highest evaluations were Ingratiators—those who used friendliness or flattery—and Bystanders.

Supervisors described male Tacticians and female Ingratiators as deferential and thoughtful—that is, males were perceived as thoughtful when they used reason and logic; females were perceived as thoughtful when they used friendliness and flattery or were passive. "The inevitable conclusion," these researchers pointed out, "is that men's ideas are valued and women's are not."[11] These results should *in no way* encourage the use of an ingratiating communication style by female workers; however, they do reflect the fact that the business world is primarily male dominated. The point is, however, that less vigorous influence styles tend to work best for *both* males and females who are trying to exert influence in the workplace.

Most adults spend more of their time on the job than in any other setting. Much of this on-the-job time is spent communicating with peers, bosses, subordinates, customers, clients, and others. While technical skills are important, they obviously are not enough to ensure success. In this section, the skills essential to communicating effectively on the job were discussed. These factors may well make the difference between success and failure not only for us as individuals but also for the organizations that employ us.

Consider This

Well, let us begin by getting motivated.

There is a vast world of work out there, where 116 million people are employed in this country alone—many of whom are bored out of their minds. All day long. Not for nothing is their motto TGIF—"Thank God It's Friday." They *live* for the weekends, when they can go do what they really want to do.

There are already more than enough of such poor souls. The world does not need you or me to add to their number. What the world does need is more people who feel true enthusiasm for their work. People who have taken the time to think—and to think out what they uniquely can do, and what they uniquely have to offer to the world.

This is, of course, where you come in. If you are willing to sit down and do this task of inventorying what you most love to do, you will be on the way to giving the world what it most needs.

The world needs you to be doing work that you love to do; moreover that is your birthright, and your destiny. But, it doesn't just fall into your lap. *You have to put in some time to make it happen.* That time begins with inventorying your skills.

—Richard Nelson Bolles, *What Color Is Your Parachute? A Practical Manual for Job-Hunters & Career Changers* (Berkeley, Calif.: Ten Speed Press, 1989), pp. 64–65.

Looking for the Right Job

What skills are important for getting a job? You should have a pretty good idea by now. Numerous studies indicate which factors are most important. John Hafer and Carolee Hoth surveyed 250 business students at the University of Nebraska and 37 major business firms representing a broad range of industries from manufacturing to public service. They concluded that the two most important factors in getting hired were oral communication skills and motivation.[12] (Motivation includes those external and internal forces that incite, impel, or drive you in a specific direction. What is it that makes you want a job? That makes you want to do outstanding work on the job? That compels you to strive for excellence?)

Gary L. Benson, director of business and management programs at the University of Wyoming-Casper, surveyed 175 personnel managers in the Wyoming area.[13] He discovered that oral and written communication skills are the most important factors or skills in helping graduating business students obtain employment. These two sets of skills were followed by work experience and energy level. (He defined energy level as enthusiasm.)

Curtis, Winsor, and Stephens, in the survey of Kansas City area personnel managers cited earlier, discovered that oral communication skills were *the* most important factor in helping graduating college students obtain employment.[14] (See table A.4.)

Preparing for the Job Search

When we look for a job, we invest a good deal of our time, energy, and hope in the search. Effective interpersonal communication is crucial to finding a job—the right job.

It is never too soon to begin preparing for the job search. The purpose of this preparation process is to assemble as much information as you can before you begin applying for specific jobs. This means reviewing your personal interests, qualifications, and expectations as well as learning every-thing you can about the particular company or work situation that interests you.

Personally, you should begin to consider your own professional needs and goals.[15] What are *you* looking for? Try to narrow both your goals and your occupational choices. It is almost certain that you will be asked questions in this area. What are your interests and attitudes? Your answers to questions like this one will indicate how interested you are in professional growth. What past experience, education, or training have you received? You will undoubtedly be seeking a career that will build on your expertise. Your qualifications will, then, add to your confidence and self-worth. What considerations need to be made with respect to your physical stamina and general health? Certain jobs may overextend you, inundate you, or box you

Rank/Order	Factors/Skills Evaluated	Score
1	Oral (speaking) communication	4.441
2	Written communication skills	4.081
3	Enthusiasm (energy)	4.076
4	Listening ability	4.052
5	Technical competence	4.040
6	Appearance	3.959
7	Personality	3.930
8	Work experience	3.811
9	Poise	3.744
10	Work-related recommendations	3.744
11	Résumé quality	3.649
12	Grade point average	3.418
13	Specific degree held	3.397
14	Part-time or summer employment	3.382
15	Leadership in campus/community activities	3.270
16	Accreditation of program	3.257
17	Participation in campus/community activities	3.169
18	School attended	2.771
19	Personal recommendation	2.377

Table A.4
Factors most important in helping graduating college students obtain employment.

From "National Preferences in Business and Communication Education" by Dan B. Curtis, Jerry L. Winsor, and Ronald D. Stephens, in *Communication Education,* 38 (January 1989). Copyright © 1989 by the Speech Communication Association. Reprinted by permission of the Speech Communication Association and the authors.

in. Knowing this ahead of time will help ensure that you do not get into the wrong type of job.

Knowing in advance of a job interview your most valuable educational experiences, your most rewarding work experiences, your most successful projects and accomplishments, and your strengths and capabilities will help you avoid hesitating if you are asked any of these questions. Your forthright answers to such questions will indicate self-confidence and strength.

To find out about a company may require some digging. You may have to consult reference publications in the library. Sometimes, the local chamber of commerce can provide information. The *Industrial Index* may be another source, as may the public relations department of the company you are investigating. The kinds of information you might wish to know would include the following:

1. How long has the firm been in business?
2. What is its product line?
3. What have been its sales over the past five years?

Try This

Take a moment right now to do a self-assessment. If you were going to apply for a job right now—one that meant a great deal to you, and could result in long-term employment—what are the various skills that you have to offer at this moment?

1. What is it that you do well and enjoy doing?
2. Currently, what is your strongest skill?
   A. Are you good at using data? (Synthesizing, coordinating and innovating, analyzing, compiling, computing, copying, and comparing)
   B. Are you good at dealing with people? (Mentoring, negotiating, instructing, supervising, diverting, persuading, speaking, signaling, serving, taking instructions, and helping)
   C. Are you good at handling things? (Setting up, precision working, operating, controlling, driving/operating, manipulating, tending, and handling)
3. What do you want to do out in the world?
4. What do you want to be?
5. What are your interests, wishes, and the things that make you happy?
6. What is it that your career or job must include to make you truly happy, used, and effective?
7. If there were one skill (or a set of skills) that you would like to acquire that would help you achieve the job that you consider "ideal for you," what would this skill or set of skills be?

4. What is its growth potential?
5. Who are the company's biggest competitors?
6. What reputation does the company have?
7. How many employees are there? What training do they receive?
8. What are the company's future plans?
9. What are the company's expectations? Traditions? Regulations?
10. What is the company's financial profile? Size of payroll? Amount of debt?
11. Who are the major shareholders? Who owns the company?

These questions are only a beginning. The more background information and knowledge you have, the better your letters, phone conversations, and interviews are likely to be. If you have completed this kind of investigation, your future employer will surely discover that you have done your homework. This indicates not only your enthusiasm but also your sincerity and determination.

If you think of this job as a permanent, lifetime commitment, you can see how important such answers are. The better prepared you are, the more intelligent and specific will be your questions in the interview. The more likely, too, that you will be able to get just the information you need without wasting an interviewer's time. In business, as in many other facets of life, time is money!

Besides personal preparation, information about the company and job, you should also think about *other possible areas* that should be investigated. For example, what about the locality and environment? How about churches, schools, and recreational facilities? What about the cost of living? Desirable housing? Do you find the climate desirable? Tolerable? What are the social and cultural norms of the local society? Would you and your family be accepted there? How about educational opportunities? Could you pursue your hobbies and sports interests there?

The Initial Inquiry

Once you have completed your background research, you are ready to contact a potential employer. The purpose of your initial inquiry is to obtain an interview. There are three ways to do it: (1) the inquiry by letter, (2) the telephone inquiry, or (3) the in-person inquiry.[16] Because first impressions are so important, the way you conduct yourself in that initial inquiry can make a significant difference.

No matter which of the three methods of inquiry are used, you will need a "home" base from which to operate. That is, there must be some way for prospective employers to contact you. It is a good idea to establish

Consider This

Being a succinct communicator will earn you high marks with others, since this is a prized skill. Train yourself to organize your thoughts in advance so you can speak more concisely. Don't take seven sentences to explain a problem when one sentence would do, followed by a brief presentation of a *solution* (if possible). If you operate on the assumption that no one will want to listen to you for more than one minute, you'll be on safe ground. Besides, if they are sufficiently interested in what you have to say, they can always ask for more detail.

—Reprinted from *Put Your Degree to Work: The New Professional's Guide to Career Planning and Job Hunting,* Second Edition, by Marcia R. Fox, Ph.D., by permission of W. W. Norton & Company, Inc. Copyright © 1988, 1979 by Marcia R. Fox.

Try This

Select a local company in which you might have some interest. Do a complete profile on this company answering the questions on pages A–11 and A–12. From where did you get most of your information? How reliable or accurate do you think this information is? Would you want to work for this company based on what you know now? What are its major strengths? Weaknesses? Are there things that you would still like to know? Are there questions that you could ask an interviewer? Can you see the advantage of doing a company profile before engaging in a job interview?

regular hours, to let others know those hours, and to stick to them. If there are times when you cannot keep regular hours, use an answering service, a telephone answering device, or provide the number of a friend who can take messages for you. You need to be businesslike in responding to telephone calls and letters, just as you do in setting hours. Respond promptly. Consider such responses necessary commitments that convey a businesslike attitude.[17]

The **inquiry by letter** is, perhaps, the most common inquiry. It is usually accompanied by a brief résumé. It is best if it can be addressed to a specific person rather than to "Personnel Director," "Department Chairperson," or "To Whom It May Concern." If you do not know a person's name, it is worthwhile placing a telephone call to determine this information. Make certain you get the proper spelling of the name and the person's title.

The inquiry by letter should:

1. Be brief.
2. Be businesslike (serious and formal).
3. Reveal a positive attitude about the firm.
4. Show what you can offer the company.
5. Indicate confidence (but maintain your distance).
6. Be courteous in its opening and closing greetings.
7. Give some indication of your individuality.
8. Have no typing, spelling, or grammatical errors.
9. Stimulate the reader's interest.
10. Explain why you want to work for this company.

The **telephone inquiry** requires forethought. Before placing or receiving a call, make certain you have a paper and pencil handy. If numerous inquiries are going to be made, these could be recorded on index cards for easy filing. Essential information that should be recorded would be:

1. Name of firm.
2. Name of person to be contacted (or contacting). Be sure to get this name down exactly right, with the correct spelling and pronunciation.
3. Address.
4. Phone number.
5. Days and hours person can be contacted.
6. Short job description, if known.
7. Impressions or suggestions about how to proceed next time.

Think about what you plan to say. The telephone inquiry is usually brief; every word is important. Prepare a *short* summary of who you are, your background, and what you can do. You should not have to flounder when asked for your credentials. But you should not offer a full résumé either. Because you know the facts well and have probably repeated them before, be careful not to rush. Speak loudly, enunciate clearly, and avoid sounding either bored or as if you have memorized your speech.

If the person you want is out when you call, be certain to get the name of the person who answered the phone. You might also jot down the time you called. It may be useful later when you *do* make contact. For example, it sounds responsible and mature to say in response to a question about when you tried to call, "I called yesterday at 2:15, but Mrs. Smith said you were in a conference." Also, you will then be able to greet Mrs. Smith by name if you come in for an interview. Going out of your way to be courteous and polite is not just good manners, it is appropriate behavior in the business world.

The **in-person inquiry** has several advantages. It will allow you to learn what positions are available, the various job requirements, and a little about the firm as well. You can also find out who the people are that you will need to see. By observing the organization and the people who work there, you will learn a great deal about the company that will help you in the job interview. If you can talk to anyone on the job, this will also help.

In the in-person inquiry, make certain you:

1. Present yourself professionally in both appearance and manner.
2. Get the information you need efficiently and record it succinctly. Be prepared to write down the necessary facts.
3. Repeat names, places, times, or other data to make certain you recorded them accurately.
4. Plan to collect the same information outlined previously under telephone inquiry.
5. Come prepared for an interview at once, if you can get one. This may save you another trip. Do not let this circumstance take you by surprise.
6. Leave a copy of your résumé, if possible.

The Résumé

There is no single right way to prepare a résumé, but it is an essential part of the job-application process. The nature of a résumé will be determined by your qualifications and by the job. Its purpose is to provide other people with a concise summary of your qualifications. Minimal requirements for the résumé include:

Try This

Create the dialogue for a telephone inquiry. You are attempting to secure an interview for a job. Pretend that this is <u>the</u> job that you really want— your ideal position. Provide both sides of the dialogue—your side as well as the person on the receiving end.

In an actual telephone contact, you should make certain that you are clear and to the point. In telephone situations there is a need for instant understanding as well as immediate recall. Pay particular attention to your:

1. Voice. Do not be abrupt or harsh.
2. Manner. Do not be tactless, unkind, or unpleasant.
3. Articulation and enunciation. Because telephone conversations do not include nonverbal elements, you must be sure that the sounds of the language are formed carefully (articulation) and, also, that they are clear and distinct (enunciation).

If you have a tape recorder available, tape your inquiry. When you play it back, check yourself on the factors: voice, articulation and enunciation, and feedback. How did you measure up?

Consider This

One of the shortcomings of the English language is the lack of a snappy word for a summary of your professional history and accomplishments. We are stuck with using foreign terms. There's "résumé," which I always have to look up to make sure I've got the accent marks running the right way, and "curriculum vitae," which is hard to spell and sounds awful even when you say it right.

If you wanted to be breezy about this listing of your professional and academic life, you could entitle it "Me." Acronym fans might vote for WIB (Where I've Been) or WID (What I've Done) or maybe WIB&WID. . . .

To my mind a perfect WIB&WID should be organized like a Henny Youngman two-liner. No fat. Get to the point and then say goodbye. The middle managers of this world are not dying to know every little detail about you. Remember: You're trying to get us to hire you, not marry you.

—From "Tell Me About Yourself . . . That's Enough!" by Larry McCoy in *The Wall Street Journal* (April 5, 1989), p. A10. Reprinted with permission of *The Wall Street Journal.* Copyright © 1989 Dow Jones & Company, Inc. All rights reserved.

1. Overall neatness.
2. No misspellings, typographical errors, or grammatical errors.
3. No erasures.
4. Typed or professionally printed presentation.

Since most people send in résumés printed on white-stock paper, a résumé printed on light-colored paper could give the applicant an edge. Remember, above all, that an employer will accept your résumé as an indication of the type of person you are. Present your résumé as you would yourself. Let it be an accurate reflection. Most often, a one-page résumé is sufficient. Employers usually skim the page for the information they are seeking; don't hide the relevant facts about yourself in a jumble of unnecessary details. Do not include such details as race, religion, marital status, or age on your résumé; it is illegal for employers to base hiring decisions upon such factors. Detailed suggestions for preparing résumés are in many English handbooks or may be obtained from the Career Development office at your college.

The Job Interview

Now that you have secured basic information, written the letters, sent out the résumés, and made the telephone calls, you are ready for the interview. So far you have dealt with basically inanimate objects; now you have to perform. You will be meeting a person face-to-face. Based on this meeting, a decision about you will be made.[18]

The nature of the situation, of course, varies with the job, the location of the interview, and the company holding the interview. But whatever the variations in these factors, personal appearance is always important in establishing the first impression. You should dress as others do in the occupation you are seeking. In addition, be clean and neat. Your hairstyle should be conservative. Go easy on the perfume or cologne. Shine your shoes, and clean your fingernails. It is probably advisable to be more conservative in dress than liberal in these situations. Avoid faddish styles, garish colors, and junk jewelry. Simplicity and appropriateness help others know that you are mature, thoughtful, and responsible. If you care about your attire, others are likely to assume that you will probably care about your job.

An interviewee must also be sensitive to the tone of the interview. An interview can be positive or negative. The tone is often reflected in feedback from the interviewer. The interviewee may detect indicators of tone in face, bodily position, muscular tension, vocal quality, and eye contact. Interviewers have bad days, long days, or troublesome interviews, just as you do. If you detect tension or fatigue you can sometimes change the tone by:

1. Relaxing. Try to enjoy the interview and learn from it.
2. Adding a bit of humor.
3. Asking a question.
4. Striving, despite the circumstances, to give a good impression.[19]

The interviewer's job is to hire someone, not to play games. The intent is to hire the person who will best fit into the organization and have something important to contribute. The interviewer is usually prepared to give the interviewee a fair hearing. After all, he or she is taking the time to interview you.

In most cases interviewers will have carefully reviewed applicants' résumés and applications to familiarize themselves with the basic information. It is always wise to have an extra copy of your résumé in case the first one has been misplaced. During the initial interview, an interviewer will attempt to fill gaps, explore ranges of experience, determine expertise in certain areas, discuss the interviewee's career goals and potential usefulness to the organization, probe the interviewee's attitudes toward the company, its products, or its services, and assess the prospective employee's personality and character.

Employment interviews often follow progressive stages of development. In many cases there will be an initial screening interview. This interview is designed to decrease the total pool of prospective candidates. Depending on the size of the pool, it can be reduced by narrowing the job specifications, or simply eliminating those who do not meet certain criteria, such as level of education or job experience. Once the pool is substantially reduced, second-stage screening interviews can take place. The number of stages involved is likely to depend on the size of the reduced pool at each stage and the difficulty in finding just the right person for the job.

Interviewers often look for interpretive information that is not conveyed on a résumé or application. They are likely to ask openended questions: "How do you feel about . . . ?" "What would be your reaction to . . . ?" or "What would you do if such-and-such happened?" Two frequently asked questions of this type are "What can you offer this company?" and "Why are you applying for this job?" or they might ask closed questions: "Did you take any courses in business?" "Have you any job experience in this area?" or "Based on what I have outlined, then, does this job still interest you?" Frequently a combination of both open and closed questions is used.

After interviewers get an answer to a question, they will often use a follow-up, or secondary, question to probe the interviewee more deeply. "Why did you choose to do that?" "Did you find that experience meaningful?" or "Can you see the benefits of this?" are some examples.

Secondary questions also help interviewers "measure" attitude and personality. Certainly no single question provides a direct line into another person's soul, but such questions as "How do you feel about that?" "What difference do you think such-and-such makes?" or "How would you respond in that situation?" help them gauge commitment, responsibility, maturity, and other leadership qualities.

Interviewers also work under certain restraints. Title VII of the Civil Rights Act of 1964 forbids discrimination on the basis of race, sex, religion, nation of origin, or age in personnel decisions. The Equal Employment

Consider This

Ironically, all the time and effort you invest in prepping for these questions will have an implicit reward even more significant than your acquired ability to respond adroitly at every turn. When you've built a series of answers that links with your résumé and letters of reference, you will be fully prepared. That preparation builds confidence, and confidence builds excellence under pressure. You will send off nonverbal signals to the employer that you're a pro, ready for anything they can throw at you in the interview. We call this the *positive expectation of success.* Your non-verbal, dress, grooming, and confidence levels will close the credibility gap within fifteen to twenty seconds of the interview opening. Everyone walks in with this credibility gap. If you don't close it within a few seconds, you'll be struggling uphill for the entire session.

—Kenneth M. Dawson and Sheryl N. Dawson, *Job Search: The Total System* (New York: John Wiley & Sons, 1988), p. 134.

Opportunity Commission (EEOC) enforces Title VII, getting its power to take companies that do not follow Title VII guidelines to court from the Equal Employment Opportunity Act. Unless certain characteristics regarding a person's ethnic origins, race, sex, religion, age, or marital status are directly related to effective performance on the job, questions on these areas are illegal. This means that an interviewer cannot ask you if you are married, single, or divorced; whether or not you attend church; if you and your spouse plan to have children; if you have been arrested (but you *can* be asked about convictions); what your age, height, or weight is; whether or not you own your own home; if you are living with anyone; whether or not you practice birth control; what social clubs or lodges you belong to; how your parents earn their living; how you might feel working with people of other races, or those of the opposite sex; or even how your spouse may feel about your having a career.

Your job as interviewee is to make a good impression. If you have thought about the interview and job in advance, you will be prepared to get the information you need. One thing you can plan to find out from the interview is whether or not you really want this job. Interviews are not one-sided. Not only does the interviewee have a choice, but he or she also has a certain personal responsibility to find out information. How often are performance reviews conducted? What are the chances for promotion or advancement? How does the organization promote employee advancement? Through educational grants? Training programs? Are employees unionized? Do union and company administrators cooperate or work amicably together? Are there contract difficulties? No-strike clauses in the contract? What are company policies regarding layoffs? Are there grievance procedures? Are clear channels set up whereby employees can communicate with superiors? What are the future plans of this organization?

Asking intelligent questions indicates that you have already thought about the interview and position. Also, it lets the interviewer know that you are serious. A serious job-seeker wants to know more than how long the working week is, how much the job pays, and what fringe benefits are available. To limit yourself to such questions—as important as they are—provides interviewers with a fairly clear set of interviewee motives and attitudes—a set that is unlikely to result in a job for the applicant.

An interviewee can make other decisions during the interview as well. For example, you can decide which questions should be answered briefly and which require elaboration. If questions are ambiguous, you should ask for clarification and avoid responding too hastily. It is a sign of good judgment to make sure that you understand the exact nature of a question before you answer it.

You can also make certain that the questions asked are relevant to professional or personal qualifications only. Finally, you can decide if the job requirements outlined by the interviewer are too restrictive. Sometimes interviewers may entertain unreasonable expectations for a prospective employee. If the interviewer has provided a fairly complete job description, the interviewee has a right to question responsibilities that go along with the job. You can also show how your own special qualifications or abilities make up for not satisfying some of the other qualifications the interviewer has outlined.

When the interview appears to be coming to an end, you should summarize what you have to offer the company. And you should not leave without determining what further information the interviewer may want. What follow-up steps are likely to be taken? How will the outcome of the interview be determined? How will you learn about the outcome? Can you call next week for an answer? You need to know what is going to come next and who is to be responsible for it.

Some writers specializing in job-hunting techniques suggest following up the interview with a "thank-you" letter or phone call. Such a letter or call can also be used to clarify ambiguous points or offer further information about your qualifications.

No matter what type of career interests you, interpersonal communication skills are likely to be important, if not essential, to your success. From getting a job to getting ahead on the job, your ability to communicate well with others will be your greatest asset.

Try This

Conduct a practice interview session with a friend. Tell your friend about the ideal kind of job you would like. Provide as many details as you can. Then ask your friend to ask you any appropriate questions—playing the role of the future employer. In your answers to your friend's questions, make certain that you:

1. Avoid any nervous habits.
2. Speak up.
3. Refrain from giggling.
4. Avoid gum chewing.
5. Speak to the point.
6. Avoid being too abrupt or curt.
7. Give an adequate answer, but not an overlong one.
8. Make no offensive or off-color comments.
9. Appear confident, alert, and responsive.

If a tape recorder is available, tape the practice interview. Then listen to the tape, analyzing your responses. How did you sound?

Notes

[1] The study was based on a questionnaire filled out and returned by 168 randomly selected graduates of the College of Business Administration at the University of Nebraska, Lincoln. See Vincent DiSalvo, David C. Larson, and William J. Seiler, "Communication Skills Needed By Persons in Business Organizations," *Communication Education*, 25 (November 1976): pp. 269–75. See especially pp. 274–75.

[2] V. Lindquist, *Northwestern Endicott Report 1986* (Evanston, Ill.: Placement Center/Northwestern University, 1985).

[3] William J. Bennett, "The Humanities Pay Off," *Across the Board*, 20 (1985): pp. 61–63.

[4] A. Howard, "College Experiences and Managerial Performance," *Journal of Applied Psychology*, 71 (1986): pp. 530–52.

[5] Dan B. Curtis, Jerry L. Winsor, and Ronald D. Stephens, "National Preferences in Business and Communication," *Communication Education*, 38 (January 1989), pp. 6–14.

[6] David R. Brandt, "On Linking Social Performance with Social Competence: Some Relations Between Communicative Style and Attributes of Interpersonal Attractiveness and Effectiveness," *Human Communication Research*, 5 (1979): pp. 223–37.

[7] Brandt, "Linking Social Performance with Social Competence," p. 227.

[8] It should be noted that little research exists that relates communicative style to variables investigated in a work setting. Patricia Hayes Bradley and John E. Baird, Jr., "Management and Communicator Style: A Correlational Analysis," *Central States Speech Journal*, 28 (Fall 1977): pp. 194–203, found that managers were perceived as democratic and likable when they displayed an attentive and friendly style. These characteristics are consistent with those reported by Brandt.

[9] Stuart M. Schmidt and David Kipnis, "The Perils of Persistence," *Psychology Today*, 21 (November 1987): p. 32.

[10] Schmidt and Kipnis, "The Perils of Persistence," p. 32.

[11] Schmidt and Kipnis, "The Perils of Persistence," p. 34.

[12] John C. Hafer and Carolee C. Hoth, "Selection Characteristics: Your Priorities and How Students Perceive Them," *Personnel Administrator*, 28 (1983): pp. 25–28.

[13] G. Benson, "On the Campus: How Well Do Business Schools Prepare Graduates for the Business World?" *Personnel*, 60 (1983): pp. 61–65.

[14] Curtis, Winsor, and Stephens, "National Preferences in Business and Communication," pp. 6–14.

[15] The suggestions in this section have been adapted from Melvin W. Donaho and John L. Meyer, *How to Get the Job You Want: A Guide to Resumes, Interviews, and Job-Hunting Strategy*, © 1976, p. 77. Reprinted by permission of Prentice-Hall, Inc., Englewood Cliffs, New Jersey.

[16] Marion Sitzmann and Leroy Garcia, *Successful Interviewing: A Practical Guide for the Applicant and Interviewer* (Skokie, Ill.: National Textbook Company, 1976), p. 1.

[17] Sitzmann and Garcia, *Successful Interviewing*, p. 1.

[18] H. Anthony Medley, *Sweaty Palms: The Neglected Art of Being Interviewed* (Belmont, Calif.: Lifetime Learning Publications, 1978), p. xi.

[19] Sitzmann and Garcia, *Successful Interviewing*, p. 8.

Further Reading

Kathleen S. Abrams, *Communication at Work: Listening, Speaking, Writing, and Reading* (Englewood Cliffs, N.J.: Prentice-Hall, Inc., 1986). The purpose of this textbook is to help students develop skills while showing them how these skills interact throughout the entire communication process. Abrams begins the text with an overview of the communication process as it applies to both spoken and written messages and concludes it with a chapter on job-seeking skills. A practical textbook with numerous examples.

Ronald B. Adler, *Communicating at Work: Principles and Practices for Business and the Professions*, 3rd ed. (New York: Random House, 1989). Adler offers an introduction to the principles and skills of effective face-to-face communication in business and professional settings. He provides a useful survey of on-the-job communication skills. This is a thorough, well-written, practical textbook.

Warren Bennis and Burt Nanus, *Leaders: The Strategies for Taking Charge* (New York: Harper & Row, 1985). The authors have divided the book into seven chapters, four of which are strategies. They introduce us to "Mistaking Charge," and "Leading Others, Managing Yourself," first; then the strategies of "Attention Through Vision," "Meaning Through Communication," "Trust Through Positioning," and "The Deployment of Self"; and, finally, "Taking Charge: Leadership and Empowerment." Bennis and Nanus have identified the essential qualities of leadership that anyone can practice. An insightful, thoughtful book on the management process.

Kenneth Blanchard and Spencer Johnson, *The One Minute Manager* (New York: Berkley Books, 1982). This is a brief look at how people work best with other people to produce valuable results and to feel good about themselves, the organization, and the others with whom they work. It is an inspirational, classic best-seller full of practical, specific advice. This is must reading for all those who manage others.

Richard Nelson Bolles, *What Color Is Your Parachute? A Practical Manual for Job-Hunters & Career Changers* (Berkeley, Calif.: Ten Speed Press, 1989). This is one of the most useful manuals for job-hunters and career changers. Updated annually, it is full of sound, detailed advice on life/work planning, self-assessment, and career planning. Written in a light, cheery style and full of interesting illustrations, this book holds the reader's attention while showing that job hunting need not be a dull, arduous, awesome task. Extensive footnotes and a lengthy bibliography are included.

Kenneth M. Dawson and Sheryl N. Dawson, *Job Search: The Total System* (New York: John Wiley & Sons, 1988). The authors, of Dawson & Dawson Management Consultants, offer a practical, direct, candid, analysis of how to handle the complexities of finding a job. Numerous illustrations and effective practical advice help readers mold their job search into a cohesive campaign that is likely to lead to a better job and better pay.

Lois J. Einhorn, Patricia Hayes Bradley, and John E. Baird, Jr., *Effective Employment Interviewing: Unlocking Human Potential* (Glenview, Ill.: Scott, Foresman and Company, 1982). The authors present fundamental communication principles and show how they apply to the employment interview. They examine the interview from the perspective of both applicant and employer and, thus, provide a comprehensive understanding of the whole process.

Marcia R. Fox, *Put Your Degree to Work: The New Professional's Guide to Career Planning and Job Hunting*, 2nd ed. (New York: W. W. Norton & Company, 1988). Fox is a senior vice president in the Corporate Development Group of Drake Beam Morin, Inc., the world's largest career-consulting firm. The value of this book is the space she devotes to advice on career management during a student's college years. She includes sections on academic advisement, career counseling, acting like a professional, professional manners, building a dossier, the importance of a mentor, the value of a contact network, and fieldwork experience during school.

Michael Ray and Rochelle Myers, *Creativity in Business* (New York: Doubleday, 1986). This book is included because of the inspiration it provides. For example, Ray and Myers suggest that business can offer a workable, productive, and enjoyable opportunity to wed practical skills with creative intuition. The authors discuss business as art, how to create curiosity, pay attention, and ask dumb questions. Ray and Myers not only offer the motivation to be creative, they suggest ways to nurture your creativity and to celebrate it.

R. Wayne Pace and Don F. Faules, *Organizational Communication*, 2nd ed. (Englewood Cliffs, N.J.: Prentice-Hall, 1989). Pace and Faules offer a perspective for thinking about organizations, human beings, and the world. The five major parts of the book include (1) the study of organizational communication, (2) organizational theories, (3) issues in organizational communication, (4) human resources and organizational systems, and (5) strategies for improving human resources and organizational systems.

Index